Foundations
of
Family and Consumer Sciences

Second Edition

*Careers Serving
Individuals, Families,
and Communities*

Sharleen L. Kato, EdD
Professor and Family and Consumer Sciences Department Director
Seattle Pacific University
Seattle, Washington

Janice G. Elias, PhD
Professor, Department of Human Ecology
Youngstown State University
Youngstown, Ohio

Publisher
The Goodheart-Willcox Company, Inc.
Tinley Park, Illinois
www.g-w.com

MW00799257

Library of Congress Catalog Card Number 2013049051

ISBN 978-1-61960-254-0

3 4 5 6 7 8 9— 15 —19 18 17 16 15 14

The Goodheart-Willcox Company, Inc. Brand Disclaimer: Brand names, company names, and illustrations for products and services included in this text are provided for educational purposes only and do not represent or imply endorsement or recommendation by the author or the publisher.

The Goodheart-Willcox Company, Inc. Safety Notice: The reader is expressly advised to carefully read, understand, and apply all safety precautions and warnings described in this book or that might also be indicated in undertaking the activities and exercises described herein to minimize risk of personal injury or injury to others. Common sense and good judgment should also be exercised and applied to help avoid all potential hazards. The reader should always refer to the appropriate manufacturer's technical information, directions, and recommendations; then proceed with care to follow specific equipment operating instructions. The reader should understand these notices and cautions are not exhaustive.

The publisher makes no warranty or representation whatsoever, either expressed or implied, including but not limited to equipment, procedures, and applications described or referred to herein, their quality, performance, merchantability, or fitness for a particular purpose. The publisher assumes no responsibility for any changes, errors, or omissions in this book. The publisher specifically disclaims any liability whatsoever, including any direct, indirect, incidental, consequential, special, or exemplary damages resulting, in whole or in part, from the reader's use or reliance upon the information, instructions, procedures, warnings, cautions, applications, or other matter contained in this book. The publisher assumes no responsibility for the activities of the reader.

The Goodheart-Willcox Company, Inc. Internet Disclaimer: The Internet listings provided in this text link to additional resource information. Every attempt has been made to ensure these sites offer accurate, informative, safe, and appropriate information. However, Goodheart-Willcox Publisher has no control over these websites. The publisher makes no representation whatsoever, either expressed or implied, regarding the content of these websites. Because many websites contain links to other sites (some of which may be inappropriate), the publisher urges teachers to review all websites before students use them. Note that Internet sites may be temporarily or permanently inaccessible by the time readers attempt to use them.

Cover photo: Konstantin Sutyagin/Shutterstock.com

Library of Congress Cataloging-in-Publication Data

Kato, Sharleen L.

Foundations of family and consumer sciences ; careers serving individuals, families, and communities / Sharleen L. Kato, EdD, Professor and Family and Consumer Sciences Department Director, Seattle Pacific University, Seattle, Washington, Janice G. Elias, PhD, Professor, Department of Human Ecology, Youngstown State University, Youngstown, Ohio. -- 2nd Edition.

    pages cm.

    Includes bibliographical references and index.

    ISBN 978-1-61960-254-0 (alk. paper)

1. Vocational guidance. 2. Occupations. 3. Family services. I. Elias, Janice G. II. Title.

HF5381.K368 2014

362.82023'73--dc23

2013049051

About the Authors

Sharleen L. Kato, EdD, loves teaching as well as learning. She is a professor at Seattle Pacific University where she encourages students to become creative and successful in their chosen career field. She believes that the mission of family and consumer sciences is the key to a myriad of meaningful and fulfilling careers. Dr. Kato has taught undergraduate students for over 25 years. She currently serves as the Family and Consumer Sciences Department Director. Dr. Kato holds a doctorate in education, a master's in human ecology, and an undergraduate degree in home economics. She travels extensively spending at least two weeks each year serving in an orphanage, teen home, and prenatal clinic in the Philippines.

Janice G. Elias, PhD, is professor emeritus at Youngstown State University where she previously served as professor of family and consumer sciences, chairperson of the Department of Human Ecology, assistant provost for academic planning, and interim dean of the College of Health and Human Services. Dr. Elias has taught family and consumer sciences in middle school, high school, and adult education settings and continues to teach part-time at the college level. She earned her undergraduate and master's degrees from Ohio University, a doctoral degree in human ecology from The Ohio State University, and a certificate in higher education management from Harvard University. Her particular interest is the interaction of family life and work life. She is a member of the American Association of Family and Consumer Sciences, Kappa Omicron Nu, and Phi Upsilon Omicron.

Acknowledgments

Many people contributed to this book and should be recognized. The following professionals reviewed the text and provided valuable input:

Dr. Sue Bailey, CFCS
    Professor (retired)
    School of Human Ecology
    Tennessee Technological University
    Cookeville, Tennessee

Dr. Wanda S. Fox
    Associate Professor
    College of Education
    Purdue University
    West Lafayette, Indiana

Sandra Hartje
    Professor of Interior Design and Housing
    College of Family and Consumer Sciences
    Seattle Pacific University
    Seattle, Washington

Dr. Carol E. Kellett
    Professor
    College of Human Ecology
    Kansas State University
    Manhattan, Kansas

Dr. Judith Rae Kreutzer, CFCS, CFLE
    Professor Emerita Family and Consumer
    Sciences
    Fairmont State University
    Fairmont, West Virginia

Dr. Cheryl L. Lee, CFCS
    Professor
    Department of Family and Consumer Sciences
    Appalachian State University
    Boone, North Carolina

Dr. Sharon Y. Nickols
    Janette Barber Distinguished Professor
    University of Georgia
    Athens, Georgia

Dr. Penny A. Ralston
    Professor and Dean Emeritus
    College of Human Sciences
    Florida State University
    Tallahassee, Florida

Dr. Cheryl M. Robinson, CFCS, CFLE
    UC Foundation Assistant Professor
    The University of Tennessee at Chattanooga
    Chattanooga, Tennessee

Dr. Jody L. Roubanis, CFCS
    Lecturer in Family & Consumer Sciences
    Point Loma Nazarene University
    San Diego, California

Introduction

What does family and consumer sciences have to do with life today? Everything. Families and communities still exist, and the desire to live a quality life while providing for the basic needs of food, clothing, and shelter is as relevant today as it was 100 years ago. From designing accessible housing for an aging population to helping children complete their high school education, all areas of specialization with family and consumer sciences are called on to help individuals, families, and communities adjust to a changing environment.

This is a book about life, education, and career stories. It is the story of Ellen Swallow Richards and her visionary contemporaries who founded the family and consumer sciences discipline. It is about home economists and family and consumer sciences professionals who improved the quality of life for individuals, families, and communities in the century since the inception of the discipline. It is the story of family and consumer sciences professionals currently working in the field. It is also your story.

This text is also about possibilities. Career prospects for each family and consumer sciences specialization area are presented. Contemporary trends and issues are discussed with an emphasis on possibilities for family and consumer sciences professionals of the present and future. Trends that will affect families of the future are discussed. As these and other trends emerge, family and consumer sciences professionals will adapt and change with the environment in order to improve the quality of life for individuals, families, and communities.

This text provides guidance about how to move into the workplace and how to make a difference in the lives of others. The text focuses on ways you can excel in the workplace and make an impact on your world. This includes work habits, attitudes, and healthy habits that lead to career success. Professionalism and lifelong learning are also important to career success.

Whether designing or selling fashion or offering hospitality services, family and consumer sciences emphasizes improving the quality of life. You will be encouraged to reflect on the profession, your skills, talents, and interests. After reading this text, you should have a solid understanding of the mission and philosophy of the profession, the current state of family and community life, career possibilities in the profession, and an assessment of your potential for making a difference in the world as a family and consumer sciences professional.

Brief Contents

Contents

Unit 3
Launching a Career in Family and Consumer Sciences   251

Unit One

Foundations and Trends in Family and Consumer Sciences

This unit will introduce you to the family and consumer sciences profession. It begins by introducing you to Ellen Swallow Richards and other early leaders and their contributions to family and consumer sciences. The unit examines how the discipline has evolved. You will explore current trends in family and consumer sciences as well as develop an awareness of career opportunities and related professional organizations, including the American Association of Family and Consumer Sciences (AAFCS). This unit will introduce you to the process of public policy making as it relates to family and consumer sciences through the development and promotion of strong families and healthy communities.

Chapter 1

The Birth of a Discipline

After studying this chapter, you will be able to:

- describe Ellen Swallow Richards, the historical setting in which she lived, the life events that shaped her professional development, and her contributions to the home economics discipline.

- outline the major events that contributed to the development of home economics, now called family and consumer sciences, as a discipline and profession.

- identify influential pioneers who contributed to the early development of the home economics profession, later known as family and consumer sciences.

This chapter introduces the history, literature, and contributions of the family and consumer sciences profession by setting the scene: life in the household circa 1850 as Ellen Swallow Richards, the founder of family and consumer sciences, is introduced in a biographical sketch. The following questions will be answered as the history, mission, careers, and emerging trends in family and consumer sciences are explored:

- How did the family and consumer sciences discipline begin?

- Who were the founders and what were their intentions as well as their contributions to the field of study?

- How has the discipline changed over the past 150 years? In what ways have the discipline and the related professions remained the same?

The Life of Ellen Swallow Richards, Founder of Family and Consumer Sciences

She could feel it in the air. When Ellen Swallow walked into her first class at the Massachusetts Institute of Technology (MIT), she could feel the tension that came from both her classmates and professors closely watching her. She was the first and only female to study at MIT, and the pressure to fit in and to perform well was evident. Would she lose her "womanly qualities"? Would she crack under the pressure? Were women really capable of learning at a higher level? Would she be "ruined" as a potential wife? All eyes were carefully watching for any sign of weakness or defect in Ellen Swallow. Over the next few years, she would not only prove her competence and worth as an exceptional scholar of chemistry but also would open the world of higher education to women in a time when higher education was reserved for men only.

Although many girls were not educated, some states and communities did allow girls to attend school. Also, there were special academies and finishing schools for girls in some cities. Higher education for women became available at private colleges and in the land-grant colleges, where the Morrill Act supported education and research in practical areas (Reuben, 1996) such as home economics (domestic science).

Who was Ellen Swallow Richards and how did she earn her place in the Smithsonian's exhibit showcasing the most influential women in America? Also, the Women's Hall of Fame credits Richards as the founder of ecology as a discipline of study. Ellen Swallow Richards was the first woman in the nation to graduate from the Massachusetts Institute of Technology with a graduate degree in chemistry. She also played a major role in opening scientific education and the scientific professions to women. Applying scientific principles to domestic life, she pioneered the new study and profession of home economics, later to be renamed family and consumer sciences. However, to fully understand and appreciate the impact Ellen Swallow Richards had on women in science, quality of life for families, and higher education, it is necessary to first understand the context of her life (Hunt, 1942).

Ellen Swallow Richards lived from 1842 to 1911. In the United States, these years were marked by many great events that left their indelible mark on the way of life in the United States. In the 1840s, the Oregon Trail was opened and vast areas of land were added to the United States. After gold was discovered in California, the expansive West gave many people new hopes and dreams of finding their fortune. By the turn of the century, the United States had experienced and survived several major events. The country had been divided and had survived the Civil War; women gained more individual and collective rights; European immigrants flooded the nation's cities; and the country progressed and changed during the Industrial Revolution. This tumultuous time in history has been called both the end and the beginning of creativity in America (Garraty & McCaughey, 1989). These were the life and times of Ellen Swallow Richards.

Ellen Swallow was born in Dunstable, Massachusetts, the daughter of Peter and Fanny G. Swallow. As the only child of parents who were former teachers, she was taught the importance of a good education as she grew up on their farm with very little contact with the outside world. Experiences that children take for granted today, such as childhood playmates, shopping trips, and even attending school, were not a part of her life. Life on a Massachusetts farm was not lacking in stimulation. Because the labor of children supported the work of farming, hard work was the order of the day and idleness was not tolerated (Hunt, 1942).

Life on a farmstead in the 1850s was predictable, and the role a person played in a family was usually determined very early in life. The first factor to be considered in establishing family roles was gender. Born a boy, certain rights and responsibilities were bestowed. Born a girl, certain expectations and responsibilities were determined. The typical rural farm family was composed of a husband, wife, and children with sometimes an aged grandparent or an unmarried relative living with them. Although we think of marriage happening at a very young age during this era, many young men sought to venture into the West before settling down. Others stayed close to home in the East but needed time to establish themselves before marriage.

Typically, men were the head of household on farms, where they cultivated and harvested the land, tended animals, and made sure there were enough resources available for the long winters. As husbands and fathers, men made most of the major decisions and were responsible for the economic well-being of the family. Sometimes men possessed craft skills that brought home additional income.

Women typically fulfilled the roles of wife and mother. Taking care of the home and family involved hard, physical work and very long hours. Baking bread, churning butter, cultivating the family vegetable garden, sewing, laundering clothing, bearing and rearing children, and nursing the sick at home were considered the accepted roles for women. Many women worked in the fields according to the seasonal demands of the crops and tended the livestock. Others helped operate shops for payment to supplement the household income. Daughters were socialized to learn wifely skills just as sons were socialized to do the work of a future husband and breadwinner. It is no wonder it was said, "Man works from sun to sun, but woman's work is never done" (American saying, source unknown).

It was a man's world in those days, and women played a subordinate role. In fact, women didn't have the right to vote until 10 years after Ellen Swallow Richards' death in 1911. For a farm girl in the mid-nineteenth century, there was little opportunity beyond marrying and occupying the role of "wife." However, Ellen Swallow wanted more. Ellen Swallow, a very bright child, was home-tutored by her parents. In her biography written by early home economics philosopher Carolyn Hunt, she was described as energetic and intellectually inquisitive (Hunt, 1942).

By the time Ellen Swallow was 17, her parents realized she had exceeded their abilities to intellectually challenge her and decided the only way to continue her education was to leave the farm and move the family to the nearby town of Westford. Her parents sold their farm and moved in order to provide her with the opportunity to enroll at the town's academy (by completing what we would consider the equivalent of a high school education). A few years later, her family moved again to nearby Littleton, Massachusetts, where she helped her parents run the family store. A growing number of girls were offered the opportunity of attending academies with the understanding that they could become teachers, one of the few acceptable forms of employment for young women. After graduation, and befitting a young unmarried woman, she took a position as an elementary schoolteacher. For two years she persevered and bided her time, longing for an opportunity to further challenge her mind.

Ellen Swallow set her sights on attending college. She applied to Vassar College with the goal of immediately beginning study. However, instead of studying at Vassar, the next few years were filled with caring for her ailing mother, teaching school, tutoring, and cleaning houses. The world was changing. Ellen Swallow spent her time teaching young children and hoping for her chance at higher education.

The 1850s brought the country closer to civil war. Harriet Beecher Stowe wrote *Uncle Tom's Cabin*, opening up the minds of many U.S. citizens to the grave injustices of slavery. For a few, life at home began to ease with new inventions such as the Singer sewing machine, the washing machine, and evaporated milk. The 1860s were the Lincoln years, and the Civil War claimed many lives in both the North and South. Midway through the decade, slaves were freed and a whole way of life had to be restructured for many. *Alice in Wonderland* reached America, and literature that was fanciful and innovative became the pastime of some.

Frugality and thrift were the hallmarks of the average family. A use was found for everything. Nothing was wasted or thrown away. For example, clothing was darned and patched until it could no longer be used, and then it became rags for household quilts and cleaning. Any scrap was used for patching other clothing or making quilts or rugs. Finally, if no further use could be found at home, rags were sold to the ragman and eventually ended up as paper. It wasn't until the late 1860s that paper was made from wood pulp.

Educating a young woman was considered frivolous and excessive as a woman's role in society was firmly established. That role was to marry, bear and raise children, and maintain the proper running of a household. Societal and economics changes in the United States during the early part of the 1800s resulted in opportunities for women in higher education by the time the century was at its midpoint. For example, westward expansion relocated many men, rendering fewer available for marrying in the East. Families became interested in having self-supporting daughters; and in order to relieve financial pressure on families, many young women were sent to college. It should be noted that Oberlin College in Ohio was the first college in the United States to admit women as degree candidates in 1837 (Kleszynski, May, & Alderman, 1994).

The Dream of Higher Education

In 1868, Ellen Swallow's dream of higher education came true as she was admitted to Vassar College in Poughkeepsie, New York. She was called a "special student" (Hunt, 1942). Majors were not chosen. Instead, all students studied the Bible, church history, Latin, Greek, calculus, and astronomy. Ellen Swallow was far away from home in new surroundings but found her intellectual home in studying astronomy and chemistry with Vassar astronomer Maria Mitchell (Hunt, 1942).

As Ellen Swallow concentrated on proving she was capable of studying at a higher level, the world around her continued to change. However, young women like Ellen Swallow weren't the only ones pursuing new opportunities. In 1868, when Ellen Swallow entered Vassar, the 14th Amendment was adopted, giving African Americans the right to citizenship. Work life changed as Congress also passed an eight-hour federal workday. Ellen Swallow was admitted to the senior class of Vassar in 1869 and completed her requirements for graduation in 1870. In this short time span, African Americans were allowed to serve in Congress, Rockefeller founded Standard Oil, and rail refrigeration cars made transport of fresh produce and meats feasible. From 1860 to 1870, the population of the United States grew from 31 million to 39 million, Massachusetts passed the first mandatory school law, and the Gadsden Purchase completed the Mexican border at the Rio Grande. For many U.S. citizens, the increasing number of women attending college was a sign of changing social order (Kleszynski et al., 1994).

After graduating from Vassar, Ellen Swallow sought employment with various industrial chemists but in each case was turned down. The country was becoming comfortable with educating women but not with employing them as professionals. One chemist, however, recognized her talent and encouraged her to further her education at the Massachusetts Institute of Technology (MIT) in Cambridge, Massachusetts. Doing so would make her the first woman in America to be accepted as a student by a scientific school. Ellen Swallow decided to pursue this challenge.

To be a woman and hold a college degree was an exceptional circumstance in the 1800s. Ellen Swallow's educational experiences reflected the importance of her goal of expanding her mind. Since no woman had ever been admitted to MIT, Swallow's task was to convince the administration that she had what it took to compete in rigorous graduate study. Ellen Swallow was socially and politically shrewd in making the proper contacts. After repeated requests, MIT's president agreed she could attend classes and attempt to study at this advanced level. Since she wasn't charged tuition, the school was not indebted to her if the "experiment" didn't work out. It was noted that she would be under careful observation for signs that she was being "wrecked as a woman" by her advanced studies (Hunt, 1942).

The following is an excerpt from Records of the Meetings of the MIT Corporation ("Ellen Swallow Richards and MIT," 2006) concerning the admittance of Ellen Swallow into MIT:

December 14, 1870

It was voted to confirm the recommendation of the Committee on the School of Industrial Science that Miss Ellen H. Swallow be admitted as a Special Student in Chemistry—it being understood that her admission did not establish a precedent for the general admission of females.

It was voted that other applications from females to enter the various departments of the School be referred to the Committee on the School of Industrial Science, with full power to admit or reject, without consulting the Corporation.

It is difficult to imagine the environment and the pressure Ellen Swallow was under at MIT. Daily, she had to prove that advanced study was not "ruining" her. Male students made requests for clothes to be darned, buttons to be sewn on, and cleaning advice. She persevered, and even though she graduated at the top of her class, her honor was not acknowledged due to the fact she was a woman. Although she was disrespected on many fronts, her hard work paid off with the honor of assisting the renowned chairman of the mining engineering department, Dr. Robert Richards, in his on-location scientific investigations. This was an honor many students desired.

After three years of intense study, Ellen Swallow earned a second bachelor's degree—a Bachelor of Science from MIT. Her degree was in chemistry. In a memorandum she sent to school officials, she indicated she could make a greater impact on people's lives in chemistry than in other fields of study. This same year, she also submitted her thesis on the chemical analysis of an iron ore and received a master's degree from Vassar. She then continued her studies at MIT with the goal of earning a Ph.D. in chemistry. However, MIT did not award the degree even though she completed all of the requirements. Later, her future husband reflected that this was probably due to the reluctance of the school to award the very first doctorate to a woman. The school did not award a doctoral degree until 1886 and it was to a man.

The following is an excerpt from Records of the Meetings of the MIT Corporation ("Ellen Swallow Richards and MIT," 2006) concerning the conferring of a degree on Ellen Swallow:

May 14, 1873

It was voted to adopt the recommendation of the Committee on the School that Miss E. H. Swallow be allowed to present herself as a candidate for the Degree of the Institute, and to take the examinations necessary for the Degree in Chemistry.

It was voted to confirm the recommendation of the Committee on the School that Miss Ellen H. Swallow, a special student in Chemistry, be permitted to enter the examinations for the Degree of the Institute.

Ellen Swallow realized how fortunate she was to have experienced such rich educational opportunities. She was convinced all women should have the same opportunities. As the first woman to study at the Massachusetts Institute of Technology, Ellen Swallow developed MIT's Women's Laboratory so more women could come to MIT to study science. Although it may seem unfair that women were not encouraged to participate in the "regular" lab, Ellen Swallow knew the Women's Laboratory was a significant step toward providing educational opportunity for women. She was dedicated to providing the same or better quality education to women enrolled in the program as was offered to men in the regular laboratory program.

Impacting the World

Ellen Swallow was very aware of the changing world around her and the impact education could make at both the personal and global level. Besides increasing opportunities for women, she was aware of the many needs of less-advantaged men and women. Her innovative studies of air, water, and food contributed to the creation of national public health standards and the new disciplines of sanitary engineering and nutrition. She was an inspiration to many. Serving as a pioneer for women in science and higher education, she was followed by many to MIT through the years.

In 1875, at the age of 33, Ellen Swallow married Professor Robert H. Richards, head of the department of mining engineering at MIT. Together they collaborated in the chemistry of ore analysis. (Incidentally, as a result of this work, she was elected the first woman president of the American Institute of Mining and Metallurgical Engineers in 1879.)

The Richards' Italianate-style home, which they generously shared with MIT students, still stands in a suburb of Boston. The home was systematically remodeled to incorporate many of their pioneering environmental concerns. For example, windows were installed that allowed air to travel in and out depending on air temperature through openings at the top and bottom of the window. Lead pipes were removed and plants were grown indoors to produce oxygen, and the waste system was redirected away from the drinking well. Ellen Swallow Richards invited MIT students to experiment in her home kitchen by calculating fuel, time, and money needed for each kitchen task.

Together the couple formed an important alliance that made a great impact on Boston's well-educated elite. People readily listened to their innovative ideas. Teaching, research, and social activities filled their time. Ellen Swallow Richards was a fascinating "working woman," a rarity among socially elite Bostonians. She continued to solicit funds for starting the Women's Laboratory at MIT while at the same time writing books and articles that applied chemistry in a practical way (Hunt, 1942).

After working as an instructor at MIT for several years, without pay, Ellen Swallow Richards passionately petitioned the Women's Education Association of Boston to pay for instruments, equipment, and books to create a research laboratory for women on the MIT campus. In the autumn of 1876, the Women's Laboratory opened. However, despite all her effort in establishing the lab, MIT Professor John M. Ordway was named director. Richards was named his assistant. Twenty-three students, most of them nondegree candidates and nearly all public school teachers, enrolled the first term. Students studied chemistry, mineralogy, and animal physiology. Over 500 women studied at the facility during its seven years of existence. With the changing times, some were able to secure jobs as government or industrial consultants. Within this time frame, women became accepted as capable regular students. When MIT opened additional labs in a new building, space was made available to both men and women.

The following is the Women's Laboratory announcement from the Massachusetts Institute of Technology's Twelfth Annual Catalogue of the Officers and Students, 1876–1877, ("Massachusetts Institute," 1999):

At the request of the Woman's Education Association of Boston, and with their generous cooperation, new laboratories have been recently provided for the special instruction of women. The design is to afford every facility for the study of Chemical Analysis, of Industrial Chemistry, of Mineralogy, and of Chemistry as related to Vegetable and Animal Physiology. These courses are intended for such as may be able to devote their whole time to the work, as well as for those who, by reason of other engagements, can spend only a few hours a week in these exercises. The laboratories, which are in the Annex to the main building, are open from 8:30 A.M., till 5:30 P.M. Students in these laboratories will pay the same fees as other students of the Institute.

The Women's Laboratory had many critics. Despite the critics, the laboratory was a success. In an 1877 transcription of the first report to the Women's Education Association ("Massachusetts Institute," 1999), Ellen Swallow Richards reported the following:

It is always pleasant to us to have our prophecies fulfilled and especially pleasant when some doubt has been expressed as to the probability of fulfillment. I hope to be pardoned therefore if I seem to boast of the fulfillment of my own predictions. I recall so clearly a conversation with two officers of the association on the morning on which we paid over the last installment of money collected for the Laboratory and while both of the ladies were very much interested in the plan and delighted with the hearty response given to their appeal they both expressed their doubts as to the result. One said to me: I wish I could feel as sure as you do that there are women who do really want this kind of opportunity. When I said that I felt perfectly sure of 15 students during the first year; both exclaimed oh if there are 8 or 10 I shall be quite happy and think the money well spent. The rooms were not open until the last of October and were not advertised outside of the Association except by a few circulars sent to friends of the members and to contributors. At this date we have had 23 students in the Chemical Laboratory, 10 or 12 other applicants failed to come by reason of sickness, inability to pay, or insufficient preparation. Some 15 are already enrolled for next year.

Following are excerpts from Minutes of the Executive Committee of the Corporation at MIT concerning the establishment of the Women's Laboratory ("Ellen Swallow Richards and MIT," 2006):

September 29, 1883

Voted: that in view of the facilities afforded by the new chemical laboratories,
and in pursuance of the wishes of the benefactors of the Woman's Laboratory, the present so-called Woman's Laboratory will be discontinued and students will be admitted to the Kidder Laboratories without distinction of sex.

November 6, 1883

The President was requested to express to Mrs. Ellen Swallow Richards the thanks of the Corporation for her past service and their regret that for the moment there seems to be no place where she can be employed. It was directed that the name of Mrs. Richards should be maintained in the Catalogue.

April 15, 1884

On motion of Dr. Williams it was voted that Mrs. Ellen Swallow Richards be appointed assistant under Professor Nichols for one year at a salary of $600 per annum her duties to be to give instruction in a course of Sanitary Chemistry.

May 6, 1884

So much of the vote found at the meeting of this Committee April 15, 1884 and recorded page 237 as determined the salary of Mrs. Ellen Swallow Richards was rescinded, and said salary was fixed for one year at $1,000. This Committee regards the work to be done by Mrs. Richards under the direction of Professor Nichols as an experiment, and in no way commits itself to the continuance of this instruction in Sanitary Chemistry unless encouraged by the results of this year of trial.

Ellen Swallow Richards' impact on MIT and subsequently on higher education for women is astounding. Beginning in 1876, she was head of the science section of the Society to Encourage Studies at Home. In 1882, she cofounded the Association of Collegiate Alumnae (later known as the American Association of University Women). In 1884, she worked in sanitation chemistry as an assistant to Professor William Nichols. For the first time since teaching at MIT, she was paid for her work. Prior to this time, she donated her time without pay. With her leadership, biology was introduced to the MIT science curriculum and the oceanographic institute, Woods Hole, was created. Richards always found a way to apply her scholarly pursuits to the well-being of families and the environment, whether it involved testing foods and home furnishings for contaminants, conserving energy, or investigating water pollution.

During this intellectually stimulating time, Ellen Swallow Richards first coined the term *oecology*, which later became *ecology*, a term widely used today (Clarke, 1973). She also noted that the interaction between people and their environment could lead to future environmental crises. Would the increasingly mechanized ways of producing goods with their inherent pollutants forever change the delicate balance of the natural environment? Would industrial by-products adversely affect the health of people? How would substandard working conditions affect the spread of disease? Despite her forward thinking, the concept of ecology as an environmental science was an idea not widely accepted until almost another century had passed.

A Century Draws to a Close

During her professional career, the changes and the challenges of family life inspired much of the work of Ellen Swallow Richards. The family landscape and typical household were changing rapidly. Between 1880 and 1920, half of the rural population in America had abandoned farming and moved into the more populated towns and cities. Over one-third of the population lived in poverty despite the doubling of per capita income and the gross national product. Fifteen million new immigrants came to the country between 1890 and 1915, arriving primarily from Ireland, Italy, Germany, Scandinavia, and Eastern Europe. As the immigrants embarked on a new life, different sounds, smells, and sights greeted the newcomers. Racism and xenophobia were becoming more prevalent as each immigrant group fought over scarce resources.

Although Ellen Swallow Richards was a member of a well-educated elite family, the majority of women at the turn of the century did not have access to education. In her social circle, women were privileged by class, and educational opportunities were within reach. There was much talk about the possibility of women gaining the right to vote, which promised a future filled with new opportunities. For the first time, some traditionally male occupations were opened to more educated women. Ellen Swallow Richards was a tangible example of the highly educated professional woman. According to U.S. census figures in the early twentieth century, employment in building trades in such positions as carpenter, stonecutter, or teamster, or in professional trades in positions such as detective, banker, or undertaker, became possible for some women. A growing number of women could realize their dream of contributing in the professions—primarily the clergy, law, medicine, teaching, nursing, and

journalism. As a result, women's enrollment in colleges and universities increased dramatically (Henretta, Brownlee, Brody, Ware, & Johnson, 1997).

The majority of women of the Boston elite were native-born, middle-class white women. For these women, fashion was a method of showing the rise in their societal stature. For the first time in U.S. history, hemlines were rising, corsets were being discarded, and hair was being worn shorter than ever before. So extensive and far-reaching were the changes that even by the early 1890s, the expression "New Woman" had become commonplace. Of course, not all women had access to the ideal, and this standard often varied depending on race, class, ethnicity, religion, region, or politics (Henretta et al., 1997).

Dramatic population growth occurred in U.S. cities during the two decades between 1880 and 1900. The Industrial Revolution held the promise of paid work for many and spurred the exodus from farms to densely populated urban areas. Combined with the steady stream of immigrants—many lacking usable skills, education, or financial resources—cities became seas of filth, poverty, and rampantly spreading disease. Yellow fever, cholera, smallpox, and infant diarrhea were spread through close contact, lack of indoor plumbing, and lack of knowledge about how diseases spread (Henretta et al., 1997).

How did the former rural families and new immigrants fare in the burgeoning cities? In their former lives, they provided most of the family's needs by their own labors, and very few items had to be purchased. Meat, milk, butter, cheese, vegetables, fruits, cornmeal, and maple syrup, among other staples, were all produced on the farm. These families were now purchasing food items, and many tried to find ways to preserve food without the benefit of refrigeration, cold cellars, or available ice. They were accustomed to making clothing at home out of purchased cotton or woolen goods. The average farmer owned several sheep whose wool was spun into yarn to be knit into clothing or woven into blankets. Shoes were purchased and were mended and mended again. Quilts, rugs, pillows, and mattresses were made in the home. Having immigrated from overseas or from the farm to cities, the new urbanites found factory work a foreign concept. Many household tasks had to be relearned. Long work hours did not allow time for many household tasks, and resources—including space—were not available in urban residences. Also, family life changed dramatically as many children labored long hours in factories alongside their parents rather than attending school.

The way of life in the United States continued changing at a rapid pace with increased migration to cities in the 1890s. The Industrial Revolution and the rapid population growth changed the face of the nation's cities. New problems emerged as noise, traffic jams, slums, air pollution, poor sanitation, and health problems became commonplace. Housing was crowded for those who resided in the cities because many lived in crowded tenement housing. Ethnic neighborhoods and communities formed, and these neighborhoods, especially for immigrant populations, were often the centers of family and community life.

For Ellen Swallow Richards, lifestyle differences between her group of educated, wealthy men and women and the plight of the typical city-dwelling family were pronounced. The difference in opportunities afforded the women in her circle compared to others in the working class was vast. However, Richards advocated tirelessly for education as well as economic, social, and political changes that supported a better quality of life. She was convinced that if women had access to financial resources and education, the impact would be of great benefit to struggling families (Hunt, 1942).

As social empathizers, Ellen Swallow Richards' social circle would discuss the plight of the impoverished and uneducated. Never one to sit idly by and talk of "what if," she came up with a plan and "sold" it to her circle of friends. Since few women could attend college and the professions were only an option for a few, Ellen Swallow Richards proposed to teach science in the community and public schools in order to expand the mind and offer applied knowledge

that would enhance the quality of life for families. With the financial backing of her friends, she began offering home, school, and community studies in sanitation, nutrition, child development, and food preservation. Her popular community "courses" taught men and women how to care for themselves and their families through applying the principles of science and economics (Hunt, 1942).

Richards' unending energy and enthusiasm spawned Boston's first school lunch program and successfully introduced courses in domestic science into the city's public schools. Under her leadership, the New England Kitchen opened in Boston. Science was applied to family eating habits as the staff offered low-cost, nutritious food to working-class families and instruction in sanitary food preparation. She also led the creation of the Rumford Kitchen at the 1893 World's Columbian Exposition in Chicago. This showcase kitchen was a popular exhibit that served inexpensive, nutritious meals and educated people about nutrition and proper food preparation. She also authored over a dozen books, including *The Chemistry of Cooking* (1882), *Home Sanitation: A Manual for Housekeepers* (1887), *Laboratory Notes on Industrial Water Analysis: A Survey Course for Engineers* (1908), and *Euthenics: The Science of Controllable Environment* (1912).

Ellen Swallow Richards later served (1884–1894) as a chemist to the Manufacturers Mutual Fire Insurance Company, where she conducted studies on the potential danger from spontaneous combustion of various oils in commercial use. During the same time period, she also served on the State Board of Health of Massachusetts where she began a survey of water supply contamination that laid the groundwork for water testing today (Hunt, 1942).

In 1899, Ellen Swallow Richards and like-minded colleagues organized a summer conference in Lake Placid, New York. Their goal was to define standards for teacher training and certification in the new field of home economics and establish a philosophical and theoretical foundation for the new discipline. At the Tenth Lake Placid Conference in 1908, the entourage formed the American Home Economics Association and elected Richards as the first president. In 1910, she spearheaded the inception of the *Journal of Home Economics* and was also named to the Council of the National Education Association. Although she never received her Ph.D. from MIT, Smith College awarded her an honorary doctorate (Hunt, 1942).

At 69 years of age, Ellen Swallow Richards lived much longer than the projected life expectancy for her time. She died after a brief illness on March 30, 1911, at her home in Boston, Massachusetts. Her grave is in Gardiner, Maine. She spent her last days in public service, speaking out for better standards of living. Her far-reaching influence, pioneering spirit, and professional achievements are still felt today.

Building a Discipline and Profession

Domestic science, human ecology, and human environmental sciences are a few of the many alternative names used for home economics over the years. Although still called home economics and home science in some nations, the discipline is officially known in the United States today as *family and consumer sciences*, and specialized terms are used for its many subdivisions. See **Figure 1-1**. *Family and consumer sciences* is a discipline and a profession that focuses on an integrative approach to the reciprocal relationships among individuals, families, and communities, as well as the environments in which they function. The history of family and consumer sciences is filled with men and women who were willing to use their talent, knowledge, and skills to provide more opportunities for others to improve their quality of life.

Although Ellen Swallow Richards is known as the founder of the family and consumer sciences discipline and the American Home Economics Association (now named the American Association of Family and Consumer Sciences), there were many other forward-thinking pioneers.

Selected Areas of Specialization in Family and Consumer Sciences
Food and Nutrition
Dietetics Food Safety Food Science Food Service Management Hospitality and Tourism Management Nutrition and Exercise (Kinesiology)
Hospitality
Food Service Lodging Recreation Travel and Tourism
Textiles and Apparel
Apparel Design Apparel Management Apparel Marketing Apparel Production Textile Design Textile Science
Interior Design and Housing
Commercial Interior Design Housing Policy Interior Marketing and Management Interior Merchandising Residential Interior Design Residential Property Management
Family and Consumer Sciences Education and Extension
Consumer Journalism Education Extension
Family and Community Services
Adult Development and Aging (Gerontology) Child Development Child, Family, and Community Services Early Childhood Education Family Relations Lifespan Human Development Youth and Adolescent Development
Consumer Resource Management
Consumer Affairs Family Finance

Figure 1-1 Family and consumer sciences encompasses a wide variety of specializations.

The 1890s through the 1920s were decades of great change for America. The men and women highlighted in **Figure 1-2**, and many others, made major contributions to reform, politics, and national life during this time called the Progressive Era. Some historians believe that the Progressive Era is the time when the United States of America "came of age." However, the development of family and consumer sciences did not stop at the Progressive Era. The discipline and related professions have continued to change, reflecting the times of each era. In the following sections, changes from the Progressive Era to the present time are highlighted.

Influential Pioneers in the Early Development of the Profession	
Catherine Esther Beecher (1800–1876)	Catherine Esther Beecher lived in an era that was known as the "cult of domesticity." As a part of a very large family, her educational opportunities were limited to self-study at home. She was convinced that curriculum should be developed for women and, as a result, she opened a private school for young women in Hartford, Connecticut. Later, she organized the Western Female Institute in Cincinnati, Ohio. Beecher is recognized as one of the early promoters of higher education for women as she was instrumental in the founding of women's colleges at Burlington, Iowa; Quincy, Illinois; and Milwaukee, Wisconsin. Catherine Beecher became a national authority on domestic well-being with her many books including *A Treatise on Domestic Economy* and *A Study In American Domesticity*, the treatise that explained the various aspects of domestic life published in the 1840s and reprinted for decades after. The success of the book was astonishing. (Her younger sister, Harriet Beecher Stowe, wrote *Uncle Tom's Cabin: Or, Life Among the Lowly*.)
President Abraham Lincoln (1809–1865)	In 1862, under President Abraham Lincoln, Congress approved an act that required all states to designate one state college that was utilizing land given by the federal government toward the dissemination of practical and useful information relating to agriculture, home economics, and rural energy. This important act is called the *Morrill Land-Grant Act*.
Isabella Mary Beeton (1836–1865)	Isabella Mary Beeton is best known for her *Book of Household Management* that was the most widely read of all household advice books in the 1800s. The middle-class of the United States was a new phenomenon, and Beeton wrote to this audience. In her book, she acknowledged that she was motivated to help women achieve the perfect home. Home management was arduous in the 1800s. Although her ideas may seem outdated today and far from contributing toward the betterment of women, she provided one of the first texts written to and for educating women to lead a higher quality of life.
Mary B. Welch (1841–1923)	In 1871, Mary B. Welch was assigned the task of teaching home economics to women at Iowa State College. This is believed to be the first effort in the United States to teach home economics to college students. She had no prescribed curriculum, no books, and very little money to do her work. She developed a system in which all students rotated through laboratory settings simulating the kitchen, dining room, and laundry where women were given training in preparing and serving meals and in maintaining clothes. She also gave lectures on cooking, sewing, water sanitation, and nutrition. She believed the best way to learn was by doing and her innovative teaching practices helped the program flourish. During her 15 years of service, her lectures and laboratory teaching covered cooking, sewing, house furnishings, health, care of the sick, ventilation, water supply purity, etiquette, child care, hospitality, and entertainment. Besides teaching at the college level, Welch took her curriculum into the local community.

Figure 1-2 In addition to Ellen Swallow Richards, these individuals contributed to the early development of family and consumer sciences.

(Continued)

Influential Pioneers in the Early Development of the Profession	
W.O. Atwater **(1844–1907)**	Wilbur Olin Atwater received his PhD in chemistry from Yale in 1869. He is most known for his pioneering work developing the caloric table and an instrument to measure caloric values in food. He is also known for beginning several of the Agricultural Experiment Stations across the country. Atwater recommended proscribed dietary studies to establish how nutrient intake affected metabolism and muscular effort. He believed United States citizens consumed too much food and exercised too little—a revolutionary thought in his day. He attended several of the Lake Placid Conferences and believed in the profession's call to apply science to everyday living.
Annie Godfrey Dewey **(1850–1822)**	Annie Dewey, librarian and educator, was instrumental in getting home economics into higher education and into public schools. Professionally, she was the first librarian at Wellesley College and cofounded the International Library of Congress. Both she and her husband, Melvil Dewey, attended the Lake Placid Conferences.
Melvil Dewey **(1859–1952)**	Melvil Dewey is remembered as the originator of the Dewey Decimal Classification (DDC) system, the founding member of the American Library Association, and founding editor of the *Library Journal*. Among the many concerns that attracted Dewey's support was women's suffrage and pioneering the creation of career opportunities for women. He attended the Lake Placid Conferences along with his first wife, Annie Dewey. Together they developed the Lake Placid Club, a resort for social, cultural, and spiritual enrichment in the Adirondack Mountains.
Marion Talbot **(1858–1949)**	As a contemporary of Ellen Swallow Richards and a fellow alumna of MIT, Marion Talbot was involved with many of the same activities in and around the Boston area. She was a writer and served as Dean of Women at the University of Chicago where she administered a home economics program. She also attended the Lake Placid Conferences.
Alice P. Norton **(1860–1928)**	Alice P. Norton worked alongside Ellen Swallow Richards in providing home economics education to the community throughout New England. She was a graduate of Smith College and was an attendee at the Lake Placid Conferences. She served as the second editor of the *Journal of Home Economics*. She also taught and worked in the field of dietetics.
Isabel Bevier **(1860–1942)**	Isabel Bevier conducted nutritional research while on the staff of the University of Illinois, where she also served as the head of the department. She helped develop the new field of home economics along scientific, rather than utilitarian lines, and served as the second president of the organization. She was a chemist and writer, known nationally for her book, *Home Economics in Education* (1924), which pushed for home economics in higher education.
Martha Van Rensselaer **(1864–1932)**	Martha Van Rensselaer was a pioneer home economist in upstate New York. She developed courses for women in rural areas of New York during the later 1800s. These courses, with others, developed into New York State College of Home Economics, of which she was a director. Later, in 1900, she joined the faculty of Cornell University. Van Rensselaer was considered a leading authority on issues affecting women and families. She understood the value of the mass media in disseminating her knowledge to millions. In addition to her widely read 1919 text, *A Manual of Home Making*, she also wrote regularly for the *Ladies Home Journal*, *Children's Magazine*, and *Boys and Girls*.

Figure 1-2 Continued.

(Continued)

Influential Pioneers in the Early Development of the Profession	
Caroline Hunt **(1865–1927)**	Caroline Hunt was a philosopher, writer, and scientist. She attended the Lake Placid Conferences and helped form the philosophical underpinnings of the profession. She was the only female full professor at University of Wisconsin and established the Home Economics program there. She is also remembered for writing *The Life of Ellen Swallow Richards*, a book that has been reprinted for decades.
Benjamin Andrews **(1878–1963)**	Benjamin Andrews was a professor of home economics for over 40 years at Columbia University. One of his books, *Economics of the Household. It's Administration and Finance* (published in 1923) is considered a classic. He served as the chairman of the editorial board for the *Journal of Home Economics* and spread the mission of home economics through a long career giving lectures, writing, and teaching. He attended the Lake Placid Conferences, serving as Secretary-Treasurer of the new AHEA.
Beatrice Paolucci **(1920–1983)**	Beatrice Paolucci was an educator and a visionary. As a professor at Michigan State University for many years, she made significant contributions to the field through her prolific writing. Forward-thinking in her transdisciplinary research, Paolucci's holistic thinking conceptualized the idea of home economics as human ecology.

Figure 1-2 Continued.

Era of the Land-Grant Universities: 1862–1890

In the last half of the 1800s, a significant legislative act was passed that forever changed the face of colleges and universities in the United States. This act was called the *Morrill Act of 1862*. During the later decades of the 1800s, the federal government was rich in land, even if not rich in tax dollars. The vast, empty land in the west and the social interest in education motivated the federal government to designate a parcel of land in each state to be used for establishing a university. These universities, called *land-grant universities*, were to extend educational opportunities that promoted agricultural, industrial, and domestic economy, which was later known as home economics (East, 1980). The intent was to make educational opportunities available to the masses and to provide programs that focused on practical issues along with scholarly subjects. Nutrition, botany, geology, agriculture, mining, and engineering were typical courses of study offered (East, 1980).

Although the land-grant universities made higher education accessible for many, there were many who were still excluded. Not all land-grant universities were coeducational. Even so, less than five percent of women finished high school or attended college (East, 1980). Minorities were also excluded as many land-grant universities were designated for white students only. In 1890, subsequent legislation established Historically Black Colleges and Universities (HBCUs), many of which were land-grant institutions. Although the schools were established, they often did not receive the same level of funding as white universities.

The Progressive Era: 1909–1920

The Progressive Era was a time of business expansion and progressive reform in the United States. The era provided the perfect backdrop for the American Home Economics Association to flourish. Several pioneers who helped to shape the field had set the stage as they worked to make society a better and safer place in which to live. These forward-thinkers called themselves *Progressives*. They were joined by Progressives in other fields who tried to make big business more responsible through various regulations, to clean up corrupt city governments, improve working conditions in factories, and create better living conditions for immigrants and those who lived in poverty—often in slum tenements. This was done through application of the sciences and, as a result, many were also concerned with the environment and conservation of resources, such as water supply sanitation. During her lifetime, Ellen Swallow Richards coined the term "oecology" which is known today as the field of ecology.

Many in this generation also expected to make the world a more democratic place. Domestically, this included working toward giving women the right to vote. Internationally, it meant trying to make the world a safer place. In 1917, the United States joined the democratic Great Britain and France in their war against autocratic Germany and Austria-Hungary in the "war to end all wars" (World War I). When the war broke out in Europe three years prior, in 1914, President Woodrow Wilson declared the nation's neutrality. However, within a few months, men were being drafted into the military. Women and other workers, few of whom had ever worked outside the home, began working in factories in order to replace many of the workers who had left to serve in the military. They were instrumental in producing supplies needed for the war effort. Home economists provided nutrition education to military personnel, served as volunteers and nurses, and designed programs for conserving and preserving war rations.

Elevating women's roles in the home, family, and community shaped people's views of society and reform. This offered women the right to have a profound influence on the development of modern America (Henretta et al., 1997). Although it may appear that home economics kept women in the home, while the women's suffrage movement attempted to move women out of the home, in reality, the two forces joined and shared ideas, tactics, and mutual promotion as both had the same goal of empowering women (Brownlee, 1979). As society changed, many organizations and movements were founded to address the problems that resulted. For example, trade unions, the National Consumer League,

the Young Women's Christian Association (YWCA), and the women's suffrage movement all began during the Progressive Era. Although women had not yet been granted the right to vote, many women were involved in shaping public policy and reform. Women's rights increased in minimum wages for women, provided benefits for children and pregnant women, and established labor laws to protect children. Many of the policies and institutions created during the Progressive Era remain an important part of life in the United States today.

An important development during the Progressive Era was the expansion of the mission of land-grant colleges. Under President Woodrow Wilson, Congress approved the **Smith-Lever Act of 1914,** which established the Cooperative Extension Service. In addition to continuing the educational mission of land-grant colleges, this act required all land-grant colleges to establish an Agricultural Experiment Station—an entity dedicated to the dissemination of practical and useful information relating to agriculture, home economics, and rural communities (East, 1980). In higher education, experiment station research has expanded in areas of textile fiber science, nutrition, family relations, human development, and consumer economics.

Another significant piece of legislation followed—the **Smith-Hughes Act of 1917.** This was the first act setting vocational education apart from the regular high school curriculum and establishing federal funds to support vocational education, now called career and technical education (CTE). Home economics courses received federal funding when included in high school curriculum, and this greatly influenced the dissemination of the discipline in public high schools. Today, CTE education in high schools includes family and consumer sciences courses that prepare students for their future careers as well as their family and community roles. In addition, the **Perkins Act** was first authorized in 1984 to support secondary and postsecondary vocational education programs in agriculture, business, and technology (Pundt, 1980).

A national honor society, *Omicron Nu*, was established in 1912 at Michigan Agricultural College, later to become Michigan State University. The society later became known as *Kappa Omicron Nu* (when the organization merged with the *Kappa Omicron Phi Honor Society*). Also, *Phi Upsilon Omicron* was founded to recognize scholarship in family and consumer sciences. Advanced degrees were offered at several universities as home economics provided a critical pathway to higher education for many women.

The 1920s and 1930s

Following World War I, the United States was the most industrialized country in the world, and economic prosperity prevailed in the early and mid-1920s. The new ideas and subsequent social movements of the Progressive Era were reaching fruition. For example, in 1921, after years of struggle, women gained the right to vote. The Smith-Lever and Smith-Hughes Acts helped home economics/family and consumer sciences become subjects that were a part of curricula in public schools, colleges, and universities, and in extension programs offered in communities. Parent education was a valued program that drew audiences throughout these decades.

In the 1920s, economic prosperity contributed to increased disposable income. The middle class grew as United States citizens began to buy products, such as clothing, that were formerly produced in the home. United States citizens became consumers rather than producers of their own consumable goods, thus opening a new field of consumer education.

The American Dietetic Association was organized to support professionals who earned the credential of registered dietitian, and many women were employed as home economists and nutritionists in corporations. The Association, now called the Academy of Nutrition and Dietetics, established professional standards and the requirement of a baccalaureate degree for dietitians. Ready-to-wear fashion spread as more women became wage-earners and inexpensive apparel became available. The Roaring Twenties

was a time of growth, prosperity, and openness to new ideas (Polakoff, Rosenberg, Bolton, Story, & Schwartz, 1976).

On the other hand, the 1920s saw the decline of many Progressive Era reform activities that had been so widespread after 1900. Quotas on the number of foreign immigrants who could enter the country were set as racial tensions grew. Consumer credit issues surfaced for the first time as many learned what it meant to buy on credit or installment plans. Home economists began to teach financial literacy and consumer economics. Home economists were hired by corporations and utility companies to give a "woman's perspective," since women had become the primary consumers of products and services for the home. Many economists believed the economic prosperity would continue. Despite their optimism, on October 24, 1929, the New York stock market crashed. That day, known as Black Thursday, caused an economic panic that put the country into the Great Depression, which lasted well into the 1930s.

As money became scarce because of the Depression, money scams became more abundant. Families who lost their homes adapted to temporary living arrangements called "Hoovervilles" after President Herbert Hoover, who stated that economic relief should be a private, not a federal, endeavor (Polakoff, et al., 1976). Eventually, federal feeding, housing, and work programs were established, providing important roles for home economists. For example, home economists were supported by the Temporary Emergency Relief Administration in their work to educate impoverished families about basic nutrition and clothing maintenance using scarce resources (Stage & Vincenti, 1997).

It was difficult for those who were employed to fight for labor unions, many of which were established in the 1920s, even though they desired better working conditions. What was once the land of hope and opportunity had become the land of desperation. Home economists (family and consumer sciences professionals) played prominent roles in many social reforms, including public education, immigrant resettlement, health and hygiene education programs, and furthering the cause of trade unions (East, 1980). First Lady Eleanor Roosevelt recognized the important role of home economics (family and consumer sciences) and enthusiastically endorsed public school and higher education programs throughout the nation as essential to health and wellness. She was a major proponent of women's, children's, and family issues (Pundt, 1980).

During the Depression, it was often difficult for people to keep their families housed, dressed, and fed and their children in school. Changes in fashion slowed considerably. Simple styles, recycled fashions, and hand-me-downs were the norm. For many, food was scarce. Simple, practical foods were grown and purchased. Industrial researchers found new ways to refrigerate food, resulting in less spoilage. Public schools faced a shortage of cash, as many citizens were unable to pay their taxes. Some school districts ceased to operate, others shortened the school year, while some significantly decreased or eliminated teacher pay. The need for practical education focusing on family needs was high, and the family and consumer sciences profession responded accordingly (Pundt, 1980).

In 1926, the Home Economics Association adopted the Betty Lamp as a symbol of the association. The lamp is derived from a German term meaning "to make better." It was used during colonial times to provide light in homes. The Betty Lamp is still used today to represent "the profession's enlightenment through leadership in thought and action for family and consumer sciences professionals" (Nickols, 2001).

The 1940s and 1950s

The first half of the 1940s was dominated by another world war. As America entered World War II, war production pulled the country out of the Great Depression. As thousands of young men left each month to fight the war overseas, many jobs were opened for women. Single women were recruited and employed first to fill the spaces left empty by men, followed by married women. This is often referred to as the first great exodus of women from the home to the workplace. Job opportunities outside of agriculture opened up for African Americans as well. The end result was that after the soldiers returned from war, women and African Americans held higher status than in the past (Goodwin, 2005).

Rationing of food, clothing, and gas was another way citizens supported the war effort. Clothing was very utilitarian and simple with restrictions on fabric yardage used and types of closures. Since zippers were rationed, wrap-around skirts were designed. Food vouchers were distributed based on family size to limit the amount of food consumed. Families were encouraged to grow their own food in "victory gardens" to offset the demand for military food rations. Few toys were made, and those that were focused on military themes. Automobile production ceased as metals and rubber were used in war efforts. Families learned to live on few resources. Home economists built a reputation for educating citizens based on scientific research. Both written publications and radio broadcasts were used to disseminate the information (Goodwin, 2005).

When the war ended and the soldiers returned home, many of those who had joined the labor force had to give up their jobs for the returning veterans. Countless young families migrated to the suburbs rather than returning to family farms. Many had children right away, beginning what was known as the Baby Boom. The GI Bill offered a college education to returning veterans and, as a result, three times as many college degrees were awarded at the end of the decade as at the beginning. Neither African Americans nor women were willing to accept a lower status after their experiences in the workplace and the battlefield. The societal fabric of the country began to change. Photographs and stories confirmed that the Holocaust did take place and made people aware of the tragic effects of prejudice (Goodwin, 2005).

The new era brought changes in home technology, housing, fashion, food, parenting, and entertainment. Home technology increased with the rapid development of the refrigerator and many other home appliances. Frozen food soon followed, and the term *TV dinner* was coined. Food storage and preparation items such as aluminum foil and Tupperware® were marketed to decrease the burden on homemakers. As more products became available, industry grew, and America was employed and hopeful. Many women continued to work for pay and also manage their homes. Housing became affordable and available, especially to young veterans and their families. As families grew and a record number of children were born, parents became interested in the "right" way to raise children. New homes, jobs, fashions, and ideas for parenting and educating children marked the end of the 1940s and the beginning of the 1950s (Goodwin, 2005).

With a growing youth population, consumerism boomed. Silly Putty®, hula hoops, drive-in movies, highways, and shopping centers were popular. Despite the optimism of the era, conservatism and anticommunism prevailed. Religion was seen as an indicator of anticommunism. Playing conservative gender roles by dressing the part took on significance, and fashion followed with men dressing in masculine clothing and women in feminine clothing. Children were socialized to traditional gender roles (Bradley, 2005). The home economics profession responded to these societal trends by offering courses in stereotypical homemaking skills. As a result, male participation in the profession dropped dramatically (East, 1980).

The 1950s brought dramatic change as America adopted the policy of "separate but equal" educational opportunities for all. In 1954, Chief Justice Earl Warren and other members of the Supreme Court wrote in Brown v. the Board of Education of Topeka, Kansas, that "separate did not make equal" and began integration of schools in the United States (Garraty & McCaughey, 1989). Although public schools were affected by this legislation, professional associations were not. Black home economists and extension agents were not given the same opportunities as their white counterparts (East, 1980).

The 1960s and 1970s

The 1960s brought changes that focused on youth and energy. The national Head Start early childhood program for disadvantaged children began in 1965. As baby boomers became teenagers and young adults, they made a great impact on U.S. society. The conservatism of the 1950s was questioned, and revolutionary thinking changed life forever in the United States. These changes affected values, beliefs, lifestyles, laws, education, fashion, fads, political viewpoints, and family life. The young, charismatic President John F. Kennedy offered hope for a new society (Goodwin, 2006).

By the middle of the decade, America was fighting a war in Vietnam. Thousands were drafted to serve in the war. Many did not understand the reasoning behind the war and protested against it on college campuses. Some of the controversy surrounded the frustration on campuses that college students were not yet of the age to vote, but they could be drafted (Goodwin, 2006).

In the 1960s, the civil rights movement made great advances. It began peacefully, with Martin Luther King, Jr., leading sit-ins and protests. People from diverse backgrounds joined together to march for racial rights. Later, Malcolm X advocated self-determination for African Americans, and by the end of the decade, the Black Panthers were calling for separatism and violence. Both Martin Luther King and Malcolm X were assassinated. Following the assassinations, Stokely Carmichael was instrumental in the development of the Black Power movement (Goodwin, 2006). In 1962, Florence Low served as President of the American Home Economics Association (AHEA). She acknowledged racial tensions within AHEA and set out to find ways to eliminate them. Through her leadership, membership regulations that limited full participatory status for African Americans were eliminated. Thus, restrictions held since the 1940s were lifted, extending eligibility to Black AHEA members to hold office and participate fully in all states of the Union (Stage & Vincenti, 1997).

In 1963, the Presidential Commission on the Status of Women questioned the unequal treatment of women, giving birth to the women's liberation movement. Author Betty Friedan wrote *The Feminine Mystique* (Polakoff, et al., 1976). When the Civil Rights Act of 1964 was amended, it included gender. The civil rights movement continued and led the way to forced integration and busing for schools in the 1970s (Garraty & McCaughey, 1989).

The revolutionary ideas, fashions, and fads were mainstreamed in the 1970s as gender and racial boundaries blurred. New technology advanced quickly as NASA began developing the space shuttle, computers came closer to the home, and DNA's genetic code was discovered. The Vietnam War ended and when veterans returned, they were met with disillusionment, disgust, and apathy. Abortion was made legal. Divorces increased, and single women faced a new poverty as displaced homemakers. The energy crisis loomed as gas prices soared (Gillis, 2006).

The turbulence of the sixties and seventies redefined many traditional values, especially those related to gender roles. Canning beans, sewing the perfect collar, and stirring a lump-free gravy were no longer priorities for homemakers and did not relate to the priorities of the generation. Family and consumer sciences leaders knew changing economic and social realities for women made many practices old-fashioned and irrelevant to current societal needs. The home economics (family and consumer sciences) discipline, once again, took its lead from cultural events (Whitely, 2006).

Education in America was heavily influenced by the scientific method beginning in the 1950s and continuing throughout the 1960s and 1970s. Home economics, an applied science, did not receive the funding and support given for basic research, nor was it given the same status. Tensions emerged as leaders within the feminist movement questioned home economics as a valid profession. Feminist leader Robin Morgan, in an address given at the AHEA Annual Meeting in 1973, claimed that home economists

were manipulating women as consumers and idealizing the traditional nuclear family and that she was, in fact, addressing "the enemy" (Stage & Vincenti, 1997). Leaders within the profession critically analyzed the role of home economics in society. As a result, the profession became very career-focused. The discipline began to change to meet the needs of society offering more specialized knowledge and increasing discipline-based research in areas of specialization. Specialization areas in nutrition, housing, apparel, consumer economics, and child studies, among others, emerged (East, 1980).

Research and application of research made significant progress in the 1970s. Research in nutrition and child development expanded, and consumer product safety information increased. Specialization of studies emerged, including majors in apparel design, consumer economics, merchandising, dietetics and nutrition, child development, family studies, interior design, and others that focused on depth of knowledge in each area. Many higher educational programs became involved in women's studies, focusing on and promoting feminism. Since the profession attracted women, it was a vehicle for empowering women to achieve their educational aspirations and career goals.

The 1980s and 1990s

The 1980s were filled with growth and prosperity for some people. The rich became richer, while the poor became poorer. *Consumerism*, the idea that increased consumption of goods is good for individuals and the economy, was at an all-time high. Buying on credit was a way of life for many. Baby boomers had reached adulthood and many were splurging on pricey clothing, designer home furnishings, and even designer food. Technology made computers commonplace, and video games became the obsession of children. Medical breakthroughs were common, but AIDS became a global epidemic, and health care costs continued to rise.

More and more men and women attended college. The high school curricula were filled with required courses to assure competence in reading, writing, mathematics, and other basic subjects. Consequently, college-bound students could not fit courses such as family and consumer sciences into their schedules. College students were interested in status, wealth, and power. Business administration and management were the most popular majors. In family and consumer sciences, fashion-merchandising (or apparel marketing) and hospitality management programs drew record numbers of students. Offshore manufacturing of apparel reduced clothing costs to U.S. consumers and made the clothing retail market explode with activity. This caused concerns about social responsibility for the women and children producing the goods in harsh conditions in developing nations (Whitely, 2006).

The nature of families changed during the 1980s. For example, the high divorce rate continued, and many highly educated women chose to have fewer children. Two-earner families, in which both the husband and wife worked outside the home, were even more common than in previous decades. More money was spent on children than ever before. Niche or specialty markets in food, clothing, and shelter developed (Whitley, 2006).

The 1990s emerged as the electronic age as access to computers, cellular phones, and other technologies became affordable. Internet access and the World Wide Web changed the way many people communicated, received information, shopped, and conducted business, but a "digital divide" created by poverty and age became evident. Studies concluded that new technologies were often resisted by older adults, but were more available and acceptable to educated families with disposable income and individuals who sought new technologies. News of military engagements in Eastern Europe, Africa, and the Middle East spread quickly and both political and celebrity scandals were reported as news. Violence as seen on television, in movies, and in the news created controversy, especially with regard to the impact on children and youth. The economy

was booming, unemployment was at an all-time low, and the minimum wage was increasing. People became more interested in health and nutrition. As a result, interest in family and consumer sciences programs in dietetics and nutrition grew and became more specialized (Whitley, Bradley, Sutton, & Goodwin, 2001).

By the 1980s and 1990s, the term *home economics* seemed outdated and irrelevant. Like many feminized professions, including teaching and nursing, the discipline struggled to keep a professional identity. Due to public perceptions, some of which were based on history, the term *home economics* did not capture the essence of the many specialized majors or the unifying theme of the profession. The "stitching and stirring" reputation did not reflect the discipline and needed to be altered.

By the middle of the 1980s, leaders of the field began looking at ways to position the profession for the next century. At a conference held in 1993 in Scottsdale, Arizona, a group set forth to develop a new conceptual framework for describing the purpose, mission, and vision of home economics. At this meeting, participants concluded that a new name and identity were needed to abolish old stereotypes. In 1994, at the annual convention of the American Home Economics Association held in San Diego, California, members voted to change the name of the organization to the American Association of Family and Consumer Sciences. The Association faced the new millennium with an open, diversified, and optimistic view (Stage & Vincenti, 1997).

Summary

Ellen Swallow Richards is recognized as the founder of home economics, a discipline that subsequently became family and consumer sciences. Born in 1842, Richards became the first woman to graduate from the Massachusetts Institute of Technology (MIT). Armed with a graduate degree in chemistry, Richards was visionary in her desire to apply scientific concepts to home and family life.

Ellen Swallow Richards was aware of the changing world around her and the impact education could make on both the personal and global level. She was especially attuned to the needs of the less fortunate. Her pioneering studies of air, water, and food led to the creation of national public health standards and the creation of new fields of study. She inspired many women to pursue science and higher education.

Ellen Swallow Richards always found a way to apply her scholarly pursuits to the well-being of families and the environment, whether it involved testing foods and home furnishings for contaminants, conserving energy, or investigating water pollution. She was passionate about bringing knowledge "to the streets" by offering community and school classes in which the principles of science and economics were applied in areas of sanitation, nutrition, child development, and food preservation.

Although Ellen Swallow Richards is known as the founder of the family and consumer sciences discipline and the American Home Economics Association, there were many other forward-thinking individuals who shared her vision and helped shape the discipline. In 1899, these like-minded colleagues organized a summer conference in Lake Placid, New York. Their goal was to establish a philosophical and theoretical base for home economics and to identify educational standards. In 1908, they formed the American Home Economics Association and elected Ellen Swallow Richards as the first president. The first meeting of the newly formed American Home Economics Association was convened in 1909, with Ellen Richards presiding.

During the Progressive Era, the women's suffrage movement attempted to move women out of the home and obtain the right to vote. Many home economists supported the goals of empowering women. Home economics courses received federal funding when included in high school curricula, which supported the growth of course offerings in the discipline in public high schools. During the Depression, it was often difficult for people to keep their families dressed and fed and their children in school. Two world wars created new stresses and changed the needs of individuals and families. Home economists responded with practical solutions related to food, clothing, shelter, and other needs of families.

The home economics (family and consumer sciences) discipline reflects constant change throughout the last century. Instead of offering one general area of study, home economics evolved into many areas of specialization, some of which include child development, family studies, dietetics, hospitality management, consumer economics, interior design, and apparel merchandising. With the movement toward women's rights and equality, home economics became more gender-balanced. Near the end of the 1900s, home economics had undergone so much change that a new name was chosen to better represent the breadth and central core (also known as a common body of knowledge) of the discipline. In 1994, the American Home Economics Association changed its name to the American Association of Family and Consumer Sciences.

So what does family and consumer sciences have to do with life today? Families and communities still exist, and the desire to live a quality life by providing for the basic needs of food, clothing, and shelter is as relevant today as it was 100 years ago. From designing accessible housing for an aging population to helping youth complete their high school education, all areas of specialization within family and consumer sciences are called upon to help individuals, families, and communities adjust to a changing environment.

Questions for Thought

1. Describe the significant events in the life of Ellen Swallow Richards that led to her personal development as well as the development of the Family and Consumer Sciences discipline.

2. How has the way family and consumer sciences been taught in high schools changed in the last 20 years?

3. Briefly describe several of the significant changes that have occurred in the family and consumer sciences profession over the past 50 years.

4. Family and consumer sciences is founded on the philosophy that teaching life skills will improve the quality of life for families and

individuals. In today's world, what would you consider to be essential life skills? What life skills do most college freshmen lack? When, where, and how should people learn these concepts and skills?

5. Why do professional organizations such as the American Association of Family and Consumer Sciences (AAFCS) exist?

References and Resources

American Association of Family and Consumer Sciences. (1996). American Association of Family and Consumer Sciences: 1995–2000 strategic plan. In C. B. Simerly, H. Light, and D. I. Mittsford, (Eds.), *A book of readings: The context for professionals in human, family, and consumer sciences.* Alexandria, VA: Author.

Baugher, S. L., Anderson, C. L., Green, K. B., Nickols, S. Y., Shane, J., Jolly, L., & Miles, J. (2000). Body of knowledge of family and consumer sciences. *Journal of Family and Consumer Sciences, 92*(3), 29-32.

Bois, D. (1997). *Distinguished women of past and present: Ellen Henrietta Swallow Richards.* Retrieved December 1, 2006, from http://www.distinguishedwomen.com/biographies/richards-es.html

Bowden, M. E. (1997). *Chemical achievers: The human face of the chemical sciences.* Retrieved December 1, 2006, from http://www.chemheritage.org/classroom/chemach/environment/richards.html

Bradley, B. (2005, June). *American cultural history, 1950–1959.* Retrieved December 1, 2006, from http://kclibrary.nhmccd.edu/decade50.html

A brief history of AAFCS. (2003). Retrieved December 1, 2006, from http://www.aafcs.org/about/history.html

Brown, M. (1981). Our intellectual ecology: Recitation of definition: A case in point. *Journal of Home Economics, 73,* 14-18.

Brown, M., & Paolucci, B. (1979). *Home economics: A definition.* Washington, DC: American Home Economics Association.

Brownlee, W. E. (1979). Household values, women's work, and economic growth, 1800–1930. *The Journal of Economic History, 39*(1), 199-209.

Byrd, F. M. (1990, Summer). Home economics: Reflections on the past, visions for the future. *Journal of Home Economics, 82,* 43-46.

Clarke, R. (1973). *Ellen Swallow: The woman who founded ecology.* Chicago: Follett.

East, M. (1980). *Home economics: Past, present, and future.* Boston: Allyn and Bacon.

Ellen Swallow Richards and MIT. (2006, May). Retrieved December 1, 2006, from Massachusetts Institute of Technology Archives and Special Collections website: http://libraries.mit.edu/archives/exhibits/esr/esr-mit.html

Ellen Swallow Richards Residence. (1998). Retrieved December 1, 2006, from National Park Service, Places Where Women Made History website: http://www.cr.nps.gov/NR/travel/pwwmh/ma67.htm

FCS body of knowledge: Shaping the next 100 years. (2010). *Journal of Family and Consumer Sciences, 102*(2), 7-13.

Garraty, J., & McCaughey, R. (1989). *A short history of the American nation.* New York: Harper and Row.

Gillis, C. (2006, September). *American cultural history, 1970–1979.* Retrieved December 1, 2006, from http://kclibrary.nhmccd.edu/decade70.html

Goodwin, S. (2005, September). *American cultural history, 1940–1949.* Retrieved December 1, 2006, from http://kclibrary.nhmccd.edu/decade40.html

Goodwin, S. (2006, December). *American cultural history, 1960–1969.* Retrieved December 1, 2006, from http://kclibrary.nhmccd.edu/decade60.html

Henretta, J., Brownlee, W., Brody, D., Ware, S., & Johnson, M. (1997). *America's history.* New York: Worth.

Hunt, C. (1942). *The life of Ellen H. Richards.* Washington, DC: American Home Economics Association.

Johnson, D. (2008). Studying the past of family and consumer sciences to develop a vision for the future. *Journal of Family and Consumer Sciences, 100*(2), 53-54.

Kleszynski, M., May, M., & Alderman, P. (1994). *Cultural, economic, and social influences on coeducation in the United States and implications for student services.* (ERIC Document Reproduction Service No. ED388154). Washington, DC: U.S. Department of Education.

Massachusetts Institute of Technology, Women's Laboratory, 1876–1883. (1999). Retrieved December 1, 2006, from Massachusetts Institute of Technology Archives and Special Collections website: http://libraries.mit.edu/archives/exhibits/esr/esr-womenslab.html

Nickols, S. Y. (2001). Keeping the Betty lamp burning. *Journal of Family and Consumer Sciences, 93*(3), 35-44.

The organization and purpose of KON. (n.d.) Retrieved December 1, 2006, from http://www.kon.org/orginfo.html

Polakoff, K., Rosenberg, N., Bolton, G., Story, R., & Schwartz, J. (1976). *Generations of Americans: A history of the United States.* New York: St. Martin's.

Pundt, H. (1980). *AHEA: A history of excellence.* Washington, DC: American Home Economics Association.

Reuben, J. (1996). *The making of the modern university: Intellectual transformation and marginalization of morality.* Chicago: University of Chicago.

Stage, S., & Vincenti, V. B. (Eds.). (1997). *Rethinking home economics: Women and the history of a profession.* Ithaca, NY: Cornell University.

Swierk, M. (2010). 100 years of sharpening our professional scissors has kept us on the cutting edge. *Journal of Family and Consumer Sciences, 102*(2), 6.

Whitely, P. (2006). *American cultural history, 1980–1989.* Retrieved December 1, 2006, from http://kclibrary.nhmccd.edu/decade80.html

Whitely, P., Bradley, B., Sutton, B., & Goodwin, S. (2001). *American cultural history, 1990–1999.* Retrieved December 1, 2006, from http://kclibrary.nhmccd.edu/decade90.html

Chapter 2

Improving the Quality of Life for Individuals, Families, and Communities

After studying this chapter, you will be able to:

- explain the mission of family and consumer sciences.
- compare various definitions of the term *family* and varied structures of the family unit.
- explain how the family functions as a social unit.
- provide an example of how the human ecosystem model and other theories are applied to meeting basic human needs.

Family and consumer sciences is a discipline and profession that focuses on people and families. Stories are what connect people with each other and with themselves. In Chapter 1, you read the story of Ellen Swallow Richards and her involvement in the formation of the family and consumer sciences discipline along with the information about other pioneers in the field. The remainder of this book is filled with stories of current leaders who exemplify excellence in the field and stories of practicing family and consumer sciences professionals. As you read, your own story will begin to unfold as you explore possible careers in family and consumer sciences.

To understand family and consumer sciences, it is essential to first understand the family as a social unit. Although families always existed in various forms, the breadth of family diversity has increased significantly in United States culture since the 1960s. For example, the two-parent family is but one of many variations today. This chapter explores the changes in family structure,

roles, and relationships. Questions such as the following arise:

- How is *family* defined?
- How has the family in the United States changed over the past half-century?
- How does the family operate within a socio-economic-political system?

This chapter provides the reader with an understanding of the family and consumer sciences profession today and its mission to improve lives of individuals, families, and communities.

What Is a Family?

"All happy families resemble one another, but each unhappy family is unhappy in its own way" (Tolstoy, 1877/1994, p. 1). When do you think this was written? ten years ago? last year? You may recognize these as the opening words of Russian novelist and philosopher Leo Tolstoy's 1877 novel *Anna Karenina*. Surprisingly, concern about dysfunctional or "unhappy" families is not just a new hot political topic. Although we do hear a great deal in the news about the "demise of the American family," the concern for family stability has spanned the centuries.

Various psychologists and sociologists have attempted to define the functional family unit. This has not been an easy task. In our society, the term *family* is used loosely and frequently. For example, teachers and coaches often talk about classroom communities and sports teams being a "family." The concept of family may be used freely, but a common definition is often illusive.

Almost everyone has strong feelings about his or her own family and families in general. Quite often, since families can be a source of great joy, pain, love, support, frustration, and dependence, our responses can be emotionally based. Since we all have personal experiences in dealing with families—some positive, some negative—individual experience is used to filter and formulate personal definitions of "what a family ought to be." Just what is a family, and, if families and family images are so prevalent in society, why is it so difficult for people to agree on a common definition? Is there an objective, value-free definition of family? These questions will be addressed in this chapter.

The original use (the etymology) of the word *family* dates to the fifteenth-century Middle English *familie*, from Latin *familia*, meaning "household" (including servants as well as kin of the householder), and from *famulus*, meaning "servant" (Harper, 2001). George Peter Murdock, an early anthropologist who conducted large ethnographic studies, defined the family in his book *Social Structure* (1949), as:

> ...a social group characterized by common residence, economic cooperation, and reproduction. It includes adults of both sexes, at least two of whom maintain a socially approved sexual relationship, and one or more children, own or adopted, of the sexually cohabiting adults.

In 1976, *Webster's New World Dictionary* defined the family as 1) all the people living in the same house, 2) a social unit consisting of parents and the children they rear, 3) a group of people related by ancestry or marriage, 4) all those claiming descent from a common ancestor, 5) a criminal syndicate under a single leader, and 6) a commune living in one household especially under one head.

Many people today would find the Murdock and Webster definitions narrow and exclusive. There are many groups of people readily accepted as families who don't fall under any of these definitions. Accepting diversity in family form is not a new phenomenon. In fact, families have always come in diverse forms, reflecting the many societal changes in the larger culture. It is the social conditions and the economic environment that affect the way people think about and value specific family characteristics and the way they are played out in everyday lives of individuals. For example, when more women entered the workforce in the 1970s, egalitarian marital relationships became more mainstream in society.

The increases in family diversity since the 1960s are more striking than during any time in previous history. This diversity is easy to spot in popular media images of family. The late 1960s and early 1970s promoted acceptance of such diversity with the newly blended Brady family in *The Brady Bunch* television show and the female head-of-household in *The Partridge Family*. Syndication allows new generations to observe the "new" family forms as depicted during these historic decades. Although the 1980s boasted the traditional two-parent Huxtable family of *The Cosby Show*, several other family forms were also presented. The fictional television character Murphy Brown decided to bear a child as a successful, unmarried, professional woman. Some people heralded her portrayal of a single parent by choice as a breakthrough in the media, whereas others saw it as an abomination. In another 1980s situation comedy, *Diff'rent Strokes*, a single father of one biological child adopted two African-American children and formed one of the first interracial families seen on television.

Fictional television families continued to reflect changing families in more recent years. *Two and a Half Men* depicted a family made up of two adult brothers raising the son of one brother. *Modern Family* showed the diversity of an extended family that included a heterosexual couple with three biological children, a gay couple raising adopted children, and a cross-cultural, cross-generational couple raising both their biological child and a child from one partner's previous relationship.

Today, most adults do not live in a traditional heterosexual two-parent family with minor children (Fields, 2004). Instead, diverse possibilities make the "traditional family" one of many forms. Despite the enormous diversity in family structure, the online edition of *Merriam-Webster's Dictionary* (2013) still defines family in a similar way as it did decades ago:

> 1) a group of individuals living under one roof and usually under one head, 2) a group of persons of common ancestry, 3) a group of people united by certain convictions or a common affiliation, 4) the basic unit in society traditionally consisting of two parents rearing their children; *also*: any of various social units differing from but regarded as equivalent to the traditional family (a single-parent family)

The key change can be seen in the *Webster* definition in the addendum *"also*: any of various social units differing from but regarded as equivalent to the traditional family (a single-parent family)." These differing forms have caused Americans to engage in emotional debates over whether shared genes and blood relationships, a shared household, or other shared resources, including emotional support, define a family. These debates force us to reconsider our concepts of what roles a mother, father, parent, child, and sibling should play. Must families be based on marriage? Can people, especially children, simultaneously move in and out of multiple families? Must everyone claim one primary family or can a person be a part of multiple and equally important families? Is a parent more legitimate if identified by biology or legality? Must emotional and social support be present to constitute a family? Such questions have resulted in heated debates, both at the personal and the political level about the family and "family values."

The junction of old and new ways of thinking about families has made it impossible to pretend all families can be defined in the same way, especially if moral values and beliefs are attached. Some political leaders claim the "breakdown of the family" is a result of the absence of the biological father in the home. Others believe lack of economic resources is the primary determinant of family breakdowns. Some people claim that what many people term the "family crisis" is really a socioeconomic class problem that starts with dysfunctional families and their destructive behaviors. Other observers believe "nontraditional family" structures are not dysfunctional, but highly adaptive and flexible units responding to societal changes. These observers assert that family dysfunction is not a result of diversity but a result of race and socioeconomic class inequalities (Vander Zanden, Crandell, & Crandell, 2007).

Although it is nearly impossible to achieve a specific, descriptive, all-encompassing definition of the family, a working definition is important for family and consumer sciences professionals who seek to improve the quality of lives of families. Before family and consumer sciences professionals attempt to meet the needs of the family, they need to understand what a family is. For the purposes of this text, *family* is defined as:

> The basic unit in which two or more people are sharing emotional, social, physical, and economic resources.

Using this definition, families may be very different from each other. For example, families can form in a variety of ways. Many people choose to marry, while others choose to remain single or opt for cohabitation (Vander Zanden et al., 2007). Intimate partners may include two persons of the same gender as well as heterosexual couples. Children may be a part of the family unit through biology or adoption. Some couples, through choice or infertility, may remain childless. Other couples, whose children are grown and out of the household, are "empty nesters." Some children may be born to a single woman. Single fathers may parent children by function rather than by birth, adoption, or legality—making their relationship a family. Many marriages come to an end through divorce; although if children are present, it is not the end of the family unit. The death of a partner or members leaving home in a one-parent family does not lead to the dissolution of a family. The family unit proceeds through life's developmental milestones. The family formation process starts again as adult children cohabitate or marry or as a divorced or widowed person remarries.

The remainder of this chapter looks at the family as a social unit that takes from and contributes toward society. Lastly, the family will be discussed in the context of life experiences and transitions. This chapter's focus on the family provides the reader with background to Chapter 3, which examines the current state of the family and consumer sciences discipline and/or profession.

The Family as a Social Unit

Life depicted on television is rarely an accurate portrayal of life experienced by most families. You have probably heard it said that in real life, problems are not resolved in a 30- or 60-minute time slot as often happens with fictional television families. In this next section, a theoretical model for family interaction with their environments will be presented. This model will explain how families are affected by the environment around them. The model presented is called the *family ecosystem model*. Understanding family ecosystem theory is essential to appreciate the complexity of everyday family functions that take place in their environmental context, and a hallmark of the family and consumer sciences discipline is this "holistic" approach.

Although variety in family structure is nothing new, the breadth of family diversity has skyrocketed in the past 50 years. However, families have always come in various forms, reflecting the societal changes in the world around them. Whatever is happening socially, economically, and politically produces the cultural values and norms in which individuals and families exist. In other words, families exist within a social system. Since it is always easier to understand theory in the context of an example, the Hernandez family will be used as an example throughout the discussion.

The Hernandez Family

Fidelio and Gloria Hernandez have been married for eight years. They met in college as Fidelio was preparing to become a high school social studies teacher. Fidelio is bilingual in English and Spanish. Gloria is a social worker for the department of social and health services in their state. She is fluent only in English but has a basic understanding of several languages, including Spanish. The couple has two daughters. Ava is six years old, and Christina is four years old. After Fidelio and Gloria graduated from college, the Hernandez family moved away from most of their extended family in the Pacific Northwest to Southern California to secure employment. They do not have grandparents living nearby. The family is devoutly Catholic and very involved in their parish. Ava is involved in group sports, and Gloria is volunteering as an assistant soccer coach for her daughter's recreational league team. Both Fidelio and Gloria play on a coed softball team. They also volunteer at their local Boys and Girls Club. Most of their social contacts and friendships have begun through their work circles or their parish. Gloria also keeps in contact with an infant support group with which she was involved when Ava was a baby. She and the other mothers in the group continue to get together for "play dates" with their children. Two years ago, Gloria was diagnosed with multiple sclerosis, a potentially debilitating disease that affects the nervous system. So far, Gloria has started drug therapy, and the disease is in remission. If asked, both Fidelio and Gloria would say their two-career family lifestyle is very full. Although this description only scratches the surface of the Hernandez' family life and gives no insight into the influence of their upbringing, it will serve as a reference point for explaining family theory.

The Social System Concept

Before beginning a discussion of how the social system concept helps in understanding families, a few definitions are necessary. A *system* is an informal network of elements that are interrelated in a more or less stable fashion within a given time period. *Informal* does not mean casual. The separate parts of a system are generally coordinated, play a functional role in the greater environment, and operate as a whole or in unison. The family fits this definition well.

The family unit can be compared to a small manufacturing company that combines capital goods, raw materials, and labor to clean, feed, create, and produce useful commodities. The commodities for a family include tangible products such as food, clothing, and shelter as well as the emotional health of the family members from quality relationships both within and outside the family. Just as a manufacturing company has goals, families also have goals, even if they are not consciously identified.

The family is a task performance group that meets the needs of its members (termed *organisms*) as well as other societal groups. This is why it is called a *social system*. For example, families play a huge role in identity development of individual members, including both adults and children. The family members establish selective boundaries with the surrounding environment, therefore maintaining the family's separateness. Families, as a whole unit as well as the individuals who make up a family, choose with whom to interact in the larger environment by establishing boundaries. These boundaries are constantly changing as the tasks of the family unit change. Some boundaries are self-selected, whereas other boundaries may be imposed by circumstances or culture. For example, a family with school-age children begins interacting with the school system once a child enters school. Educating children is a requirement in the United States. However, a parent has the choice to use the public school system, private schools, or schooling in the home. Notice how the definition of a social system suggests both stability and change.

In describing human ecosystem theory, Nickols (2003) shows the characteristics of a family system that processes inputs to meet family goals. See **Figure 2-1**. The processing activities are known as *throughput*. The quality of the

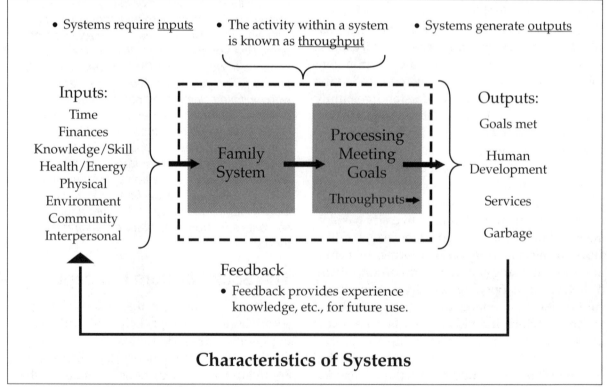

• Systems require <u>inputs</u>

• The activity within a system is known as <u>throughput</u>

• Systems generate <u>outputs</u>

Inputs:
Time
Finances
Knowledge/Skill
Health/Energy
Physical
Environment
Community
Interpersonal

Family System → Processing Meeting Goals (Throughputs→)

Outputs:
Goals met
Human Development
Services
Garbage

Feedback
• Feedback provides experience knowledge, etc., for future use.

Characteristics of Systems

Nickols, S.Y. (2003). Human ecosystem theory: A tool for working with families. Journal of Family and Consumer Sciences, *95*(2), 15–18.

Figure 2-1 A family system processes inputs to meet family goals.

system outputs is dependent on the quality of input and processing mechanisms. Since families are dynamic social units, feedback happens during the throughput. *Feedback* gives future perspective and knowledge based on previous experiences. For example, when a family's second child enters school, prior experience with the educational system now plays a part in their decisions. In this case, the family, school system, and community are important components of the social system.

Ecological Theory of Development Model

As humans, we depend on many factors in our *environment* (factors both inside and outside the family unit) for survival. This interdependence both within and with the environment is referred to as the *ecosystem*. Psychologists base developmental theory on the *venue* (time, place) of a person's maturation. Developmental psychologist Urie Bronfenbrenner, in his 1979 treatise *The Ecology of Human Development*, used the environmental approach to describe a person's development socially, emotionally, physically, and cognitively within the context of his or her environment. See **Figure 2-2**. He called this the *ecological theory of development*.

Bronfenbrenner described the individual's environment as a set of nested structures. His analogy of a set of Russian dolls visually demonstrates how one environment encapsulates the next. Four levels of environmental systems, distinguished on the basis of their propinquity with respect to the developing person, are the micro-, meso-, exo-, and macrosystems. The family is the primary microsystem in which development takes place. Relationships between the family and other venues for development, such as the neighborhood childcare center or school, constitute a mesosystem. External environments, such as social networks and religious groups in which the family participates, are a part of the exosystems. For the Hernandez family, their parish, work colleagues, athletic teams, and other social organizations are a part of their exosystem. Lastly, the micro-, meso-, and exosystems

are embedded in the macrosystems. These are the greater ideological values, norms, beliefs, and general ways of behaving and thinking that are esteemed in a particular culture. The Hernandez family subscribes to a value system esteemed by their extended family and their church. On a larger scale, they hold many beliefs and values similar to those of their neighbors and fellow Americans. Family, education, and religious freedom are a few of the values they esteem.

The Human Ecosystem Model

Family and consumer sciences uses developmental psychology theory, but applies it in a more holistic manner. In the *human ecosystem model* (Nickols, 2003) depicted in **Figure 2-3**, each of the environmental systems is further differentiated into three distinct environments that include the natural environment, the human constructed environment, and the human behavioral environment.

The *natural environment* includes all of the available natural resources. Humans interact with the available natural resources to create other resources that sustain life. For example, unprocessed food from plants is a part of the natural environment. Since food is a basic human need, these components have a huge influence on the quality of life for individuals and families. As for most Americans, food is readily available to the Hernandez family at local grocery stores if financial resources are available. Government assistance and charitable sources of food can also be accessed if financial resources are not available, but the original source is plant material, soil, and water in the natural environment.

The natural environment also includes genetic makeup of individuals as well as sources for and quality of air, energy, water, land, and plant life. For instance, if a genetic disorder is passed from one generation to the next, it may have great implications on the health and quality of life for family members. The effect of Gloria Hernandez' struggle with multiple sclerosis on the family falls into the natural environment. Although the cause of multiple sclerosis is

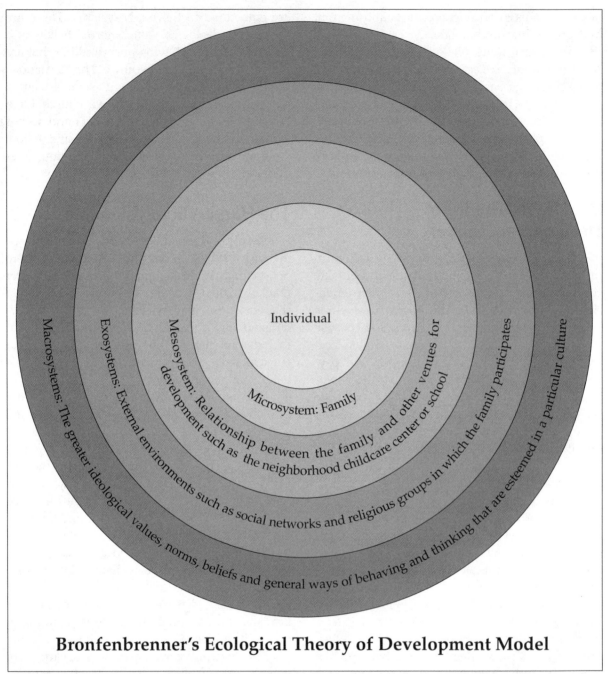

Bronfenbrenner's Ecological Theory of Development Model

Figure 2-2 Bronfenbrenner used the environmental approach to describe human development. As humans, we depend on many factors in our ***environment*** (factors both inside and outside the family unit) for survival. This interdependence both within and with the environment, is referred to as the ***ecosystem***. Psychologists base developmental theory on the ***venue*** (time, place) of a person's maturation.

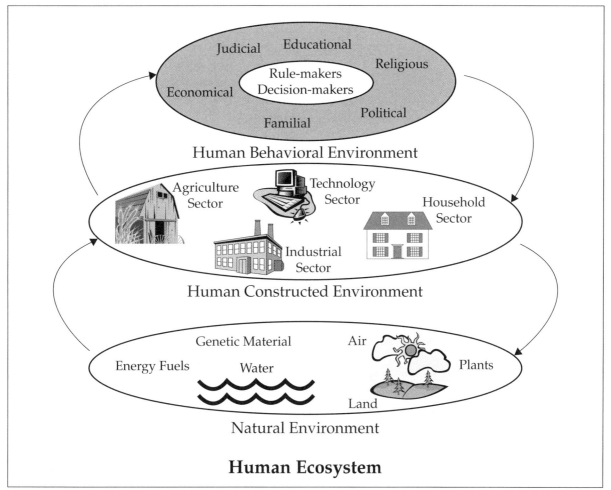

Nickols, S.Y. (2003). Human ecosystem theory: A tool for working with families. *Journal of Family and Consumer Sciences, 95*(2), 15–18.

Figure 2-3 In the human ecosystem model, each of the environmental systems is further differentiated into three distinct environments.

not known, researchers believe it has something to do with the natural environment. According to the National Multiple Sclerosis Society (2006), it may be genetic, it may be climatic, or it may be related to a virus that is passed between individuals. Air pollution, availability of food from plants, and the climate of the land are other examples of human interaction with the natural environment.

The *human constructed environment* includes the transformation systems that turn energy and information into products for human consumption. Products found in agriculture, technology, industry, and the home are all part of the

human constructed environment. These are the resources humans have produced from natural resources. Tractors, breakfast cereal, designer jeans, cell phones, public transportation, and refrigerators are a few examples of the endless products made for human consumption. This environment has a great impact on the family unit as material products are produced and consumed. As a family unit, the Hernandez family is constantly making choices as consumers of the human constructed environment. Their home and furnishings, the clothing they wear, the car they drive, and the various other consumer products they use are all a part of this environment. Like most citizens of the United States, they are bombarded with an abundance of potential resources in the human constructed environment.

The *human behavioral environment* includes all the societal systems that regulate relationships between people and their behavior. The judicial, educational, economic, familial, religious, and political systems all play a part. Within these systems are laws, rules, and policies that regulate human behavior. Family customs or rules, traffic laws, and school policies are examples of social systems that regulate the human behavioral environment. City, county, state, and federal laws are all part of this environment as are school rules and employment rules and employer expectations. Influences from Fidelio and Gloria's upbringing could also play a role. Certainly the desire to be effective parents plays a role, as is evident in Gloria's involvement with a parent support group. Fidelio values education and has dedicated his career to educating young people. Gloria believes in caring for others through her work as a social worker, and her work parameters are influenced by agency policies, community resources, and laws. She believes all people have the right to basic food, clothing, and shelter, but she encounters many families who do not have them because of their experiences with various elements in the human behavioral environment, such as bankruptcy laws and the juvenile court system. Their strongly held religious convictions guide much of their behavior. The influences in the human behavioral environment are too numerous to mention here. Reread the Hernandez family profile. What would you add here?

Addressing Basic Human Needs

The Hernandez' family situation is one that is probably familiar to you. Sometimes it is easier to apply theory to a situation different from your own. In the following story, you will read about the life of a young Ethiopian woman, Nafisia, as told by an American relief worker. As you read the story, identify how the availability of natural resources (the natural environment), the availability of goods and services (the human constructed environment), and the social system including customs and regulations, the greater political arena, and personal values (the human behavioral environment) interact to affect the quality of life of Nafisia and her family.

A Story of Survival: Nafisia

The year after I graduated from college, I decided to devote a year to working as an international relief worker. It is a choice that always sounds impressive, but the fact is, I could not figure out what to do with myself after graduation. Sure, I could look for a traditional job and begin my climb up the corporate ladder, but I figured I had years ahead of me to do that. Besides, I graduated right when unemployment was at a peak in my region of the country. I also had college loans to pay. Working as a relief worker would allow me to defer payments for a year. Besides, my parents had divorced while I was in college so I really no longer had a "home base." I thought if I was going to see the world, I had better find an economical way to do it. I figured somewhere in the Caribbean might be a nice place to serve—and it would have been, but I was not sent there. Instead, I heard the words: "Welcome to Ethiopia." But this is not a story about me, it is a story about a young Ethiopian woman named Nafisia and her dignified struggle to care for her family.

We have all heard of Ethiopia, "the poster child for famine." This African country has been in the news as dramatic scenes of emaciated children fill television screens. Every part of Ethiopia does not look like the horrific scenes on television, but there are millions of starving and hungry people throughout the Horn of Africa—the easternmost projection of Africa that includes Somalia, Ethiopia, and Eritrea. Most regions are suffering from a severe drought. Half of the region's drought victims are Ethiopians.

Is the drought really such a concern? Isn't that the natural climate of the Horn of Africa? Is the climate any different than it was years before? I learned the answer to all these questions is yes. One hundred years ago there was a drought in this region every 10 to 15 years. Now, there is a drought every five or fewer years. In many areas, this is the third year in a row without significant rain. Recent flooding in Mozambique was caused by rain that was supposed to have fallen in Ethiopia, but instead, it fell in the north.

Climatic changes play a big part in the lack of food, but Ethiopians are also vulnerable to food shortages due to the high population growth rate, dwindling farm size, unjust patterns of land tenure, inefficient farming techniques, and deforestation. It is a complex problem complicated by local and international politics.

For me, seeing hunger came down to trying to help individual people cope. In particular, it came down to a young woman named Nafisia whom I have grown to greatly admire. Nafisia looks like a young girl to me. Physically, she is tiny in stature. She claims to be 16 but I cannot imagine her being over 14. She is already a mother and has the responsibility of caring for her young son. Her husband serves in the military, and she and her son live with her aunt. She doesn't know if or when she'll see her husband again. Both of her parents died of HIV-AIDS, and her younger sister died of pneumonia two years ago. When her husband left, they owned a cow. Today, the cow is gone. It was sold when it became sick from starvation.

While politicians worry about who will be blamed for people starving to death, Nafisia worries about what she will feed her three-year-old son. Normally, this time of year, the fields around her village are green, but the drought has kept them brown. She, her son, and her aunt feel fortunate to afford one meal a day that they share in the evening. When food supplies are tighter, Nafisia's aunt often doesn't eat so her nephew can. They have witnessed many villagers who, weakened by an insufficient diet, suffer from chronic respiratory problems. Nafisia gathers wood during the day and sells it at the market to buy food. Although they are not starving, they are often hungry. Nafisia's primary concern is to keep her family fed. On most nights, Nafisia makes a small fire and cooks a little bit of wheat, stirring in some moss and leaves, to give the wheat more substance. For now, she is collecting enough wood to buy the wheat, but as less wood can be found, she will rely on our relief agency to provide the wheat—that is, if the shipment comes

in. Today, the warehouse sits empty as political events delay relief shipments. Although collecting wood is hard work, even at her young age, Nafisia would prefer to provide for her family on her own rather than receive a hand-out from me. She has dreams beyond providing food for her family, though. She hopes her husband will return home. She hopes that her son will be in good health and not contract a life-threatening disease as so many children do before the age of five, and, perhaps, he might even go to school someday.

Everyone is not hungry or starving in Ethiopia. Food is available for people who have money. Markets stock tomatoes, onions, beans, and potatoes. However, for most, the combination of drought and poverty make life difficult at best. It's not just the lack of food. The drought makes it difficult to find drinking water, and bathing is almost unheard of. Some people walk miles for fresh drinking water.

I often find myself thinking about how this year's experiences will affect me for the remainder of my life. After my year of service is over, friends will probably ask me if I feel I have had an impact on the world. That is a hard question to answer. My part is so small, and the problem of hunger is so complex. The food relief provided by agencies is currently holding mass starvation at bay in some villages like Nafisia's, but the meals are not substantial, and people like Nafisia and her family continue to be hungry. The problem is compounded by AIDS and treatable diseases, such as diarrhea, pneumonia, and tuberculosis, that destroy the lives of people who are needed to help communities recover from drought and natural disasters. The world is currently concerned with wars and crises in other countries, but people in Ethiopia continue to go hungry.

For many, Ethiopia brings to mind hopeless images of starving children in a faraway country in Africa. They may see Ethiopia as a country that can't take care of its own problems and repeatedly begs for help from developed countries. For me, Ethiopia is a country filled with people like Nafisia who are trying to survive and hope for the future.

Many factors play into Nafisia's situation. How would a family and consumer sciences professional analyze the situation? Family and consumer sciences focuses on improving the quality of life for individuals and families through the basic human needs of food, clothing, shelter, and relationships within the context of their environment. Food, clothing, and shelter come from resources available in the natural environment and are produced in the human constructed environment within the framework of the human behavioral environment. Family relationships, both inside and outside the family unit, cross the boundaries of the three eco-system environments. Family and consumer sciences professionals look at all three environments to assess needs. The basic human needs include the following:

- food
- clothing
- shelter
- relationships

Food

Food is a basic need of individuals and families. Food consumption patterns both within families and the greater society are influenced by complex, interrelated factors including the biological, social, economic, cultural, and political environment. For Nafisia, like everyone else, food is a biological need. However, the social and political environment that allows some to receive food while others do not as a result of political power plays have made meeting the biological need for food difficult. In other parts of the world, over-abundance and supply of food can lead to health issues. As a basic need, food can become a social and political power tool. Cultural differences in what constitutes food also play a part. For example, in United States food banks that attempt to service people from very diverse cultural backgrounds, some items are simply not acceptable as food due to strong cultural taboos and beliefs. Recently, advances in nutrition have greatly enhanced population health and well-being.

Clothing

Clothing is another basic need of individuals and families. It serves to cover and protect the body from the elements. In advanced societies, however, clothing also serves to meet basic human social and psychological needs. This differentiates clothing from fashion with its constant cycles of change in style. Clothing, accessories, and body adornment are important clues for understanding who we are as individuals and as a family. Clothing, accessories, and body adornment are also how we express culture, show social status, and communicate gender and religious values.

Shelter

Shelter or housing is the third basic need of individuals and families. As families progress through the life cycle, they generate different needs for housing. Although the focus of needs is often dependent on income, housing needs are affected by family values, attitudes, composition, and the housing market itself. In the United States today, affordable housing is an issue, especially in urban areas. Individuals and families are also affected by the interior spaces of shelter. From couches to paint color, design provides the artifacts for understanding who we are as individuals and as a family, which issues and topics are of importance in the present, and where we hope to go.

Relationships

The modern nuclear family is shaped by three sentiments: romantic love between adult partners rather than a partnership based on function only, parental love for children, and the belief that bonds among nuclear family members grow more intense and binding. Because of this, the modern family compared to family units throughout history is often termed the *psychological family*. In many cultures throughout the world, personal relationships inside the family and satisfaction with these relationships outside the family have become important cultural indicators of family success. In recent years, more focus has been placed on the relationships and interactions of a family unit with the outside culture. This has broadened the definition of the family to include the *global family,* and at the same time, this boundless worldwide interaction has caused the nuclear family, in some instances, to become more insulated from the effects of what a family may consider negative influences on individual members within the unit; there's a weakening of the whole unit. Humans are destined to be in relationships with others. We need other people. Family and consumer sciences has always focused on relationships as an essential human need.

Summary

We are all familiar with the concept of family and most have extensive personal experience with families, but defining the family unit with one simple definition still proves to be difficult. In this chapter, the family unit is defined as *the basic unit in which two or more people are sharing emotional, social, physical, and economic resources.* This defines the modern family and is inclusive of various living arrangements and values. It also forms a basis for further study of family needs.

Families exist within a social system, and theoretical models help professionals visualize how various factors impact individuals, families, and communities. The human ecosystem model provides a structure for explaining how each successive environment plays a part. This model demonstrates how the major areas of study in family and consumer sciences—food, clothing, shelter, and relationships—all contribute to the well-being of individuals and communities.

The next time you are with a group of friends, try this experiment. Ask each of your friends to succinctly define the term *family.*

Questions for Thought

1. How are families depicted in television and film today? Which fictional television family do you see as most realistic?

2. What will families be like in 10 years? in 25 years? What changes may occur? How will families remain the same?

3. Why does the United States lag behind other industrialized countries regarding family-friendly policies such as parental leave for child care, child care facilities, and teacher pay?

4. Write your own definition of the family. How does your definition differ from the definition given in this chapter?

5. After reading the description of Nafisia's life, identify factors affecting her family's quality of life in the:

   A. natural environment

   B. human constructed environment

   C. social behavioral environment

6. Identify and give examples of how factors from each of the three environments in the human ecosystem affect your own quality of life.

References and Resources

Aldous, J. (1996). *Family careers: Rethinking the developmental perspective.* Thousand Oaks, CA: Sage.

Baugher, S. L., Anderson, C. L., Green, K. B., Nickols, S. Y., Shane, J., Jolly, L., & Miles, J. (2000). Body of knowledge of family and consumer sciences. *Journal of Family and Consumer Sciences, 92*(3), 29-32.

Bronfenbrenner, U. (1979). *Ecology of human development: Experiments by nature and design.* Cambridge, MA: Harvard University Press.

Bronfenbrenner, U. (1986). Alienation and the four worlds of childhood. *Phi Delta Kappa, 67,* 430-436.

Brown, M. (1981). Our intellectual ecology: Recitation of definition: A case in point. *Journal of Home Economics, 73,* 14-18.

Brown, M. M. (1985). *Philosophical studies of home economics in the United States.* East Lansing: Michigan State University.

Brown, M., & Paolucci, B. (1979). *Home economics: A definition.* Washington, DC: American Home Economics Association.

Bulbolz, M. M., & Sontag, M. S. (1993). Human ecology theory. In P. G. Boss, W. J. Doherty, R. LaRossa, W. R. Schumm, & S. K. Steinmetz (Eds.), *Sourcebook of Family Theories and Methods: A Contextual Approach.* New York: Plenum.

Coontz, S., & Song, S. (1999). The American family. *Life, 22*(12), 79-83.

East, M. (1980). *Home economics: Past, present, and future.* Boston: Allyn and Bacon.

Exploring 100 years of family-related products, organizations, events, and concepts. (January 01, 2009). *Journal of Family and Consumer Sciences, 101*(2), 15-17.

Fields, J. (2004). *America's families and living arrangements: 2003.* Retrieved December 12, 2006, from http://www.census.gov/prod/2004pubs/p20-553.pdf

Harper, D. (2001). *Family.* Retrieved December 12, 2006, from the Online Etymology Dictionary Website: http://www.etymonline.com/index.php?term=family

Hitch, E. J., & Youatt, J. P. (1995). *Communicating family and consumer sciences: A guidebook for professionals.* Tinley Park, IL: Goodheart-Willcox.

Huston, P. (2001). *Families as we are.* New York: City University.

Laszloffy, T. (2002). Rethinking family development theory: Teaching with the systematic family development (SFD) model. *Family Relations, 51*(3), 206-214.

Melson, G. F. (1980). *Family environment: An ecosystem perspective.* Minneapolis, MN: Burgess.

Murdock, G. P. (1949). *Social Structure.* New York: MacMillan.

National Multiple Sclerosis Society. (2006). *What causes M.S.?* Retrieved December 12, 2006, from http://www.nationalmssociety.org (Path: about MS; what is MS?).

Nickols, S. Y. (2001). Family and Consumer Sciences in the United States. In P. B. Baltes, & N. J. Smelser (Eds.), *International Encyclopedia of the Social and Behavioral Sciences* (Vol. 8, pp. 5279-5286). Oxford, England: Elsevier Science.

Nickols, S. Y. (2003). Human ecosystem theory: A tool for working with families. *Journal of Family and Consumer Sciences, 95*(2), 15-18.

Paolucci, B., Hall, O. A., & Axinn, N. (1977). *Family decision making: An ecosystem approach.* New York: John Wiley.

Simerly, C. B., Light, H., & Mittsford, D. I. (1996). *A book of readings: The context for professionals in human, family, and consumer sciences.* Alexandria, VA: American Association of Family and Consumer Sciences.

Stage, S., & Vincenti, V. B. (Eds.). (1997). *Rethinking home economics: Women and the history of a profession.* Ithaca, NY: Cornell University.

Tolstoy, L. (1994). *Anna Karenina.* East Rutherford, NJ: Penguin Books. (Original work published in 1877).

U.S. Bureau of the Census. (2004*). Percent of households that are married-couple families with own children under 18 years: 2005.* (Report No. R1102). Retrieved December 12, 2006, from http://factfinder.census.gov (Path: people; relationships).

Vander Zanden, J., Crandell, T., & Crandell, C. (2007). *Human development.* New York: McGraw-Hill.

Webster's new world dictionary (2nd college ed.). (1976). Cleveland, OH: Williams Collins.

Winton, C. (1995). *Frameworks for studying families.* Guilford, CT: Duskin.

Zimmerman, S. L. (2001). *Family policy: constructed solutions to family problems.* Thousand Oaks, CA: Sage.

Chapter 3

The Current State of the Family and Consumer Sciences Profession

After studying this chapter, you will be able to:

- articulate the mission and body of knowledge in family and consumer sciences.

- explain what it means to be a professional.

- describe or demonstrate the components of professional ethics in words and actions.

- identify the importance of leadership and professional organizations in family and consumer sciences.

- make a personal commitment to being an active member of at least one professional organization.

In the first two chapters of this book, you learned about the history of the family and consumer sciences profession, defined *family*, and explored how the family is a social unit that interacts within a given culture or environment. How has the discipline of family and consumer sciences evolved since the days of Ellen Swallow Richards? How has its mission stayed the same? In this chapter, readers will learn about these questions and will explore the current state of the discipline and profession, analyze the contemporary mission of family and consumer sciences, and identify organizations that support family and consumer sciences students and professionals. Other information in the chapter focuses on professionalism, the role of ethics, and leadership.

Aaron's Questions

Professor Hardy sat down to talk with Aaron, a prospective apparel design major, about the program offered at the state university. Aaron had been drawn to the ever-changing world of fashion since he traveled to Europe as a part of his high school French studies. He was anxious to make his way into the fashion industry, but knew that he wanted a college degree. As Professor Hardy went over the curriculum, potential career opportunities, and questions about the apparel design program and the university in general, Aaron stopped her and asked, "So why is apparel design a part of the school of family and consumer sciences? What does that mean? How is this program different from a technical degree program in apparel design, and why do I need to take a course introducing me to family and consumer sciences? And while I am asking those questions, why do I need a degree? Can't I just learn apparel design skills on my own?"

How would you answer the questions Aaron posed to Professor Hardy? Maybe you have asked these questions yourself. These and other questions will be answered in this chapter.

The Mission of Family and Consumer Sciences

Why are apparel design and other specializations placed within the academic unit of family and consumer sciences? The answer to this question is reflected in the mission of family and consumer sciences, which has been expressed in various ways over the years, as shown in **Figure 3-1**. The common thread in these mission statements is improving the quality of life for individuals, families, and communities.

Apparel designers with a family and consumer sciences background combine knowledge of fashion and technical skills in design with knowledge of basic human developmental needs and the management of individual and family resources. In other words, it is a more comprehensive or holistic view of apparel and fashion than is offered in an academic unit such as art or design.

How does training in apparel design within the context of family and consumer sciences

differ from technical training in apparel design? If Aaron chooses to pursue a career in fashion design for young urban men, his family and consumer sciences background will give him a deeper understanding of their physical, emotional, social, and cognitive development as well as the context of an urban environment. He will understand the socioeconomic strata of his clientele as well as financial resource allocation and the decision-making dynamics of his intended customers. In addition to his talent and creativity, he will have the technical skills in pattern drafting, textile science, and fashion forecasting required in the fashion industry.

In both programs, a student learns how to draft patterns, how to do computer-aided

---

Definitions and Mission Statements for the Family and Consumer Sciences Profession

1902
"…study of the laws, conditions, principles and ideals which are concerned on the one hand with man's immediate physical environment and on the other hand with his nature as a social being, and is the study specifically of the relations between those two factors" (Fourth Lake Placid Conference, 1902; cited in East, 1980, p.10)

1909
"…improve the conditions of living in the home, the institutional household, and the community" (American Home Economics Association, 1909; cited in Stage & Vincenti, p.28)

1979
"…to enable families, both as individual units and generally as a social institution, to build and maintain systems of action which lead (1) to maturing in individual self-formation and (2) to enlightened, cooperative participation in the critique and formulation of social goals and means for accomplishing them" (Brown & Paolucci, 1979, p. 23)

1994
"…an integrative approach to the relationships among individuals, families, and communities and the environments in which they function" (American Home Economics Association, 1994)

2011
"Essence of Family and Consumer Sciences: Creating healthy and sustainable families" (American Association of Family and Consumer Sciences, 2011)

2012
"…the comprehensive body of skills, research, and knowledge that helps people make informed decisions about their well-being, relationships, and resources to achieve optimal quality of life" (American Association of Family and Consumer Sciences, 2012c, "What is FCS?")

Figure 3-1 What key ideas are contained in these statements?

design, how to evaluate the serviceability of textiles, and how the apparel industry runs. When apparel design concepts are taught within the realm of family and consumer sciences, however, apparel becomes more than a mere material good. Instead, apparel is viewed as an artifact of life that can increase the quality of life for an individual, family, or community. In doing so, clothing becomes much more than color, fit, and line. It is an important social, emotional, and physical tool that supports individual identity and self-concept.

Aaron's last question about why he needed a degree rather than just learn apparel design skills on his own is a question many students have. While it is true that knowledge and skills can be learned through life experience, employers value general knowledge and critical thinking skills as well as specialization in a specific discipline. In some family and consumer sciences specializations, such as dietetics and early childhood education, certification or registration that is based on a baccalaureate degree plus a supervised professional internship is required to work in the field. The trend in employment markets and, subsequently, higher education is toward increased specialization in specific majors. Employers want very specific knowledge and skills, and they also want employees who can solve problems and think on a larger scale. In other words, it is not enough to have only technical skills. Employers want employees who can think. It is predicted that this trend will continue well into the future as technology increases the depth and breadth of knowledge in each specialization area. Consequently, enrollment in higher education programs continues to grow (Lerman & Schmidt, 1999).

Hotel and restaurant management, interior merchandising, dietetics, nutrition and physical activity, family and financial counseling, fashion merchandising (apparel marketing), textile science, and child development are just a few of the careers offered in the profession today.

Even with the increase in specialization areas, leaders in the family and consumer sciences profession continue to uphold the unifying body of knowledge that connects each of the separate specializations. That is, the social context within which families exist has changed dramatically, but the mission of the discipline remains much the same. Family and consumer sciences specializations provide opportunity for students to develop thinking skills that are interdisciplinary and integrative, giving them the ability to meet human needs and solve the complex issues that challenge individuals, families, and communities in today's global society. Thus, the needs of individuals, families, and communities remain at the center of the discipline.

The Family and Consumer Sciences Body of Knowledge

With so much variety among family and consumer sciences specializations, is there anything that family and consumer sciences specialists have in common in addition to the mission? The answer is yes. The family and consumer sciences' unifying body of knowledge connects the specializations together in an integrative manner. This body of knowledge provides a foundation for professional practice no matter what the specialization. The body of knowledge includes three categories: integrative elements, core concepts, and cross-cutting themes.

- The integrative elements are *human ecosystems* and *life course development.*

- Core concepts include *basic human needs, individual well-being, family strengths,* and *community vitality.*

- The cross-cutting themes are *wellness, appropriate use of technology, global interdependence, resource development and sustainability,* and *capacity building.*

The following sections discuss each of these concepts (American Association of Family and Consumer Sciences, 2010).

Integrative Element: Human Ecosystems

Use of a human ecosystems perspective has been evident in family and consumer sciences from the early days of the field. Note the 1902 definition, which emphasizes the connections between people and their environments. This integrative element was examined in detail in Chapter 2. No matter what your specialization, you are learning to use an ecosystems perspective. For example, interior designers create human-built environments to meet the needs of the clients who will use them. When a preschool teacher is concerned about a child's development, he must analyze how the child's family and school (human behavioral micro-environments) can work together to support the child. A nutrition researcher may examine how a nutrient (from the natural environment) may affect the progress of a disease in a patient. Can you think of examples in your career field?

Integrative Element: Life Course Development

In addition to the human ecosystems framework, a life course development perspective is another way to understand individuals and families. A life course perspective looks at an individual or a family over time. Three different kinds of time influence human behavior: individual time, generational time, and historical time. Individual time is usually referred to as chronological age. An individual's age is a good predictor of a person's interests, privileges, and roles played in society. For example, one must attain a certain age to be allowed to drive a car because a degree of maturity is required. We don't expect teenagers to be interested in retirement planning or middle-age adults to watch cartoons on Saturday morning. Adults in a family are supposed to support and care for the children (Price & McKenry, 2003).

People who were born during the same time period tend to share certain characteristics because they have been shaped by the same social and economic conditions during their formative years. Members of generation Y, born roughly between 1982 and 2003, grew up during the digital age and are more likely than their grandparents to be comfortable in adapting to new electronic technologies (Pendergast, 2009). Significant historical events also have an impact on those who experience them. For example, the traumatic events of September 9/11 affected Americans' feelings of security (Price & McKenry, 2003).

The life course development perspective also includes the major concepts of stages, tasks, and transitions. A stage is a period in a person's or family's life. In everyday language, people speak of the "teenage years" or the "empty nest" stage of a family. You may have studied, or will likely study, different individual and family development theories with formal names for stages. Examples include Erikson's psychosocial theory of human development and Duvall's family life cycle. At each stage, the individual or the family needs to accomplish certain tasks for healthy development. For example, infants in Erikson's first stage need to develop trust in their caregivers. Young married couples in Duvall's first stage of the family life cycle need to learn to get along with their spouse's relatives. Events, such as the birth of a child or the youngest child leaving for college, propel people to the next stage. The move from one stage to the next is called a transition, and transitions tend to be stressful (Benokraitis, 2012; Price & McKenry, 2003).

Using the life course development approach helps professionals successfully meet the needs of their clients, students, patients, or customers. A dietitian, for example, would be aware that understanding the developmental tasks of adolescence is critical to planning a weight-loss program for obese teenagers. An interior designer can use knowledge of child development to design a playroom appropriate for preschoolers. A restaurant owner in a retirement community may choose music from the 1960s to appeal to his baby boomer customers. A financial counselor would recognize that a couple with young children may be more focused on planning for their children's college education than on their retirement needs. What other examples in your career field illustrate that considering individual time, generational time, life stages, or developmental tasks is helpful?

Core Concept: Basic Human Needs

Basic human needs are "components of human existence that must be satisfied for individuals to develop their human capacity" (Nickols et al., 2009). They are central to this discussion. In Chapter 2 you learned how the field of family and consumer sciences helps improve quality of life by focusing on meeting people's needs for food, clothing, shelter, and relationships. How will you do that in your specialization? One way to examine this question is to consider the hierarchy of human needs developed by Abraham Maslow. Maslow classified needs as physiological, safety, love and belonging, esteem, and self-actualization.

Self-actualization refers to a person's drive to reach his/her full potential, to become the best person one can be. In **Figure 3-2**, these needs are pictured in a pyramid with physiological needs at the base and self-actualization at the top. The pyramid illustrates Maslow's contention that one must first meet a lower need before needs higher on the hierarchy become motivating factors. For example, when a person has an unmet physiological need, such as food, the person is not concerned with the higher need of self-respect (McLeod, 2007).

There are other ways to classify needs, and Maslow's theory has been criticized as not applicable in all cultures (Wachter, 2003). However, it can be a useful framework. Considering Maslow's hierarchy, how does your career field help people meet their needs and eventually arrive at self-actualization? Some examples are obvious. The hospitality industry meets customers' needs for food and shelter. How does the industry address safety needs or the desire for

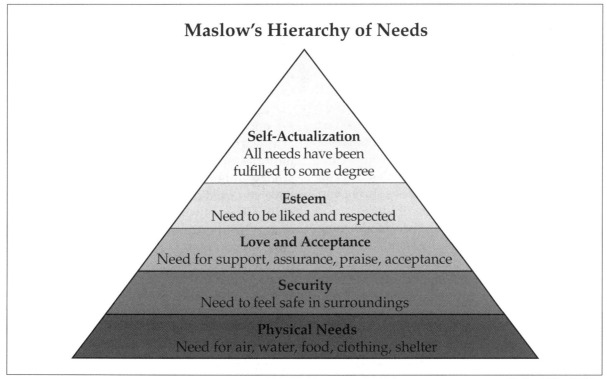

Goodheart-Willcox Publisher

Figure 3-2 Abraham Maslow believed physical needs must be met before all other needs and wants.

love and belonging? The apparel industry provides protective clothing for safety. How does it satisfy the human need for self-esteem? What examples can you think of in food and nutrition, resource management, human development, and family and consumer sciences education?

Core Concept: Individual Well-Being

The promotion of individual well-being is one of the clear goals of professional practice in family and consumer sciences (Nickols et al., 2009). Individual well-being, family strengths, and community vitality are overlapping considerations in the body of knowledge model. They are interrelated. Without healthy individuals, there cannot be strong families or vital communities. On the other hand, healthy families and supportive communities are needed for individuals to develop their unique potential. There are many types of well-being, including physical, emotional, material, social, and spiritual well-being. In what way will you contribute to individual well-being in your future career?

Core Concept: Family Strengths

The development of strong families is another goal of the profession. As you learned in Chapter 2, the concept of family has evolved over time, and there are many different structures that can fulfill the basic functions of the family. Researchers have found that certain protective factors help keep families strong and able to cope with the challenges of life.

These protective factors include an affirming communication style that enables families to solve problems calmly, rather than an incendiary style that features yelling and blame. Families who can draw on hope and spirituality in times of crisis are more resilient. Equality and truth are also important factors in family resiliency. During difficult times especially, truthfulness within the family and from those who interact with the family is necessary. Families who are flexible and change their roles and lifestyle to adapt to new circumstances

can return to harmony and balance. On the other hand, maintaining family routines and rituals helps people cope with adversity. Some families are hardier than others. In other words, they see a hardship as a challenge, have a sense of control over the situation, and forge a strong commitment to solve the problem together. Families whose members are healthy and who have a strong social network are also more able to cope with the inevitable stresses of life (McCubbin, McCubbin, Thompson, Han, & Allen, 1997).

Core Concept: Community Vitality

Family and consumer sciences looks at the whole person, the whole family, and its surrounding community. Communities provide resources that most families alone cannot. These include, for example, schools, libraries, health and safety services, parks, museums, and cultural and civic organizations. Without these resources families would not be able to meet their basic needs, individual well-being would be compromised, and it would be difficult to build strong families. Likewise, healthy individuals and strong families contribute to community vitality, the capacity of the community to develop (Nickols et al., 2009).

Keep in mind that geographic communities are not the only type of community. There are also learning communities, professional communities of practice, and online communities, among others. What community resources have you used during your life? How has your ability to meet your goals been affected by the quality of the community in which you live? How do you plan to contribute to the community where you live and to your professional community?

Cross-Cutting Theme: Wellness

If you are not sick, does that mean you are well? Not necessarily. Wellness is not the absence of disease but, rather, optimal functioning in every dimension of life. The National

Wellness Institute defines wellness as "an active process through which people become aware of, and make choices toward, a more successful existence" (National Wellness Institute, n.d., "Defining Wellness"). When hearing the word *wellness* people often think first of physical wellness, but wellness has several other components, including emotional, social, occupational, intellectual, and spiritual wellness (Fain & Lewis, 2002).

Optimal physical wellness results from good exercise and eating habits, self-care, appropriate use of medical services, and avoiding the abuse of drugs and alcohol. Emotional wellness has to do with recognizing, accepting, and managing one's feelings. Emotionally healthy individuals express feelings appropriately, cope with stress, form close relationships with others, and develop an optimistic outlook. The occupational dimension of wellness includes pursuing a career that best complements your interests, values, and abilities and finding satisfaction in your work. Social wellness refers to developing friendships, contributing to the community, and living in harmony with other people and nature. Spiritual wellness is developed through personal reflection to find meaning in your life and clarify your own truth and values. It may or may not have a religious component. Intellectual wellness involves challenging one's mind, learning new things, and expanding your creative and critical thinking abilities (Hettler, 1976; Fain & Lewis, 2002).

The FCS profession has a long history of promoting physical wellness, especially by those who practice dietetics and nutrition education. These contributions are recognized by other professions. An article in the *Journal of the American Medical Association* pointed out the important role that family and consumer sciences teachers have in the nation's fight against obesity (Lichtenstein & Ludwig, 2010). When a preschool teacher says, "Tell Victor why you are so angry; you don't need to hit him," she is helping a child learn to express emotions appropriately. What other examples show that FCS professionals help others optimize wellness?

Cross-Cutting Theme: Appropriate Use of Technology

Thirteen-year-old Anna Schiferl was still in bed when she texted her mom, who was in the kitchen, that she wanted cinnamon rolls for breakfast. Her mother reminded her that she is not allowed to text people who are in the same house. Communication experts are becoming concerned that people are losing the ability to have the face-to-face conversations that build personal relationships (Associated Press, 2012).

Throughout the history of the field, family and consumer sciences professionals have examined the relationship between technology and the people who use it. In the early years of the profession, home economists helped introduce technology into homes as a way to reduce labor. Labor-saving devices such as vacuum cleaners and automatic washers were seen as ways to free women from the burdens of housework. As systems thinking became central to the field, awareness grew that the implementation of new technologies usually had unforeseen consequences. By the 1970s, some home economists were questioning the high-energy lifestyle that was being promoted by the extensive use of technology. Over the past 100 years, the field has moved beyond the unquestioning use of technology to solve problems, to also examining the problems caused by technology (Elias, 1987).

FCS professionals today recognize that technologies are generally neither good nor bad; they can be used in ways that harm or help. The challenge for the profession is to "question whether the actual and possible applications of technology improve well-being and at whose expense" (Makela, 2008) and to match the technology appropriately to the task (Braun, 2008).

For example, genetic modification research utilizing genome exploration and DNA knowledge will offer new health alternatives, eliminating some diseases and curing others. Drug companies are frequently introducing new drugs that can help treat symptoms or even cure many illnesses and ailments. Even our food is changing. Crop and animal food products will continue to be genetically modified to offer better nutrition, including lower-fat alternatives. In the area of human biology, questions regarding cloning, parental rights, and reproduction techniques are in the forefront. Many genetic engineering techniques are already available, raising ethical, moral, and medical decisions that individuals and families will have to make.

Digital technologies will continue to revolutionize and transform society at a fast rate. Although the advancement of technology on the industrial and personal level has been astounding during just the past decade, the rate of increase in technological development in the coming years is predicted to speed up. New ways of living, working, and learning will recreate life as we know it. We have already seen great changes in education where coursework has moved outside traditional classroom walls and is delivered in various electronic forms. Expectations in work life and culture have been revolutionized through telecommunications such as the Internet and wireless devices. Even expectations in personal and home technology have completely changed. Upcoming changes will force individuals to consider how to balance or perhaps integrate human contact with technology. *High-touch environments*—that is, places where relationships are esteemed and a sense of community prevails—will be desired. Although, initially, some believed that more technology would lead to more leisure, this has not been true for most people. Increased technology has subsequently increased expectations for being connected and generating greater output. Telecommunications has had a positive effect on families, resulting in more frequent contact and leading to strengthening relationships. On the other hand, technology has also made it possible to extend bullying from the school yard into the home and to easily trade child pornography around the world.

Cross-Cutting Theme: Global Interdependence

In the past few decades, we have seen communication increase around the world. We have also seen that what happens in one country or region quickly influences another. In the next few decades, it is predicted that the world will seem smaller as more people travel internationally and see media images of cultures around the world. Communication is instantaneous. Global crises and skirmishes will continue to divide and separate people. However, people will also be more interested in developing a sense of community around them.

How will basic human needs be met around the world? How will choices made by one person affect someone in another part of the world? An apparel designer may choose to have clothing he or she designed produced in another country to reduce labor costs. A family and consumer sciences specialist is trained to consider this decision, not just from his or her own perspective, but from the perspective of the manufacturing company and the people whom the decision could harm or benefit. Some considerations may include employee work conditions and pay. For example, the decision to produce a sweater in a country with very low labor costs could affect employment in the United States as jobs are lost in the sweater production industry. On the other hand, moving the sweater production to a low-wage country would provide employment for its workers, putting food on the table for many families.

Cross-Cutting Theme: Resource Development and Sustainability

The current interest in protecting the environment will continue to increase while accommodating building growth. Designing affordable, self-sustaining communities will be a challenge. Sustainability means meeting today's needs without endangering future generations. As the world becomes further digitized and physically separated in the work environment, a need for community at home and in neighborhoods may grow. This will open up new issues and questions. How can we provide affordable housing to a growing population while not depleting the land of natural resources? How should natural resources be used? Who should decide? These are questions about sustainability that will face all families and communities.

FCS professionals in all specializations can incorporate sustainability into their practices. Here are some examples.

- A hotel manager institutes a program that encourages guests to reuse towels, thus reducing the environmental impact of laundry.

- A family and consumer sciences educator teaches students the eight Rs: refuse, reduce, reuse, recycle, repair, restore, repurpose, redesign (Thompson, Harden, Clauss, Fox, & Wild, 2012).

- A fashion buyer responds to consumer demands by expanding the store's selection of organic clothing.

- An interior designer encourages a client to follow LEED (Leadership in Energy and Environmental Design) standards for a new building.

What are some other examples that come to mind?

Cross-Cutting Theme: Capacity Building

As far back as the founding pioneers, family and consumer sciences has been a prescriptive and educational discipline. That is, it focuses on teaching and finding solutions to problems before they happen rather than only on fixing problems after they occur. Providing education and offering recommendations empowers people to make moral, ethical, and even spiritual decisions that will improve their quality of life as they see fit. Empowering people in this way is an example of capacity building, defined by Buck (2003) as "developing knowledge and skills for an individual, a family, or a community to meet their full potential." Building capacity in oneself or others requires critical thinking, good communication skills, an appreciation for diversity, and the willingness to become engaged in public policy development.

Whether working with clothing, food, or shelter or helping people with relationships, family and consumer sciences specializations use critical thinking to solve life problems. Say, for example, that an early childhood educator is working with a three-year-old who seems to have problems navigating socially in the classroom. A trained educator will look at the problem in several ways and consider the child's social, emotional, cognitive, and physical spheres. Finding information about these spheres could include interacting with the child's family, other teachers, the child, and perhaps, a medical doctor. Creative thinking skills play a large part in critical thinking and problem solving. Family and consumer sciences draws from a number of core disciplines such as psychology, sociology, economics, biology, and chemistry to creatively solve everyday problems faced by individuals. This is why it is called an *applied* discipline. Vincenti and Smith (2004) discuss the role of critical science theory that applies to all family and consumer sciences specializations as knowledge that focuses on "human interests, communicative theory grounded in dialogue, and actions based on moral consciousness."

Understanding and utilizing communication skills is essential in applying concepts and solving life problems in all family and consumer sciences specializations. For example, if an interior designer cannot effectively communicate a creative solution to his or her client, the idea is lost between conception and potential implementation. Likewise, if a hospital dietitian cannot communicate a nutritional analysis to other professionals on his or her diagnostic team—including physicians, nurses, therapists, and the patient—the expertise goes to waste. People hone their communication skills over time, responding to new methods of sending and receiving information. Even though communication methods change with technological innovations, the ability to listen, understand, and clearly articulate ideas remains at the core of good communication.

To build capacity of individuals, families, or communities, family and consumer sciences specialists must be comfortable with and appreciate human diversity. Without an appreciation for diversity, client needs will not be met. Take, for example, a nutritionist who is working with individuals from a culturally diverse background. If his or her client considers particular animal protein sources unethical or even sinful, and the nutritionist does not appreciate cultural values concerning food choices, the advice and expertise may go unheeded. Even if the food item is not considered taboo, the client may have no experience preparing or eating it.

Capacity building also means using "internal and external leadership skills in order to move an individual, a group, or a project forward" (Buck, 2003). Many challenges faced by families cannot be solved through individual or family efforts alone; participation in public policy may be needed. Family and consumer sciences professionals are not content with impacting their own small sphere of influence; they seek to change the greater community through larger policy-level efforts. They are motivated by a deep interest in developing the community. For example, an interior designer may work with a client to design a home that is accessible for individuals with physical disabilities. He or she may expand this work by sharing resources and knowledge with other interior designers, architects, and builders. This builds a larger network of people sharing resources to enhance life for members of the community. The designer may eventually help develop building laws and regulations that require housing to be accessible for all people through his or her work testifying at hearings or writing legislators about proposed bills. Many family and consumer sciences professionals work diligently to change and formulate public policy at the local, state, and national levels. Chapter 5 will further explore public policy.

Professionalism

What makes a person a professional? Is it a college degree? an advanced degree? Is it competence in a field? skills? character? a certain salary level? expertise in a field? The answer could be "all of the above" or "some of the above" depending on the profession. The term *professional* is used frequently in the English language to denote an expected level of behavior, but it also denotes skills and competence. Sometimes competence is measured in academic degrees obtained. Sometimes it is a combination of both experience and training. Whether a person is considered a professional may vary by field, but certain expectations are denoted with the concept.

According to the *Merriam-Webster's Collegiate Dictionary*, **professionalism** is defined as the "conduct, aims, or qualities that characterize or mark a profession or a professional person." General principles that underpin a definition of professionalism include competence, complex decision making, decisiveness, and community awareness.

Professionals demonstrate a continuing commitment to excellence by pledging to develop competence in their field. That is, they are prepared technically with the skills needed to perform the job well. These may be specific task-oriented skills, or they may be skills related to the facilitation of getting a job done. Competence is measured differently in each profession.

Sometimes competence is measured through competency exams, apprenticeships, academic degrees, internships, and length of experience. For example, a registered dietitian must hold a baccalaureate degree, have completed an approved supervised practice, and have passed the Registration Examination for Dietitians to demonstrate competency in the nutrition field. An interior designer must pass an exam to receive national or state certification. On the other hand, an apparel merchandiser can demonstrate competence through on-the-job performance, successful internship completion, a college degree, or a combination of the above depending on the requirements of the position. Professionals are not only competent in their field, but also dedicated to developing their competence and influencing environmental changes around them. Competence generally increases over time with experience and lifelong learning.

Professionals are also identified by their ability to deal with high levels of complexity and uncertainty. Tasks are not always spelled out clearly and concisely, but a professional can work in an environment that is not always transparent. Professionals develop confidence to act in uncertain situations and exhibit thoughtful decisiveness. This means they are thoughtful about their actions and decisions. However, in their decisive action, professionals respond to societal needs and their behaviors reflect a social bond with the communities they serve. This community awareness prompts a greater good than just serving his or her own needs. Professionals also demonstrate core humanistic values. Family and consumer sciences professionals adhere to high ethical and moral standards and are accountable for their actions and for those of their colleagues.

So what is professionalism? Here is a summary of what it is and what it is not. Professionalism in the workplace has to do with technical skills or level of expertise. It may not be about having the highest level of expertise, but it is about the desire to continue learning and developing expertise. It is not related to a person's education level or grade point average, but does relate to a desire to learn, grow, and adapt to changing and complex environments. It is not exclusive to certain types of jobs or occupations because professional behavior can be found in any occupation or service. Professionalism includes being considerate and respectful in dealing with coworkers, customers, and management while maintaining the highest standards possible in your field. It is about being the best you can be. It is about having an optimistic attitude toward work and life. It requires maturity, regardless of age or experience.

Professionalism has many benefits. First, it offers respect and consideration among people. Second, it gives confidence and assurance to both the professional and his or her constituents. Third, it builds trust that decisions made will be ethically sound and will serve the greater good. However, what is considered moral or ethical or even what is considered "for the greater good" is far more complex in today's global environment than you might expect.

Professional Ethics

Professional ethics involve making moral decisions. Making the right decision is not always easy, however. What is ethical, moral, or right may not be clear in every situation. Ethics are demonstrated in an individual's words and actions. Take, for example, the story of Kathy, a recent graduate in family finance.

Kathy's Ethical Dilemma

Graduation was a big celebration as Kathy's parents, siblings, friends, and classmates honored her achievement. Now the time had come to find a job. Six months ago, Kathy completed her family and consumer sciences degree in family finance. It had been a hard road. As a single, divorced mom of two school-age children, it was not easy going back to school in her mid-forties. She received some government financial aid and support from family, yet times were lean over the past two years. Her kids were ready to have their mom back—no more studying late into the night and having little money.

Kathy chose family finance as a major because she personally experienced the heart-wrenching decisions that come with declaring personal bankruptcy. As a young woman, she frequently overused her high-interest credit cards, and by the time she married, both she and her husband were in serious debt. They found financing that required no down payment and bought a house, two new cars, and home furnishings to fill their home. When their marriage broke up after declaring bankruptcy, neither she nor her husband had any assets to speak of. Kathy sought counseling from a family finance counselor in her community whom a friend recommended. It was difficult for Kathy, but her counselor helped her to set goals, establish a budget, and live within her means. After seeing first-hand how a family finance counselor can impact a person's life and future, Kathy decided that was the career path for her. She had empathy for people struggling financially and wanted to help improve the quality of life for others.

The timing of Kathy's graduation was unfortunate. Although the family finance field was growing by leaps and bounds and there was great need for people with her education and skills, her small town was suffering from plant closures and high unemployment. Her plan had been to move from her rural college town to a suburban area, but after her father's recent heart attack and her mother's struggle with diabetes, she knew she needed to stay close until things stabilized. Besides, she felt she owed it to them. She never would have made it through the last two years of school without their constant help—financially, emotionally, and in practical ways such as with child care and meals.

Kathy has been jobless for a total of 18 months, including the six months since graduation. Two months ago, she started looking outside her field, increasingly willing to take any job. However, even minimum wage positions were scarce, and they did not pay enough for one person to live on, much less three. She has school loans that she needs to begin paying off and does not want to get into financial trouble again. Her biggest worry, however, is her lack of medical coverage for her children. She has somehow paid her rent for the last six months, but now that her savings are running out, she desperately needs a job. She has been trying to keep a cheerful, hopeful attitude for her children, who are unaware of the family's financial distress.

Now, a job Kathy never applied for has come up. She received an unsolicited call from a national lending store that markets "payday loans" through storefronts at strip malls. The company makes it very easy for people with poor credit to take out loans. However, the interest rates are astronomical— sometimes as high as 500 percent. From her educational training, she knows that people who take out these easy loans rarely recover financially. She is offered a high salary and a benefits package that covers her whole family, but Kathy believes it is absurd and hypocritical to encourage people to take out these easy loans. However, her own financial situation is worsening and just one unforeseen event could devastate her family. Should she take the job to support her family and prevent financial ruin? As a professional, shouldn't she guide people in solid financial decision making? To whom is she responsible?

Few choices we face are as difficult as the one Kathy is facing, but being ethical is often hard. We are surrounded with choices

personally and professionally. Everything we say and do represents a choice. This makes sense on a personal level, but in a culturally diverse environment, how can people come to agreement on ethical choices? This has been a debated topic in schools for many years. Ethics entail values, and in Western culture, values are viewed as personal. Yet, decisions we make determine the shape of our lives and the lives of those around us. Across cultures and belief systems, six common pillars of ethical decision making emerge (Josephson, 2002).

- Trustworthiness: This includes honesty, courage to do the right thing, and loyalty.

- Respect for others: This involves using good manners and being considerate of the feelings and culture of others.

- Responsibility: A common theme in ethical behavior, this means not only persevering in tasks but also doing your best. Self-control, self-discipline, accountability, and reflective action all play a part in responsible behavior.

- Fairness: This is not only about playing by the rules, but also involves being open minded and using equity as a principle when dealing with others.

- Caring: This includes being kind and compassionate to others, expressing gratitude, forgiving others, and helping people in need.

- Citizenship: This involves doing what you can to make your community a better place. Sometimes, all that is required is simple cooperation. Other times, it takes personal involvement with issues in the community. The community can be as small as a two-person friendship or as large as a society. Citizenship includes obeying laws and rules and also respecting authority. It means being a good neighbor to other people and the environment.

Although the six pillars of ethical behavior may be somewhat universal, beliefs about whether a specific action is ethical may vary by cultural group. For example, in the United

States, it is considered unethical (and illegal) to exactly replicate a clothing designer's work with the intention of selling a "fake," (an item that passes off as the original). In other cultures this is not considered unethical but instead is shrewd business, and many exact copies of designer clothing and accessories are sold at much lower prices than the originals. It is illegal to sell such copies in the United States. However, it is an accepted practice and an important part of the United States apparel industry to "knock off" (make close copies of) designer goods. These knockoffs are sold under a different label and often use inferior materials or construction techniques. Thus, in the United States, it is not considered unethical to mimic a designer's work or to reproduce it as an inferior product. It is considered unethical to replicate goods and falsely use the original designer's name, trademark, or logo. Professionals must always be aware that culture and the specific situation can place a filter on what is considered ethical behavior.

Ethics in a professional setting concerns conduct of behavior and practice when carrying out professional work. Many professional organizations and businesses have a code of conduct. These codes or guidelines usually address the professional's obligations to the employer, to the client or customer, and to society as a whole. They include principles such as honesty, nondiscrimination, confidentiality, competence, and the avoidance of conflicts of interest or abuses of power.

- Honesty: Professionals do not misrepresent their qualifications or the services that they offer.
- Nondiscrimination: Professionals provide services without discrimination based on ethnicity, country of origin, gender, race, religion, or age.
- Confidentiality: Professionals protect confidential information they obtain in the course of their work. This is especially important in health care settings, where violations of confidentiality are not only unethical but also illegal.

- Competence: As a professional you are expected to stay up to date in your field to provide the best possible service to your employer and clients, customers, patients, or students. If you are unable to perform competently due to substance abuse or mental illness, for example, you are obligated to remove yourself from situations where you might do harm and to seek help.
- Conflicts of interest: A conflict of interest is a situation in which you may be tempted to put your personal interest above that of your employer or client (patient, student). Two situations in which conflicts of interest frequently arise are in hiring and purchasing. For example, your responsibilities may include hiring. Suppose a member of your family is one of the candidates for the position. Your evaluation of the candidates may be biased, and your relative may have an unfair advantage. In this situation, it is important to make your employer aware of the relationship and allow someone else to make the hiring recommendation. Purchasing items for your employer from businesses in which you have a financial or personal interest is another example of a conflict of interest. In some situations, it is also illegal.
- Abuse of power: Sexual harassment is an example of the abuse of power, but it is not the only type. Using your position of authority to force employees to perform personal services that are not part of their job duties is also an abuse of power. The employer is not paying your administrative assistant to address and mail your personal holiday cards or political campaign flyers. Public employees have lost their jobs for this kind of ethical violation.

Professional behavior and, specifically, professional ethics are crucial in establishing the ideals and responsibilities of the family and consumer sciences profession. Professional ethics serve to protect the professional and his or her clients, motivate and inspire high performance levels, and improve the quality and consistency of professional services rendered.

You are expected to exhibit ethical behavior as you prepare for your profession. For example, students demonstrate honesty by avoiding plagiarism and correctly giving credit to sources. When you are placed in a field site for internship or clinical experiences, you may have access to confidential information, which should not be shared. The Code of Ethics of the American Association of Family and Consumer Sciences (available at the organization's website) applies throughout the field, but there are also specific codes in dietetics, early childhood education, interior design, education, and other related fields. Check the websites of professional organizations to find the applicable codes.

Leadership: Past, Present, and Future

Leadership involves knowing what is happening in the world around you and responding to make a difference. There are many definitions of leadership. A simple one states that *leadership* is the process of leading others toward an established goal. Other definitions are more complex. For example, Bennis' (1989) definition of leadership focuses on the personal capabilities of the leader. He advises leaders to know themselves, to communicate a well-articulated vision of where they want to go, and to build trust among followers in the process.

Family and consumer sciences has moved forward since its inception because of its past leaders and practicing professionals. In Chapter 1, you read about Ellen Swallow Richards and her involvement in the formation of the family and consumer sciences discipline, as well as stories of other pioneers in the field. Family and consumer sciences is a discipline that focuses on people and families. It is also about their stories. The remainder of this book features stories of contemporary leaders in the field, as well as practicing family and consumer sciences professionals. Stories connect people with each other and with themselves and will help readers become the future leaders of family and consumer sciences.

Family and Consumer Sciences Organizations: Providing Opportunities for Leadership

One of the best ways to know what is happening in your field and to hear from leaders in your interest area is to join a professional organization. Several "umbrella" organizations for family and consumer sciences serve as good sources of information. See **Figure 3-3**. Each of these organizations is described in the following paragraphs. Visit these organizations online or read some of their publications.

Websites for Family and Consumer Sciences Organizations	
American Association of Family and Consumer Sciences	aafcs.org
Association for Career and Technical Education	acteonline.org
International Federation for Home Economics	ifhe.org
Kappa Omicron Nu	kon.org
National Coalition for Black Development in Family and Consumer Sciences	ncbdfcs.org
Phi Upsilon Omicron	phiu.org

Figure 3-3 Access these websites for information about family and consumer sciences organizations.

The American Association of Family and Consumer Sciences

The American Association of Family and Consumer Sciences (AAFCS), organized by Ellen Swallow Richards and others in 1909, is still a strong voice for families today. AAFCS is the only professional association that brings together family and consumer sciences professionals and students across practice areas and content specializations. Members include early childhood, secondary, university, and extension educators; administrators and managers; human services professionals; researchers; community volunteers; business people; and consultants. The AAFCS mission is

> To provide leadership and support for professionals whose work assists individuals, families, and communities in making informed decisions about their well-being, relationships, and resources to achieve quality of life (AAFCS, 2012a).

Today, the AAFCS endeavors to improve the quality of life for individuals, families, and communities by providing educational programs and resources and by influencing public policy. The AAFCS continues to react and adapt to the needs of individuals within the context of society as it has throughout its history. There are also state affiliates of the AAFCS. Each state affiliate has its own officers and meetings or conferences. The AAFCS is the professional organization that represents all areas of family and consumer sciences in the United States.

International Federation for Home Economics

The International Federation for Home Economics (IFHE) was founded in 1908 in Switzerland as an International Non-Governmental Organization (INGO) in consultative status with the United Nations and with the Council of Europe. There is a national coordinating body in each participating country, including the United States. The purpose of IFHE is to facilitate and increase opportunities in family and consumer sciences throughout the world. The mission of the IFHE is "to provide an international forum for home economists to develop and express the home economics concerns for individuals, families, and households at the United Nations and among other international non-governmental organizations whose interests parallel those of home economics. The ultimate goal of the IFHE is the improvement of the quality of everyday life for individuals, families, and households through the management of their resources" (International Federation for Home Economics, n.d., "Mission").

The Association for Career and Technical Education

The Association for Career and Technical Education (ACTE) was founded in 1926 and is currently the largest national education association dedicated to preparing youth and adults for successful careers. Part of the organization's strength is in its numbers. It has over 28,000 members (Association for Career and Technical Education, 2006). Another strength is its diversity. Career and technical educators, administrators, researchers, and counselors from secondary through adult levels participate. Career and technical education includes employment preparation skills as well as specific trade skills. The organization plays a key role in assuring growth and funding of educational programs at the local, state, and federal level. An important part of this task is communicating with legislators and government leaders about the programs and offerings in career and technical education. When a concern related to technical or career education is at issue, ACTE becomes involved. Members are also kept up to date through news briefs and conferences.

Family and consumer sciences secondary and post-secondary educators are well represented within the organization and constitute one of the largest and strongest divisions within ACTE. It is an active division that serves its members well. For example, the family and consumer sciences division of ACTE keeps educators abreast of current issues and legislation affecting the profession.

Kappa Omicron Nu

Kappa Omicron Nu is an honor society for undergraduates, graduate students, and professionals in family and consumer sciences. Its mission is to empower family and consumer sciences leaders through scholarship, research, and leadership development. Many opportunities for training, showcasing work through publication and presentations, and funding are offered through Kappa Omicron Nu. Members are nominated on the basis of their scholarship and character by current members. They are initiated into the organization through a ceremony and participate in local affiliates of the organization. Many universities and colleges that have family and consumer sciences programs (or human sciences programs, sometimes called human ecology) sponsor local Kappa Omicron Nu chapters. An undergraduate research initiative by the organization provides opportunity for students to publish and present research (Kappa Omicron Nu, n.d.).

Phi Upsilon Omicron

Phi Upsilon Omicron is a national honor society in family and consumer sciences that was founded in 1910 at the University of Minnesota. In fact, it was the first student organization formed in family and consumer sciences (Phi Upsilon Omicron, 2006). The purpose of the honor society is to recognize and encourage academic excellence, to promote professional and leadership opportunities and resources for development, and to provide service to the profession. Chapters include both alumni and collegiate groups.

National Coalition for Black Development in Family and Consumer Sciences

The National Coalition for Black Development in Family and Consumer Sciences (NCBDFCS) was formed in 1980 as the Coalition for Black Development in Home Economics. The Coalition works with the American Association of Family and Consumer Sciences to promote the profession. It provides networking and professional development opportunities. The organization's goals include strengthening family and consumer sciences programs at historically black colleges and universities (HBCUs) and promoting black participation in all aspects of family and consumer sciences. Membership is open to individuals with degrees from any of the specialized areas of the field and to students pursuing degrees. The NCBDFCS awards student scholarships and support for students to attend professional meetings (National Coalition for Black Development in Family and Consumer Sciences, n.d.).

Specialized Organizations

Many other associations exist that support the mission of family and consumer sciences. Professional associations that focus on specific specializations within family and consumer sciences include the American Society of Interior Designers, the International Textiles and Apparel Association, the Academy of Nutrition and Dietetics, and the National Council on Family Relations. These associations will be explored further in later chapters. Many of these organizations offer discounted student membership rates.

The Value of Joining Professional Organizations

There are many advantages to joining a professional organization, especially while you are still a student. First, professional organizations link you to the most current trends in the profession. Through newsletters, journals, online postings, and conferences, both students and professionals are able to keep up with current events and new trends. Second, professional organizations offer opportunities for students and professionals to interact in a business setting as well as in informal settings at conferences and meetings. Leadership positions are often available for both students and professionals, and serving in these positions reflects initiative, responsibility, and commitment on your résumé. As noted earlier, the AAFCS has a student member section that provides leadership training in officer positions. These positions offer useful networking opportunities as well as the opportunity to hone your leadership skills.

The third reason to join a professional organization is to access job banks and career networking opportunities that are available only to members. Employers who post jobs on professional organization websites or in their printed material are looking for future employees with the same professional interests or background as many of the organization's members.

Also, as a student member of a professional organization, you may be eligible for several financial benefits. Membership dues are often reduced for student members. Some associations even offer lower membership rates for new professionals. Scholarships and fellowships are frequently offered to student members as well. Overall, joining a professional organization is a wise investment in your future.

Current Issues in Family and Consumer Sciences

Where is family and consumer sciences today, and where is it going? The family and consumer sciences discipline of today is very different from the days of Ellen Swallow Richards. The very nature of the discipline demands change. Thus, as society changes, so does the emphasis of the educational and research programs in family and consumer sciences. However, the profession is not just reactionary. The profession's leaders are forward-thinking, anticipating changes that will affect the family in the coming years. These changes and trends will be discussed in detail in Chapter 4. Chapter 5 explains how the profession influences public policy to deal proactively with societal changes and concerns.

Summary

The mission and definition statements of family and consumer sciences have evolved over time, but certain ideals have remained constant.

FCS professionals work in a holistic and integrative way with individuals, families, and communities to improve quality of life. The profession considers the context in which people are situated and seeks to change societal conditions that may hamper optimal development.

From designing accessible housing for an aging population to helping children make good nutrition choices, all areas of specialization within family and consumer sciences are unified by a common body of knowledge. This shared knowledge includes several core concepts: basic human needs, individual well-being, family strengths, and community vitality. Professionals use two overarching theoretical perspectives in their work: life course development and human ecosystems. Several themes cut across all of the specializations: wellness, appropriate use of technology, global interdependence, resource development and sustainability, and capacity building.

Professionalism also binds the specializations together. Professionalism is defined as the behavior, aims, or traits that characterize a person as meeting the standards of the profession. Family and consumer sciences specialists are family advocates and professionals in their field. Professionalism intrinsically carries with it an expectation of moral or ethical decision making. Although ethics are hard to define in a multicultural society, six pillars of ethical decision making were identified in this chapter. These include: trustworthiness, respect, responsibility, fairness, caring, and citizenship. Ethical principles are specified in codes of conduct developed by professional organizations.

Family and consumer sciences needs people who can act as ethical professionals and leaders to carry the discipline forward. How can you play a part? Professional organizations play a major role in leading the future of the family and consumer sciences profession. There are many benefits for both student and professional members of associations, including timely communication, policy formation, family advocacy, financial benefits, networking, and leadership opportunities. They also serve as employment resources.

Family and consumer sciences is alive and well. Family and consumer sciences leaders and organizations are forward-thinking, anticipating and adjusting to changes that will affect the family in the coming years. The profession is setting practices in place that will meet the needs of families today and in the future.

Questions for Thought

1. Reread the story about Kathy, the recent family and consumer sciences family finance graduate seeking employment. What would you do if you were in her situation?

2. Look at the website for two or three of the family and consumer sciences professional organizations described in this chapter or in the chapter on your career field. Answer the following questions for each:
    - What is the mission of the organization?
    - Who is eligible for membership?
    - How much does membership cost?
    - Is there a student rate for membership?
    - What benefits are afforded to members?
    - What resources are available online for members and nonmembers?

3. It is easy to agree that people should have their basic needs met, but ethical questions sometimes arise in meeting those needs. In recent years, homelessness has found a new face in America. It is not only the face of single men choosing to live on the streets but also men, women, and children who have no permanent place to live. They survive on streets, in cars, and in shelters. They are often poor, socially isolated, sometimes ill, and sometimes alcohol or drug addicted. Some are fleeing abusive relationships. In many communities across the country, conflict has arisen between the homeless, those who have homes, and advocates for both sides. Fundamental questions surround the issue of homelessness. Is there a morally right or wrong response? Respond to the following questions:
    - Do homeless people have a right to be homeless if they want to be?
    - Do homeless people have the right to populate public spaces such as parks and parking lots?
    - Do people with homes have the right to ban homeless people from their neighborhoods?
    - Do people choose to be homeless, or is it always involuntary?
    - Should homelessness be accepted as an alternative lifestyle that is a part of American diversity?
    - What is the role for family and consumer sciences professionals to play in addressing the issue of homelessness?

4. Find a code of ethics for your intended career field. How does it address the ethical issues of honesty, competence, nondiscrimination, confidentiality, conflicts of interest, and abuse of power?

5. Discuss the following questions with other students in your career or specialty area: How are you learning to use technology appropriately, sustain resources, promote wellness, build capacity, and deal with global interdependence? How will you use the life course development or ecosystems perspective in your work? How does your field support individual well-being, strong families, and vital communities? To what extent will you be involved with meeting basic human needs?

References and Resources

Adams, L. (2001). The family and its well-being. *Journal of Family and Consumer Sciences*, *93*(3), 19-21.

American Association of Family and Consumer Sciences. (2012a). *About us*. Retrieved from http://www.aafcs.org/AboutUs/index.asp

American Association of Family and Consumer Sciences. (2012b) *Code of ethics*. Retrieved from http://www.aafcs.org/AboutUs/CodeEthics.asp

American Association of Family and Consumer Sciences. (2012c). *What is FCS?*. Retrieved from http://www.aafcs.org/AboutUs/FCS.asp

American Association of Family and Consumer Sciences. (2011). *Family and consumer sciences, AAFCS, co-branding toolkit*. Retrieved from http://www.aafcs.org

American Association of Family and Consumer Sciences Council for Accreditation. (2010). *Accreditation documents for undergraduate programs in family and consumer sciences (2010 ed.).* Retrieved from http://www.aafcs.org/education/accreditation.html

American Home Economics Association. (1994). *The Scottsdale Meeting: Positioning the profession for the 21st century, proceedings.* Alexandria, VA: American Home Economics Association.

Associated Press. (2012, June 4). Is texting killing the art of conversation? *The Vindicator*, A2.

Association for Career and Technical Education. (2006). *Who we are.* Retrieved December 30, 2006, from http://www.acteonline.org/about/whoweare.cfm

Baugher, S. L., Anderson, C. L., Green, K. B., Nickols, S. Y., Shane, J., Jolly, L., & Miles, J. (2003). *Body of knowledge of family and consumer sciences.* Retrieved December 1, 2006, from http://www.aafcs.org/about/knowledge.html

Bennis, W. (1989). *On becoming a leader.* New York: Addison Wesley.

Bennis, W. G., & Nanus, B. (1997). *Leaders: The strategies for taking charge* (2nd ed.). New York: Harper and Row.

Bennis, W., Spreitzer, G. M., & Cummings, T. G. (Eds.). (2001). *The future of leadership: Today's top leadership thinkers speak to tomorrow's leaders.* San Francisco: Jossey-Bass.

Betts, S. C. (2006). A worldview of FCS teaching, scholarship, and practice. *Journal of Family and Consumer Sciences, 98*(3), 14-16.

Bolman, L. G., & Deal, T. E. (1991). *Images of leadership:* NCEL Occasional Paper No. 7. (ERIC Document Reproduction Service No. ED332345). Nashville, TN: National Center for Educational Leadership.

Bolman, L. G., & Deal, T. E. (1995). *Leading with soul: An upcoming journey of spirit.* San Francisco: Jossey-Bass.

Braun, B. (2008). Point of view: Appropriate technology. *Journal of Family and Consumer Sciences, 100*(2), 1.

Brown, M., & Paolucci, B. (1979). *Home economics: A definition.* Washington, DC: American Home Economics Association.

Buck, S. (2003). Building capacity through leadership development programs. *Journal of Family and Consumer Sciences, 95*(3), 8-11.

Deal, T. E. (1996). Capturing the spirit of leadership. *Kappa Omicron Nu Forum, 9*(1), 11-19.

Doherty, W. (2000). Family science and family citizenship: Toward a model of community partnership with families. *Family Relations, 49*(3), 319-325.

Earnest, G. W. (2003, Winter). Study abroad: A powerful new approach for developing leadership capacities. *Journal of Leadership Education, 2*(2). Retrieved April 17, 2007, from http://www.fhsu.edu/jole/issues/JOLE_2_2.pdf

East, M. (1980). *Home economics: Past, present, and future.* Boston: Allyn & Bacon.

Elias, J. G. (1987). Home economics and the growth of household technology. *Home Economics Forum, 1*(2), 6-8.

Fain, N. C., & Lewis, N. M. (2002). Wellness: The holistic approach to health. *Journal of Family and Consumer Sciences, 94*(2), 6-8.

Fletcher, K. (2008). *Sustainable fashion and textiles.* London: Earthscan Publications, Ltd.

Greenleaf, R. (1991). *Servant leadership: A journey into the nature of legitimate power and greatness.* Mahwah, NJ: Paulist Press.

Hettler, B. (1976). *Six dimensions of wellness model.* National Wellness Institute, Inc. Retrieved from http://www.nationalwellness.org

International Federation for Home Economics (n.d.). *Mission statement.* Retrieved June 10, 2012 from http://www.ifhe.org/127 html

Jax, J. A. (2000). A critical interpretation of leadership for the new millennium. *Journal of Family and Consumer Sciences, 92*(1), 85-87.

Josephson, M. (2002). *Making ethical decisions.* Los Angeles: Josephson Institute of Ethics.

Kappa Omicron Nu. (n.d.). *Publications.* Retrieved December 1, 2006, from http://www.kon.org/publications/pubs.html

Keegan, C., Gross, S., Fisher, L., & Remez, S. (2004). *Boomers at midlife: The AARP life stage study executive summary.* Washington, DC: The American Association of Retired Persons.

Langone, C. A. (2004, Summer). The use of a citizen leader model for teaching strategic leadership. *Journal of Leadership Education, 3*(1). Retrieved April 17, 2007, from http://www.fhsu.edu/jole/issues/JOLE_3_1.pdf

Lerman, R., & Schmidt, S. (1999). *An overview of economic, social, and demographic trends affecting the U.S. labor market.* Washington, DC: The Urban Institute.

Lichtenstein, A. H., & Ludwig, D. S. (2010). Bring back home economics education. *Journal of the American Medical Association, 303*(18), 1857-1858.

Makela, C. J. (2010). Point of view: Communities make a difference. *Journal of Family and Consumer Sciences, 102*(3), 3.

Makela, C. J. (2008). Point of view: Technology and media: The privacy factor. *Journal of Family and Consumer Sciences, 100*(2), iii-iv.

McCubbin, H. I., McCubbin, M. A., Thompson, A. I., Han, S., & Allen, C. T. (1997). Families under stress: What makes them resilient? *Journal of Family and Consumer Sciences, 89*(3), 2-11.

McLeod, S. (2007). *Maslow's hierarchy of human needs.* Retrieved from http://www.simplepsychology.org/maslow.html

Michael, J. A. (Ed.). (1994). *For the common good: A strategic plan for leadership and volunteer development.* Washington, DC: U.S. Department of Agriculture, Cooperative Extension Service.

National Coalition for Black Development in Family and Consumer Sciences. (n.d.). Retrieved from http://ncbdfcs.org

National Wellness Institute. (n.d.). *Defining wellness.* Retrieved from http://www.nationalwellness.org/index.php?id_tier=2&id_c=26

Nickols, S. Y. (2001). Keeping the Betty lamp burning. *Journal of Family and Consumer Sciences, 93*(3), 35-44.

Nickols, S. Y., Ralston, P. A., Anderson, C., Browne, L., Schroeder, G., Thomas, S., & Wild, P. (2009). The family and consumer sciences body of knowledge and the cultural kaleidoscope: Research opportunities and challenges. *Family and Consumer Sciences Research Journal, 37*(3), 266-283. DOI: 10.1177/1077727x08329561.

Pendergast, D. (2009). Generational theory and home economics: Future proofing the profession. *Family and Consumer Sciences Research Journal, 37*(4), 504-552. DOI: 10:1177/1077727X09333186.

Phi Upsilon Omicron. (2006). *What is Phi Upsilon Omicron?* Retrieved December 1, 2006, from http://www.phiu.org/about_information.htm

Price, S. J., & McKenry, P. C. (2003). Sustaining families: Why the life course development approach works. *Journal of Family and Consumer Sciences, 95*(2), 11-14.

Richards, M. V. (2000). The postmodern perspective on home economics history. *Journal of Family and Consumer Sciences, 92*(1), 81-84.

Rost, J. C. (1991). *Leadership for the twenty-first century.* New York: Praeger.

Shaklee, H., Laumatia, L., Luckey, B., Traver, S., Nauman, A., Tift, K., Liddil, A., & Hampton, C. (2010). Building inclusive communities: A social capital approach. *Journal of Family and Consumer Sciences, 102*(3), 44-48.

Simerly, C. B., Ralston, P. A., Harriman, L., & Taylor, B. (2000). The Scottsdale initiative: Positioning the profession for the 21st century. *Journal of Family and Consumer Sciences, 92*(1), 75-80.

Stage, S., & Vincenti, V. B. (Eds.) (1997). *Rethinking home economics: Women and the history of a profession.* Ithaca, NY: Cornell University Press.

Stevens, G., & Martin-Hernandez, A. (1999). Community collaborative problem solving—cross cultural lessons. *Journal of Family and Consumer Sciences, 92*(1), 79-82.

Theobald, R. (1997). *Reworking success: New communities at the millennium.* Gabriola Island, British Columbia, Canada: New Society.

Thompson, N. E., Harden, A. J., Clauss, B., Fox, W. S., & Wild, P. (2012). Key concepts of environmental sustainability in family and consumer sciences. *Journal of Family and Consumer Sciences, 104*(1), 14-21.

Vincenti, V., & Smith, F. (2004). Critical science: What it could offer all family and consumer sciences professionals. *Journal of Family and Consumer Sciences, 96*(1), 63.

Wachter, K. (2003). Rethinking Maslow's needs. *Journal of Family and Consumer Sciences, 95*(2), 68-69.

Wentworth, D. K., & Chell, R. M. (1997). American college students and the Protestant work ethic. *Journal of Social Psychology, 137*(3), 284-286.

Professional Journals and Trade Publications

Family and Consumer Sciences Research Journal

Human Ecology Forum

International Journal of Home Economics

Journal of Family and Consumer Sciences

Chapter 4
Environmental Trends Affecting Individuals, Families, and Communities

After studying this chapter, you will be able to:

- describe the major societal trends forecasted for the next 50 years.

- explain how the aging population will affect society.

- analyze the impact of demographic change, including increasing diversity in the United States in upcoming years.

- depict the effect of a global economy on society over time.

- discuss current issues and future trends in digital technology.

- predict and analyze relevant work/life issues of the future.

- describe changes in family composition.

It has been said that the only thing constant is change ("Heraclitus," 2007). Families exist in an ever-changing environment, and the institution of the family has changed over time. While you can look backwards and see how societal changes have changed family life over the past 50 years, it is more difficult to look ahead and forecast how society will change in the future.

A Busy Family

Matt moved another load of laundry from the washer to the dryer. Later, he would run to the grocery store to pick up a few items for his children's school lunches tomorrow and the last-minute items his daughter needs for a science project. Matt's wife, Martha, was helping their two children with homework. Hopefully, the family will find some time to relax and enjoy a game or watch television tonight and will get to bed at a reasonable time. Morning always comes too fast.

It seems to Matt that every day is a balancing act. Each workday, Matt leaves for work at 5:30 a.m. He is usually in the office at 6:00 a.m., skips lunch, and leaves work by 3:00 p.m. He picks his two children up from school on the way home. Typically, they have several after-school activities. Today it's soccer and trumpet lessons. Tomorrow it's math tutoring and a play date. By the time he and the children get home, it's around 6:00 p.m. Martha will be home from work preparing dinner. Martha starts her workday later in the morning after getting the children ready and taking them to school. Between Matt and Martha, they are keeping up with family and work demands. They both know, however, that the slightest change in routine, such as a child who has a fever, can cause a minor crisis.

Matt wonders how life became so busy. He doesn't remember life being this way for his parents when he was young. His dad worked outside the home and was responsible for yard work and car care. His mother worked part-time and was responsible for all child care and housework. He wondered if life felt as busy and stressful to them as it does for him. As a child, he remembered hearing how technology would make for more leisure time, lessen household tasks, and make office work much more efficient. This was not his experience, and it did not seem to be the case with those around him, either. In fact, it seemed like the opposite was true. If less leisure time and more stress was the trend, he wondered what life would be like for his children and grandchildren in 50 years. How will society change in the next 50 years?

Although trends may be followed, predicting the future is more difficult. Since creativity spawns further creativity, many future innovations and trends have not yet been fathomed. History has shown this to be true. In a 1949 *Popular Mechanics* magazine article, the following was predicted about computers of the future: "Where a calculator on the ENIAC is equipped with 18,000 vacuum tubes and weighs 30 tons, computers in the future may have only 1,000 vacuum tubes and perhaps weigh 1.5 tons" (Hamilton, 1949). Obviously, this scientist could not specifically forecast the future of technology. However, this scientist was accurate in the projection that computers would use fewer vacuum tubes and that they would weigh considerably less. World events, natural disasters, and environmental changes also cannot be forecasted. However, trends can be projected from information available in the present. Recognizing current trends and extrapolating future trends is the work of futurists. Are family and consumer sciences professionals also futurists? Why or why not?

Family and consumer sciences professionals have always concerned themselves with the environment in which families and individuals live. In Chapter 2, the influence of the environment on family life was introduced using the human ecosystem model. To fulfill the mission of improving quality of life for families and individuals, it is imperative that family and consumer sciences professionals understand the environment in which they exist and plan for future changes in the environment. Some family and consumer sciences professionals will also be engaged in creating that environment as they work in product development and research. In this chapter, you will explore trends and future projections in the human behavioral, human constructed, and natural environments. Specific trends that are explored include the demographics of the aging population, changing family structures,

the projected increase of diversity, the global economy, technological changes, and work/life issues. Public policy in relation to these trends in the United States will be addressed in Chapter 5.

The Aging of the Population

As people go through life, they age. Despite heroic efforts some may use to appear younger than their biological age, aging is inevitable. Globally, the number of people who are 65 years of age or older has already increased dramatically over the last 50 years. This age group will continue to increase rapidly. In fact, many futurists believe there is no end in sight. Why? When the natural aging process is combined with a decrease in fertility and an increase in available health care, the number of older people and their representation in the population increases rapidly (Haupt & Kane, 2004).

The U.S. population is continuing to age. In the United States following World War II, approximately 77 million babies were born between the years of 1946 and 1964. This generation, known as the baby boom generation, has influenced trends from a very early age. During infancy and childhood, increased attention was placed on parenting, nutrition, and education. Later, when this generation entered adolescence and early adulthood, their ideas, opinions, and politics forever changed society. Corporations, government, and the educational system are currently led by this generation. As the baby boomer generation grows older, the number of people over 50 years of age will expand to over 50 percent of the total population. The oldest of this generation began turning 65 in 2011. Currently, their average life expectancy is 83 years of age, although with improved health care and healthy lifestyles, many will live into their nineties and beyond.

What impact will the aging baby boomers have on society? Many people believe they will redefine the meaning and purpose of older adulthood. They want to remain active and to continue to participate in society. Baby boomers will demand more development of accessible, affordable housing for older adults. They want to be financially secure and to maintain strong emotional and social health. How do these goals change the public agenda? Health care, independent living, workforce participation, and retirement are hot topics as baby boomers age.

Aging and Health Care

A growing, older adult population can be seen around the world. This is partly due to better health care resulting in a longer life expectancy. In fact, the reduction in deaths due to heart disease is one of the largest contributing factors toward increased life expectancy. Older adults are concerned about increasing the quality and years of healthy life and eliminating health disparities. Many diseases can be prevented or at least symptoms can be relieved with proper nutrition, physical activity, weight management, oral health, and vision and hearing care.

It is clear that older adults wish to remain healthy and independent to ensure a positive quality of life. However, as people age, they often experience greater need for medical care. They may need more doctor visits, hospitalization, rehabilitation, and prescription drugs. As more and more people enter older adulthood, health care costs will increase. For older adults who are unable to afford medical care, who is responsible for their health care costs? Is it the individual's family, or should society (state or federal government) or private organizations be responsible?

In the United States, Medicare and Social Security have offered financial aid to older Americans for many decades. Medicare, a government health insurance program, helps older adults pay for medical costs. Social Security, a government retirement fund, provides supplemental income to Americans who have met age requirements and employment contribution eligibility standards. Other assistance programs are available for special-needs populations.

Assistance programs for older adults are receiving tremendous attention, and many Americans are concerned about their future Social Security and Medicare benefits. There are several reasons for their concerns, including uncertainty about their own future employment earnings, the formula that is currently used to determine benefits, insufficient funds for these programs, and the future structure of the assistance programs. Health care issues will continue to be on political agendas as these issues will be of personal interest to large segments of the population who are either patients or caregivers (Keegan, Gross, Fisher, & Remez, 2004).

Aging and Independent Living

The greatest fear of many older adults is losing their independence and no longer being able to care for themselves. Imagine you or a loved one is in a situation where you are contemplating whether or not it is safe to live alone. How would you tell your elderly mother you are worried about her leaving the stove turned on and unattended or falling down the stairs? Where would you want to live if you could not live by yourself any longer? How would you feel if you were asked to give up your driver's license?

In many cultures, these questions are not a concern because older adults often live with family members or friends. For example, three or more generations may cohabit. Moving from semi-independent living to dependent living is seamless as generations depend on each other throughout the lifespan. In societies that promote independence of each generation, however, many older adults want to grow old in their own homes. They struggle to not give up their independence. Quality of life is often measured by the amount of independence they perceive in their living conditions.

Many older adults are not able to live independently because of poverty and poor health. Sometimes, the decision is made by others for older adults if their mental or cognitive status is impaired. Older people requiring assistance from caregivers are often dependent on others for their physical, psychological, social, and economic needs.

The transition of older adults from independence to increasing dependence is a major family life transition. As the population ages and life expectancy increases, it is quite possible for families to have two or more generations over the age of 65. Older adults may play the role of caregiver for an older generation as they adjust to their own aging and mortality.

Kathleen's Dilemma

Kathleen woke up every night this week at 3:00 a.m. to give her mother her medicine. She has a looming deadline at work. Even though she needs time to work, she will need to leave the office early this afternoon to take her mother to her doctor appointment. She feels like she is letting her coworkers down, but she knows her mother needs her. Her mother needs full-time care, but Kathleen cannot afford care or to quit her full-time job.

For many adults, taking care of their parents is a daily concern. Caregivers can become emotionally drained, physically exhausted, and distracted at work. In the United States, a federal law called the *Family and Medical Leave Act (FMLA)* offers some support for working caregivers. This law allows eligible workers up to 12 weeks per year of unpaid leave for family caregiving without loss of job security or health benefits. The law helps people who can afford to take unpaid leave, but it does not help those who cannot afford to be without pay. Restrictions such as the size of the company and the employee's length of employment also limit its usefulness.

Growing older is one stage of the life process. However, the later years can become lonely and difficult for many older adults and a stressful time for their families. With a growing older adult population, how will society accommodate the desire of older adults to maintain their independence and dignity? How will caregivers be supported? What role should families play? What role should society as a whole play? These are a few of the questions society will face in upcoming years. Each requires careful thought and planning, and

family and consumer sciences professionals will be providing education and support to older adults and their families as they make very complex and difficult decisions. Career opportunities related to aging are discussed in Chapter 12.

Aging and Workforce Participation and Retirement

When psychologist Erik Erikson described his theory of development during the lifespan, he described the final stage as a reflective, retrospective viewing of a person's life. He asserted that this final stage begins around 60 years of age and involves evaluating integrity in a person's life versus despair over reaching the end of life. Later, when Erikson observed the projected life expectancy of the baby boomer generation, he warned against early retirement followed by years of nonproductivity. He stated that a prolonged retirement and lack of engagement would have a negative effect on older adults (Erikson, 1986).

When Erikson gave his warning in the 1980s, the decades-old trend toward early retirement was beginning to turn. The average age for retirement was rising. The strong economy in the United States during the 1980s and 1990s supported longer employment. Longer employment began other related trends such as changes in mandatory retirement, changes to Social Security benefit eligibility that discouraged early retirement, and changes in the occupational gender mix as both men and women worked later in life (Erikson, 1986).

Baby boomers are more likely to continue working longer than previous generations in the last century. Retirement will likely not be a one-time event but a gradual move toward complete retirement. Will the economy support additional workers, especially when a large younger generation follows? Will covert age discrimination in the workforce decrease or increase? Will new jobs become available for younger workers if older adults fill positions longer? These are a few of the questions society will face as the population ages (Ervin, 2000).

The Next Boom: Generation Y

However, as much impact as baby boomers have had and will continue to have on the culture of the United States; a second population wave is following. Although the focus in the past half-century has been on baby boomers, they produced another large generation—their children and grandchildren—who are often referred to as echo boomers, the millennial generation, or generation Y. Members of this generation were born between 1982 and 2003. This new wave is creating a very large young adult population. Although not quite as large as the baby boom generation, generation Y is making a huge impact on society. Their large purchasing power is affecting clothing, food, and home markets. In between these two generations is generation X, born between 1965 and 1981.

As baby boomers grew up and left the public schools, a glut of classroom space and a surplus of teachers were left in their wake. Generation Y has been filling classrooms once again, and a teacher shortage has been seen and felt for a number of years. Colleges and universities have also been filling up as a result of this generation entering young adulthood.

The labor market is expecting a surplus of workers. The problem has been intensified by the economic downturn that began in 2007. One resulting concern is that the projected large number of unemployed young adults will fuel crime and social unrest. A considerably larger number of youth will be wholly unequipped for the workforce. For example, people who have grown up in poverty will be far less likely to have access to technology. Therefore, they will be lacking critical technology skills. The labor force will have to attempt to simultaneously meet the needs of both the younger generation and the older generation (Lerman & Schmidt, 1999).

With two competing, powerful generations at both ends of the age spectrum, there will naturally be competition for resources. Should money be spent on Social Security and Medicare or for schools and health insurance for children living in poverty? Education and resource allocation that meet the needs of both older and younger adults will be required.

Growth in Human Diversity

The United States has often been called the "great melting pot society." For generations, diverse individuals have assimilated into a single heterogeneous society. Different backgrounds, languages, ethnicities, religions, and socioeconomic classes have lived in one society, although not without conflict. In recent decades, many people have contested the melting pot ideal. They propose that a more realistic and appropriate "ideal" is one of multiculturalism or cultural diversity and multiracialism. *Multiculturalism* is based on the idea that cultural identities should not be discarded or overlooked but instead should be maintained and valued. *Multiracialism* refers to the trend of more people becoming heteroracial rather than representing one race category. For example, a person may claim both Caucasian and Asian racial ancestry. At the same time that cultural diversity is being more highly valued, globalization is accelerating cultural homogenization. Cultural barriers around the globe are breaking down due to travel and the Internet (Baugher, 2012). Individuals have more contact with persons from other countries, races, and religions, increasing the need for cultural competence. In the following sections, multiracialism, multiculturalism, and cultural competence in a diverse labor market will be discussed.

Multiracialism

What race are you? This is a common, although not an always appreciated, question that may be asked of multiracial individuals. (*Multiracial* means being of more than one race.) People often have a desire to label and categorize people by race. Must people be categorized by race? The answer varies by whom you ask.

By the year 2020, it is expected that the United States will no longer have a racial majority group. Instead, the population will be more racially diverse than at any time in previous history. The majority (white) ethnic group will decrease, while ethnic minorities, especially multiracial ethnic minorities, will increase. Why? There are several reasons. First, immigration from Asia, Eastern Europe, Africa, the Middle East, Mexico, and Central and South America continues to increase. During the 1800s and early 1900s, most immigrants came from Western Europe and Russia. Although this brought great ethnic, cultural, and religious diversity, a majority white culture grew. In recent decades, immigrants have come from all regions of the world. Second, fertility rates differ by ethnic group. By July 2011, racial and ethnic minorities made up more than half of all U.S. births (Baugher, 2012). Third, international adoptions have increased, with most adopted children coming from countries that do not represent the white majority group. Fourth, in the 1970s the U.S. Supreme Court declared all laws prohibiting interracial marriages unconstitutional.

Although interracial marriages have existed throughout time, the changed laws and more accepting societal attitudes of the last several decades have resulted in a steady increase of interracial marriages and multiracial offspring in the United States. In fact, between 1970 and 1998, the number of interracial couples more than quadrupled (Haupt & Kane, 2004). During the last several decades, the surge in interracial unions has resulted in an increase in multiracial children. Between 2000 and 2009, the number of Americans who identified with two or more races increased by 87 percent, to over 7 million people (Benokraitis, 2012). Celebrities and other influential people of multiracial heritage will continue to have an impact on how society views the concept of race.

Race identification has been a part of the U.S. census since its inception. Race and ethnicity are not scientific concepts; they are socially constructed concepts. Although physical features often define race, and ethnicity is defined by social and linguistic background, racial and ethnic categories vary by society and shift and change over time. For example, racial categories on the U.S. census have not remained constant. On the first census, there were two racial choices: "white" and "other." Slaves were counted in a separate category. By the middle of the 1800s, residents were classified as "white," "black," or "mulatto." By the end of the 1800s, census takers were instructed to distinguish household members as "white," "black," "mulatto" (one-half black), "quadroon" (one-quarter black), "octoroon" (one-eighth black), Chinese, Japanese, or American Indian. American Indians were asked to estimate racial percentages. By the 1900s, many racial subcategories had emerged (Haupt & Kane, 2004).

With these racial category changes, racial reporting methods have changed, too. Prior to 1970, individuals collecting census data would guess in order to identify the racial heritage of a person by sight. In 1970, with the onset of the first mailed questionnaires, people began self-reporting their racial heritage. Broad choices were given (white, black, Asian, Hispanic), and respondents could choose just one category to identify themselves racially (Jones & Smith, 2001).

On the 2000 census, for the first time in census history, people with mixed race heritage were able to choose more than one racial category when identifying themselves and their children. Over 18 racial categories and subcategories were included on the census form. What did the 2000 census find out about multiracialism? Findings indicated that multiracial identity is most likely underreported. Parents identify the racial identity of their children on the U.S. census. One of the most surprising results of the 2000 census was that most interracial couples do not report their children as multiracial. In fact, fewer than half of children living with parents of different races were identified as multiracial. Analysis of census data showed that biracial groups vary considerably. For example, children of American Indian and white parents tended to not identify their children as multiracial.

Multiracial parents were much more likely to identify their own children as multiracial, however (Jones & Smith, 2001).

The shifting labels and definitions of race used on the U.S. census reflect the growing diversity of the American population. Race may become less of an issue for future generations as the United States becomes more diverse than ever. Unique challenges, both in varying intensity and scope, may face multiracial families and individuals. Often these unique challenges are based on geographic location, family systems, and community support.

Cultural and Religious Diversity

President John F. Kennedy once said, "If we cannot now end our differences, at least we can help make the world safe for diversity" (Kennedy, n.d.). Racial diversity is just one component of diversity. The United States is also richly diverse in ethnicity, religion, life experiences, values, and socioeconomic status. For example, although Christianity is still the majority religion claimed by residents of the United States, a myriad of other faiths, belief systems, and religions are represented in growing numbers. Ethnicity, too, has become a spotlight as it focuses on national identity and life experiences more than just racial heritage.

In the early decades of the 1900s, the United States promoted quick and early assimilation into the mainstream culture. Today, many believe that this value system is inappropriate. Instead, individual identity and individual rights are valued. It is collectively held that citizens should accept and respect others who are different from themselves. Even if people are in agreement over the value of diversity, establishing and upholding everyone's individual rights can be difficult and complex. Diversity takes many forms. Some areas currently being addressed in diversity include:

- religious freedom
- gender equity
- rights related to sexual orientation and lifestyle

- ethnicity in the criminal justice system
- age discrimination
- wealth, welfare, and stratification
- residential housing segregation in communities
- disparities in educational test scores among people of varied ethnicities and races
- health and development of children, adolescents, and adults
- entrance into some professions
- media and music representation of ethnic groups and culture
- access for individuals with disabilities

Multiculturalism in the Labor Market

Multiculturalism is an approach for managing cultural diversity in a multiethnic society, stressing mutual respect and appreciation for cultural differences. In the words of prominent businessman Malcolm Forbes, *diversity* is "the art of thinking independently together" (2007). In the past several decades, the value of diversity in the workplace has been accepted and even celebrated. Since the civil rights movement occurred and the Equal Rights Amendment was proposed, diversity has moved from being a legal, moral mandate to a valued business imperative. The growing presence of racial minorities and women in the workplace demonstrates this change. Today, more minorities and women enter the workforce than any other group.

Why is cultural diversity important to successful business practices? Businesses operate in society. However, diversity in the workplace is a complex issue. To those organizations that see diversity as conflict ridden, it presents an arduous challenge. It may be viewed as something "on the side" that requires extra effort and resources. To those who embrace diversity, it can offer a competitive edge. Diversity is woven into the vision, mission, values, strategic planning, customer relationship management, work systems, and business processes of the organization. Together, this unified climate delivers a strategic advantage.

How does diversity play out in the daily business environment? In the past few decades, workplace diversity has moved from counting minorities to fostering environments where the talents and differences of all employees are valued and respected. It is not a project that can be completed in a set amount of time, but a way of doing business. It involves inclusion, value, and respect for the diversity of the population, the business sector, and the customer base.

Because professionals today interact with diverse coworkers and clientele, being culturally competent is important to career success. A culturally competent person is able to understand, communicate with, and interact effectively with people of different cultures. Developing cultural competence requires being aware of your own worldview and attitudes toward cultural differences. It means acquiring knowledge of other cultures and interpreting behavior in light of the cultural context. For example, family is not defined in the same way in all cultures (Martin & Vaughn, 2007; National Center for Cultural Competence, n.d.).

In today's global economy you may interact with many kinds of people, not only at home but in other countries as well. Business cultures around the world vary in several ways. These include communication style (direct or indirect); work style (formal or informal); attitude toward time (scheduled or flexible); decision-making style (individualistic or collective); discussion style (fast or measured); and several other dimensions. For example, a product developer who works with a Chinese factory to produce clothing will need to remember that the Chinese expect formality and courtesy in business meetings. "Yes" may mean "I hear you," not "I agree," and decision making tends to be slow because obtaining consensus from members of the group is valued. Due to these differences, it is important to study a country where you will do business and develop your intercultural

sensitivity. Intercultural sensitivity includes tolerance for ambiguity, being flexible, listening with empathy, and showing respect (Tomalin & Nicks, 2010).

The Global Economy

Look at the labels on the clothes you are wearing. Chances are the items were made in another country. Did you drive a car today? You may pride yourself on owning an American-made car, but there's a good possibility the parts came from several different countries and then were assembled in the U.S. How much did you pay for gas? Why do gas prices fluctuate so much? Wars, natural disasters, and government policies in other countries can affect how much you pay at the pump. These are all examples of globalization. *Globalization* is the "integration of economies throughout the world through trade, financial flows, the exchange of technology and information, and the movement of people" (Hodelin, 2000, cited in Hodelin, 2006). Globalization has both positive and negative consequences for consumers, workers, families, and FCS professionals.

On the positive side, globalization leads to economic growth in general. There has been an increase in international trade and investment over the past few decades. This has set the world stage and offered many developing countries opportunities to participate in the global economy. Countries viewed as "emergent markets" today are likely to fare the best tomorrow. China and India are two prime examples of countries whose present and future economy looks bright. There is a rising standard of living in developing countries, enabling their consumers to buy goods from around the world and benefiting the countries that export those products. Supporters of globalization contend that it encourages productivity and innovation as businesses compete on the world stage to lower costs. American consumers can buy many products at a lower price than if they were manufactured in the United States. Another benefit of a global economy is that it promotes intercultural understanding (Nickols, Turkki, Pichler, Kirjavainen, Atiles, & Firebaugh, 2010).

On the other hand, the outsourcing of jobs to lower-wage countries has led to unemployment in industrialized nations. In many cases workers who now perform the jobs are exploited with few safety protections or rights. Globalization has also led to destruction of traditional cultures and harm to the environment. Although many countries will do well, all will not. Poverty and regional differences will seem more pronounced as communication devices and travel open up the world to many.

The Move Toward a Dualistic Economy

As stated earlier, not all countries will benefit from global economic growth. In fact, it is predicted that many countries and regions will fall behind. Military and civilian conflicts are two factors that will contribute to economic failures. Those countries that do not diversify will also lag behind. In some countries and regions, a gap in the standard of living will widen between the lower and upper classes that will decrease the middle class and result in a dualistic economy. When critical masses can be found at the two ends of the economic spectrum with a diminishing middle class between, the condition is referred to as a *dualistic economy*.

Many futurists assert that the wealthy class will grow larger along with the poor, while those in the middle class dwindle. In some instances, this may be found within a country, such as in the United States (Lerman & Schmidt, 1999). Others predict that a dualistic economy will emerge on a global scale (Agenor, 2002). Why? It is predicted that education will be the foremost determining factor between individuals and countries. The move toward a global economy combined with the technological revolution has placed a premium on education. Education may be in the form of post-secondary school training, skill acquisition, or higher education. As a result, it is expected that school enrollments will increase worldwide. Educational gender gaps will decrease. Adult literacy will increase. What will happen to countries where educational opportunities are not available? Unfortunately, these countries will have a more difficult time competing in the world market.

Within the United States, many futurists warn of a dualistic economy that is looming in the future. In the 1990s many U.S. leaders were encouraged by the decrease in number of families living in poverty. As the century changed, however, so did the trend. In 2001, the poverty rate increased as well as the number of families living in poverty (Darling, 2005). Some caution that a high school diploma is being devalued and a college degree or graduate degree is the expected norm for trade and professional careers. The gap between rich and poor may become wider as it becomes more difficult for low-income families to educate their children beyond high school, and it does not just include formal education. Poor children are much less likely to have access or exposure to technology than their more affluent counterparts. The inequality between rich and poor in the United States may become deeper and wider in the upcoming years, creating an economy that lacks a middle class.

Unfortunately, the economic divide is predicted to widen as the gap between the rich and poor continues to grow. One factor influencing this widening gap is that perceived minimum levels of education will continue to rise and it will become more difficult for children and families in poverty to cross socioeconomic boundaries (Lerman & Schmidt, 1999).

Technological Changes

The personal computer revolution that began in the mid-1970s has profoundly changed lives. In the 1970s and 1980s, many predictions were made about the future of technology and how it would affect society. As of yet, many of these predictions have not come true. Instead, technology has changed lives in ways never predicted.

For example, computers that utilize voice recognition have been slower to come on the scene than originally predicted, but the explosion of the Internet in the 1990s was beyond most people's imagination. Some believed personal computers would put many employees out of work. Instead, technology has created its own enormous job market.

Changes in digital technology have an effect on families, too. With a plethora of information and communication possibilities at their fingertips, children may be at risk. They are often exposed and made vulnerable to electronic bullying, unwanted solicitation, pornography, and other forms of unwanted or undesirable communication (Darling, 2005).

Although some of the early promises of the technology revolution did not come to pass, a lot did change—but not as predicted. Specific predictions did not take into account the dynamic change and unexpected turns technology research would make. Innovation has spawned innovation. That said, what could we expect during the next 50 years? Change is certain, but specific predictions are difficult to make. Instead, futurists are focusing on general areas of continued development. These include added flexibility and customization, voice recognition and language conversion, accessible technology, and improved data management. These are discussed in the following section. In addition, the effects of technology on the workplace, the economy, and the world will be explored.

Improved Flexibility and Customization

Improved flexibility and customization increase the applications and uses of current technology and seamlessly integrate new and future technology. Current research and development are focusing on the two themes of flexibility and customization. It will take into account personal preferences, abilities, and different situations. Voice recognition and interactive computers, the management of data, adapting technology to the workplace, and

technology that will improve the quality of life for individuals requiring assistance will all utilize flexibility and customization.

Flexibility, Customization, and the Great American Business Venture

Imagine you are starting a business venture based on an invention you created to more easily measure and calculate caloric values of processed foods. You are in the process of hatching the perfect business plan for introducing, marketing, selling, and distributing your product. You write down ideas and conversations you have had whenever and wherever you can. The basic idea has been in your head for several years, but new ideas, and twists and turns to the idea, develop at unexpected times. Sometimes an idea will pop into your mind, and you just can't wait to write it down. The ideas come to you while watching your favorite baseball team at the noisy, crowded stadium, while waiting for your friend to arrive at a quiet coffee shop, while you are bicycling on a bike trail, and while you are shopping for groceries. Pulling out your laptop computer is cumbersome. You do not always have it with you. Sometimes a small handheld electronic notepad is all you need. At other times, you would like a full computer screen, keyboard, and mouse to concentrate on your writing. In quiet moments, you sometimes prefer handwriting, while at other times, you would like to verbalize or even just think through your ideas and have them recorded and stored. You need flexibility in your technology so it can adapt to different situations and environments. For example, in a noisy baseball stadium, voice recognition may not be feasible, but thought recognition could be. Customization would allow you to change your technology use from one situation to the next and in an intact, efficient manner.

Voice Recognition, Interactive Computers, and Language Conversion

Voice and handwriting recognition have made great strides in the past few decades, but they have not progressed as quickly as many people believed they would. Humans continue to figure out words that computers do not recognize. Computer voices continue to sound robotic rather than human. However, computers are beginning to seem less like machines and more like able-bodied assistants. For example, Siri (Speech Interpretation and Recognition Interface) software available on recent Apple products can carry on a "conversation" with you. Still, futurists believe the great breakthroughs will occur in voice and handwriting recognition and perhaps even thought recognition in the upcoming decades. Advances in voice recognition are particularly important to blind consumers who have not previously been able to take advantage of many smart phone features.

One of the frustrations for computer users is correctly following instructions for input, retrieval, and management of data. Natural language commands, the common words and phrases in a person's language choice, rather than the words and phrases of computer programmers, would enable more people to efficiently and effectively use their computer. This is different than the current assisted technology that requires users to speak predetermined phrases in exact sequence. For example, a user could say "go to the Internet and find a website that compares dishwasher prices."

Currently, there are many language conversion programs. However, future programs will convert one language into another using the full context and meaning of sentences, phrases, and paragraphs rather than just converting word by word. Even workers who do not sit in front of a computer may find that technological advances result in higher efficiency. For example, a clinical dietitian may quickly convert nutrition counseling to a language that is most expedient in communicating the message desired, or an apparel designer might instruct a computer to "grade the pattern down one dress size" rather than typing computer-aided design commands. Technology will continue to be used as a means of offering educational opportunities in new and different ways. The possibilities are endless. Just as in past decades, however, some advances will not happen as quickly as anticipated, some

will remain novelties or toys, and others will be replaced by even greater advancements that are not yet conceived.

Accessible Technology

It is important that technology adapts to the specific needs of people and their environment. This is especially true for people with disabilities. Technology has been making great strides in helping to make the world more accessible to people who need assistance. Some of these technologies are already available, others are being developed, and some are in the conception stage. The focus of future research is on *universal design*, which adapts to the needs of users in changing environments rather than being suitable only for the specific needs of one user, or in the case of accessible design, the specific needs of a particular disability. In the home and in the workplace, technology may open opportunities for people who are currently limited. Technology that improves the quality of life for all individuals will not only entail better computer systems, but will also encompass all aspects of making life easier. With an increasing aging population, the opportunities for assisting older adults with maintaining independence and self-reliance in everyday living are vast. Safety and security, communication, and physical restraints might be overcome through technology.

Managing Data: Intuitive Access to Information

Have you ever "lost" a file and spent considerable time looking for the document on your computer? Most people have. Huge improvements have been made in data storage in the past few years. Storage has become quick, inexpensive, and easy to move from one application to another. However, storage devices have also made it more difficult to find a "lost" file. Data is not always stored and retrieved in meaningful or intuitive ways. It is forecasted that data storage, retrieval, and manipulation will continue to expand beyond what is currently envisioned.

Data will be input, indexed, retrieved, and manipulated in ways that are efficient, easy, and intuitive.

Technology and Globalization

In the past several decades, technology has opened up the speed, efficiency, and frequency of communication around the world. Global industries now rely on technology for real-time communication, and business is easily conducted around the world. Today, products may be designed in one country, manufactured in another, and customer support offered from still another country. Futurists contend that technology will only increase the ability to communicate and real time will be replaced with virtual reality—being present and face-to-face even when thousands of miles apart. Language barriers will be lessened as voice translation technology increases. The distribution, production, and delivery of food, clothing, and shelter will be immediate and efficient.

Family Changes

Compared to the 1950s, Americans today are more likely to never marry or to delay marriage and parenthood, and to divorce. There are actually more households consisting of single people than married couples living with children. One of the contributing factors to the rise of single households and the decline of married households is that there are fewer unmarried men than women over the age of 18. The average age at marriage has been rising for men and women for 50 years, and couples are likely to live together before marriage. Many of these cohabiting couples never marry. The United States has one of the highest divorce rates in the Western world. However, the divorce rate peaked in the 1980s and has actually decreased slightly and stabilized (Benokraitis, 2012; Strong, DeVault, & Cohen, 2011). It is predicted that generation Y will have more interest in stable relationships than generation X before them.

Fewer children today live with two married biological parents. This is primarily due to the increase in births to unmarried women, rather than the result of divorce. As a percentage of all births, those to unmarried women grew from 11 percent in 1970 to 39 percent in 2008 (Strong, DeVault, & Cohen, 2011). Most single-parent families are headed by women, and these households have a higher rate of poverty than married couple households or those headed by single fathers. Surprisingly, over one million children live with a grandparent without a parent present. Remarriage after divorce is common, resulting in many stepfamilies. Several million children live with unmarried cohabiting couples, and same-sex couples also parent children, who may be adopted or biological children of one of the partners (Benokraitis, 2012; Strong, DeVault, & Cohen, 2011).

Changes in marriage and family law have had profound effects on the legal structure of families. For example, legalization of same-sex marriage in some states has expanded same-sex partners' rights and benefits, but without diminishing the rights of heterosexual marriages.

Work/Life Issues

What will the workforce look like in the future? Over the next 50 years, the world population is expected to grow to almost 9 billion people. Futurists project that the population in the United States alone will grow by one-half. Why is such a large increase predicted in the United States? Some of the population growth will be influenced by birth and death rates, but most of the growth will be influenced by increased immigration. Most immigrants will be of working age when they arrive in the United States.

For several more decades, the baby boom generation will continue to keep their places in the workforce. The youngest baby boomers have years of work left before them. As discussed earlier, retirement will come at a later age and the large generation Y will follow. As the workforce includes older adults, there will subsequently be a rise in the number of people with disabilities in the workforce. On the flip side, younger workers will be challenged with balancing the demands of work with caring for aging parents or other relatives.

Although the baby boom generation will continue to cause the workforce median age to rise, when they do retire, the median age will drop. Generation X, which immediately follows, is a smaller demographic group. However, the larger generation Y, combined with the increasing number of immigrants, will expand the younger workforce.

Gender will also play a part in the workforce of the future. In the past decade, more women have entered the workforce, while employment rates for men have been declining. Futurists believe that women will continue to move both in and out of the workforce as they continue to assume the lead role in childrearing.

Employment, Wages, and Benefits

Some industries will see changes and may even be eliminated, while new industries will emerge worldwide. Technology will play a large role in the development of a dualistic labor economy. As a result, wage gaps between those who are educated and those who are not may widen.

What will happen to wages and benefits? It all depends. If enough people are qualified for higher-paying jobs, wage inequality may shrink. In the United States, wage differences between middle- and low-income earners may also shrink. Futurists assert that the wage discrepancy between men and women will narrow in upcoming decades as more women continue to enter the workforce and the number of women with experience and education grows. This gap may decrease faster than expected if more women cross the employment gender boundaries and gender segregation of occupations. The trend may be slowed, however, by continued discrimination and by "segregation" of women in certain occupations and industries. Although employees will want increased benefits in areas

such as child care and elder care support, expansion will be slow in the current economic environment. The Patient Protection and Affordable Care Act, commonly referred to as Obamacare, will affect how employers provide insurance benefits in the future.

Family and Work Issues

Two-career families, single parents with young children, elder care, and long commutes—these are the daily realities of many people in the workforce. For many workers, there are not enough hours in a day to take care of all their responsibilities. Despite time-saving conveniences such as prepared foods, home shopping, and home appliances, families still perceive that their personal time is diminishing. In the past and in the present, many workers have limited options. For example, part-time work may not be an option if a full-time salary is needed. Child care may cost more than salaries earned. Government assistance may not be available for the elderly or children.

How will these concerns shape the future? Futurists project that these issues will continue to grow, and employers will be forced to help their workers solve their work and home life issues. Child care and elder care options will emerge. Nonstandard hours of work will increase along with flexibility of time and place of work. More affordable and available child and elder care and increased flexibility on the job will emerge. It is not possible to add hours to a day, but futurists believe employers and governments will play a larger role in helping families cope and thrive. If and how this is done, however, remains to be seen.

More variations in work and home life choices will offer greater flexibility in time, location, and quality of work. Many people have come to expect an integration of work life and personal life rather than viewing each as distinctly separate and mutually exclusive (Lerman & Schmidt, 1999). Further acceptance of personal and work life integrations will encourage more people, especially women, to start businesses in their homes. Telecommuting from across a nation or around the world will become more common. Employers will continue to divide their workforce to be physically present at very diverse geographic locations. The baby boom generation will continue to work well into the traditional retirement age and, perhaps, far past it. Changes in Social Security benefits in the United States will necessitate later retirement for many.

Workplace Conditions

In most instances, workplace conditions are improving. For example, occupation-related injuries, diseases, and deaths have decreased significantly over the past 50 years. As new occupations emerge, safety and inspection measures, training methods, incentive programs, government standards, and employee/employer expectations have improved significantly, so these expectations may be transferred to emerging workplace settings. Global government and humanitarian efforts have aided the development of safe work environments in many countries where occupational hazards remain a concern.

Although many workplace settings are physically safer, social and emotional problems continue, and, in fact, seem to be increasing. Most of these concerns are related to stress. If people are required to work longer hours and remain connected through technology during their off-hours, stress will continue to rise. For example, in the past decade, cell phones, e-mail, and text messaging have increased the actual work hours for many employees and made them accessible 24 hours a day. The "working vacation" evolved during the technological revolution. Stress also increases with family responsibilities.

Workplace conditions have improved significantly for women and minorities, but in many regions of the world, including the United States, much work still needs to be done. Will these efforts continue? Futurists believe they will. Some of the motivation comes from pure demographics. If the workforce is more racially and gender diverse, employers cannot afford not to utilize the talent from all segments of the workforce population. They must help employees balance work and family life. Put simply, it is an economic necessity. How this plays out in the next half-century remains to be seen, and futurists are unclear on specific solutions.

Summary

Family and consumer sciences leaders are looking at future trends so they can help family and consumer sciences professionals respond to the needs of families and individuals in the future. Forecasted trends include an aging population, growth in diversity, the continued move toward a global economy, advancements in digital technology, and work/life balance issues.

Around the world, the older adult population will continue to grow over the next 50 years. An aging population raises concerns such as independence and housing solutions, health care management and costs, and workforce participation and retirement. Another population boom is currently entering adulthood and will continue to do so over the next 20 years. Two large generations at the opposite ends of the adult age spectrum may create resource distribution tensions.

In the next 50 years, it is forecasted that a racial majority group will cease to exist in the United States. The primary reason for the changing racial profile is immigration from non-European regions of the world. International adoptions and the quickly growing multiracial population will further propel this trend. Cultural and religious diversity will also grow. Growing diversity over the next 50 years will subsequently change the racial profile of the family and workforce in the United States.

The family in the United States will continue to change in the next century, in concept, form, and structure. Currently, families are continuing to shrink in size, and the trend toward single-parent families is continuing. Family diversity will continue with the family taking many forms.

Over the past several decades, there has been a pronounced move toward a global economy. International trade and investment along with advancements in communication have contributed toward this trend. Countries rely on each other more and more as economies become intertwined. Around the world, the middle class is growing. Even so, a dualistic economy is developing in some societies, including the United States. A growing dualistic society is forecasted as expected education levels continue to climb, creating an economic rift between the educated or skilled and the uneducated and unskilled.

Digital technology has made enormous strides in the past several decades, recreating and defining most aspects of society. Some innovations forecasted in the past have come to fruition, whereas others have not. Many current innovations have exceeded earlier expectations and could not have been fathomed in earlier decades. Forecasters predict that digital technology will continue to change at an even faster pace. Instead of predicting specific inventions as earlier forecasters did, futurists today are looking at broader trends in digital technology. These include increased flexibility and customization along with improved voice recognition, interactive computers, and language conversion. They also forecast improved data management and more accessible technology that meets the needs of all users rather than focusing on one disability or need. Technology has played a huge role in the world economy, and forecasters believe it will continue to do so.

The trends discussed here will affect the workforce. Wages and benefits will become dominant issues as increased communication sheds light on working conditions, pay, and benefits in cultures around the world. In those countries that cannot compete, unemployment will be a great concern. In a trend that began before the turn of the century, workers around the world will struggle with balancing their work/life demands and their personal or home life demands. Child care and elder care will be pressing issues as more adults find themselves caring for aging friends and family members while rearing their own children. Workplace conditions will continue to be physically safer, but social and emotional issues, including stress, will gain prominence.

Well-known U.S. baseball player, coach, and manager Yogi Berra once said, "The future ain't what it used to be" (Berra, 1998). Change is inevitable. Family and consumer sciences professionals of the future must have the skills and education to help individuals and families improve their quality of life in a changing environment and to influence public policy and institutional change with the interests of families in mind.

Questions for Thought

1. If the population is aging, what new fields of specialization will open up to family and consumer sciences professionals and what areas of collaboration will emerge in the following areas?
   - food and nutrition
   - apparel and textiles
   - housing and interiors
   - family services and child development
   - education
   - hospitality

2. Who should be responsible for supporting health care for older adults? Why? What effect could your answer have on families? on government? on individuals?

3. Who should be responsible for child care expenses? parents only? the employer? the government? other organizations? On what do you base your answer? What effect could your answer have on the workforce?

4. With two large adult population groups (the baby boomers and generation Y) at opposite ends of the adult age spectrum, what tensions do you think will develop in the workforce? Which group will have more power? Why?

5. What benefits will cultural diversity in the United States bring? What problems may occur as a result? What measures should employers—and family and consumer sciences professionals—take in view of multiculturalism?

6. Of all forecasted trends in digital technology, which one do you think is the most important and deserves the most research and development resources? Why?

7. If a dualistic economy prevails in the United States in upcoming decades, how will it affect the work of family and consumer sciences professionals in these areas?

- food and nutrition
- clothing and fashion
- housing and interiors
- family services
- education
- hospitality

References and Resources

Agenor, P. (2002). *Does globalization hurt the poor?* (Report No. WPS2922). Retrieved April 17, 2007, from www.worldbank.org (Path: publications; documents & reports; search on report number).

Alun, J. (1999). Ageing in rural China: Impacts of increasing diversity in family and community resources. *Journal of Cross-Cultural Gerontology, 14*(2), 153-169.

Baugher, S.L. (2012). Cultural competency: Globally and locally. *Journal of Family and Consumer Sciences, 104*(2), 10-12.

Belden, Russonello, Stewart, & Research/Strategy/Management. (2001). *In the middle: A report on multicultural boomers coping with family and aging issues.* Retrieved April 17, 2007, from http://assets.aarp.org/rgcenter/il/in_the_middle.pdf

Benokraitis, N.V. (2012). *Marriages and families: Changes, choices, and constraints.* Upper Saddle River, NJ: Prentice Hall.

Berra, Y. (1998). *The Yogi book: I really didn't say everything I said.* New York: Workman.

Bianchi, S.M. (2011). Changing families, changing workplaces. *Future of Children, 21*(2), 15-36.

Cherlin, A. (2004). The deinstitutionalization of American marriage. *Journal of Marriage and the Family, 66*(4), 848-862.

Darling, C. (2005, January). Changes and challenges: Families in a diverse culture. *Journal of Family and Consumer Sciences, 97*(1), 8-13.

Daugherty, R. A., & Williams, S. E. (2004, July). *Leaders and public deliberation: A study in citizen involvement.* Paper presented at the Association of Leadership Educators Annual Conference, Memphis, TN. Retrieved April 17, 2007, from http://leadershipeducators.org/2004/Daughertywilliams.pdf

Department of Economic and Social Affairs, Population Division. (2002). *World population and ageing: 1950–2050.* New York: United Nations.

Dortch, S. (1995). The future of kinship. *American Demographics, 17*(9), 2-4.

Erikson, E. H., Erikson, J., & Kivnick, H. (1986). *Vital involvement in old age.* New York: W. W. Norton.

Ervin, S. (2000, November–December). Fourteen forecasts for an aging society. *The Futurist, 35*(6), 24-28.

Fields, J. (2004). *America's families and living arrangements: 2003.* Washington, DC: U.S. Census Bureau. Retrieved December 12, 2006, from http://www.census.gov/prod/2004pubs/p20-553.pdf

Forbes, Malcolm. (2007, April 17). In *Wikiquote, The Free Online Compendium of Quotations.* Retrieved April 19, 2007, from http://en.wikiquote.org/wiki/Malcolm_Forbes

Frey, W. (2003). Married with children. *American demographics, 25*(2), 17-20.

Hamilton, A. (1949, March). Brains that click. *Popular Mechanics,* 162-167, 252-266.

Haupt, A., & Kane, T. (2004). *Population handbook* (5th ed.). Washington, DC: Population Reference Bureau.

Heraclitus (2007, April 18). *In Wikiquote, The Free Online Compendium of Quotations.* Retrieved January 1, 2007, from http://en.wikiquote.org/wiki/Heraclitus

Hildebrand, V., Phenice, L. A., Gray, M. M., & Hines, R. P. (2000). *Knowing and serving diverse families (2nd ed.).* Upper Saddle River, NJ: Prentice-Hall.

Hodelin, G.B. (2006). Globalization and world hunger: The role of FCS. *Journal of Family and Consumer Sciences, 98*(3), 8-13.

Jones, N., & Smith, A. (2001). *The two or more races population: 2000.* Census 2000 Brief, U.S. Census Bureau. Retrieved April 17, 2007, from http:www.census.gov/prod/2001pubs/c2kbr01-6.pdf

Keegan, C., Gross, S., Fisher, L., & Remez, S. (2004). *Boomers at midlife: The AARP life stage study executive summary.* Washington, DC: The American Association of Retired Persons.

Kennedy, J. F. (1963, June 10). *Commencement address at American University, Washington, DC.* Retrieved January 1, 2007, from http://honors.umd.edu/HONR269J/archive/JFK630610.html

Lee, S. (1998). Asian Americans: diverse and growing. *Population Bulletin, 53*(2), 1-40.

Lerman, R., & Schmidt, S. (1999). *An overview of economic, social, and demographic trends affecting the U.S. labor market.* Washington, DC: The Urban Institute.

Leslie, C.A., & Makela, C.J. (2008). Aging as a process: Interconnectedness of the generations. *Journal of Family and Consumer Sciences, 100*(1), 6-13.

Moller, V. (1998). Innovations to promote an intergenerational society for South Africa to promote the well-being of the black African elderly. *Society in Transition, 29*(1-2), 1-12.

National Center for Cultural Competence. (n.d.) *Conceptual frameworks/models, guiding values and principles.* Retrieved from http://nccc.georgetown.edu/foundatins/frameworks.html

National Intelligence Council. (2000). *Global trends 2015: A dialogue about the future with nongovernment experts.* (Report No. NIC 2000–02). Langley, VA: Author.

Our families—changing roles. (2004). *Canada and the World Backgrounder, 70,* 18.

Pendergast, D. (2009). Generational theory and home economics: Future proofing the profession. *Family and Consumer Sciences Research Journal, 37*(4), 504-522.

Schvaneveldt, P., Kerpelman, J., & Schvaneveldt, J. (2005). Generational and family changes in cultural life in the United Arab Emirates: A comparison of mothers and daughters. *Journal of Comparative Family Studies, 36*(1), 77-92.

Smith, D. (2003). *The Older Population in the United States: March 2002.* Washington, DC: U.S. Census Bureau.

Strong, B., DeVault, C., & Cohen, T.F. (2011). *The marriage and family experience.* Belmont, CA: Wadsworth.

Theobald, R. (1997). *Reworking success: New communities at the millennium.* Gabriola Island, British Columbia, Canada: New Society.

Tomalin, B., & Nicks, M. (2010). *The world's business cultures and how to unlock them.* London: Thorogood Publishing.

Weston, R. (2003, Spring/Summer). Australia's ageing but diverse population. *Family Matters, 66,* 6-14.

Whitehead, B., & Popenoe, D. (2004). *The state of union: The social health of marriage in America.* Piscataway, NJ: The National Marriage Project.

On the Internet

http://www.aoa.gov—Administration on Aging provides information for older adults and the families and professionals who work with them

http://nccc.georgetown.edu—National Center for Cultural Competence provides resources to promote diversity and cultural competence, particularly among health and human services workers

http://www.urban.org—The Urban Institute, a nonpartisan policy center with research information about children, families, poverty, work, health, and many other issues

http://www.familiesandwork.org—Families and Work Institute, a nonprofit, nonpartisan research institute that provides information about changing families and workplaces

http://web.worldbank.org—The World Bank hosts the Open Knowledge Repository with access to thousands of documents related to eradicating poverty around the globe

Chapter 5

Public Policy Affecting Individuals and Families

After studying this chapter, you will be able to:

- Define public policy.
- Explain the process of public policy development.
- Describe public policy affecting individuals, families and communities.
- Provide examples of family and consumer sciences public policy issues.
- Describe future public policy issues that address emerging needs of individuals, families and communities.

Thomas Jefferson, a Founding Father and third president of the United States (1743-1826), once wrote that "A nation, as a society, forms a moral person, and every member of it is personally responsible for his society" (Lipscomb, 2001). In other words, he believed that it was the responsibility of citizens in a democratic society to play a part in the development of society as a whole.

From the beginnings of the profession, family and consumer sciences professionals have focused beyond the individual household to the community at large. Ellen Swallow Richards and her colleagues focused early on the role of home in the larger social setting. They knew that the family could not exist outside the community environment and that the inputs and outputs of the family and community interaction formed the framework for society as a whole (Hunt, 1942).

During the 1900s, there are many examples of family and consumer sciences professionals connecting the home and family with the larger community. Teaching the importance of hand washing and germ theory, rationing in war times, and advocating for product standardization and funding for vocational training in public schools are a few of the many examples of the involvement of family and consumer sciences professionals in the community. The idea of family within community has remained the focus of the discipline throughout the decades. In the later 1900s, family and consumer sciences professionals advocated for many issues related to families and the community, and they influenced legislation including textile flammability standards, removal of lead in residential paint, early childhood brain development education, and nutritional labeling.

Presently, family and consumer sciences professionals are even more intentional, directed, and active in advocating for family and community well-being. Acting as both private citizens and in professional groups, family and consumer sciences professionals focus on improving family life through changing public policy in child development and family relations, consumer protection, housing and interior design, clothing and textiles, food and nutrition, and education. In the following sections, public policy is defined, examples are given, and the process of affecting change is outlined.

Public Policy in Action

Read the following four scenarios. What is the issue being addressed? At what level is the issue being addressed – local, state or federal? What do the scenarios have in common?

Scenario 1: The small business owners that surrounded Jared's high school were not the most hospitable toward high school students who skated in front of their stores after school. As Jared and his friends saw it, the problem was not that they wanted to disturb the local business customers but for kids who were not involved in after school sports, there was no energy outlet for them immediately after school. And it was not that he and his friends were not physically active, either. They just were not attracted to any of the organized sports offered by the school. Jared and his friends brainstormed about the problem and the increased complaints by business owners. There were rumors about establishing anti-loitering laws. Jared and his friends came up with an alternative. They proposed that the city fund and build a skate park that would allow kids to get needed physical activity while keeping them from loitering around surrounding businesses. They wrote a plan, met with the city council, and in the end, were involved in a focus group that helped design the new skate park. It seemed that everyone was pleased with the results—teens, business owners, school administrators, store patrons, and parents.

Scenario 2: It all started when Julie got a job in food service on her college campus. She soon noticed that at the end of the day, the on-campus delis and coffee shops discarded dozens of prepackaged sandwiches, pastries, and salads even if they were barely past their expiration date. Julie asked the store manager and then the director of campus food services if the food could be collected and redistributed to hungry families in the surrounding community. At first her request was rebuffed. However, as Julie shared her idea with more and more students, the idea took on a life of its own. The university newspaper ran a story about the discarded food along with statistics about hunger in the community. Soon university faculty became interested in her idea. Eventually, Julie and her cohorts received permission to pick up the discarded food at the end of the day. They then distributed to the campus food bank. From all over the city and even the suburbs, hungry people come to pick up free food. And it was good food—food that was being thrown out daily until Julie and her friends got into the act. Dozens of volunteers including students, faculty, and staff now contribute their time toward the pick up and distribution of food. There is little paperwork, no red tape, and food is distributed to those who need it.

Scenario 3: After years of living in low-income rental apartments and finally, a rental house, Susan's two young daughters were experiencing elevated blood lead levels. Their doctor explained that children who have elevated blood lead levels often have reduced attention spans, are hyperactive, and can exhibit behavior problems. She warned Susan that continued exposure might lead to kidney damage, damage to the central nervous system, a number of other serious health concerns or even death. Where did the lead exposure come from? After testing the paint in her rental home, it was determined that the paint contained high levels of lead.

Susan had never heard about the danger of lead in older paint. Since the 1970s, it was no longer legal to sell paint with lead additives, but in 1990, many homes still contained the original paint that was produced long before the government restrictions. Since many low-income housing units receive little maintenance and care, these are the residences where lead paint is most prevalent.

Many citizens and professionals came to realize that the legislation that made lead paint production and use in the United States illegal was not enough. Lead still existed in many homes, especially rental units which served as residences for low income families with children. Citizens lobbied for change and the federal government responded. As a result, the Residential Lead-Based Paint Hazard Reduction Act was enacted in 1992. Lead disclosure information, monetary grants to aid organizations and communities in lead reduction, and research and education are addressed by this law. Subsequent legislation in the latter 1990s further provided help and incentives for communities to reduce lead in residences. Today, there are far fewer homes that have lead-based paint compared to the early 1990s when the program began. Many cities have implemented higher standards that call for removal of lead paint from residences.

Scenario 4: When planning an assembly in honor of Martin Luther King Jr. Day, a club comprised of fourth-, fifth-, and sixth-grade students at an elementary/middle school in Washington state studied civil rights and learned much more than they could share during the assembly. They wanted fellow students to understand the history of civil rights in the United States.

This group worked with a state legislator in 2010 to create a bill encouraging schools to teach about civil rights history. A state Senator supported the cause and worked hand-in-hand with the students to draft the bill, which did not make it past its first hearing due to the lateness of it being introduced. That did not deter the students or the Senator, who brought the bill back the following year of the legislative session.

The opportunities this afforded the students to learn more about the legislative process were endless. The students participated in a hearing through a conference call and visited the state capital for the full Senate reading of the bill. The club advisor stated that the students learned a lot about the process of a bill becoming law and what it's like to be in the legislature.

Both the state House of Representatives and the Senate approved the bill and it went on to the governor for signature and to become session law. This is one example of civic engagement in the political process of policy making by a group of dedicated students around a topic they cared about.

The scenarios presented all involve creating or changing public policy. More importantly, all four involve private citizens who decided to make a change to improve their environment.

Civic Engagement and Public Policy in the United States

Civic engagement is a process by which different voices, opinions, and perspectives are shared and oriented toward mutual understanding, with the goal of making a difference in the life of the community. In other words, it is a public conversation between individuals. It can include anyone—concerned citizens, experts in a related field, politicians, and government officials. Civic engagement works best when citizens combine knowledge, skills, values, and motivation to improve the life of the community, rather than furthering individual agendas.

Civic engagement involves both political and nonpolitical activities. A nonpolitical activity is volunteering or community service. Political activities include voting, advocacy on specific social issues, contributing resources of time or money to a public policy or political campaign, and communicating with elected officials. The opportunity to become involved in public policy formation at the grassroots level is also an important activity. Although rules of order may be used in public forums, civic engagement is still considered an informal process. Individuals may participate in civic engagement as average citizens, policy educators, policy analysts, or policy advocates. Because public policies are undergoing continual change, civic engagement is appropriate and effective at many points during the public policy process.

Public Policy and Family Policy

Should government regulations require the removal of all old lead paint in housing? Should health care be provided to all families despite income level or employment status? Should cell phone use be restricted while driving? Should the textile trade be regulated so that all countries can compete equally in the global marketplace? Do parents have the right to eavesdrop on their children's telephone and Internet conversations? The questions are endless. Everyone makes choices as new questions arise. This is true of all individuals and organizations, including families.

In democratic societies, all citizens are responsible to observe, evaluate, and if necessary, impact government in a way they deem intellectually and morally correct. Public policy is the process of formulating questions, evaluating alternatives, and determining answers. The results are new guidelines, regulations and laws enacted by the government, at the local, state or federal level. These are called public policies. *Public policy* involves action that is intended to accomplish a goal. It is not always easy as every policy involves choosing between alternatives.

Whether it is working with food, clothing, shelter, family relationships, or education, or preventing consumer fraud, family and consumer sciences public policy activists specifically evaluate complex questions affecting families and communities. This area of concentration is called *family policy*. The purpose of family policy is to improve the lives of individuals, families and communities. Just like in the larger arena of creating public policy, in family policy current government programs, laws and regulations are evaluated based on how they affect the family unit. Questions that might be asked regarding a specific family policy include: How does current policy affect the structure of the family? How does it affect the functions performed by the family unit? How does it affect the behavior of family members? What are the overall consequences of the policy on the family? Once a policy is created, it is implemented and evaluated. If needed, new policies may need to be created or existing policies revised. In the process, several questions must be asked, including: is the proposed policy economically feasible? Does it have a benefit to individuals, families, and society as a whole? Is the policy morally defendable? And is it politically feasible?

Process of Public Policy

Sometimes the process of changing public policy seems overwhelming and too complex for average citizens. The American Association of Family and Consumer Sciences (AAFCS) offers support, training, and resources to learn skills in affecting public policy. AAFCS utilizes a policy analysis organizing tool developed by Braun and Bauer (2001) to explain the process of impacting public policy. See **Figure 5-1**. This tool is built around five "I's". These include:

- Information
- Issues
- Impacts
- Implications
- Imperatives

These "Five I's" represent stages in affecting public policy change.

Information

The information stage involves general fact-finding. This includes researching the current legislation on an issue, finding out who needs information and when, the type of information needed, and the preferred media format for information delivery. During the information stage, fact-finding is on a very general level when values and needs are assessed, costs and benefits are weighed, and current legislation is evaluated based on needs. For example, during the information stage, a person who is concerned about the sharply increasing rate of high school drunk driving incidents in the local community would begin the information stage by researching the current legislation on teen driving requirements, sale of alcohol to minors and legally adult teenagers, and other legislation affecting teens. The next step would be to find out who needs to know about the dramatically rising rates of teen drunk driving incidents, what type of information would get the message across to them, and how the information should best be delivered. The benefits and costs of changes to legislation that might curb the rising trend would need to be assessed, as well as the values and needs of the community.

Issues

In the second stage, the issues involved in the situation are analyzed. This is the stage when feelings, opinions, and attitudes of people who consider themselves stakeholders in the issue are considered. Does the issue have a history? For example, does a change in the community play a part in the dramatic increase in teen drunk driving incidents? Where has the alcohol been purchased? Have school or community activities changed in hours of operation or availability to teens? Are more teens unemployed

"Five I's" Policy Analysis Organizing Tool

Policy under analysis: _____

Analysis done by _____ Date _____

Information Gather the facts about the situation—Legislation (existing, proposed, pending); Values; Needs; Assets; Capacity; Costs; Benefits.	**General Questions to answer:** What information exists? What is needed? Who needs the information? Why is the information needed? When is the information needed? In what media is the information needed? Who can obtain the information? At what cost? When?	**Findings and Source:**
Issues Identify the issues involved in the situation.	What issues have a history? What issues are emerging? Who agrees? Disagrees? Are the issues changing?	
Impacts Analyze the likely consequences for people.	Who will be affected by the legislation? Intentionally? Unintentionally? What are the short-term and long-term effects?	
Implications Consider the possible effects on people and organizations.	What might the legislation, as is or as proposed, mean for: People targeted? People not targeted? Other federal, state and/or local legislation? Community nonprofit and faith-based groups? Government agencies?	
Imperatives Ponder the call for action presented by the situation.	What's the reason(s) for action? Why should we act in a timely manner? Why us? Why now? What might happen if no action is taken?	

Source: aafcs.org Developed by Bonnie Braun, 2001

Figure 5-1 AAFCS uses this policy analysis organizing tool in impacting public policy.

and subsequently are more teens faced with idle hours? What is the opinion of community teens? What about community parents? What do local school teachers think is the cause? In this stage, alternatives to the current legislation are considered and discussed among stakeholders. Should there be a community curfew for teens? Should legal punishment be stronger for retailers who sell alcohol to minors? Should adults who provide alcohol to minors, either directly or unwittingly, be held responsible? Since most teen accidents that involve alcohol happen when there are two or more teens in the car, should the number of vehicle occupants be limited?

Impacts

In the third stage, the impact of the proposed legislation is assessed. The question is asked, who will be affected by the proposed legislation? Some people will be affected intentionally by policy changes whereas others will be affected unintentionally. There will be both long- and short-term effects with any public policy change. In this stage, these impacts are made clear.

Implications

In the fourth stage, the potential implications of the proposed legislation will be judged from the viewpoint of all who are directly and indirectly involved. How will it change the lives of those involved? Will it have a positive or negative affect? Will it affect the larger community, state, or federal requirements? How will nonprofit and faith-based groups react to the proposed legislation? Are there economic, social, political, or physical ramifications of the proposed legislation? In hotly debated issues, discussions often take place through a number of media formats. The greater the impact of the proposed legislation, generally the more media attention the proposed legislation receives.

Imperatives

The last stage, the imperative stage, is evaluating the timeliness and urgency of the proposed legislation. In the example used here, this stage involves considering the impact of not changing legislation. Would the trend in teen drunk driving incidents continue to increase? Is it a matter of saving lives? Are there financial incentives for moving quickly on the proposed legislation?

Role of Family and Consumer Sciences Professionals in Public Policy

How can you affect change in public policy? The answer to this question is slightly different based on whether you are acting as a family and consumer sciences professional or as an individual citizen. As an individual citizen, there are many ways to be actively involved in public policy change. First, be a registered voter and regularly vote during elections. Voting and electing candidates that represent your values consistent with the well-being of individuals and families is the first step toward public policy change. You may choose to campaign for or against particular issues, especially issues that relate to your expertise and interests. This could include writing, telephoning, or e-mailing legislators, speaking at public forums, or contacting organizations that are involved in legislation such as local government or school boards. Becoming actively involved in campaigns and initiatives by lobbying, donating money or time, and attending public meetings are all an important part of citizenship in a democratic society. As an individual, your personal values, religious or faith-based beliefs, and personal best interests may play a large part in your activities and interests.

As a family and consumer sciences professional, your role is slightly different. Personal values, religious or faith-based beliefs, and interests should play a minor role in your activities and interests unless they are consistent with the objectives of the professional group you represent.

There are some general recommendations for ways in which family and consumer sciences professionals can be involved in shaping public policy that concerns families. First, be well informed about all of the issues involved. For example, if you are concerned about affordable, quality child care, find out what the issues are and what the current standards or policies are in your city, county, or state. Shortages of affordable quality child care may stem from long-term and sustained unemployment opportunities, current guidelines and regulations concerning child care, a lack of educational programs that prepare child care workers, low wages for child care workers, high insurance premiums, government funding limitations, or any number of other factors unique to your area. Second, voice your support for or opposition to current programs and policies that affect families.

Working to educate others on the implications of current or proposed public policy is another way to be involved. As a professional, your role as an educator should be facilitating discussions and explaining points of view of various constituents. You can identify objectives and help decision makers sort through the details and data that supports or disputes a particular stance.

Research, collaborations and evaluation also play a role in how family and consumer sciences professionals engage in policy.

The Role of Research

Family and consumer sciences professionals are well qualified to contribute their expertise in public policy issues that affect the family. Expertise in housing, textiles and clothing, food and nutrition, education, family services, child care, consumer protection, and hospitality is frequently needed in public policy formation. Collaborative research into various aspects of U.S. politics and public policy has resulted in many changes that have led to an improved quality of life. There are many examples of family and consumer sciences professionals contributing their specialized knowledge to public policy formation. A partial list of contemporary

public policy issues that include family and consumer sciences specific knowledge include:

- financial literacy
- textile flammability
- safe and affordable housing
- poverty and homelessness
- nutrition supplemental program for women, infants and children (WIC)
- Head Start early childhood school preparation
- food stamp recipient education programs and the Expanded Food and Nutrition Education Program (EFNEP)
- child nutrition programs
- Child Care Development Block Grant (CCDBG)
- Dependent Care Tax Credit (DCTC)
- right to privacy
- private school vouchers

The Role of Collaboration

For civic engagement to work effectively, participants must collaborate together. Collaboration is the process of partnering with others to accomplish a goal. Collaborative learning has been the focus in schools for the past several years. As a result, more and more adults feel comfortable with the collaborative process.

When people work together, more is accomplished. This is because unified efforts can utilize limited resources to their fullest extent. And with different voices in the conversation, problems and goals can be more clearly defined. Public policies often involve very complex issues. Collaboration helps stakeholders to share the load and address complex issues.

The Role of Evaluation

Public and family policy makers focus on the outcomes of government decisions. Since evaluation of outcomes cannot be value-free, professionals must evaluate public policy from a variety of perspectives. For example, as a professional, you might ask about the advantages and disadvantages of providing subsidized housing in an affluent suburban neighborhood. As a professional, you would provide your expertise on housing issues and their effect on families. However, as a private citizen, your involvement may be different. As a private citizen your involvement may be less objective and more value-laden. Both professionals and those acting purely as private citizens are needed in public policy formation.

In order for many government programs to continue, politicians have to know if the programs are effective. They often call on family and consumer sciences professionals to show evidence that the programs have effected change. They need personal anecdotes and, more importantly, hard data. For example, when politicians evaluate the effectiveness of an educational program, they want to know the effect the program has had on children, schools, and the community. Did the program help to lower the high school drop out rate? Did it change attitudes? Did it involve more parents in the learning process? These are typical evaluative questions that must be addressed.

Examples of Public Policy Benefiting Children and Families

Family and consumer sciences professionals are concerned with improving the quality of life for families and individuals. Public policy found in laws, guidelines, and budget lines can be used to enhance or detract from this mission. Much work has been done in the past and is continuing in the present to create public policy that will improve quality of life. Family and consumer sciences public policy activists concentrate on issues important to the family and carry out research suited to their particular strengths. For example, public policy that improves the quality, affordability, and accessibility of child care

ultimately improves the overall quality of family life. In the following section, several select public policy initiatives are highlighted.

Head Start

Young children who live in poverty are often less prepared than their more affluent counterparts to attend school, especially in the early years. Why? Poverty is a disadvantage in many ways. The lower availability of nutritious food, lower-quality day care, less frequent health and dental care, and fewer enriching cultural experiences combined with higher family stress often make it difficult for young children to succeed in school. Difficulties during the early school years often lead to difficulty in later years of school. Head Start is a U.S. program that helps prepare low-income preschool children attend school. The program was started in 1965 as a result of grassroots efforts and eventual public policy change that occurred as the result of the work of many individuals. Educators, nutritionists, health professionals, social and family service professionals, and many other professionals came together to provide comprehensive services for economically disadvantaged children. The result has been children who are better prepared to enter the traditional kindergarten and benefit from their education through high school system. Some Head Start programs are coordinated with other social programs to provide all-day child care. These programs provide a positive high-quality environment for preschool children and, at the same time, afford their parents the opportunity to seek full-time employment. Today, hundreds of thousands of children are served each year in the United States.

21st Century Community Learning Centers

In the 1970s, significantly more women entered the workforce. The number of families with two incomes increased significantly throughout the next couple of decades. As a result, the 1980s were known as the decade of "latch key" children, meaning that many children were unattended during after-school hours. Traditionally, child care has been available for infants and preschool children. Spending many hours unsupervised, countless schoolage children used their idle hours sitting in front of the television or computer, or out on the streets. The result was not good for the children or their communities, especially in large urban areas and remote rural areas that lacked neighborhood and community support systems. In the 1990s, community activists, educators, and others concerned with the quality of life of schoolage children pulled together and sought change. The result was a program called 21st Century Community Learning Centers. This program provides federal funding for inner city and rural schools to remain open past regular school hours. During these extended hours, recreational and learning-based activities are provided. In general, this program offers a safe place for children during after-school hours. Funds are awarded in the form of grants. Community organizations and independent service providers are encouraged to partner with schools.

Child Care and Dependent Care Grants and Tax Credits

During the 1990s, several state and federal programs were made available to families with dependent children. Three significant policy changes include the Dependent Care Tax Credit (DCTC), The Child Care Development Block Grant (CCDBG), and the Title XX Social Services Block Grant (SSBG). The Dependent Care Tax Credit provides tax relief to tax-paying families with children under the age of 13. The intent of the tax credit is to offset child care costs. The tax credit varies depending on the number of children in the family and is based on a percentage of child care costs. The program is income based. A majority of states also provide state dependent care tax credits. The Child Care Development Block Grant was passed in 1990 and was later merged with child care funding that was part

of the welfare program. This program requires states to provide at least a set percentage of dependent care support to low-income families. Of this support, some must be earmarked for child care including early childhood and before- and after-school programs. The Title XX of the Social Services Block Grant also provides financial support for a broad range of social services, including child care for families in need.

Food and Nutrition Programs

In 1999, the U.S. Department of Agriculture (USDA) published a report on hunger in America. According to the report, at any given time, approximately 10 percent of citizens do not have access to enough food to meet their needs. About half of these households face hunger in any given year. Of even greater concern, nearly 30 percent of children under the age of 12 in the United States are either hungry or at risk for being hungry. Since children are undergoing tremendous physical and cognitive growth, hunger puts them at risk for poor development. Hunger also puts them at risk for increased incidence of disease, and for the youngest children, a higher risk of infant morality.

The USDA and the Food Research and Action Center (FRAC), an anti-hunger group, along with other organizations and thousands of individuals have worked to plan and implement several federal anti-hunger programs including food stamps, child nutrition programs, and the Special Supplemental Program for Women, Infants, and Children (WIC). The Food Stamps program serves millions of United States citizens each year although the number of participants has dropped in the past decade. Why? Proponents believe that a drop in participation represents a decrease in need. Opponents counter that the program has made it more difficult for people in need to access the program and the lower number of participants does not reflect the growing need for assistance.

It is generally accepted that learning is difficult when a person is hungry. Hunger makes it difficult to concentrate and slows cognitive processing. Child nutrition programs provide school lunch and breakfast programs for children in qualified schools and child care centers. Federal guidelines specify nutritional expectations of school lunches. The Special Supplemental Program for Women, Infants and Children, more commonly referred to as WIC, provides food assistance to women and children with an emphasis on pregnant and lactating mothers and infants. Although these programs have been around for many years, they are continually modified and updated as public policy advocates evaluate and push for changes that meet the needs of a changing society.

Other federal programs focus on individuals and families that may or may not include young children. The USDA supports the Expanded Food and Nutrition Education Program (EFNEP) in all 50 states. The EFNEP provides assistance to individuals and families with limited resources by providing nutrition, meal planning, and food budget education in communities. Audiences may be found in schools, after-school programs, camps, churches, libraries, or other community centers. Family and consumer sciences professionals working for government extension services train community volunteers to teach these courses.

With an increase in the elderly population and a concern for quality of life issues, the federal Elderly Nutrition Program (ENP) was established to provide home- and community-based long-term care, including nutritional resources, to avoid premature hospitalization or nursing home care of the elderly. The purpose is to provide resources so that the elderly may choose to live independently in their own homes for as long as desired. A recent evaluation of this program demonstrated success in several areas. Participants report high satisfaction with the program, higher daily intake of key nutrients, and increased social contact. ENP meals often provide up to half of the participant's daily nutritional intake ("First Evaluation," n.d.).

Family and consumer sciences professionals work through many organizations and groups to affect change. One forum for affecting change is through the American Association of Family and Consumer Sciences and its many state affiliates. In the following section, current public policy issues that AAFCS is actively pursuing are described.

AAFCS Public Policy Issues

The American Association of Family and Consumer Sciences is actively involved in public issues affecting the family today. The organization focuses on public issues that affect the quality of life for families rather than public policy in general. For example, early childhood parent support and/or intervention that educates parents on early childhood brain development has long-term positive effects on family life. Another example is a bill that impacts career and technical training in public high schools. When bills are being heard in the United States Congress, the House of Representatives, or the Senate, family and consumer sciences professionals can move quickly to make their voices heard. AAFCS focuses both on immediate public policy initiatives that are time dependent and long-term resolutions that promote advocacy, coalitions, and partnerships with other individuals and groups who share the organization's mission. The AAFCS Public Policy Committee directs the public policy actions of the organization (2003).

As the Public Policy Committee scans the news and public forums for issues that relate to families, they also look for long-term trends. These long-term trends often result in AAFCS public policy initiatives that include strategic plans, issue monitoring, and resource development for individual members and affiliate groups. In order to focus the organization's energy in strategic areas and to not spread its resources too thinly, basic principles are used for screening public policy issues before they become AAFCS initiatives. The Public Policy Committee may bring it before AAFCS as a proposed initiative if the issue involves these principles (2003):

1. **Family support and responsibilities:** This involves the necessary tasks of families including nurturing members, maintaining shelter, food, and clothing needs, and managing resources. It also includes community and hired support such as child care and employer family leave.

2. **Family memberships and stability:** The definition of family has changed over the past several decades and family stability has ebbed and flowed as demonstrated in marriage, divorce, and cohabitation data. Issues such as marital rights, employee benefits, and laws and regulations concerning divorce and marriage are included in this.

3. **Family involvement and interdependence:** This includes the roles of individual family members and the support, reliance, and independence/dependence among them.

4. **Family partnerships and empowerment:** How can government agencies, community programs, schools, and other public and private organizations partner with families? Empowerment rather than instruction or other prescriptive methods are preferred.

5. **Family diversity:** Families are changing. These changes include foster parent and adoption laws, sexual orientation laws and mores, and other diversity issues.

The AAFCS Public Policy Committee focuses its efforts on both education and advocacy in public policy efforts. It prepares briefs and statements for members' use, publishes a two-page article on public policy issues in the *Journal of Family and Consumer Sciences* each year, and works with AAFCS state affiliates and other units to assist them in their work on the earmarked issues. The committee also creates partnerships with other groups. Each year, the AAFCS "Friend of the Family" award is given to an outstanding individual who is making an impact on the quality of family life. Three public policy initiatives have been supported by AAFCS in recent years: health and wellness, financial literacy, and child care.

Health and Wellness

The health and wellness initiative focuses efforts of AAFCS affiliates, divisions, sections, and individual members on the long-term effects of health and wellness on quality of life for families. AAFCS recognizes evidence that lifestyle choices such as smoking, overeating, lack of physical exercise, stress, and other changeable patterns increase the risk of disease and ultimately reduce quality of life. It also acknowledges that the poverty and education level play a large role in available health care and knowledge of lifestyle choices that promote disease prevention. The objective of this initiative is to reduce the physical, social, and emotional consequences of poor or misinformed lifestyle choices related to health and wellness. Through education, research, and advocacy, AAFCS is placing long-term efforts into helping families make better and more informed choices.

Financial Literacy and Family Financial Planning

The second AAFCS public policy initiative is financial literacy. The increased complexity of the economic marketplace, ease in obtaining personal credit, increase in personal bankruptcy filings, and the result of surveys that indicate a lack of individual competence in financial literacy together sparked this initiative. After reviewing and evaluating a number of data resources, the Public Policy Committee determined that personal financial education and resources were not available to many citizens. As lifespans increase, the need for personal money management is greater than ever before. In short, money has to last longer. The objective of this initiative is to reduce the number of individuals and families facing poverty and to increase financial stability among families. By creating financial stability, families have a better ability to meet their basic needs of food, clothing, and shelter. Family financial security also affects society as a whole. AAFCS has joined with other organizations such as the Jump$tart Coalition for Personal Financial Literacy to lend a broader voice to the concern. Work is being done in communities by partnering with local school boards and media to promote financial literacy.

Child Care

The third AAFCS initiative calls for accessible, available, and affordable quality child care and for economic restructuring that allows one parent to be present full-time in the home if he or she desires. The issue of quality child care is not new. It is, however, complex. Personal values, beliefs, and expectations all play a part in the issue. AAFCS uses three basic guidelines for public policy activities:

- Government should support the traditional mothering role by making it easier for mothers to choose not to enter the workforce, to leave the workforce and reenter, or to provide child care financial support for mothers who choose to financially support their families through employment.

- Government should provide quality child care assistance to families and children at risk.

- Government should play a role in helping families access and secure affordable quality child care. This will offer long-term benefits to families and society as a whole.

As more and more women enter the workforce, the prevalence of mothers who are working outside the home and who have dependent children increases dramatically. For many, staying at home, full-time is not a financial option. At the same time, quality child care for young children and after-school care for older children is unavailable and/or unaffordable. Child development research supports the need for quality child care. For young children, there are great social, emotional, and cognitive benefits. It also lowers stress among family members. For older children, being unattended during after-school hours may promote risky behaviors. Most

crimes occur among youth during these hours (Hofferth & Sandberg, 2001).

As with the previously described initiatives, the AAFCS Public Policy Committee strives to provide education and advocate, support, and lobby for public policy that leads to affordable and available quality child care. It also seeks to join with other like-minded groups to provide solutions to families who desire to have one parent at home full-time in a child-rearing capacity.

Future Public Policy Issues

Family and consumer sciences professionals must understand the changing environment in order to meet family needs. The individual and/or family is the center of the human ecosystem model. The human constructed, human behavioral and natural environments surround the individual and family and create the context for which decisions are made and resources are used. In response to environmental changes, public policy advocates adapt to meet the changing needs of the family.

In a highly populated, diverse world, it is difficult to make global predictions regarding family structure and change, but there are universal global trends related to population and aging. These are clear. The world population is growing and aging. However, marriage, divorce, birth rates, household size, and family roles are highly dependent on culture.

What will happen to the family in the next 50 years? It is easy to look back and see trends of the past, but looking ahead is more difficult. Economic, social, environmental, political, and technological changes may occur that are beyond forecasters' comprehension. Despite the difficulty of seeing ahead, current trends point to several potential changes in the family unit in upcoming decades. These include changes in the institution of marriage, age at first and subsequent marriages, birthrates and household size, age of first-time parents, single-parent families, and family roles.

So who should be involved in public policy? Everyone should. Everyone has a voice, an opinion, and everyone can make a difference. In fact, public policy begins with local movements and initiatives. Schools, churches, neighborhoods, and workplaces are the common places where critical initiatives begin. Family and consumer sciences professionals can make a significant difference in the lives of individuals and families simply by getting involved on a personal and local level. Since they hold credible research-based information, they are well equipped to aid decision makers by providing relevant data.

Summary

Family and consumer sciences professionals have influenced public policy for over 100 years. Ellen Swallow Richards, family and consumer sciences founder, and others influenced the quality of life for families on a community scale from the profession's inception. Thousands of leaders in the profession have followed in their steps by advocating for public policies that improve family life. Some early examples include personal hygiene and food sanitation education and legislation, war-time rationing, and career training in public schools.

Public policy includes community and government policies, laws, standards, and regulations. Family and consumer sciences specialists are concerned about public policy that affects families. Throughout the decades, they have participated in family policy formation. Examples include textile safety and trade legislation, food labeling, housing standards, and early childhood child care and education.

The process of public policy formation includes five stages. These stages include information gathering, issue formation, impact review, implication assessment, and assigning an imperative. The American Association of Family and Consumer Sciences promotes specific and directed initiatives, which include advocating for increased focus on health and wellness, financial literacy, and affordable quality child care.

The family is the center of the human ecosystem model. Environmental trends affect the quality of life for families. Changes in the family unit itself are also predicted for the future. These include changes in the make-up of the family; marriage, divorce, and birth rates; and household roles. As families and the environment in which they exist continue to change, so will the need for new family policies. For family and consumer sciences professionals, it is imperative that they advocate for public policies that improve the quality life.

Questions for Thought

1. Why it is important to participate in government as a private citizen? as a family and consumer sciences professional?

2. Name at least three ways individuals can influence the development, formation, and implementation of public policy issues.

3. Identify your United States Congressional representatives in the House and in the Senate, your state governor, and your state legislators. Describe three ways you can communicate with them. Give specific contact information.

4. Secure a copy of your local newspaper and read it thoroughly. As you do, look for public policy issues in your community that specifically impact families.

5. Name one individual who has influenced public policy in the past year. This person could have influenced policy at the local, state, or federal level. Write a short synopsis describing how he or she has participated in public policy formation.

6. Visit the American Association of Family and Consumer Sciences website and go to the public policy (advocacy) link. What are the current public policy initiatives supported by the organization? Identify and describe two ways you could participate in the AAFCS public policy initiatives.

7. With three or four of your classmates, design and implement a community service project that contributes toward one of the AAFCS public policy initiatives.

8. The third AAFCS initiative calls for accessible, available, and affordable quality child care and for economic restructuring that allows one parent to be present full-time in the home if he or she desires. AAFCS uses three basic guidelines for public policy activities. Do you agree with the three AAFCS child care initiative guidelines? Why or why not?

References and Resources

Anderson, C. L. (Ed.). (2004). *Family and community policy: Strategies for civic engagement.* Alexandria, VA: American Association of Family and Consumer Sciences.

Anderson, C., & Braun, B. (2001). *Engaging in public policy decision making: A strategic direction.* Alexandria, VA: American Association of Family and Consumer Sciences.

Anderson, C., & Miles. C. S. (1990). Policy education: Making the difference in the public arena. *Journal of Home Economics, 82*(2), 7-11.

Bogenshneider, K., Olson, J. R., Linney, K. D., & Mills, J. (2000). Connecting research and policymaking: Implications for the theory and practice from the family impact seminars. *Family Relations, 49*(3), 327-339.

Braun, B. (1998). *Reflective leading in the public interest: A dialogue about practice.* East Lansing, MI: Kappa Omicron Nu Honor Society.

Braun, B. (2001). *AAFCS presents the "Five-I's" policy analysis organizing tool.* Retrieved January 12, 2007, from http://www.aafcs.org/policy/res/5I_Policy_Analysis_Tool.pdf

Braun, B., & Benning, L. (2001). Welfare reform four years later: The mobilization of the land-grant system. *Journal of Extension, 39*(4).

Lipscomb, A. (Ed.). (2001). *The writings of Thomas Jefferson* (Vol. 1). Washington, DC: Bank of Wisdom.

Mathews, D. (1999). *Politics for people: Finding a responsible public voice.* Chicago: University of Illinois Press.

Meszaros, P. S., & Cummings, P. (1983). Roots in public policy formation. *Journal of Home Economics, 75*(2), 34-37.

National Council on Family Relations. (2001). *Public policy through a family lens: Sustaining families in the 21st century.* Minneapolis, MN: National Council on Family Relations.

Pundt, H. (1980). *AHEA: A history of excellence.* Washington, DC: American Home Economics Association.

Travers, K. S. (1997). Reducing inequities through participatory research and community empowerment. *Health Education and Behavior, 24*(3), 344-356.

Williams, S. (2001). Citizen engagement through public deliberation. *Journal of Family and Consumer Sciences, 93*(2), 12-13.

Unit Two

Exploring Careers in Family and Consumer Sciences

Career opportunities that involve meeting basic needs of individuals and enhancing the quality of life of individuals, families, and communities will be explored in Chapters 6 through 13. Each of these needs is a specialization area within family and consumer sciences. Career opportunities in food and nutrition, hospitality, textiles and apparel, interior design and housing, family and consumer sciences education and extension, family and community services, early childhood and human development, and family and consumer resource management are explored. Chapters begin with a "slice-of-life" career spotlight that features a first-person vignette. It sets the tone for the chapter and gives you insight into the day-to-day application related to the specific need. Development of each career field will be explored, trends will be surveyed, family needs discussed, and a survey of career opportunities within the specialization will be presented. *Issues in the News* will also be presented to give you an idea of future trends. *Professional Profiles* provide insight into careers within each specialization. The end of each chapter includes questions and exercises that will encourage further exploration of the specialization area.

Chapter 6

Careers in Food and Nutrition

After studying this chapter, you will be able to:

- describe the field of food and nutrition.
- discuss the various career opportunities in the food and nutrition field.
- explain what academic training is needed to work in the food and nutrition field.
- describe typical working conditions in the food and nutrition field.

Just a few minutes ago, as I walked out of my patient's room and into the bustling hospital hallway, I knew that she was coming close to the end of her ability to taste, swallow, and enjoy food. Soon I would be recommending the placement of a feeding tube that would assure her of the necessary nutrients her body needs. I know that she will resist this move, but I will work to convince her and her family that proper nutrition is critical to fighting the aggressive cancer in her body. I have seen many patients recover and go on to live very active lives, and I want to provide my patient with every chance for the same opportunity.

I am a registered dietitian in a large university hospital. As a medical nutrition therapist, I work with cancer patients in an oncology ward. I work with a team of physicians, nurses, therapists, and social workers to provide the best care and treatment for our patients. I am an expert in nutrition. I specialize in the care and feeding of cancer patients.

What do I do in an average day? I usually begin my day by answering and sending e-mail and by taking stock of the day ahead. If any of my patients are being discharged, I plan extra time

for the multidisciplinary discharge meeting. I will be consulting with the patient, his or her family, and the community dietitian who will monitor the patient after discharge. For example, one of my patients had surgery and chemotherapy for cancer of the stomach and can only manage liquids. She, too, needs to be fed by tube. She is also diabetic, which further complicates the situation. Since she lives alone, I must make sure she fully understands her dietary needs and work with a social worker to find an in-home care assistant. This is a complicated case, and it takes quite a bit of my morning.

The remainder of my morning is filled with "rounds"—patient visits and consultations with medical staff. I review the patient charts, including blood levels and any other health indicators, new drugs that may create nutrient/drug interactions, and patient status. My pager keeps me moving from consultation to consultation, and even with the best of planning, my schedule is hectic. Although the pace can sometimes be hurried, I always take time to keep meticulous records of each patient.

In the afternoon, I continue to consult with patients as needed, but I spend most of my time participating in staff problem solving and consultations. A team of physicians, nurses, therapists, social workers, and other specialists review cases together. These sessions are invigorating as our team works together to provide the best health care possible for our patients.

Late afternoons are spent doing paperwork and comparing notes with other staff dietitians. When one of us is challenged by a new patient health issue, another usually has some experience or insight to share. I will coordinate with the food service department to make sure diet orders are updated.

I am really proud of my profession. Dietitians help people in a very tangible way. As a registered dietitian, I have many career options. There are always new procedures to learn, new research to apply, new drug therapies to explore, and new patients who present new and unique challenges.

Are you really what you eat? Does the belly truly rule the mind? Why are there so many hungry and starving people around the world? When the media bombards us with images of food abundance, why do so many people struggle with anorexia and bulimia? Is the newest fad diet healthy? Are genetically modified food products safe to eat? Is food the way to a person's heart and emotions? Is it a coincidence that *desserts* spelled backwards is *stressed*? Food and nutrition are sources of provocative and sometimes humorous questions that have no easy answers.

There is no denying that food consumes a tremendous amount of our time and energy. It is one of the basic human needs. Obviously, we need food for survival, as our bodies cannot run without it. However, food has meaning that goes far beyond providing nourishment. Food has carried a message in every society throughout time. It informs us about social standing, social relationships, and social significance of events, and it communicates societal values. Symbolic food references are a part of every language. For example, "You can't have your cake and eat it too" is a common expression in the English language. People assign both spiritual and physical meaning to food. Food from past cultures is often studied as an artifact—where it came from, how it was a part of the economy, and how it was prepared.

Food also holds spiritual and mythical meaning in many societies. The spiritual and mythical importance of food is evident in several films. For example, the films *Waitress, Julie & Julia, Soul Food,* and *Eat, Pray, Love* all exemplify how food is embedded in our relationships, language, and art. This is true today just as it has been throughout history. As novelist Virginia Woolf (1929) wrote, "One cannot think well, love well, and sleep well, if one has not dined well."

The Food and Nutrition Field

The food and nutrition field has three distinct segments—nutrition, food production, and hospitality. First, the field of nutrition will be explored. Second, the food production segment of the industry will be discussed. Finally, hospitality will be briefly discussed in this chapter, but covered in greater depth in Chapter 7. Typical careers in the food and nutrition field are listed in **Figure 6-1**.

Nutrition

Nutrition is the study of how nutrients interact with biological organisms and how an organism assimilates food and uses it for growth and maintenance. It encompasses food science, food preparation, food nutrients, digestion, and the physical, social, and emotional implications of food and eating. Dietitians help people apply this knowledge to improve their health and wellness. The science of doing so is termed *dietetics*.

Nutrition as a field of study began in the 1800s when scientists such as Ellen Swallow Richards began applying scientific knowledge to daily living. As discussed in Chapter 1, some of the early pioneers in family and consumer sciences specialized in nutrition. For example, Wilbur Olin Atwater was best known for his pioneering work developing the caloric table and an instrument to measure caloric values in food. He recommended dietary studies to establish how nutrient intake affects metabolism and muscular effort. He also predicted one of the main health concerns of today: that Americans consume too much food and exercise too little. He attended several of the Lake Placid Conferences and was an FCS founder. Isabel Bevier was another early influence in

Sample Career Areas in the Food and Nutrition Field		
Catering	Food engineer	Marketing research
Clinical nutrition	Food inspector	Media relations
Community education	Food labeling	Nutrition writer
Consumer affairs	Food scientist	Product development
Consumer safety officer	Food service management	Public health
Counseling/consultant	Food service sanitarian	Research
Critical care nutrition	Food stylist	Retail management
Curriculum development	Government affairs/policy	Sensory analysis
Diabetes education	Health education	Sports nutrition
Dietitian	Home health care	Test kitchen manager
Eating disorders	Hotel/restaurant management	University extension
Food buyer	Legislation	University teaching
Food critic	Long-term care	Weight management

Figure 6-1 The food and nutrition field offers a variety of careers.

the field of nutrition. She conducted nutritional research while she was a faculty member at the University of Illinois in the late 1800s and early 1900s.

In 1917, in the midst of World War I, a group of visionary women formed the American Dietetic Association (ADA) in an effort to not only conserve food for military purposes, but also to improve the general health and welfare of the American public. Today, the organization is known as the *Academy of Nutrition and Dietetics (AND)* and is over 70,000 members strong. It represents the largest organization for food and nutrition professionals. The organization's mission is to lead the future of dietetics. An important part of this mission is carried out by the Accreditation Council for Education in Nutrition and Dietetics (ACEND). This governing body grants accreditation status to approved higher education programs. The Academy also serves as an educational forum for nutrition professionals by providing educational programs and conferences, research updates, and information on current trends. In addition, the Academy credentials individuals through the Commission on Dietetic Registration.

Food Production

Food production includes the natural or human-constructed sources of food and the production, product development, distribution, marketing, and sales of food products. It also includes the hospitality and food service industry. Each area alone is an enormous agricultural or industrial segment of the economy.

Food production goes beyond the domestication of animals or the cultivation of plants. Today it includes the emergent reliance on genetic engineering of food products. Food production has moved far beyond a purely agricultural enterprise into mega-agribusinesses. New food production technologies and an increased ability to transport food products in a timely fashion have increasingly made food production an international business. Careers in food production combine knowledge and expertise in agriculture, food chemistry, and business.

Hospitality

The *hospitality industry* meets food, shelter, entertainment, and other needs of people who are

Issues in the News
Organic Food

Is it organic, or is it all natural? Do the terms mean the same thing? No. FDA has not developed a definition for use of the term *natural* or its derivatives. However, the agency has not objected to using the term if a food does not contain added color, artificial flavors, or synthetic substances. Since it is a rather loose term, the consumer does not know how the product was grown or raised.

To be termed *organic*, foods must follow strict guidelines established by the U.S. Department of Agriculture:

- **100 Percent Organic:** Contains only organically produced ingredients and may use the USDA organic seal of approval.

- **Organic:** Contains 95 percent organic ingredients and may use the USDA organic seal of approval.

- **Made with Organic:** Contains at least 70 percent organic ingredients but cannot use the USDA seal.

- **Some Organic Ingredients:** Contains less than 70 percent organic ingredients. These products may only list the organic items in the ingredient panel on the side of the package, and cannot display the USDA seal.

Why are people interested in organic foods? There are several reasons. First, organic products are free from artificial preservatives and chemicals, and they are not genetically modified. Organic plants must be grown on land that has been pesticide free for at least three years. This includes all synthetic pesticides and fertilizers. Also, irradiation or sewage may not be used on the plants. In addition, no part of the food product may contain any genetically modified parts. Any animal food products must be from animals that are fed strict vegan diets. Since no animal by-products are used, certain diseases such as mad cow disease are eliminated. Animals may not be fed antibiotics or hormones. Organic food products may be healthier, but they are not more nutritious than nonorganic food products.

Second, some say organic foods taste better, although this is not always the case. Many organic growers use "heirloom" or old-fashioned varieties of plants rather than the more modern varieties. Over generations of plant life, flavors may have been bred out of some plant varieties.

Organic foods usually cost more than other foods. In fact, they may cost between five and fifty percent more, depending on the type of product. Price seems to be a major obstacle that is keeping organic foods from being more widely accepted. Despite the added cost, the organic food market continues to grow. What used to be a niche market that was run by a handful of small farmers has now become a large and growing industry. Large wholesale and quantity retailers have aided this market growth. In addition, concerns over genetically modified food products have encouraged some consumers to seek out organic foods.

---

away from home. In a sense, hospitality vendors create a home away from home for people. Food and physical well-being play a central role in the hospitality industry, and this field is increasingly conscious of the nutritional issues influencing consumer choices. The types of services provided in the hospitality industry are broad and range from five-star gourmet restaurants to beverages served at a convenience store. Careers in hospitality will be discussed in Chapter 7.

Career Opportunities in Food and Nutrition

Two groups within the general population are forecasted to grow in numbers: the elderly and the very young. As a growing percentage of the population ages and as more children are born, people will become more interested in health issues. This public interest will most likely result in more emphasis on health education and healthy lifestyles, especially nutrition and healthy eating. The increase in interest will further contribute to a demand for dietitians and nutritionists, especially in management areas. From food technology to nutrition counseling, the food and nutrition field provides a wealth of job opportunities.

Clinical Nutrition

Clinical dietitians are health care professionals who hold the credential of registered dietitian. Clinical dietitians are vitally important in the medical industry because they assess the needs of patients and plan medical nutrition therapy to promote health and wellness. Their expertise is needed through all stages of the lifespan, from beginning to end. For example, they help newborns with nutrition problems to thrive. They work with teens and adults on sports, fitness, and obesity issues as well as eating disorders. They may be there at the end of life. Dietitians often assist families in moving terminally ill patients from a hospital setting to home, working with a hospice team and the patient's family to ensure proper feeding of the patient.

Clinical dietitians may be found in research institutions, hospitals, medical clinics, public or private medical organizations, or in private practice. As the health care field has become more specialized, so has the field of nutrition. Clinical dietitians often specialize in particular areas of expertise. Some of the specialized areas of clinical nutrition include pediatrics, critical care, diabetes, renal, geriatric, sports nutrition, and research. Each of these specializations is briefly described here:

- *Pediatric dietitians* specialize in the nutritional health and care of children. A clinical dietitian specializing in pediatrics would be very familiar with the developmental stages, common illnesses, and typical taste and feeding preferences of childhood. For example, a pediatric specialist may be trained to work with specific medical needs of a preschool-age child with cystic fibrosis. Pediatric specialists are also experts in prenatal nutrition and the needs of newborns in neonatal intensive care.

- *Critical care specialists*, sometimes called *nutrition support dietitians*, work with patients who are critically or terminally ill. They must understand the nutritional needs of the patient, the disease or condition, and the social and emotional concerns of the patient and family. They are experts in drug-nutrient interaction and nutrition support. They may specialize in working with cancer patients, burn patients, or other types of seriously ill people.

- *Renal specialists* counsel patients experiencing kidney problems, such as those who have had transplants or require dialysis. They typically work in the renal unit of a hospital or at an outpatient dialysis center. Some of their responsibilities include interpreting laboratory results, understanding fluid electrolyte management, and educating patients, families, and other health professionals.

- *Diabetes specialists* develop nutrition care plans and help the patient and family manage this chronic condition through nutrition and exercise.

- *Sports nutritionists* are clinical dietitians who specialize in the specific needs of athletes in sports and physical activity. They must understand how the body operates under physical stress and how nutrition can be used to enhance healthy performance.

- *Geriatric nutrition* focuses on the needs of older adults. Practitioners in this specialty work in long-term care, assisted living facilities, home health care, community meal programs, and other settings that serve older adults.

- *Research dietitians* may work in health care or academic institutions, exploring and defining the role of nutrition in acute and chronic diseases. They may also work in the food industry or for pharmaceutical or nutraceutical companies to examine the role of functional foods, supplements, and/or drugs on food and nutrient intake and eating behavior. Research dietitians are instrumental in identifying preventive care strategies that are more timely and less costly than treatment-driven health care.

Often these subspecialties require advanced training and education. Clinical dietitians work in research, education, government, and health care organizations. They may work directly with patients or on a policy level in which patients are rarely seen. They may work for an organization or in a private practice. Although there is great diversity in career paths, clinical dietitians share the common mission to provide nutritional health care for individuals and families.

Community Nutrition

Most clinical dietitians work with patients in health care facilities, whereas community dietitians work with individuals and groups in the community to improve health and prevent disease. The terms *community dietitian* and *public health nutritionist* are sometimes used interchangeably, but they are not exactly the same. *Public health nutritionists* work specifically for government agencies, such as a county health department. *Community dietitians* work in a variety of practice settings, including government agencies, worksite wellness programs, home health services, fitness centers, private practice, community clinics, and health organizations (Boyle, & Holben, 2013). Whatever their title, community dietitians and public health nutritionists identify nutrition and food consumption issues and help individuals and families resolve problems and improve their quality of life.

The work of professionals in community nutrition may be focused at the individual or program level. At the program level, community nutrition involves assessing needs of diverse populations and planning, implementing, and evaluating programs to meet those needs. Responsibilities may include collaborating with community organizations in research and public policy development, designing surveys, and writing grants. For example, the federal government's Special Supplemental Nutrition Program for Women, Infants, and Children (WIC) focuses on connecting nutrition to health care for women and children. The original purpose of the program was to provide quality prenatal care for expectant mothers and to reduce the occurrence of low-birth-weight babies. Public health nutritionists are needed to plan, manage, and evaluate the program, while at the individual level, WIC nutritionists apply maternal and child nutrition principles through direct work with clients.

From nursing homes to day spas, community dietitians meet people with varying needs. They may help people modify their diets to gain weight, lose weight, improve health, manage chronic illness, transition from hospital to home, extend their food budgets, or prepare healthy meals. These are complex problems. For example, working with a patient who is struggling with obesity involves not just the client's physical needs, but emotional and social needs as well. The nutritionist must work with both the family and the patient and assess the context in which the client lives. A plan is then developed that supports the values and goals of the patient. If finances are a concern, educating the patient to prepare nutritious, low-cost meals is included. The dietitian helps his or her patients identify emotional triggers for overeating or medical reasons for weight gain. He or she also teaches the client to critically assess diet and physical activity information reported by the media.

Nutrition Education

In some sense, almost all dietitians are nutrition educators. Much of their time is spent helping people to unlearn poor dietary habits and learn more nutritious ways of eating. They help others to apply nutrition knowledge to their own lives. Nutrition education is also a large, growing area in which some professionals specialize.

Traditional *nutrition educators* provide nutrition information to students and food service workers in both public and private education, from child care centers through universities. Some nutrition educators do not work directly with students but are employed by the government to set up nutrition programs at the city, school district, or state level. For example, a nutrition educator might establish guidelines and implement a before-school breakfast program for low-income children. He or she might work with food service administrators to establish a menu that offers nutritious choices for children.

Nutrition educators may also follow the traditional teaching route. They may teach nutrition in a high school, at a college or university, or in a cooperative extension program. College and university nutrition educators must have highly specialized knowledge and generally must hold graduate degrees in nutrition. However, they are not employed only in nutrition or family and consumer sciences fields. Nutrition educators may also teach in other health-related organizations, such as medical schools, hospitals, clinics, and health maintenance organizations (HMOs).

Nutrition education does not always happen in a traditional setting. Private businesses, such as health clubs and spas, also offer classes on nutrition and healthy eating. Nutritionists may also work for pharmaceutical companies, food product sales companies, supermarkets, or industry associations, such as the National Dairy Council. Through promoting products, they serve as educators on the health benefits of the products. Sales of the products often take place at educational seminars and training sessions.

As technology continues to develop, so too will the desire for faster and more up-to-date nutrition information. Nutrition educators serve as the link between nutrition research, practice, and communication of nutrition knowledge.

Food and Nutrition Management

Administrative dietitians manage food service operations. They often work in noncommercial food service, which is offered in organizations whose main purpose is something other than making a profit from the sale of food and beverages. These organizations include educational institutions, health care facilities, correctional institutions, businesses and industries, government agencies, and the military. The dietitian may be employed directly by the organization or by a for-profit company that is contracted by the organization to provide food service. Organizations that contract food service may employ a *food service liaison* to deal with the contract company (Ninemeier & Perdue, 2008).

Food service administrators in health care facilities are responsible for providing meals that meet the nutritional needs of the patients. However, patients are not their only clientele; they also must meet the needs of visitors and employees. They supervise cafeterias and snack bars as well as provide catering for special events. The administrative dietitians may collaborate with clinical dietitians in providing nutrition education. In a small organization, the food service director may also be the clinical dietitian.

School systems and universities are other work settings for administrative dietitians. *School food service directors* may work with teachers in nutrition education programs or serve on the district's wellness committee. *School food service consultants* work for a state department of education or other government agency, such as the U.S. Department of Agriculture. They help schools comply with government regulations through activities such as staff training. In postsecondary settings, a campus food service director may oversee multiple cafeterias, snack bars, concession stands, full-service restaurants, and catering services.

Whatever the setting, the responsibilities of administrative dietitians include menu planning, purchasing, and supervising staff in food preparation and delivery.

Dietetic Technician

A *dietetic technician, registered* (DTR) is a trained food and nutrition professional who works under the supervision of a registered dietitian when providing nutrition care. Dietetic technicians offer personalized service to clients, helping them to ensure a balanced diet and select nutritious foods. They work in the same settings as dietitians and assist dietitians in several ways. Typical work settings include hospitals, nursing homes, and community health organizations. For example, registered dietetic technicians may develop, implement, and review nutrition care plans established by a hospital clinical dietitian. They may assess the nutritional status of a client and document the care in his or her medical record. They talk with clients and learn their food preferences and diet histories. Sometimes they design specialized meal plans or work with families to apply specialized diet restrictions to their daily lives.

Dietetic technicians also work independently as part of the food production and food service industries. They are involved in all aspects of food production and service, including quality service, safety standards, food service supervision, menu design, and food production. Dietetic technicians serve in the front-line and mid-level management positions in food service settings such as schools, universities, long-term care facilities, hospitals, and hospitality settings.

Food Scientist

Is the food safe to eat? Does it taste good? Is it convenient to prepare? Is it healthy for the body over the long term? These are some of the questions that food scientists study and answer. Food science is the application of scientific principles to create and maintain a wholesome food supply. *Food scientists* usually work for food processing companies, government agencies, universities, or research institutions to develop new products that are healthy, safe, palatable, and convenient. They apply knowledge of biochemistry, human biology, microbiology, toxicology, biotechnology, and other sciences to determine new or better ways to prepare, distribute, package, use, and store foods. Sometimes they perform basic research into the composition of food products, focusing on the nutritional composition of foods. Other times, food scientists look at the way food is processed to determine the healthiest and most tasteful, convenient, or efficient method of preparation. Some food scientists are involved in enforcing government regulations, food inspection, sanitation, and other safety measures. Food scientists are often working on the forefront of the food industry, offering new and interesting food products for consumers. Frozen foods, shelf-stable foods, and microwavable meals are just a few of the food products introduced by food scientists over the years. They are concerned about using food resources wisely with as little waste as possible.

There are numerous career opportunities for food scientists, and they go by many names, including product development specialist, sensory scientist, and quality control specialist. Food scientists may also work as technical sales representatives in businesses where food science knowledge is critical. *Food science technicians* assist food scientists in tasks such as maintaining safe and sterile laboratories, preparing and analyzing samples, and testing food components or containers.

Food Product Development

Food product development involves the research and production of new food products. For example, when a soup manufacturer plans to add a new flavor, much time and energy is devoted to discovering the newest trends in food as well as customer preferences and concerns.

Professional Profile

Clinical Dietitian

Sarah Zarelli, RD
Children's Hospital and Medical Center

How did you get into your line of work?

When I was in high school, my school had a career day. My friend and I decided to explore careers in health services. Although my main intent that day was to have a day off from school, I was intrigued with the field of nutrition. From that point on, I knew I would pursue a career in food and nutrition. When I began exploring college options, I intentionally looked for a school with a good dietetics program.

In college, I majored in dietetics and minored in Spanish. This was a perfect combination for me as my dietetic internship was with a community organization that served native Spanish speakers. After completing my degree and internship and passing the RD exam, I began my career as a hospital clinical dietitian.

What does your "typical" day entail?

One of my favorite things about my job is that it never stays the same. I begin my day answering correspondence and catching up on the status of my patients. I spend the mornings checking in on patients and their families. The afternoon is spent meeting new patients. I spend a lot of time during the day on my feet, interacting with people. This is very people-oriented work.

My two specialty areas are working with children with brain tumors and children who have suffered serious accidents. Since a brain tumor can affect many parts of the body, I need to work with nutritional issues as well as the mechanics of eating. For example, I can provide food that meets a child's nutritional needs, but if it is not in a form that can provide nourishment for the body, my work is in vain. Physicians, nurses, occupational and physical therapists, and other health care providers work together to provide care for each patient. Since my patients are children, I also work with family members. Since I am a "people person," I thoroughly enjoy all the interaction that my job entails. I also enjoy being a member of a problem-solving team. I feel respected by the other health care professionals with whom I interact, and because my role is so important, I spend a lot of time researching information. My day also entails a lot of record keeping and interacting with food service staff.

The hardest part of my job is not becoming so emotionally involved that I cannot function at my best. Children often stay in the hospital for an extended length of time, and over this time, I build relationships with them and with their families. Because I work in health care, the result of our efforts is not always what we hope it might be. Nevertheless, I know that my work is important to the well-being of many children.

How do you fulfill the mission of family and consumer sciences— that is, how does your work improve people's quality of life?

Every day I help people get the food and nutrition their bodies need. When children are sick, our goal is to get them healthy, and food plays a vital role in this endeavor. Our desire is to give each child the best quality of life possible, and since food is a life-sustaining resource, my work as a dietitian plays a vital role in achieving this goal.

Issues in the News
Obesity

You hear about it all the time. Americans are eating too much and exercising too little. The number of overweight and obese Americans has been increasing at an epidemic rate during recent decades. The concern is not just about appearance. It is an epidemic health concern for Americans. For example, overweight and obese individuals are at increased risk for physical ailments such as coronary heart disease, congestive heart failure, and stroke, among others. Children are of particular concern because excessive weight and obesity in childhood can lead to a lifetime of chronic diseases. Some of the health concerns include high blood pressure, hypertension, high blood cholesterol, and type 2 diabetes. Data from national surveys indicate that more than two-thirds of Americans are overweight or obese and over 16 percent of children age 2 to 19 are obese (Boyle & Holben, 2013).

This problem did not occur overnight. Being obese or overweight are conditions that are complex health issues, and one simple remedy will not suffice. Eating too much and exercising too little are not the only causes of overweight. The environment and the constant availability of high-calorie foods may play a part. The social environment can influence health concerns, too. In addition, researchers have found that genetics may also play a large part in overweight and obesity conditions.

Why do overweight and obesity health concerns continue to persist? They are complex issues that require collaboration among individuals, dietitians, health care providers, businesses, insurance companies, government, and communities. Besides improved health, there is a huge economic incentive for all involved to halt and reverse this growing trend using both prevention and treatment measures.

Product development also includes sensory analysis of the perceived appearance, aroma, texture, and flavor of the food product. The packaging, production plans, and the overall marketing concept and sales plan must be decided. Product development requires a huge investment on the part of the manufacturer.

Food Sales, Marketing, and Distribution

Food sales, marketing, and distribution is the part of the industry that examines food trends and the eating and shopping habits of both potential and current customers and offers appropriate food products to meet consumer needs. Just like any other consumer product, food is trendy and follows fads. Food is developed and marketed with a specific niche market in mind. Because food involves such an enormous industry, sales and marketing must be carefully and constantly monitored. Food production is not always about big business, however. Many in the food distribution field are concerned about providing equitable food resources around the world. In this case, equitable food availability, not profit, is the motivation.

Additional career opportunities in food service management exist in food sales, marketing, and distribution. These careers will be highlighted in Chapter 7.

Media and Business Opportunities

Individuals with strong communication skills and expertise in food and/or nutrition may find a career in media. The media are important tools for distributing nutrition information. Television news shows often carry food, nutrition, or health segments that feature nutrition educators. Newspapers and magazines may employ nutrition educators who write health and wellness features or columns. Newsletters distributed by HMOs, health care providers, and human resource departments may also carry articles written or edited by nutrition educators.

Magazines, television, newspapers, and websites are information outlets for people who are creative with food and words. For example, you might develop recipes in the test kitchen of a magazine. *Food editors* are responsible for the food-related content in magazines, newspapers, or websites. *Food writers* produce copy for magazines, newspapers, and websites or write their own blogs. The digital world is full of food content. *Food stylists* make food look appealing for the camera. Their work appears in cookbooks, advertising, television programs, and movies. Authors are also needed for textbooks, curriculum materials, and software. Some food journalists are employed by an organization, but others

Professional Profile

Food and Nutritional Sciences Educator

Joey Kathleen Freeman, MS, RD
University, college, and public school settings

How did you get into your line of work?

I became interested in the nutritional sciences in high school. My parents both influenced me in different ways to take this career path. Beginning in middle school, my dad and I ran long distance together, and over the years, we explored optimal nutrition intake for runners. Although I initially planned to major in premedicine with an emphasis in psychiatry, my plans were modified during my sophomore year in college when a newspaper article highlighting the exciting career possibilities in dietetics influenced my decision to change my major to dietetics. After taking my first nutrition class, I knew a career in dietetics was for me. I quickly realized that medicine and psychology were two of the major backbones of dietetics and that I could continue to use my knowledge of those fields as a registered dietitian. Throughout my 10 years as an RD, I have enjoyed working in many areas, including research, school food service management, and nutrition education. My passion is being a nutrition educator.

What does your "typical" day entail?

Currently, I teach nutrition courses to dietetics majors at a university. I teach medical nutrition therapy, community nutrition and education, and human nutrition classes. I also taught food service management at other schools and summer nutrition seminars to school food service personnel.

A typical day entails preparing for class lectures by conducting research, cross-referencing nutrition materials, and thinking about the most effective strategies to use to teach the course material. I am a strong

are freelancers who market their work to a variety of outlets.

Freelance writing is not the only opportunity for self-employment. Dietitians may have their own consulting businesses or provide nutrition counseling through a private practice. For example, a restaurant might hire a consultant to analyze a menu's nutrient content, or a dietitian in private practice might design and deliver a series of weight-loss seminars. Consultants are hired for specific tasks and paid by the hour or job.

Preparing to Enter the Food and Nutrition Field

Whether working as a nutrition educator, a registered dietetic technician, or a nutrition researcher, those working in the nutrition field should be calm, precise, and creative problem solvers, able to work through complex issues to ensure the overall health of their clients. They must be able to work with a variety of people and have well-honed interpersonal and people-helping

believer in the fact that there are many different types of learners and many different teaching strategies that can be used to reach all learners. I am also a big believer in hands-on learning. Whenever possible, I will engage my students in class activities that involve solving problems in case studies. So I take a lot of time prepping for lectures to decide on the best delivery form of the material. Other tasks during my day as a nutrition instructor include helping to connect students with field experiences, discuss internship and job opportunities, help them through the dietetic internship application process, go over assignments and exams, and anything to help them prepare to succeed as a nutrition professional.

I also spend time writing and grading papers and assignments, keeping up with my continuing education through reading professional journal articles, going to conferences, and reviewing textbooks.

How do you fulfill the mission of family and consumer sciences— that is, how does your work improve people's quality of life?

As a nutrition educator, I strive to keep up with the ever-changing field of dietetics in hopes of delivering the most up-to-date knowledge of the field to my students. Keeping up to date allows my students to be prepared going into their dietetic internships and will help them be prepared to practice dietetics once they receive their RD. I also believe that teaching is so much more than purely relaying information. In order for the students to learn effectively and carry that learning with them into their careers, I believe that information must be taught in ways that reach students. I believe the assignments and activities I require in my classes increase the retention rate of the material, which increases the likelihood that students will retain the knowledge into their careers. Through my efforts as a nutrition educator, I believe my students will become competent dietitians and will be able to effectively provide medical nutrition therapy and nutritional counseling to the public, and thus improve lives.

Professional Profile

Administrative Director

Mary Angela Miller, MS, RD, LD, FADA

Ohio State University Wexner Medical Center

University & Ross Heart Hospital Administration

How did you get into your line of work?

The best thing about earning a food and nutrition degree is that it has fostered a career that allowed growth, change, and influence while combining science and service, nutrition and health. In the first decade of my career, I focused on physiological and biological aspects of dietetics. In the second decade, I honed my management, communication, and food skills. Now I spend most of my time in leadership, strategic planning, and administrative activities.

After graduating from Youngstown State University, I gained valuable experience as a dietitian in a community hospital. I next worked at the Cleveland Clinic, where I was the first dietitian assigned to the intensive care units. It was there that I obtained my first management position as a nutrition care coordinator, supervising dietitians and dietetic technicians. During that time, I completed my master's degree at Case Western Reserve University.

After relocating to Columbus, I accepted a position as Weight and Wellness Director in a large medical practice. Running a small business from start-up to execution was among the most challenging and valuable experiences I've ever had. We had to offer a safe and effective program so that patients would achieve their goals, physicians would trust us, and both would refer clients. It was the first time I supervised other allied health personnel, such as nurses and medical assistants.

The success of this program prompted an invitation from the Ohio State University Medical Center to apply as director for their new weight management program. In an interesting turn of events, I was asked during the process to interview for the Food Service Director position, the job I was

---

skills. Since they act as resources, they must be confident, up to date in their nutrition knowledge, and able to apply nutrition principles to a number of different settings.

Making food taste and look great and delivering it in a timely manner are important tasks in the food service industry. Doing so takes a tremendous amount of ingenuity, flexibility, and problem-solving skill, especially when multiple issues arise and the pace is hectic. Food service managers must be creative, adaptable, calm in the event of emergencies,

eventually offered. It entailed managing a multimillion-dollar department with over 200 employees. In this position, I learned how to handle human resource issues, negotiate contracts, organize for efficiency, and most importantly, foster and develop a skilled management team.

Ten years later, I was asked to also assume oversight of the outpatient Ob/Gyn Clinic. It had an experienced clinical team and nurse manager, but the business organization required some attention. Fast-forward another decade: I now administer most of the larger hospital-owned outpatient clinics, including Wellness and Prevention, Wound Care Clinics, and the Heart Hospital Ambulatory Care Center, along with several more clinical inpatient departments and support services. OSU supported my development in many ways, including selecting me to complete a certificate program in health care management offered through the college.

What does your "typical" day entail?

Because I've been a department director, I have a keen appreciation of the challenges involved in delivering services in a 24/7 environment. My experience has taught me about both the business and clinical components of health care. I've learned how to navigate in a complex academic medical center, meet national quality standards, and never lose sight of the patients as well as the staff who care for them. My main purpose is to support my directors in delivering services that fulfill our mission. I may coach them through a particularly challenging issue and connect them with a colleague who has dealt with a similar one. I accompany them on rounds in their department to connect with and learn from patients and staff. Today, I'm meeting with an ambulatory clinic director to review current financial and efficiency metrics and have a preliminary discussion on goals for the coming year.

How do you fulfill the mission of family and consumer sciences— that is, how does your work improve people's quality of life?

The areas I work with touch every patient, visitor, and employee every day. Everyone eats and breathes. Two of my services, nutrition and respiratory care, support these basic essentials. The scope of my work envelops the entire continuum of care across the life cycle. We cover birth in the obstetrics clinic and the bereavement staff support our dying patients and counsel their families. In between, wellness and prevention services heal and rehabilitate. The OSU Wexner Medical Center is one of the country's best performers in delivering quality patient care, and I feel privileged to be part of that effort.

and supportive leaders of the personnel they supervise.

The qualities needed by workers in the food and nutrition field include solid scientific grounding, creativity, an eye for detail, and health consciousness. Employees must be pas-sionate about the product or service they are offering, whether it entails nutritional advice or food products and services. All food and nutri-tion professionals must consider the needs of the end user. Consider the academic training needs and working conditions discussed in the following sections and compare them to your own academic and work environment goals and interests. Professional organizations can give you insight into the food and nutrition field. Several professional organizations, their websites, and descriptions are shown in **Figure 6-2**.

What Training Is Needed?

There are several training routes to careers in food and nutrition. The level of expertise and the education credentials required depend on the type of work. For example, there are very stringent guidelines and specific requirements for becoming a *registered dietitian* (RD). These include earning a bachelor's degree from a program accredited by the Accreditation Council for Education in Nutrition and Dietetics, completing a supervised practice, and achieving a passing score on the national examination administered by the Commission on Dietetic Registration. Supervised practice may be obtained through a postgraduate internship, or it may be coordinated with an undergraduate or graduate degree. To maintain their credentials, registered dietitians must complete continuing education requirements. Additional board certifications may be required for specialized work. Most states require dietitians to be licensed, and the requirements are generally the same as for becoming registered. Students should be aware that the term *nutritionist* is unregulated and be

Professional Organizations Supporting the Food and Nutrition Industry		
Professional Organization	**Web Address**	**Description**
Academy of Nutrition and Dietetics	eatright.org/Public	The largest professional organization in the nutrition field with over 70,000 members. Educational opportunities, conferences, job banks, scientific papers, and current news reports are some of the services offered.
American Society for Nutrition	nutrition.org	A nutrition research society established in 2005 by the merging of three nutrition research groups. The focus is on nutrition research, education, and clinical practice.
American Society for Parenteral and Enteral Nutrition	nutritioncare.org	An association for health care professionals involved with clinical nutrition therapies, such as providing nutrition through liquids or "tube feeding." Provides peer networking, educational opportunities, and a peer-reviewed research journal.
Association for Healthcare Foodservice	healthcarefoodservice.org	An organization for professionals who manage food service in health care facilities that operate their own food service rather than outsourcing.
Association of Food Journalists	afjonline.com	An organization that offers education, networking, and ethical standards for food writers.
Association of Nutrition & Foodservice Professionals	anfponline.org	A professional association that provides education and services specifically for dietary managers.
Institute of Food Technologists	ift.org	An organization for food science and food technology professionals, IFT is dedicated to assuring a safe and abundant food supply.
Society for Nutrition Education and Behavior	sne.org	Nutrition educators find support in this professional organization directed toward teachers, community educators, and professors of nutrition.

Figure 6-2 Check out the websites of these professional food and nutrition organizations.

Issues in the News
Genetically-Modified Foods

Potatoes that absorb less oil when fried, bananas that carry vaccines against polio and other diseases, increased crop yield to feed an exploding world population, and coffee with less caffeine—all are biotechnology projects aimed at producing genetically modified foods to meet the world's needs. Many scientists in the food industry, government, and educational research settings promote the great benefits of genetically modified foods. Fewer pesticides may be needed in the future as crops are engineered to withstand pests. Food may be successfully grown in drought areas where people

are currently starving and can be enhanced with vitamins to provide better health.

While there are many advocates for genetically modified foods, there are also many others who are passionately against them. Consumer groups, environmental activists, and some scientists strongly believe that genetically modified foods will have a long-term negative effect on the world's environment, people's health, and the socioeconomic status of many populations. For example, some believe genetically modified foods may introduce foreign genes into food products

that put humans at risk. Others believe that genetically modified products place the power of food control in the hands of very few organizations.

The debate over genetically modified food products affects personal, community, national, and global levels. In spite of negative views about modern biotechnology methods, scientists use them to advance these ambitious goals: to develop food varieties that grow more abundantly under stressful conditions, mature more quickly, taste better, last longer, and are more nutritious.

wary of organizations offering certification for nutritionists.

Dietetic technicians who are registered can work in clinical settings under the guidance of registered dietitians. There is now more than one educational pathway to becoming a registered dietetic technician (DTR). One way is to complete a two-year associate's degree in a Dietetic Technician program accredited by the Accreditation Council for Education in Nutrition and Dietetics (ACEND) and have supervised practical experience. Another route is to complete an ACEND-accredited Didactic Program in Dietetics and receive a bachelor's degree. Just like registered dietitians, DTRs must pass a national exam and complete continuing education requirements. Additional educational and training information for registered dietitians and

registered dietetic technicians may be obtained from the Academy of Nutrition and Dietetics. Dietetic technicians who are not registered can work in the food service industry.

Educational requirements and training in food service management are highly dependent on the particular job position. Some organizations require the registered dietitian credentials. Others require a degree in business administration or hospitality management. In specialized occupations such as food preparation and hospitality, culinary training may be required. Overall, training and knowledge are needed in food products, nutrition, business management, and food service. Because of the wide diversity in educational requirements and desired experience and training, it is wise to seek advice from professionals in the food service management and

Director, Consumer Group

Jan Roberts
Darigold, Inc.

How did you get into your line of work?

I work for Darigold as a product manager, which involves the research and production of new food products. Darigold is a producer and distributor of quality dairy products that are fresh from local, farmer-owned dairies. These dairy products—including milk, butter, yogurt, sour cream, cottage cheese, and frozen dairy products—are sold to the consumer, commodity, and specialty markets.

Food and nutrition became my passion in junior high school and remained so as I went on to college. When I attended college, I chose to pursue a degree with nutrition as my major and education as my minor.

The most influential person who helped to shape my career choice was a classroom guest speaker, Darigold's home economist. Darigold had a program available to FCS teachers that offered their home economist to visit classrooms and guest lecture on the nutritional value and the use and care of dairy products. As a student, I was fascinated with her specialized knowledge and expertise and with the dairy products themselves.

I began my career as a high school FCS teacher. Remembering how much I enjoyed the experience as a student, I likewise invited a Darigold home economist to be a guest speaker for the classes I was teaching. It was her passion for Darigold and the company's commitment to good nutrition that finally encouraged me to ask her if the company would ever hire another home economist. In 1979, I joined the Darigold company as a spokesperson in the field of food and nutrition. It was my job to act as the liaison between the consumer and Darigold. Over the years, my

hospitality field to determine desirable training and education. Several credentials are available, including Certified Foodservice Management Professional (FMP), awarded by the National Restaurant Association Educational Foundation.

Food scientists often have doctoral degrees. Their preparation includes coursework in chemistry, biology, food science, and research. Food science technicians work under the direction of food scientists and typically have associate degrees. People who work in food science need skills in data analysis, critical thinking, and communication. Certification is available from the Institute of Food Technologists.

What Are the Working Conditions?

Whether providing nutritional assessment, planning the school food service menu, or researching a new food additive, successful food and nutrition professionals work in a variety of settings. Because the career opportunities are so vast in this field, typical working conditions in the food

job has changed as have the consumers the company serves. However, some things remain the same. We still offer quality local dairy products to consumers, and I still offer sound nutrition information. I am still passionate about the nutritional value of dairy products, too. The field of food product development has grown and expanded. Today, my job title is Product Manager for both Darigold brand and the private label products we produce.

What does your "typical" day entail?

Like most professionals, it is hard for me to describe a "typical" day as no two days are alike. On any given day, I may work with our sales, marketing, or research and development teams. I am involved in the product development process from product conception to roll-out. For example, when a new frozen dairy product is introduced to the consumer, I will have participated in the process of idea conception through product testing to final placement on supermarket shelves. I will know just about everything there is to know about the product. Within Darigold, I have developed and implemented competitive products and consumer sensory panels. I am also responsible for nutrition education and food application programs with health and food service professionals throughout the Northwest. I am the technical sales advisor in sales presentations to customers. I work with vendors on ingredients and technology for new products. I also work with the media and direct promotional events.

How do you fulfill the mission of family and consumer sciences— that is, how does your work improve people's quality of life?

The passion that developed for my work started with the passion that my predecessor had for her work with Darigold. Her passion contributed to guiding the company to be genuinely committed to the health and well-being of consumers through the delivery of nutritious, high-quality dairy products.

---

and nutrition field vary widely. For example, a food product developer may work in a kitchen laboratory setting with a team of researchers. His or her day may include tweaking a muffin recipe repeatedly and analyzing a muffin from each batch until the desired results are achieved. For a clinical dietitian, the day may involve working with patients, their physicians, nurses, and other health care professionals in a health care facility such as a hospital or clinic. Nutrition researchers may work with animals or cells in a laboratory, or they may interview people about their food habits and analyze the data.

Many in the food and nutrition field work a traditional eight-hour day, 40 hours per week. Others in the field, such as nutritionists in private practice or managers in the food service industry, may have longer, less conventional and more flexible work hours. Food service workers may be among the first to arrive in the morning and the last to leave at night. They often work very long hours. Food service environments vary greatly, from school cafeterias to hospital dining rooms to government food service programs to fast-paced retail outlets and restaurants.

Summary

Food is one of the basic needs of families and individuals. It provides nourishment to the body. The study of food as nourishment is termed *nutrition*. Food also meets emotional and social needs of people. In developed societies, food is an artifact of societal trends just as clothing and shelter are. In other situations, just securing basic nutrients is the priority.

The development of the field of food and nutrition coincided with the founding of the family and consumer sciences profession in the early 1900s as several founders focused their interest on applying scientific concepts to food and nutrition. Then, as today, research and a growing information base expanded nutrition knowledge. The food and nutrition industry is a multibillion-dollar global enterprise that provides food products to meet the physical, social, and psychological needs of people. It is a complex industry that spans a wide range of products and services, from providing nutrition health care to manufacturing the newest convenience food products to feeding the hungry. Because of its very nature, it is a fast-paced, dynamic, and creative industry. However, it also requires some in this field to be methodical and patient.

A variety of career opportunities exist in the food and nutrition industry. Careers in clinical nutrition, nutrition education, community nutrition, media, and research are just a few of the opportunities that exist in the field of nutrition. Food service management, food science, and food product development and marketing opportunities are available in the retail and marketing segments of the food industry. How can you know if a career in this field is right for you? Evaluate your strengths, weaknesses, skills, and interests in food and nutrition. If you are considering a career in this field, contemplate increasing your knowledge of the profession.

Pursuing a Career in Food and Nutrition

1. **Interview a professional.** The food and nutrition field offers a vast array of professional opportunities. However, due to the sheer number of possibilities, finding a career track can be overwhelming, especially in the less regulated field of food service. To get a better idea of career possibilities in nutrition, refer to the Academy of Nutrition and Dietetics website. To get a clearer understanding of the many career routes in nutrition and in the food product and food service industries, refer to Figure 6-1. You can get a "real-life" view of being in the food and nutrition area by interviewing a professional in your chosen field. For example, you could interview a clinical nutritionist, food service manager, food journalist/critic, or nutrition educator. Ask the person how he or she entered the field, what the advantages and disadvantages are, and what a typical day entails. What personal qualities are needed for success? Be sure to solicit any advice for your career decision making.

2. **Shadow a professional.** Seek permission to job-shadow a food or nutrition industry professional. Often, you can arrange this through your university. The more you observe, the more you will become familiar with this diverse and complex industry. Observation times could range from a few hours to several days. Internships, part-time employment, summer employment, and volunteer experiences will also help you decide if this is the field for you.

3. **Read about the daily work of food professionals.** Search the website of the U.S. Food and Drug Administration for information on Science and Research. Look for a source that provides information about one or more food science careers. Other websites as well as library resources can be accessed to explore other food and nutrition careers.

4. **Become acquainted with professional organizations.** Since their mission is to educate and support professionals, professional organizations provide a wealth of industry information. They also provide relevant industry research and review innovations. Many professional organizations include job banks for prospective employers and employees. Generally, they do not try to sell anything to members. Look up each of the websites listed in Figure 6-2.

5. **Become acquainted with professional publications.** Review some recent issues of

journals in your field. What are current topics of interest in food science? in nutrition? How can professional publications be useful to you as a student and in your future career?

Questions for Thought

1. Access the U.S. Department of Labor, Bureau of Labor Statistics website. Choose two related career profiles listed here and report on their career descriptions, typical working conditions, job outlooks, and expected earnings:
   - dietitians and nutritionists
   - food service managers
   - agricultural and food scientists
   - dietetic technicians

2. What are college students eating today? Identify three food trends for college students. What factors influenced these trends? Will the trends be sustained over several seasons or are they short-term fads? How will these trends affect future food interests, fads, and careers?

3. Review major trends that are described in Chapter 4. How do you predict these changes will affect the work of professionals in food science and nutrition? Which health and fitness trends will define this decade? How will this decade be described by future historians in regard to health, nutrition, and fitness? What new jobs may emerge from these trends?

4. The most commonly cited reason for not buying organic food products is cost. Those who do choose to buy organic foods cite health benefits as their number one reason for purchasing. If you were to develop a marketing campaign that encouraged consumers to buy organic foods, which segment of the consumer market would you choose to direct your advertising toward? Why? What would be the central theme of your marketing campaign?

5. The Public Broadcasting Service in a joint effort with NOVA/Frontline produced and aired a television show called *Harvest of Fear*. Access this site and go through the links that ask the question "Should we grow GM crops?" You will be asked the same question seven times. Each time, you will be asked to either support or disclaim the argument for or against genetically modified food products. Depending on your answer, you will then be presented with a counterargument for or against. You will be presented with six arguments for growing GM crops and six against. At the end, you will be asked to decide whether you are for or against growing genetically modified products.

6. Imagine that your community is providing a free health fair for schoolchildren and their families. You have been asked to provide a program on childhood physical fitness and nutritious snacks that children can prepare. What will you focus on? What types of activities will you include? How will you make an impact?

7. The effects of childhood malnutrition are devastating. The lack of proper nutrition has long-term effects on physical, social, and cognitive development and the onset of various diseases. For some families, malnutrition is a result of lack of education. For many, it is from a lack of financial resources. What can and should various sectors of society do to combat childhood malnutrition? Consider the role of government agencies, schools, community groups, medical professionals, and private organizations such as charities or religious organizations.

References and Resources

American Dietetic Association & Pennington, J. (1999). *The essential guide to nutrition and the foods we eat*. New York: Harper Collins.

Bennett, J. (1987). *The hunger machine: The politics of food*. New York: Basil Blackwell.

Berdanier, C. (2006). *CRC desk reference for nutrition*. Boca Raton, FL: CRC/Taylor & Francis.

Bickerstaff, L. (2008). *Careers in nutrition*. New York: Rosen Publishing Group.

Bordo, S. (1993). *Unbearable weight*. Berkeley: University of California Press.

Boyle, M.A., & Holben, D.H. (2013). *Community nutrition in action: An entrepreneurial approach* (6th ed.). Belmont, CA: Wadsworth, Cengage Learning.

Busch, F. (2000). *The new nutrition*. Hoboken, NJ: Wiley.

Caldwell, C.C. (2005). *Opportunities in nutrition careers*. New York: McGraw-Hill.

Civitello, L. (2003). *Cuisine and culture: A history of food and people*. New York: John Wiley & Sons.

Clark, R. (1990). *Our sustainable table...Essays*. San Francisco: North Point Press.

Commission on Dietetic Registration. (n.d.). *Certifications and licensure*. Retrieved from http://www.cdrnet.org/certifications

Duyff, R. L. (2002). *American Dietetic Association complete food and nutrition guide*. Hoboken, NJ: Wiley.

Eisman, G. (2006). *A basic course in vegetarian and vegan nutrition*. Watkins Glen, NY: Vegetarian and Vegan Association.

Ephron, N. (Director). (2009). *Julie & Julia* [Motion picture]. United States: Columbia Pictures.

Gabaccia, D. R. (1998). *We are what we eat: Ethnic food and the making of Americans*. Cambridge, MA: Harvard University Press.

Gladwell, M. (2001, March 9). The trouble with fries: Fast food is killing us, can it be fixed? *The New Yorker Magazine, 77*(2), 52-58.

Insel, P., Ross, D., & Elaine, R. (2003). *Discovering nutrition*. Boston: Jones and Bartlett.

Kittler, P., & Sucher, K. P. (2000). *Cultural foods: Traditions and trends*. Belmont, CA: Wadsworth/Thomas Learning.

Larson, R., Wiley, A., & Branscomb, K. (Eds.). (2006). *Family mealtime as a context of development and socialization*. San Francisco: Jossey-Bass.

McHughen, A. (2000). *Pandora's picnic basket: The potential and hazard of genetically modified foods*. Oxford: Oxford University Press.

Murphy, R. (Director). (2010). *Eat, pray, love* [Motion picture]. United States: Columbia Pictures.

Ninemeier, J.D., & Perdue, J. (2008). *Discovering hospitality and tourism: The world's greatest industry* (2nd ed.). Upper Saddle River, NJ: Pearson Prentice Hall.

Nottingham, S. (1998). *Eat your genes: How genetically modified food is entering our diet*. London: Zed Books.

Paine, A. (Ed.). (1935). *Mark Twain's notebook, prepared for publication with comments by Albert Bigelow Paine*. New York: Harper & Brothers.

Raeburn, P. (1995). *The last harvest: The genetic gamble that threatens to destroy American agriculture*. New York: Simon & Schuster.

Schlosser, E. (2001). *Fast food nation*. Boston: Houghton Mifflin.

Seltzer, B. (2011). *101 careers in public health*. New York: Springer.

Shelly, A. (Director). (2007). *Waitress* [Motion picture]. United States: Fox Searchlight Pictures.

Shils, M. (Ed.). (2006). *Modern nutrition in health and disease*. Philadelphia: Lippincott, Williams, & Wilkins.

Tillman, G. (Director). (1997). *Soul food* [Motion picture]. United States: Edmonds Entertainment.

Timberlake, L. (1987). *Only one Earth: Living for the future*. New York: Sterling.

Woolf, V. (1929). *A room of one's own*. New York: Harcourt, Brace.

Professional Journals and Trade Publications

Journal of Child Nutrition and Management

Journal of Food Science

Journal of Human Nutrition and Dietetics

Journal of the Academy of Nutrition and Dietetics

Journal of Nutrition Education and Behavior

Today's Dietitian

On the Internet

http://www.fda.gov—home of the U.S. Food and Drug Administration, which provides a wealth of information on food topics, especially food safety

http://www.cnpp.usda.gov—site of the U.S. Department of Agriculture, Center for Nutrition Policy and Promotion, which disseminates the Dietary Guidelines for Americans and other key nutrition education information

http://www.nutrition.gov—a portal to reliable nutrition information from government agencies

Chapter 7

Careers in Hospitality

After studying this chapter, you will be able to:

- analyze opportunities, challenges, and trends in the hospitality field.

- discuss the various career opportunities in the hospitality field.

- explain what academic training is needed to work in the hospitality industry.

- describe working conditions in the hospitality field.

This morning I was up at the crack of dawn. I like my guests to wake to the smell of fresh-brewed coffee and fresh-baked pastries. As I sat in the warm morning sun, I reflected on my choice of life work. As most bed-and-breakfast establishments usually are, my business is my home. It is located in a beautiful Northeast setting of trees, a creek, and mountain backdrop.

Running a bed-and-breakfast is really a labor of love, as most small hospitality business owners, like myself, work very long hours. However, running my own bed-and-breakfast has also been my dream for many years. Every day I meet new visitors, and as I say goodbye to new acquaintances, I know, many will be repeat guests.

When my guests wake this morning, I will give them a choice of breakfast in their rooms or breakfast at the family table. Conversation will usually center on my guests' plans for the day. They often ask for my advice on local tourist activities or local history. Most guests will then leave for the day to pursue their activities. A few will stay behind to read or relax. This is my time to

plan dinner, prepare rooms for incoming guests, shop for supplies, and oversee the housecleaning crew that I contract for hire. I have two part-time employees who monitor the desk during the day to take and confirm reservations. Another employee does the bookkeeping. I keep tabs on items to be ordered, customer complaints, and staff scheduling conflicts, all of which are taken care of during the day. I study the accounting records daily to stay on top of the financial situation. I must also find time to glance through tourism trade papers and websites, and I read the travel review section in the newspaper. I am frequently asked to donate a night's stay to local school auctions and other charity events. This is a good way to market our business to new customers.

I serve an evening meal for guests who choose the option of a home-cooked meal. Although it requires quite a bit more time and commitment from me, I really enjoy this aspect of my business. I love to cook and entertain, as well as meet new people. We chat over family-style meals. This is when I really connect with my customers and get to know them.

It is extremely important that I have exceptional name and face recollection. The most successful owners report the majority of their clientele are regular customers. The easiest way to gain repeat business is by offering special treatment. Remembering a customer's name, favorite room, food, or interests always impresses my guests. I act as a host, chatting with customers and making sure they are satisfied.

How did I prepare for my career? I graduated from college with a degree in hospitality management. During my college years, I also worked in a restaurant and had an internship with a catering company. After college, I worked in management for a national hotel chain. Between my college coursework, internship, and work experience, I gained a lot of knowledge about the hospitality industry.

It has been two years since I began my bed-and-breakfast venture, and the steep learning curve has started to level out. Word-of-mouth advertising, my networking with local business owners, plus a user-friendly website have given me one less thing to worry about. Most of my guests now come to me rather than me going out and drumming up business.

I am in charge of and responsible for every aspect of my business. If I take vacation time, I have to either close my business or leave it in the hands of someone I trust completely to maintain my high standards while maintaining a genuine interest in my guests and their welfare. Is this a lifetime career? I think so. For me, it is a perfect fit between my family life, my personal passions, skills, interests, and my love for people.

The beaches of Rio, the buildings of New York, the museums of London, the shops of Taipei, or the opera house of Sydney—the urge to see new and different places lures thousands of people to explore the world each year. Hotels, airlines, trains, cruise ships, food service establishments, retailers, tourist attractions, and cultural events all play a part in encouraging people to explore the world. For ease and efficiency, the travel and tourism, lodging, food service, recreation, and event and meeting management industries are often referred to simply as the hospitality industry, one of the largest industries in the world.

Novelist and poet Robert Louis Stevenson (1879) once said, "We are all travelers in the wilderness of this world, and the best we can find in our travels is an honest friend." The hospitality industry deals with complex issues that focus on providing a temporary "friend" for individuals and families. It involves much more than offering a decorated room, clean bed linens, and bath towels, or even serving a good meal. The hospitality industry serves to meet food, shelter, recreational, and other needs of people who are traveling. In a sense, hospitality vendors create a home away from home for travelers, even if it is only for an hour or two.

The Hospitality Field

Hospitality. The word itself conjures up images of comfort, friendliness, and feeling welcome. The **hospitality industry** is multifaceted and includes several major segments: food service, lodging, travel and tourism, recreation, and event and meeting management.

People have many different needs, interests, and preferences; and the hospitality industry attempts to provide products and services that honor diverse customer requests. Recently, a number of issues have emerged in the hospitality industry. The issues are complex and although the hospitality market continues to grow, it has been profoundly altered in the last decade by these changes. For example, travel agents or personal contacts used to be the norm for booking reservations. Today, many hospitality reservations are made using the Internet. As a result, a large number of industry careers were eliminated while new career paths flourished. In addition, many current concerns have grown out of lifestyle changes, globalization, and safety and security issues. Lifestyle changes, particularly those brought on by an aging population, have made a major impact on the hospitality industry as a whole.

Career Opportunities in Hospitality

Career opportunities in hospitality range from owning a restaurant or convention planning to catering or running a bed-and-breakfast. The hospitality industry offers careers with theme parks, cruise lines, restaurants, hotels, and resorts, just to name a few. The hospitality industry falls under the broad umbrella of family and consumer sciences because the industry

Issues in the News
Lifestyle Trends

Even after terrorist attacks, natural disasters, and financial failures, the hospitality industry continues to flourish. Why? Many observers attribute the growth to lifestyle trends that began after World War II, flourished in the 1980s, and continue today. Lifestyle trends affecting the hospitality industry include rising education levels, increasing age and early retirements, increases in disposable income, reduced leisure time, the economic contributions of women, and the proliferation of travel options.

After World War II, education levels began to rise in the United States and many other parts of the world. Women in particular entered colleges and universities at an unprecedented rate. Higher education levels stimulated curiosity about the world. At the same time, media and communication technology provided vivid images of distant places. This, too, piqued many people's curiosity. As a result, more people, especially the educated, began to travel to more exotic places.

As the average age in the United States and around the world began to climb, more people in their prime of life decided to travel. The baby boomers began to reach middle age and with their decreased parenting responsibilities, peak career income, and a desire to see the world, they began traveling more. Baby boomers have more free time than they had previously, and those with children choose to expose them to enriching experiences. As a result, heritage and cultural tourism is growing as families visit a community to learn more about history and their own heritage.

As more people entered the workforce over the past several decades, they earned more money and controlled more discretionary income. In families, women often make financial decisions, and they are more likely than men to support cultural and heritage activities (Cushner, 2004).

Many working people have less leisure time than did workers a generation or more ago. The average number of weeks worked per year by full-time employees in America has increased, and nonwork time is filled with commuting, family duties, and other responsibilities (Drago, 2007). Thus, the time spent away on vacation becomes more important and travelers often look for quality in their vacations. Quality can be interpreted many ways, such as by the accommodations, transportation, leisure activities available, or environment. Since many people take shorter trips or weekend escapes, they may maximize vacation experiences. In addition, concerns about exposure to the sun have made alternatives to time at a beach more interesting to travelers.Last, the proliferation of travel options has increased hospitality opportunities. When people arrive at their destination, they need food and lodging. Many travelers want to be entertained. Subsequently, the hospitality industry is flourishing in many parts of the world as a result of changing lifestyle trends.

focuses mainly on meeting basic human needs, including food and shelter, and it contributes to an improved quality of life. Typical careers in hospitality are listed in **Figure 7-1**. Career opportunities in the following areas will be explored:

- Food service
- Lodging
- Travel and tourism
- Recreation
- Event and meeting management

Sample Career Areas in Hospitality		
Banquet manager	Convention and visitors bureau director	Reservations supervisor
Bed-and-breakfast manager	Country club director	Resort owner/manager
Business travel specialist	Cruise director	Restaurant manager
Campground manager	Destination management specialist	Sales/marketing director
Casino manager	Director of catering	Theme park coordinator
Chef	Executive housekeeping manager	Tour broker
Concierge	Guest services manager	Travel writer
Convention/meeting manager	Hotel manager	Wedding or party planner

Figure 7-1 The hospitality field offers a variety of careers.

Food Service

The *food service industry* includes all the establishments that serve meals and snacks prepared outside the home. Generally, the food service industry can be divided into commercial and noncommercial ventures. *Commercial food service* includes food service establishments that prepare and serve food to the general public for profit. For example, full-service restaurants offer prepared meals that are served to customers. Quick-service restaurants and specialty food providers, catering services, and services provided by hotels, spas, and other recreational facilities are also considered commercial food service.

Noncommercial food service businesses provide food service within established organizations such as schools, hospitals, and other establishments. For example, a bookstore may have a coffee shop within the store that is run by another business entity. A sports stadium may have several food vendors offering food and beverage products within the stadium. (For information about noncommercial food service organizations, refer to Chapter 6.)

Food is a basic human need, and the food service industry supports this basic human need as well as providing a special experience because of the nature of the products, menu, ambience of the environment, or nature of customer service. Because it meets a basic need, the food service industry will always exist and the career possibilities will be plentiful. Careers in management, catering, and the culinary field will be explored here.

Restaurant Management

How many times during the last month have you eaten at a restaurant, cafeteria, dining hall, or coffee stand? Buying prepared foods is a way of life in the modern United States. In fact, you would probably find it difficult to determine exactly how many times you have purchased prepared foods such as a sandwich, a fruit smoothie, or a hamburger. At each of the food service establishments you visited, a food service manager was behind the scenes making sure the product you desired was served in a timely manner and appropriately hot or cold, fresh, and convenient.

Food service managers direct and coordinate the operations of businesses that prepare and serve food. Many opportunities for food service managers can be found in the private, public, for-profit, and not-for-profit sectors. For example, the United States military serves food to hundreds of thousands of military personnel each day.

Food service managers are responsible for the daily operations of restaurants and other food service establishments. Their work includes planning, organizing, completing, and evaluating food service functions. Food service managers oversee the inventory and ordering of food, equipment, and supplies. They are responsible for the care of equipment and facilities. Like managers of any large operation, administrative and human-resource responsibilities are an important part of their work. These responsibilities include recruiting and training new employees as well as monitoring employee performance. These duties are an important aspect of a food service manager's job, as restaurants tend to hire entry-level, transient workers.

In most full-service facilities, the management team consists of a general manager, one or more assistant managers, and an executive chef. In most hospitality venues, the *general manager* performs the administrative duties and provides general business oversight in assignments that include maintaining employee work records and payroll; completing paperwork to comply with licensing, tax, wage and hour, unemployment compensation, and Social Security laws; and maintaining, ordering, and paying for new equipment. The *assistant managers* deal with the everyday running of the facility and often work on the dining floor. Assistant managers interface with customers.

Catering

Wedding receptions, retirement parties, office lunches, and museum openings are just a few of the many occasions when caterers provide food for a gathering of people. *Catering* involves working to provide food and beverages for special occasions, one-time or infrequent events, or regularly scheduled events. For example, in the movie industry, catering companies provide regular on-location meals. All caterers work closely with their clients to design, prepare, and serve menus for the planned events. For instance, caterers provide menus and the clients select menu items and work with the caterer to assemble a meal where each dish complements the others. Caterers often work around a theme and almost always within budget constraints. Flower arrangements or other centerpieces and decorations, table linens, and serving pieces may also be a part of the total package offered by a caterer.

Catering is a people-oriented profession that requires culinary arts skills, strong interpersonal communication skills, and the ability to manage a cooking and serving staff. Successful caterers are able to guide clients to make decisions that will benefit their event. Since the majority of catering businesses are owner-run, caterers must also have business skills. They need to market their business, plan for profit and minimize loss, procure ingredients, and manage employee hiring, training, and evaluation. Because caterers have many tasks to oversee, businesses rarely grow large. In fact, most catering businesses employ fewer than six employees, and most of these workers are part-time.

For people who love to prepare food and serve it in an artistic manner, catering can provide a lucrative and creative career path. There are some "seasons," such as summer weddings and winter holidays, that are busier than others. Although there are no industry-specified educational requirements for becoming a caterer, there are food-handler permits that must be obtained and commercial food service guidelines that must be followed. A business license is also required. Specific requirements vary by region, and information can usually be obtained through the local health board. Culinary academies, food service experience, and business courses in finance, management, and accounting are also important to a successful catering business.

The Culinary Field

Do you watch cooking shows on television? Do you whip up culinary masterpieces for your friends and family? Do you visualize preparing food in a state-of-the-art kitchen with gleaming appliances, readily available fresh ingredients, and a team of sous-chefs waiting to follow your orders? Becoming an executive chef is a dream profession for many people. The popularity of

Professional Profile

Chief Executive Officer, Private City Clubs

Tom Goodenow
The Harbor Clubs Seattle & Bellevue WA

How did you get into your line of work?

While living on campus during college, I became active in the campus food service. I became more interested in food service and decided to combine it with my entrepreneurial spirit. As a result, I established a campus-wide concession operation. I became known as the campus "food guy," and even the college president enjoyed the hot dogs I cooked on a camp stove and sold at school football games. Upon graduation, I returned home to Honolulu to work for my dad's private detective firm as a private eye. While this profession was filled with much excitement, I missed interacting with people.

A few years later, the college president of my alma mater called. He told me he was on the board of directors for the 1974 World's Fair (Expo '74) to be held in Spokane, Washington. He asked if I wanted to be involved in planning the fair. I jumped at the chance. At Expo '74, I wore many hats, including being a consultant to the VIP Club.

I joined my college buddy and began building taco-themed Mexican restaurants in eastern Washington and northern Idaho. Fast food led to dinner-house restaurants and I became part owner of Casa Blanca Restaurant in Spokane. At the time, Casa Blanca was serving 800 dinners on Friday and Saturday nights. It became the highest sales volume restaurant in eastern Washington.

After Casa Blanca, I decided to do it on my own. In 1982, interest rates were 23 percent. I built Tom Foolery's Restaurant in Spokane. We filed for bankruptcy after two years of operation. This very tough experience taught me a great deal, and I became very numbers oriented. I also learned how to become a people-mentoring coach. This is a skill I now use daily as I operate three separate food service operations.

I moved to Seattle in 1983. Another former college classmate was the general manager of a tennis club. The club had not returned a profit in some 100 years in the food and beverage department. He was convinced I could turn around both the sales and operating numbers. After five years of growth in annual profits, I was asked to do the same at The Harbor Club in Seattle, Washington. The Harbor Club was struggling at the time as a downtown rooftop city club.

In November of 1988, I went to work as general manager of The Harbor Club. I quickly learned why others had rejected the notion of operating the club. I was faced with my first payroll and our checking account was on empty. What I failed to see was that in the week prior, the steam water boiler had blown and all cash went to repair the boiler. I quickly began calling members asking if I could stop by and collect their accounts we had just billed. From that humble beginning, we have added a third more square footage to Seattle Harbor Club, taken over another failed private club, and now we operate another formerly failing century-old club in Arizona. Recently, we opened an employee cafeteria for a financial institution.

What does your "typical" day entail?

In food service there is no typical day. As CEO, I find my workday starting quite early. We are open for three meals a day. I find approximately 50 percent of my day is spent in meetings. Approximately half of those are with key direct-report staff, and the remainder is with members and committees of the club. I have learned the skill of coaching. I view myself as a constant coach as the team I have assembled takes my constant direction as I empower them to make the "play." The food and beverage industry is always undergoing change. We must constantly reinvent our business model. While we have a tradition to follow in regard to our menus, facilities, and marketing, our team members must all adapt to our changing society. I am charged with directing this change.

How do you fulfill the mission of family and consumer sciences— that is, how does your work improve people's quality of life?

As the coach/manager, I take great pride in putting together a team and then mentoring the team with the goal of stretching and growing people's lives when possible. Eventually, it is my hope that I will send some of my team off to new opportunities. In my many years in the food and beverage industry, I have seen employees grow beyond our organization. Thanks to individual development, I have sent employees to other larger organizations (with more pay and responsibility). Our former catering team members have gone on to run Safeco Field, the Seattle Convention Center, and Seattle Westin Hotel Banquet Departments. The same can be said of taking current staff and moving them up to higher positions. For example, I have seen dishwashers move up to talented cooks, former cooks move up to chefs, servers to banquet managers, and a server to the position of general manager of a golf club.

Thanks to my position, I feel I touch the lives of many people on a daily basis. I have been blessed in my ability to mentor and coach and, therefore, influence the lives of many people for the better.

cooking shows on television perpetuates the ideal of the "flashy" chef. However, is it a real career, and is it feasible?

The answer is yes. There are many successful executive chefs around the world who find a high level of satisfaction in what they do. The *executive chef* is in charge of the menu planning and food preparation in a restaurant. Executive chefs are interested in the ingredients, aesthetic appeal, and nutritional content of the menu. They select menu items that appeal to customer tastes and preferences and work with the general manager to place food orders, check deliveries, and establish quality guidelines.

Executive chefs often work long and chaotic hours. They "pay their dues" as sous-chefs, catering managers, kitchen or banquet managers, pastry chefs, or as other culinary staff. During

Issues in the News
Security and Safety

Growing concerns over traveler safety and security have had profound effects on the hospitality industry. Many facets of the industry have been forced to change the way they conduct business in order to provide both real and perceived safety and security. For some parts of the industry, such as airlines, this has resulted in loss of revenue due to traveler fluctuations and the cost of making travel safe and secure. For passengers, this has added to the cost of travel through higher ticket prices. Safety and security are not just a financial concern of the hospitality industry service providers; they are also a concern of government.

Tourism and the subsequent hospitality industry provide great economic resources to most developed areas of the world. Loss of tourism translates into lost jobs.

When you travel domestically or abroad, the odds are in your favor that you will have a safe and incident-free trip. However, concerns for safety and security have escalated in most parts of the world. Crime, political unrest, and violence, as well as unexpected exposure to disease or natural disasters, happen to travelers in all parts of the world.

Disease
A traveler's risk of disease or illness cannot always be determined. For example, an outbreak of a particular strain of flu on a cruise ship may not be identified until after many travelers have become ill. However, the presence of disease outbreaks, such as malaria, at travel destinations can be noted and steps can be taken to prevent infection. Sources of information include the Centers for Disease Control (cdc.gov/travel/) and the World Health Organization (who.int/ith/en/). This information is important to travelers and hospitality industry professionals who help travelers plan their trips. For food service and lodging service providers that are located in areas of concern, marketing efforts assure customers of safe travel.

Local Crime
Local crime is a concern for many travelers. For the hospitality industry, it is a matter of concern for guests and the financial well-being of their establishment. Hospitality providers can supply information about the history, culture, customs, and politics of an area so guests can be informed about potential risks. Helping guests with transportation to and from local establishments and providing readily accessible addresses, phone numbers, and directions to and from their establishments can help insure safety. Hospitality providers can also provide safety officers and escorts for tourists. Local crime is a concern for marketing and sales, as negative publicity can greatly affect the tourist trade.

Natural Disasters
Natural disasters cannot be forecast. Hurricanes, tornadoes, earthquakes, tsunamis, and other unexpected natural

meal times, the pace can be fast and grueling. However, the work is creative, detailed, rewarding, and often provides a sense of community.

Lodging

Playwright George Bernard Shaw once said, "I have always said the great advantage of a hotel is that it's a refuge from home life" ("George Bernard Shaw," 2007). People traveling for business or leisure reasons look for a "home away from home" when they travel. A good meal, a comfortable bed, and attentive staff can go a long way toward making travelers feel at home.

Lodging employees work at all kinds of establishments. *Lodging* can take many forms that vary from hotels, motels, lodges, camps, inns, and bed-and-breakfasts to ranches, resorts,

disasters can deter tourist travel, cause unexpected delays, or require refunds or extra services. In the worst cases, lives are lost, facilities are destroyed, and lawsuits prevent further business ventures. Natural disasters always cause unexpected costs, but in the tourism industry, service providers must work with guests who are displaced from their homes and familiar resources.

Political Unrest

Political unrest may be easier to forecast than crime or natural disasters. Certainly political events can take hospitality enterprises by surprise, but more often, the political climate dictates events that affect tourist business.

In the United States, the Department of State issues travel warnings and public announcements. They can be obtained in both written and electronic form. Travel warnings are issued when the Department of State recommends deferral of travel by United States citizens to a country with which the United States has no diplomatic relations or when there is civil unrest, dangerous conditions, or known terrorist activity and, therefore, the United States government cannot assist travelers in need. Public announcements are used to get information to travelers early and quickly about immediate safety or security threats. Foreign embassies or consulates in the United States can also provide current information on countries.

Security Risks/Terrorism

The threat of terrorist activity is not new. However, for Americans, terrorism has become much more of a perceived threat following 9/11. Many service providers within the hospitality industry suffered financial setbacks from increased fear of travel, especially to international destinations. New security procedures at airports, hotels, and other locations have made travel more cumbersome and less carefree.

Terrorist acts occur at random, making it impossible for hospitality service providers to fully protect their guests and their businesses. Hospitality service providers establish precautions that provide some degree of protection and serve as deterrents to would-be terrorists. In the United States, the Department of State (travel.state.gov) provides emergency warnings regarding known or suspected terrorist activity.

Safety and security issues will always be present. Safety and security issues can range from poor sanitation procedures in a local restaurant to large-scale natural disasters. For example, if customers hear that a local food establishment may present health concerns, the business may lose its customer base even if the rumors are unfounded. Fear and concern, whether based on reality or perception, can devastate a business. The financial ramifications of these events continue to be of concern to hospitality service providers.

and cruise ships. They can meet minimal standards of shelter or provide amenities such as wireless Internet access, spa or recreational facilities, food service, a concierge, and business centers. Lodging employees have many different duties as well. They make sure that guests' needs are addressed and everything is kept in order. They may also provide services for business travelers, such as helping to arrange conferences and providing meeting rooms and electronic equipment.

The larger the organization, the more personnel it takes to run a smooth hospitality venture. Hospitality is a service-oriented industry, and the service is provided by people. In large hospitality organizations involving food and lodging, service may be provided by dozens or even hundreds of employees. For example, when you check into a hotel room, employees who are working to make your stay enjoyable include the management staff, front desk, bell staff, food service workers, housekeeping, recreational facilities workers, landscapers, and maintenance workers. Food service alone includes many employee roles such as hosts, food servers, room service staff, food preparation workers and cooks, dishwashers, table bus persons, and management. Additionally there are many auxiliary workers in marketing, sales, interior design, accounting, and procurement.

So who is running the house? In the lodging industry, *general managers* run hotels and resorts.

Issues in the News
International Travel and Globalization

A cruise around the world or a summer in Europe have been fodder for classic films and novels, as affluent and educated tourists have been interested in international travel for decades. Once available only to the very wealthy, international travel has become common among the middle- to upper-socioeconomic classes. Why has it increased and how has it changed?

There are several reasons why international travel has increased, including lifestyle changes, the global economy, and advances in global communications. International travel involves extended or lengthy trips less often than it did in the past. Today it frequently involves one- or two-week voyages. Transportation accommodations can be more comfortable, convenient, and much faster than in the past.

The rise of international tourism represents a tremendous opportunity to access the educated, affluent, and sophisticated consumer. These are the prized customers who can provide repeat business to hospitality providers. Thus, they have been targeted by creative packaging of services and marketing.

International travel marketing often promises experiences that will be life enhancing. Such experiences appeal to the more mature, wealthy, and educated consumer. For example, this consumer values traveling to a remote geographic area, interacting with the residents, and learning about the local culture. Tourism dollars may benefit the local economy and promote perpetuation of the culture. This is termed *sustainable tourism.*

Many communities are finding that developing sustainable tourism activities that share a similar philosophy of respect for the host region results in a joint preservation ethic between tourists, the hospitality providers, and the local culture. This includes respect for both the history and the people and may result in enhanced understanding and appreciation of the unique heritage of a community. This relationship makes the tourism activity sustainable because the needs of both the tourist and the locals are met while not depleting the culture and

They have overall responsibility for the operation of the hotel. This includes setting standards for guest services, housekeeping, interior decor, and food service. It also includes setting room rates, managing room availability, and reviewing and approving expenditures. Most hotels are a part of large corporate operations, and guidelines are established by the owners or executives of the chain. However, when it comes to everyday operations, it is the general manager who sets the tone for the lodging experience of the guests.

Some general managers live on-site and are available 24 hours a day. Most hotels, however, employ general managers along with night or assistant managers who cover the hours that the general manager is not working. Larger hotels employ front office managers who oversee the operations of the front desk and all interactions with guests from the time they make reservations until the time they check out of the hotel. They meet and greet customers when they arrive, assign rooms, deal with complaints, meet special needs or requests, and make adjustments to bills. Since front office managers cannot always be present, they are responsible for training assistant managers and/or staff.

The responsibilities of a hotel manager are great and varied. The larger the hotel is, the more activities included as management responsibilities. For example, personnel management or human resources, accounting, recreational facilities, spas and swimming pools, maintenance,

---

eliminating future tourism. *Ecotourism* is the term used to describe sustainable tourism when the focus is on learning about and preserving the natural environment.

The move toward a global economy also influences more international travel. When both strong and weak economies co-exist throughout the world, economic variability will promote travel to some areas and discourage travel to other areas. Depending on their home economy, the number of travelers from a geographic location will also vary. For example, if the economy in Asia is weak, fewer tourists from these countries may participate in international travel. On the other hand, a strong European market may send many tourists to Asian destinations. Also, as currencies become more easily interchangeable, tourists are more likely to travel between countries. Many European countries use the euro as their currency. Tourists traveling between these countries don't need to exchange one currency for another.

Variation in the price of medical care around the world has created a demand for *medical tourism*. Surgical procedures can be obtained in India, Thailand, or South Africa at 10 percent or less of the price in the United States or Europe. Consumers can even combine a face-lift with recovery at an international resort (Cetron, DeMicco, & Davies, 2010).

Last, advances in global communications have brought increasing awareness about the world and its many cultures. Potential tourists can read about international travel destinations, view photographs, search for up-to-date information on the Internet, and view video or television stories. With this increase in information, there is an increasing awareness of issues. Tourists can now travel armed with information about everything from the current local weather to aerial view maps.

For many reasons, tourists today are interested in life-enriching experiences. International travel provides an opportunity for these experiences. Because the target market provides a lucrative future for the hospitality industry, international travel will continue to grow.

marketing and sales, and security are all under the supervision of the general manager. Each of these areas provides specialized career opportunities within the lodging industry.

Travel and Tourism

A comfortable room, good food, and a helpful staff can make being away from home an enjoyable experience for both business travelers and those traveling for pleasure, adventure, or other reasons. In the past decade, travel and tourism has become the world's largest industry. By all indications, the industry will continue to grow. For example, globalization has made travel easier as communication systems have advanced, economic systems have changed, and knowledge about other cultures has increased. It has also opened a new facet of tourism that focuses on heritage or cultural travel.

The *travel and tourism industry* is much like the manufacturing industry in that it brings together many component parts to make a product. For example, transportation, meals, hotel rooms, tours, and entertainment are packaged together to form a "product" or "package." These packages are sold to consumers through travel agents, tour operators, Internet sites, and other service segments of the industry.

Travel agency employees arrange travel and/or vacations to a specific area and act as an intermediary between the client and the providers of tours, transportation, food service, and lodging. Some companies only deal with business travel, large tour groups, or individual travelers. They may also provide educational programs on topics such as methods of travel, passports, visas, foreign currency, and cultural customs.

Other hospitality careers exist with airline, cruise, and railway companies. Tour companies, resorts, and hotels also have hospitality employees in areas related to travel and tourism. Some large corporations employ their own business travel consultants. In addition, a growing industry exists in travel safety and security. Concerns about safety and security have been magnified and publicized by terrorist acts in recent years, and segments of tourism have suffered as a result of these concerns.

Recognizing the impact of tourism on the economy, government at all levels promotes the industry through destination management organizations. These organizations include, for example, city convention and visitors bureaus and state tourism offices. Employees market the region as a tourist destination, provide information about the area, facilitate development of new tourist attractions, and conduct research.

Recreation

Hiking, swimming, reading, shopping, playing soccer, drawing, and dancing are just a few of the endless recreational opportunities people pursue during their leisure time. The *recreation industry*, which focuses on recreational, leisure, sports, adventure, and cultural activities, is a fast-growing industry. As the population ages, more people may have time for leisure activities. This is good news for recreational professionals who base their careers on organizing and providing recreational activities for people.

Recreational workers provide people with opportunities for leisure time enjoyment. They arrange recreational programs, manage facilities, provide or staff instructional workshops, and oversee the general recreational programs—including advertising and registration. They often manage recreational facilities such as health clubs, city parks, swimming pools, and community centers. They hold a variety of positions at different levels of responsibility, varying from managers and directors to instructors, counselors, and recreational therapists. They also work in a variety of settings, including senior centers, hospitals, cruise ships, camps, and college campuses. Specialized training in an area, such as early childhood education, dance, athletic training, sports management, or a particular art, is often desired. Some jobs require teacher certification or management experience. A bachelor's degree and experience are preferred for most supervisory jobs and are required for administrative jobs in the recreation field.

Gaming is a form of recreation that has grown rapidly in recent years. The gaming industry includes casinos, horse and dog track racing, and combinations of the two called *racinos*. Casinos generally include lodging and food and beverage services, and they may offer live entertainment, retail shopping, health spas, convention services, and other amenities. In addition to the career opportunities offered by other hotels, casinos have specialized positions in operations, finance, security, and surveillance. Job titles include *manager of slot operations, manager of table games, director of casino operations, cage manager, credit manager, director of surveillance,* and *director of security.* Employees must have a clear understanding of the games that are offered, an ability to deal with a large number of customers in a fast-paced environment, and willingness to work nonstandard hours.

Event and Meeting Management

In the hospitality industry, an *event* is a special occurrence, and careers in event and meeting management are focused on making those special occasions successful and memorable. Events range from a child's birthday party to international conferences attended by thousands of people. They include conventions, weddings, festivals, fundraisers, award ceremonies, inaugurations, parades, and even the Olympics! Managing these events requires familiarity with the catering, lodging, and travel segments of the hospitality industry.

Event planners may work for an event planning company or as freelancers. Corporations, nonprofit organizations, government agencies, professional associations, and universities hire event planners, although their titles may differ. Planners meet with clients to understand the purpose of the event and determine the budget, time, location, and activities. They contract for services from vendors such as florists, photographers, and musicians and arrange for food service and lodging. Event planners who work for nonprofit organizations may solicit donations from supporters to maximize the profit made from fund-raising events.

Wedding planners are event planners who work directly for the bride and groom. Have you ever fantasized about a dream wedding? The wedding planner's challenge is to reconcile the dreams of the clients with financial realities. Wedding planners consult with the couple to plan the event and are present to troubleshoot activities on the actual wedding day. Job duties can include selecting venues and negotiating rentals, choosing music, booking musicians and photographers, planning menus and choosing caterers, renting equipment and overseeing the setup of tents and tables, contracting for security, and planning audio and lighting systems. Advising on invitations, floral arrangements, favors, and seating plans are other tasks. A wedding planner may need to arrange transportation and lodging for guests.

Wedding coordinators perform some of the same functions as wedding planners, but they are not employed by the bride or groom. They typically work for a hotel, banquet facility, or other wedding venue to communicate with the bridal couple and coordinate the services provided by the site. They liaise with outside vendors, such as florists, to ensure that this special occasion runs smoothly.

Convention service managers plan, coordinate, and implement events in hotels and convention centers. These events may include conferences, meetings, trade shows, weddings, anniversary or birthday celebrations, or other special events. Convention service managers have the same responsibilities as any event planner but generally on a much larger scale. They are responsible for the lodging, food, and activities of participants throughout their stay.

Convention service managers meet with their clients or group representatives to plan hotel lodging and meeting rooms to reserve, meals to serve, and configuration of rooms to meet the goals for the event. In doing so, it is important for the convention service manager and the group representatives to establish a clear picture of the event and what plans are in the realm of possibility. The convention service manager then offers a budget proposal to the group and negotiates the event plan, including menu choices, the number of expected attendees, meeting room configurations, and any special needs such as audiovisual equipment, local tours, or transportation.

During the meeting or event, convention services managers orchestrate the fine details such as transportation and accommodations of participants, facilities, catering, signage, displays, translation, audiovisual equipment, printing, and security. They monitor spending during the event to ensure it is staying within budget guidelines and constantly check and make sure the expectations of the group are being met and any problems are quickly resolved.

To be successful in the event and meeting management sector, you must have creativity, interpersonal skills, organizational and time management skills, good written and oral communication, attention to detail, and the ability to multitask and problem-solve in sometimes stressful situations.

Professional Profile

General Manager/Hotel Manager

William Mehalco
Hotel Indigo New York City – Chelsea

How did you get into your line of work?

My fascination with hotels began when my father took my brother and me to Walt Disney World when I was seven. All I wanted to do was stay in the hotel! I still remember inspecting a guestroom hallway for cleanliness. From that experience on, whenever I stayed in a hotel, I made it a point to walk the property and learn about how it functioned.

In college I was in the hospitality management major and decided to join the Hospitality Management Society (HMS). Joining the group allowed me to attend the International Hotel/Motel and Restaurant show in New York City. When I got out of the van, I felt the energy and opportunity in New York City that I remembered from the hotel in Disney World.

From joining the Hospitality Management Society, I learned that I needed to gain experience in the hotel industry while still a student and that I wanted to get to NYC. Through HMS I was able to network and obtain a job at a well-known hotel in my area. I worked as a bellman, and in engineering and housekeeping. With NYC in my dreams, I worked hard and would stay well after my shifts without pay to gain more experience. I was promoted to front desk agent, and once I graduated from college, I became front office manager. After two years as front office manager, while also traveling with the management company assisting other hotels, I decided it was time to take my chance at the Big Apple.

They say if you can make it in NYC you can make it anywhere. Well, to "make it" in NYC is the hardest thing I have ever experienced. People are extremely talented, tough, fast, smart, and eager to do whatever it takes to succeed. I worked in a couple hotels and slowly learned the tips and met the right people to get me through my first year. Then I got my chance to

Other Areas Related to Hospitality

The areas of human resources and marketing and sales perform vital roles in hospitality organizations. The opportunities are as varied as the types of organizations within the industry.

Human Resources

Human resources professionals increase an organization's competitive strengths by linking workforce trends and characteristics with the most effective methods for enhancing the productivity, motivation, and well-being of workers. In the hospitality industry, as in other industries, human resources managers:

- build effective work teams through careful hiring
- work to provide compensation and benefits
- consult about legal issues
- design and implement employee training and development

help open the Hotel Indigo New York City–Chelsea as front office manager. Through hard work I was promoted to assistant general manager after one year and a year later, I became the general manager.

What does your "typical" day entail?

In the hotel industry there is no typical day. My day is based upon employee relations and guests of the hotel. If you treat your employees fairly and take the time to listen to them, they will feel valued and create positive experiences for your guests. I like to go around and listen to employees, get involved in morning department meetings, check in/out a few guests at the front desk, check on the breakfast service, and talk to patrons. Employees seem to really respond positively to an active manager.

For the other 50 percent of the day, I spend time in our executive offices. I analyze revenues and expenses. I need to ensure the owner is pleased with the performance and that our franchise is satisfied with our corporate and hotel involvement. Because we are a boutique hotel, we have a small management team of eight people. This means I get personally involved in reservations, revenue management, sales, events, and marketing. Larger hotels have a manager and supervisor for each of these areas. I look at it as an advantage of knowing everything about the hotel and the industry.

How do you fulfill the mission of family and consumer sciences— that is, how does your work improve people's quality of life?

I have the opportunity to improve the lives of employees and guests. I hire staff that DO NOT want to be front desk agents or servers or bellmen all their lives. I hire them because they have an interest in hotels and people. I want them to gain something here that will prepare them for their next step, whether or not that is with my company.

Each employee has the opportunity to positively impact staff and guests. If a guest needs a sewing kit, it could be to sew a button on his/her suit, the suit which he/she wears to an interview, the interview in which he/she gets the job, the job which establishes his/her future, and so forth. This sounds like a stretch, but I have been around to see some powerful moments created by the staff I hired, staff that I genuinely care about. Together, our impact on our guests creates success which pays itself forward. When we do it right, we help change the world.

- advocate for labor relations

Large organizations within the hospitality industry attract employees with diverse skill levels, experience, languages, and ethnic and educational backgrounds. Small- and medium-sized organizations are realizing the need for qualified, talented workers, and human resources managers can help them acquire, train, and retain good staff.

Marketing and Sales

If people do not know about a food service establishment or lodging facility, how can they become customers of the business? The hospitality industry is competitive and requires careful design and implementation of marketing and sales programs directed to a target audience upon which their success depends. The target audiences may be consumers, travel agents, tourism promoters, stockholders, or potential clients. Sales and marketing managers in the hospitality industry often specialize in lodging or food service.

Careers in sales and marketing within the hospitality industry include corporate marketing and sales positions, restaurant and travel reviewers, travel journalists, advertising sales for travel publications, and public relations managers. *Sales and marketing managers* use a variety of media in their efforts to reach their target market. As in the past, word-of-mouth marketing is important because consumers make recommendations to other consumers, travel agents, and tour company operators. They share positive and negative experiences with one another, and professional reviewers write and publish their critiques.

Today, the Internet provides a wealth of information to consumers about food service and lodging providers. Consumers may now browse an almost infinite number of possibilities, and hospitality service providers must find innovative ways to stand out from the crowd. Many hospitality service providers have joined together to offer "package deals" that discount lodging, transportation, food, and tourist activities if booked together.

Preparing to Enter the Field of Hospitality

The hospitality industry demands workers who are energetic, flexible, creative, savvy, service oriented, and good problem solvers. All hospitality professionals must consider the needs of the customer. Good customer service is the key to success in this industry, and an ability to work with and serve diverse colleagues and customers is essential. Consider the academic training needs and working conditions discussed in the following sections and compare them to your own academic and work environment interests. Professional organizations can provide insight into the hospitality field. Several professional organizations, their websites, and descriptions are given in **Figure 7-2**.

What Training Is Needed?

The hospitality industry is a fun and exciting career field. However, competition for management positions is often keen. In prior years, many managers were promoted from existing staff. Some hotel and food service management personnel are still promoted to high-level positions based on experience rather than formal education. In hotels, it is helpful to possess experience or education in restaurant management because many hotel operations involve food service. However, hospitality management jobs frequently require candidates with college degrees. There are many university programs that prepare students for management positions within the hospitality industry, including hotel management, restaurant management, nutrition, marketing, or retail management. A liberal arts degree may be acceptable if the applicant has experience at a hotel, restaurant, or resort. Certification programs offered by professional organizations, such as the American Hotel and Lodging Association, the National Restaurant Association, or Club Managers Association of America, may distinguish you from other applicants.

Although advanced education is an asset and a requirement for some hospitality management

Professional Organizations Supporting the Hospitality Industry		
Professional Organization	**Web Address**	**Description**
American Culinary Federation	acfchefs.org	A professional association that provides education, apprenticeships, competitions, and certification for chefs.
American Gaming Association	americangaming.org	A trade association that promotes and lobbies on behalf of the commercial casino gaming industry.
American Hotel and Lodging Association	ahla.com	A comprehensive century-old professional organization that supports the hotel and lodging industry.
American Society of Travel Agents	asta.org	A large association of travel agents and related professionals that emphasizes education, training, and profitability.
Club Managers Association of America	cmaa.org	An organization intended for managers of city, military, country, athletic, faculty, golf, and yacht clubs.
Convention Industry Council	conventionindustry.org	A federation of organizations involved in the meetings, conventions, and exhibitions industry. It promotes the exchange of information and publicizes the economic impact of the industry.
Destination Marketing Association International	destinationmarketing.org	An organization that offers educational opportunities, certification, and other resources to convention and travel bureau professionals and students.
Global Business Travel Association	gbta.org	An organization for business and government travel and meeting managers and travel service providers.
Hospitality Sales and Marketing Association International	hsmai.org	An individual membership organization committed to growing sales for hotels and their partners.
International Council on Hotel, Restaurant, and Institutional Education	chrie.org	Provides programs and services to improve the quality of hospitality and tourism education at colleges and universities.
International Hotel and Restaurant Association	ih-ra.com	An international trade organization that promotes the hotel and restaurant industry and participates in public policy advocacy on a global scale.
Meeting Professionals International	mpiweb.org	An organization that provides professional development and networking opportunities for event and meeting managers.
National Restaurant Association	restaurant.org	A large, comprehensive trade association supporting the restaurant and food service industries.
Society for Foodservice Management	sfm-online.org	An organization that focuses on the needs of executives working in the food service industry.

Figure 7-2 Check out the websites of these professional hospitality organizations.

(Continued)

Professional Organizations Supporting the Hospitality Industry		
U.S. Travel Association	ustravel.org	An organization that represents all segments of the travel industry to promote travel in and to the U.S., advocate for the industry, and conduct research and economic analysis.
United Nations World Tourism Organization	unwto.org	A specialized organization of the United Nations focusing on global tourism policy issues. It promotes sustainable, responsible, and accessible tourism, especially in developing countries.
World Travel & Tourism Council	wttc.org	An exclusive professional organization comprising top executives from 100 of the leading travel and tourism companies.

Figure 7-2 Continued.

positions, experience is also critical. Practical experience is extremely important in order to learn about as many functions of the organization as possible. In many hospitality management degree programs, one or more internship experiences are required. Also, nonmanagement industry experience can offer practical knowledge of the hotel or food service industry. Internships, employment, and volunteering also offer opportunities for networking and can significantly increase job opportunities. There are many opportunities for students to volunteer to coordinate campus events or work with community organizations.

Career possibilities are abundant for those holding a two-year (associate) degree as well. These include manager and assistant manager positions in both the food and lodging industry as well as culinary arts positions. Corporate-level positions usually require a baccalaureate or graduate degree.

Many culinary schools offer the training needed in this competitive field. However, success in the field also requires a person to gain experience and learn not only culinary skills but also basic skills needed to run a successful business.

Although there are many culinary schools across the nation and around the world, the American Culinary Federation certifies only a few that meet their high standards. The American Culinary Federation and other organizations serve as sources of industry information in the field.

Some family and consumer sciences programs in colleges and universities offer reciprocal programs that allow students to complete some course requirements at culinary schools. Because it is becoming more difficult to become an executive chef, both education and talent are encouraged in this field. Specialization in a certain ethnic cuisine or a certain type of food, such as pastries, is also beneficial.

Because there is so much diversity in the size, focus, and scope of hospitality organizations, career paths vary greatly. For example, entry-level positions in large hotel chains generally include trainees who wish to be assistant managers. Many hotels have training programs for employees that involve rotation through all operations of the hotel. Hotels that don't offer training value employees with experience. Smaller establishments usually do more on-the-job training.

The hospitality industry also requires certain personal skills. These include the desire to serve others and to seek their best interests and comfort. Qualifications of a manager include the ability to coordinate the work of many people, paying attention to detail while considering the "big picture," and skill in quick problem solving. Although hospitality professionals provide a product or a service, they work with people. This necessitates good communication skills and a genuine interest in meeting the needs of diverse people.

What Are the Working Conditions?

The hospitality industry is a service industry, and services rendered are often provided face-to-face. Thus, the working conditions often include long hours, especially during peak times of the day, week, and year. Work hours are filled with personal interactions. So much human interaction can occur that hospitality managers experience stress and need to get away from demands of the work environment.

Food service managers are among the first to arrive in the morning and the last to leave at night. Chefs and caterers spend hours planning and securing inventory and then preparing and serving food during peak dining hours. Peak dining hours are most often during midday and evenings. Noncommercial food service professionals work more traditional hours because school cafeterias, office cafeterias, and establishments located within traditional venues have limited daytime and early evening hours.

Food service requires a high level of teamwork and flexibility during peak business hours. This results in a high-energy environment that promotes creativity. Food service professionals should be friendly, service oriented, and willing to do what it takes to provide high-quality customer service. They should also be calm and able to work through "emergencies." Food service professionals use their knowledge to coordinate a wide range of activities and staff. When concerns arise, managers solve the problem with minimal disturbance to customers. Dealing with irate customers or uncooperative employees can be stressful, and an effective food service manager has excellent conflict resolution skills.

The lodging industry is similar to the food service industry in several ways. First, being a service industry, it must meet the needs of guests. Hotels are open 24 hours a day, and guests may arrive or leave at all hours of the day and night, seven days a week. Thus, long hours and careful planning for peak business periods are common. Managers tend to have more regular hours if the establishment is large enough to have assistant managers. For small business ventures such as independent hotels, inns, and bed-and-breakfast establishments, it is more difficult to schedule regular hours. The lodging work environment is also similar to food service in that it requires creative and flexible problem solvers who can resolve conflicts in a timely manner.

Professionals in the event and meeting management field also must be prepared to work nonstandard hours. Many special events, such as weddings, take place on weekends. Meeting the needs of demanding clients and tending to many details can be stressful. Most wedding planners are self-employed, and they need business management skills such as marketing and bookkeeping if they are to be successful.

Summary

The hospitality industry is one of the largest industries in the world, and its overall growth continues worldwide. Although it is growing, it has been affected by outside forces that include globalization, changing lifestyle trends, and safety and security concerns. Factors that have caused changes in the hospitality industry include terrorist attacks and international conflicts. In addition, technological changes in communication and transportation have altered the way business is conducted and the way people travel. The aging population has changed the profile of typical tourists and their desired services and destinations.

The hospitality industry includes five major segments: food service, lodging, travel and tourism, recreation, and event and meeting management. Hospitality fields are known for workforce and customer diversity, and many management opportunities exist. In the food service industry, careers include management and catering. In the lodging industry, positions include those in management and conference services. Event managers and tourism professionals often need to be familiar with both food service and lodging operations. One of the growing areas in recreation is gaming, and gaming venues also provide food service and lodging. There are many marketing and human resources positions in hospitality fields. A college degree and related work experience best prepare you for a position in hospitality management.

How can you know if a career in this field is right for you? Evaluate your strengths, weaknesses, skills, and interests in the field of hospitality. If you are considering a career in the field, contemplate increasing your knowledge of the profession by observing people in their work environment or by studying opportunities in the field. Even if you decide that hospitality is not a career path for you, the exercises/activities will give you an appreciation for the importance of excellent customer service, meeting the needs of people away from home, and fulfilling plans for a special occasion.

Pursuing a Career in Hospitality

1. **Interview a professional.** The hospitality field offers an array of professional opportunities. To get a practical view of the daily workings, interview a professional in your chosen field. For example, interview a commercial food service manager at your university, the executive chef at a restaurant, a hotel manager at a five-star hotel, a restaurant reviewer for your local newspaper, or an entrepreneur of a small bed-and-breakfast or inn. Ask the person how she or he entered the field, what the advantages and disadvantages are, and what a typical day entails. Be sure to solicit advice for your career decision making. What personal qualities are needed to be successful in the field?

2. **Shadow a professional.** Seek permission to shadow a hospitality industry professional. Often, you can arrange this through your university. The more you observe, the more you will become familiar with this diverse and complex industry. Observations could range from a few hours to several days. Internships, part-time and summer employment, and volunteer experiences also will help you decide if hospitality management is the field for you.

3. **Become acquainted with professional organizations.** Professional organizations provide a wealth of industry information since their mission is to educate and support professionals. They also provide relevant industry research and review innovations. Many professional organizations include job placement services for prospective employers and employees. Generally, they do not try to sell anything to members. Look up each of the websites listed in Figure 7-2. Do they provide opportunities to students, such as student memberships, internships, scholarships, or competitions?

4. **Become acquainted with professional publications.** Review recent issues of journals in your field, selecting from the list at the end of the chapter. What are current topics of interest in hospitality management? How can these publications be useful to you as a student and in the future?

Questions for Thought

1. Access the United States Department of Labor, Bureau of Labor Statistics website. Choose two related career profiles listed here and report on the career description, typical working conditions, job outlook, and expected earnings:
   - caterer
   - chef
   - restaurateur

2. Review major trends that are described in Chapter 4. How do you predict these changes will affect the hospitality industry?

3. Have safety and security concerns in recent years changed your views about travel? Do you know anyone who will not travel due to safety or security concerns? What do you believe will be the long-term effects of these terrorism and safety concerns on the hospitality industry?

4. Consider your best experience as a guest at a lodging facility such as a hotel or inn. What made this experience superior? How much of your positive evaluation was based on interactions or services provided by employees?

5. Describe your most memorable negative food service experience. Could the serving staff, chef, or food service manager have done anything to change your outlook on the experience? How would you change the experience to make it positive?

References and Resources

Burns, J.B. (2010). *Career opportunities in travel and hospitality.* New York: Ferguson.

Butler, R.W., & Russell, R.A. (Eds.). (2010). *Giants of tourism.* Cambridge, MA: CABI.

Cady, S., & Aron, C. (1999). *Working at play: A history of vacations in the United States.* New York: Oxford.

Centers for Disease Control. (2012). *Traveler's health.* Retrieved from http:www.cdc.gov/travel

Cetron, M. J., DeMicco, F., & Davies, O. (2010). *Hospitality 2015: The future of hospitality and travel.* Lansing, MI: American Hotel & Lodging Educational Institute.

Columbus, G. (2011). *The complete guide to careers in special events: Step toward success!* Hoboken, NJ: Wiley.

Cushner, K. (2004). *Beyond tourism: A practical guide to meaningful educational travel.* Lanham, MD: Scarecrow Education.

Drago, R.W. (2007). *Striking a balance: Work, family, life.* Boston, MA: Economic Affairs Bureau, Inc.

Eberts, M., Brothers, L., & Gisler, A. (2006). *Careers in travel, tourism & hospitality.* New York: McGraw-Hill.

Fenich, G. G. (2012). *Meetings, expositions, events, and conventions: An introduction to the industry.* Upper Saddle River, NJ: Pearson Prentice Hall.

Hall, K., & Schulz, C. (2011). *Career launcher: Hospitality.* New York: Ferguson.

Hamilton, D.C. (2009). *Love what you do: Building a career in the culinary industry.* New York: iUniverse.

Hettner, K. (2012, July 19). *With global instability, who wants to be a tourist?* Retrieved from http://www.cnn.com/2012.07/19/travel/travel-violence-tourists/index.html?hpt=tr_c2

Institute for Career Research. (2004). *Careers in hotel, motel & resort management: Hospitality industry executives.* Chicago: Institute for Career Research.

Martin, J. (2006). *Global business etiquette: A guide to international communication and customs.* Westport, CT: Praeger.

Ninemeier, J.D., & Perdue, J. (2008). *Discovering hospitality and tourism: The world's greatest industry* (2nd ed.). Upper Saddle River, NJ: Pearson Prentice Hall.

Reynolds, J. (2004). *Hospitality services.* Tinley Park, IL: Goodheart-Willcox.

Richards, G., & Hall, D. (2000). *Tourism and sustainable community development.* London: Routledge.

Shea, L.J. (2009). *Pioneers of the hospitality industry: Lessons from leaders, innovators and visionaries* (Vol.1). Richmond, VA: International CHRIE.

Smilow, R., & McBride, A.E. (2010). *Culinary careers: How to get your dream job in food with advice from top culinary professionals.* New York: Clarkson Potter.

Smith, V. (1989). *Hosts and guests: The anthropology of tourism.* Philadelphia: University of Pennsylvania.

Stevens, C. A., Murphy, J.F., Allen, L.R., & Sheffield, E.A. (2010). *A career with meaning: Recreation, parks, sport management, hospitality, and tourism.* Champaign, IL: Sagamore Publishing.

Stevenson, R. (1879). *Travel with a donkey in the Cevennes.* Retrieved on January 12, 2007, from http://robert-louis-stevenson.classic-literature.co.uk/travels-with-a-donkey-in-the-cevennes

Swatos, W. (Ed.). (2006). *On the road to being there: Studies in pilgrimage and tourism in late modernity.* Boston: Brill.

Torpey, E.M. (2006-2007, Winter). Jobs in weddings and funerals: Working with the betrothed and the bereaved. *Occupational Outlook Quarterly*, 30-45.

Torpey, E.M. (2010-11, Winter). Working vacations: Jobs in tourism and leisure. *Occupational Outlook Quarterly*, 2-11.

U.S. Department of Labor, Bureau of Labor Statistics. (2012–13). Meeting, convention, and event planners. In *Occupational outlook handbook*. Retrieved from http://www.bls.gov/ooh/business-and-financial/meeting-convention-and-event-planners.htm

U.S. Department of State. (2012). *Worldwide caution*. Retrieved from http://www.travel.state.gov

Walker, J.R., & Walker, J.T. (2012). *Exploring the hospitality industry*. Upper Saddle River, NJ: Pearson Prentice Hall.

Williams, C. (1998). *Travel culture: Essays on what makes us go*. Westport, CT: Praeger.

World Health Organization. (2012). *International travel and health*. Retrieved from http://www.who.int/ith/en/

Professional Journals and Trade Publications

Club Management

Cornell Hospitality Quarterly

International Journal of Hospitality and Tourism Administration

International Journal of Contemporary Hospitality Management

Journal of Hospitality and Tourism Research

Journal of Travel Research

Lodging Magazine

Nation's Restaurant News

On the Internet

http://www.hospitalitynet.org—A comprehensive guide to the hospitality industry with links to industry news, professional associations, job opportunities, publications, market reports, and educational programs

http://www.tourismcares.org/scholarships—Information about scholarships for travel, tourism, or hospitality students

Chapter 8

Careers in Textiles and Apparel

After studying this chapter, you will be able to:

- analyze contemporary opportunities, trends, and challenges in the field of textiles and apparel.

- discuss various career opportunities in the textiles and apparel field.

- explain what academic training is needed to work in the textiles and apparel industry.

- describe working conditions in the textiles and apparel field.

Here was my fantasy when I was a kid: I would grow up, go to college, become a wildly successful fashion designer, go to elegant parties every night, and at the end of my Paris fashion show, I would walk down the runway to rave reviews. Well, I am a fashion designer. I do consider myself successful. Perhaps not successful in the way I fantasized about in the days of my youth, but I work with a great team of highly creative, talented people. Together, we put out some pretty amazing apparel for an upscale, trendy men's line. My clothes may not be on Paris runways, but I will say it is a pretty amazing feeling to walk into a store and see our clothes on display. It is even better when I see a guy at a party wearing something I designed. We are successful. Last year, the company sales figures beat our previous year's record. Our company name has become synonymous with hip, trendy men.

When I was a kid fantasizing about being a fashion designer, I had no idea how involved the apparel design process is. It is a process

that occurs during all my waking hours, maybe even my sleeping hours! In my mind, I am always coming up with a new idea. For example, when I walk down the streets I notice unique colors and textures, new ways of combining things, and interesting patterns. Sometimes I will notice something as small as a seam on a shirt. Seeing a new fabric can inspire a whole new line of apparel. Often, I am mentally working on a couple hundred different ideas. They do not all come to fruition, but I am always thinking about possible new designs. I usually sketch my ideas, but the designs that I pursue seriously are drawn using a computer. In menswear, we do technical style drawings that are very detailed. Because menswear does not dramatically change form from year to year—a button-down shirt is a button-down shirt—I find my inspiration in fabrics and trimmings.

So where do I find interesting fabrics and trimmings? I shop a lot. I look and see what is currently on the market and forecast what may come next. Our company subscribes to a menswear fashion forecasting organization that sends styling trends and fabric forecasts to us each season. I talk to fabric vendors. Sometimes, I work with a textile designer to turn an idea or concept into custom-designed fabric print. A fabric converter then prints the fabric.

Fashion design is not just about coming up with great ideas. It is also about taking the idea to completion. I assist our pattern drafters in making sample patterns. I also work with our manufacturers in producing a sample of my design. Since we work with overseas sample manufacturers, communicating my idea can be challenging due to cultural and language differences. Communicating ideas involves more than pictures. Written and verbal descriptions are critical, too. Only after the sample is completed do I really know whether or not our communication was clear. I fine-tune the design and make sure the fit is correct. When my team of designers, the company merchandisers, and company executives are satisfied, we go into production. I wish it were always that smooth, but as in other creative endeavors, there are often setbacks and readjustments.

I do have my fantasy job. It is hard to imagine myself in any other line of work. I know I love being an apparel designer because I never stop thinking about the next great shirt. All it takes is a new color, a really interesting texture, or a great button found in some quaint little retail shop and I am off and running again. Oh, and by the way, there have been some great parties along the way!

There is ample evidence to support the notion that fashion and beauty are important to people. Apparel is far more than a body covering. Apparel is fashion and fashion is a powerful cultural and economic influence in developed and developing societies. It is an important tool of communication. Both senders and receivers use it as an effective medium of nonverbal messages. A person's appearance has an effect on that person's self-esteem, body image, perceptions of others, family and religious values, and group participation. Strong markets exist for functional and fashionable apparel.

The Textiles and Apparel Field

Because fashion is such a powerful cultural and economic influence, the economic interests of manufacturers and advertisers have been important. However, it is highly unlikely these would have been successful unless their message and products met a receptive audience. Beauty not only sells, it pays. This chapter will familiarize you with the historical development of clothing from handmade and homemade to manufactured global fashion. It will also explore

the fundamental material resource of textiles and apparel. In addition, the chapter will outline potential career opportunities for professionals and future trends of the industry.

From go-go boots to leisure suits, each historical period boasts new methods of attaining beauty and acceptance. Why? Caring about clothing and the human body is a basic human urge—as basic as building shelter. That is what makes clothing one of the basic human needs. However, apparel goes far beyond covering the human body and protecting it from the environment. When apparel frequently changes based on social, psychological, and economic factors, it is termed *fashion*. Fashion encompasses the latest and most admired styles of apparel and appearance.

Apparel speaks and generations listen. In the 1950s, poodle skirts and blue jeans were popular among teenagers. Teens were a newly recognized population group in America who gained prominence due to their sheer numbers. With their prominence came buying power. The young, sassy poodle skirt and unconventional blue jeans showcased the youth and energy of the baby boomer generation.

In the early 1960s, women across America idolized the look of Jackie Kennedy. She symbolized the hopefulness of the new decade with her simple, glamorous, feminine apparel. In the 1970s, bright colors, floral prints, and flamboyant jewelry in men's apparel symbolized the blurring gender lines promoted by the women's liberation movement. It symbolically demonstrated the move from conventional to unconventional. Men's apparel became more fashion-oriented than it had been in centuries.

Fashion is all around us. It is no coincidence that fashion is inspired and influenced by societal trends. In this chapter, the field of textiles and apparel will be discussed. The business segment that focuses on the conception, production, marketing, and sales of textile and apparel products is called the *fashion industry* or *apparel trade*. This chapter explores fashion careers and presents trends, opportunities, and issues related to fashion careers. In addition, basic questions such as what skills you will need in the fashion industry, what a typical day involves, and what the working conditions are like will be answered.

Career Opportunities in Textiles and Apparel

From fiber technology to fashion journalism, the fashion industry provides a wealth of job opportunities. Many are in retail sales, along with a smaller portion in apparel production and textile manufacturing. In the following section, the three main categories of fashion careers are explored: the textile industry, the apparel industry, and retail marketing and promotion. Career opportunities in each major segment of the fashion industry are highlighted. Typical careers in the textiles and apparel field are listed in **Figure 8-1**.

The Textile Industry

Textile fabrics are essential in meeting the basic needs of apparel and shelter. Fabrics used in clothing keep us warm or cool; protect us from impact, chemicals, and other environmental hazards; symbolically communicate who we are; and enhance our performance, both physically and psychologically. In our shelters, we use fabrics on the floors of our homes, offices, places of worship, and places of business. We use fabrics to cover furniture in our homes and places of work, as well as in our vehicles and airplanes. Protective textiles are used to guard against biomedical hazards. Fabric may be functional as well as fashionable, and its uses are endless.

Textile fabrics bring both beauty and comfort to our world. From warm bath towels to sleek evening gowns, fashion design and home furnishings would not have their appeal without beautiful and functional fabrics. Textiles are the primary material for creating fashion. In fact, many fashion designers use fabric as their starting point in the design process.

The *textile industry* is both an agricultural industry and a chemical industry. For example, cotton and flax (linen) are fibers that are grown and harvested from plants. Wool and silk are also natural fibers, but they are cultivated from animal sources. Polyester, acrylics, and nylon are just a few of the dozens of synthetic fibers that are produced in chemistry laboratories. The diverse nature of the agriculture and chemical industries that create and manufacture textile products makes the textile industry complex.

The textile industry brings scientists and artists together. Scientists are often employed at the fiber stage, especially in synthetic fiber production. Also, they are employed in the agricultural

Sample Careers in the Textiles and Apparel Industry		
Accessories designer	Fashion photographer	Sales representative
Account executive	Fashion publicist	Showroom manager
Ad copywriter	Manufacturing manager	Store planner
Apparel designer	Merchandiser	Stylist
Art director	Pattern maker	Technical designer
Boutique owner	Product developer	Textile colorist
Buyer	Product manager	Textile designer
Costume preservationist	Research scientist	Trend forecaster
Fashion editor	Retail analyst	Visual merchandiser
Fashion illustrator	Retail manager	Wardrobe consultant

Figure 8-1 The field of textiles and apparel offers exciting career opportunities.

sector in producing natural fibers. Scientists are also employed as chemical and industrial engineers in the manufacturing of textile goods. Artists are employed in the textile industry as textile designers. Finally, production managers are needed to oversee the manufacturing process of textiles. The main categories of the textile industry will be covered in this section. These categories include textile science, textile design, textile product manufacturing management, and textile sales and marketing.

Textile Science

Textile scientists work to improve the competitive edge of companies. They problem-solve ways to apply research, improve manufacturing technology, and introduce new and improved textile products. To achieve these results, textile scientists must understand the physical, chemical, and engineering properties of textile materials. They apply knowledge to various textile end-uses such as geotextiles used for road and land construction, biomedical materials used in medicine, advanced engineering composites used in building, and protective apparel used in various hazardous situations. They can also apply textile research to traditional apparel and interiors products.

Textile scientists study textiles from raw materials through manufacturing and finishing

Issues in the News
Sustainable Textiles

Producing textiles is hard on the environment. Traditional methods of producing natural agricultural fibers, such as cotton, require large amounts of pesticides and subsequent cleaning products that are released into the environment. Synthetic fiber production uses petroleum-based ingredients to produce products that can last for hundreds of years. Used clothing may be donated and given a second use by others, but eventually it must be discarded. Also, what happens to the millions of yards of carpeting that is disposed of when carpet is replaced? Most of it goes into landfills. These are complex problems that have taken years of continued research and development to explore and find potential solutions. Environmentally friendly textiles are safe, use recycled and/or safely biodegradable materials, and implement safe manufacturing processes. Environmentally friendly products are called **sustainable textiles**.

Textile fiber producers and fabric manufacturers have been working on creating sustainable fibers and fabrics. Creating sustainable or environmentally friendly textiles has been an important focus of both the agricultural and the chemical or synthetic segment of the textile industry.

Cotton fiber producers have been experimenting with new methods of producing cotton since the late 1980s. Like organic food producers, organic cotton growers began as small, privately owned niche-market businesses, but over the years they have gained momentum and have increased sales. Cotton sold as "organic" must be grown according to the federal guidelines for organic crop production. This means crops must be rotated and not grown repeatedly in the same soil. Synthetic pesticides and fertilizers may not be used. Insects must be controlled by natural means. For example, natural predators, rather than chemicals, are used to control pests. Although synthetic pesticides are not used, a growing number of biopesticides are available. Organic cotton fabrics must also use environmentally friendly methods of fabric production, coloring, and finishing. Organic proponents cite many advantages to organic fiber production, including preservation of soil and lower

of fabrics as related to durability, comfort, care, and aesthetics. They must be knowledgeable about natural and manufactured fibers, yarns, fabric construction, dyes, and finishes. They provide the means to compare fabrics that compete with each other in a specific product market through fabric testing and specifications. This is done by establishing relevant fabric testing procedures used by regulatory agencies in government as well as private testing institutions.

Textile Design

Textile design is the art of creating or changing the appearance of a fabric. The aesthetic qualities of fabrics attract us even before fabric serviceability is considered. *Textile designers* are concerned with both the structural and the surface design of fabrics. Because these two are so technically different, however, textile designers usually specialize in structural or surface design. For example, a designer may specialize in woven-in designs or a knit-in pattern. This is considered structural design. Surface designers focus on applied surface designs. For example, a textile surface designer creates a design for placing a pigment print on the top surface of a fabric that is already constructed. Polka-dots, paisleys, and floral prints are a few examples of textile surface designs. A textile designer who creates a variety of different color combinations

risks to humans and animals from chemical exposure.

Organic sheep and wool production has also been on the leading edge of organic regulations. It is also very similar to organic food production, specifically meat production. For instance, in order for their wool to be certified organic, sheep must not be fed hormones, and antibiotics may not be used on the animals. However, vaccines are acceptable. Chemical sprays for insects are not used since they could leave residues in the wool.

Producing sustainable synthetic fibers is very different from producing organic agricultural textiles. Fibers from plant or animal sources may be organically produced, but synthetic fibers are produced in chemical plants. However, today's synthetic textile fibers are more environmentally friendly than ever before. Some are made from recycled materials. For example, polyester can be made from many materials, including recycled soda bottles. Other synthetic textiles are made from postindustrial waste. That is, instead of being discarded, excess material left over from the manufacturing process is reprocessed into new fibers.

Once fibers are produced, they can be made into environmentally friendly fabrics. For example, wool fabrics may be shredded and rewoven into new fabrics. Polyester can be made into chemical chips that are then made into new fibers. Manufacturing waste by-products can be recycled or made with more environmentally friendly ingredients.

Disposal of waste products is also a concern that is receiving attention. Some manufacturers are working to create affordable and fashionable fabrics that are "closed-loop." Closed-loop means the fabric is 100 percent biodegradable, including fibers, fabric, dyes, and any chemicals that are a part of the fabric as well as every by-product of the manufacturing process.

New environmentally friendly textiles are designed for a wide variety of applications, from trendy high fashion apparel to commercial grade carpeting. Textiles are a fashion product, and producers are always looking for ways to offer sustainable textiles in a wide range of colors, patterns, and textures.

for a design is called a *colorist*. Textile surface designers both create and oversee the production of surface prints. They accomplish this task much like the apparel designer does, but computers, as a design tool, figure even more prominently in textile design.

Since textile design takes place earlier in the whole apparel manufacturing process, textile designers must be skilled in forecasting colors and trends. They must possess a good business sense, textile knowledge, and technical skills. The actual printing process is done by the fabric converter, a fast-paced, fashion-oriented segment of the textile industry devoted to printing and finishing fabrics.

Textile Product Manufacturing Management

The raw materials of textile manufacturing must go through many processes before they

Issues in the News
Textile Trade Issues

Since so many countries around the world participate in textile production, establishing trade issue agreement guidelines has been difficult. Not only is the textile industry vast, it varies greatly. For example, silk produced in China is a very labor-intensive agricultural product. Nylon produced in the United States, on the other hand, is a chemically derived product. These examples only involve fiber production. Yarn production, fabric construction, and fabric dyes and finishes are other large and varied segments of the textile industry.

Between the early 1960s and 2004, the textile trade was governed by various international agreements that established quotas limiting the importation of textile products into countries whose textile trade was threatened by the imports. For example, at one time the United States cotton industry was threatened by less-expensive cotton fibers from other countries that had lower labor costs. (Cotton is a traditionally labor-intensive fiber to produce.) Quotas were established that limited the amount of cotton fiber that could be imported into the United States, thus protecting the livelihood of cotton growers in the United States.

The World Trade Organization (WTO) is an international organization that deals with the rules of trade between nations. As a global organization, the goal of the WTO is to help producers of consumer goods, such as textiles and apparel, do business in the global export and import marketplace. They do this through lobbying for and establishing agreements between nations. The goal is to help producers, exporters, and importers of goods and services conduct their business. Beginning in 2005, the quotas came to an end, and under WTO agreements, importing countries could no longer discriminate against some exporting countries. This move will continue to have a profound and far-reaching effect on textile trade over the upcoming years. To soften the effect, the WTO established a 10-year plan to gradually phase in the new agreement. This gradual phasing-in began in 1994. There are, of course, both proponents and opponents of the new agreements. Some believe this move will unjustly discriminate against disadvantaged countries. Others believe that the new agreement will offer more opportunity to developing countries. On either side, concerns about the preservation of domestic industry and economic ramifications are weighed against concerns for the global economy, economic equity, and human rights to livelihood.

become finished fabrics. Natural fibers such as cotton and wool must be processed, and synthetic materials must be formed into fibers. From there, fibers may be spun or formed into yarns. Fabrics are constructed by weaving, knitting, or any number of other fabric construction methods. Finally, fabrics are colored and finished. Each step in the process may be performed by a different segment of the industry or, in the case of integrated corporations, one company performs all manufacturing processes from start to finish.

The textile industry is labor intensive and although it relies heavily on technology, most employees in the textile industry are directly involved in production. Textile production management involves the administration of the textile manufacturing process. This can involve research and development, implementation of automated systems, product development, quality control, environmental supervision, industrial engineering, sales support, personnel supervision, and overall plant management. Sound business management and accounting skills must be combined with technical knowledge and skills for successful textile production management to occur.

Textile Sales and Marketing

It isn't enough to make high-quality, fashionable and serviceable fabrics. They must also be made available to users. Textile sales and marketing must happen at all stages of the textile manufacturing process. For example, manufacturers of synthetic fibers must foster sales by making their product known to potential consumers. In the natural fiber markets, several promotional agencies exist that market the benefits of the fiber to users. Cotton, Inc. is one example. This organization may be familiar to you from their prolific advertising campaign proclaiming cotton as the "fabric of our lives." Fibers are sold to textile mills that produce yarns and fabrics. They may then be sold to converters. Fabrics are then sold to retailers and designers and/or manufacturers of home furnishings and apparel. At each stage of the process, textile products must be advertised, promoted, and sold to potential consumers.

There are many career opportunities in sales and marketing in the textile industry. *Textile market analysts* research the market for future trends and forecast future supply and demand of particular fibers and fabrics. They analyze sales data from competing companies and advise their clients on future trends. *Textile sales representatives* serve their clients by showing their fabric line to designers at the beginning of each season and whenever new fabrics are added. Sometimes, textile production companies employ salespeople directly. Other times, independent representatives sell one or more company's product lines to consumers.

The Apparel Industry

From design inspiration to finished fashion apparel, the *apparel industry* is responsible for the conception through the final production of fashion apparel. In this segment of the industry, apparel designers create clothing that will meet the needs of consumers, and manufacturers produce apparel that meets the functional, fashion, and financial desires and constraints of consumers. Although the designing of apparel is very creative, it is also very technical and requires precision and technical know-how. It also requires technical understanding of textiles and other materials and the human body upon which the apparel must fit and move. The production of apparel requires business savvy, skilled construction techniques, and manufacturing expertise. In this section, major career categories of the apparel industry are highlighted.

Women's fashion is the backbone of the fashion industry. Female teens and women consume more clothing and spend a higher percentage of their personal income on apparel than male teens and men do. Since money talks, the women's fashion industry has listened and responded by exploding into every small niche market imaginable. It is easiest to understand this large and complex segment of the industry by breaking it into large categories or divisions.

Professional Profile

Designer, Men's Woven Shirts

Marine Matson
Reunion Menswear

How did you get into your line of work?

My education gave me the perfect foundation for the work I do today. When I began college, I was unsure of a major. I was interested in so many areas, including the French language. Because I was in an honors program that did not have as many general education requirements, I was able to enroll in various courses that interested me. During my freshman year, I took a textiles class. I was intrigued. Next, I tried an apparel design course. I was hooked. I took every course I could in apparel design, and before I knew it, I was well on my way to completing a degree in fashion design.

Although I learned a lot in my courses, one of the most valuable parts of education was learning to network with my professors and industry professionals. My professors often invited guest speakers into our classes, and we went on many field trips. One guest speaker was a "headhunter" for the apparel industry. I got up the nerve to introduce myself, to submit my résumé, and to interview with her. By the time I had graduated, I had landed my first job as a design assistant for a major retail store. This was a big opportunity for me, but it also required great risk. My new employer was located in another state. I had to move myself to a new city, begin a new job, and develop a new social network as a brand-new graduate.

I learned a lot in my first industry job. I also learned I really missed the city I had left. I persisted in my job, however, and dedicated myself to learning as much about the fashion industry as possible. I wanted to have as many skills as possible to offer future employers.

The traditional division breakdown for women's apparel includes the apparel type or category, price range, and styling.

Until the latter half of the 1900s, women's fashion changed much faster than men's fashion. For decades, men wore somber colors, the mainstay of business wear. Fashion underwent very few changes and younger men dressed just like older men. During the 1960s, long hair, psychedelic color palettes, flowered shirts, and unisex apparel came on the scene. By the 1970s, the creative influence of forward-thinking designers created a renaissance in men's fashion that

has continued throughout the decades since. Men's fashion became brighter, changed faster, and provided a different look for the younger male. In the past few decades, the move has been toward a more casual appearance.

Following World War II, the baby boom generation caused the children's clothing market to expand. But the children's market of the late 1940s and the 1950s did not compare with the children's market that resulted from baby boomers coming of age and having their own children. In the 1980s, stereotypical young urban professionals (yuppies) were interested in dressing

After a year, I began looking for a new job in my home state. I was interested in one particular apparel company. When I contacted them, there were no job openings. I persisted. Finally, I picked up and moved home. The next day I called the company's human resources department again and inquired about a job opening. I was told a temporary position was available if I could start the next day. I did, and my "temporary" job soon became a permanent position. The moral to this story is to be persistent. Since then, I have changed jobs to the one I enjoy today. Again, networking was the way I found my job.

What does your "typical" day entail?

The fashion industry is very people-oriented, fast-paced, and creative. Because of this, a lot of communication happens during my typical day. I send and receive a lot of e-mail, especially with manufacturing contacts in Hong Kong. I meet with my other design team members to consult, review, plan, and critique our work. I also review and approve samples of handlooms, lab dips for color, and strike offs.

The creative part of my day is working on CAD patterns and experimenting with different woven shirt color ways. I design shirt silhouettes and, in general, let my creative juices flow. The creative work is tempered by creating line lists, specifications, and other detailed data.

How do you fulfill the mission of FCS—that is, how does your work improve people's quality of life?

This seems fairly straightforward with the clothing business. Everyone (or almost everyone) wears some form of clothing every day of his or her life. Sometimes people wear multiple outfits during a single day. Not only is apparel important as a form of protection from the elements, it is a form of self-expression. The clothing I design is middle-market; affordable, yet fashionable.

---

their children in the most up-to-date, fashionable clothing possible. Children's clothing became a status symbol. This was a new phenomenon. In the past, teenagers and adults typically chose clothing to convey status and prestige, but only a small percentage of children were dressed to display status for their wealthy parents. In the 1980s, showing status through clothing was no longer just for the wealthy. Because of marketing efforts that targeted youth, children became more status conscious and began to desire specific brands or labels of clothing. Many apparel manufacturers and retailers, such as The Gap,

began producing children's clothing lines that mimicked teen and adult fashions. The children's clothing market expanded rapidly, subdividing into many categories. The children's wear market is both creative and complex. The large number of sizes and size categories necessitated by the rapid growth of children and the large number of price and style levels lead to many subcategories of children's clothing. In addition, the consumer of children's clothing depends on the child's age, gender, and price level of the clothing. Sometimes the child is the decision maker in clothing choices. At other times, and certainly in infant and toddler clothing, an adult is the decision maker. Also, children's clothing is more often a gift purchase than adult clothing is.

Apparel Design

A common assumption about fashion designers is that they spend their days sketching designs or draping fabric over dress forms until the perfect garment emerges. This is a simplistic view of their work. Today, designers frequently use computers to draw their designs, especially in the ready-to-wear garment industry. Before any designing occurs, however, designers must keep up-to-date with fashion trends. Watching fashion on the streets, shopping retail stores, keeping up with international fashion trends, and scanning reports from fashion forecasters are important activities for all designers. If a designer cannot predict what the customer will want to wear in the upcoming season, there is little chance for success. After all, the purpose of apparel design is to provide clothing to meet customer needs.

Apparel design is the segment of the apparel industry that conceives and creates garments. *Apparel designers* are involved in many daily tasks. They may be involved in cutting and sewing sample garments as well as selecting fabrics, trimmings, and notions for their designs. Other activities include selling their design line (collection of related designs) to company merchandisers, working with manufacturing and production managers, and collecting sales data.

Designers are creative people who can turn their imaginative ideas into actual products. They need technical skills to produce designs through hand-sketching or using computers, create technical specifications, and understand the techniques and tools necessary to produce a garment. They must possess knowledge of textiles in order to select the most serviceable materials for the garments they design. Lastly, they must be able to communicate their ideas to others.

In addition to creative and technical skills, apparel designers must also possess business skills. Creative designs that do not sell well cannot be tolerated over the long term if a designer is to be successful in the fashion field. Understanding price points, supply and demand, fashion timing and cycles, and wholesale and retail accounting practices are some of the business skills needed by fashion apparel designers.

Most designers specialize in a particular type of clothing or accessory. For example, junior sportswear, children's sleepwear, misses' sweaters, or young men's jeans are just a few of the seemingly endless specialty markets. Other specialty markets include designing uniforms for medical, military, or law enforcement personnel or sports teams. Theater, opera, and dance companies employ resident designers. Generally, each specialty area becomes more defined with smaller niche markets. Well-defined niche markets allow designers to closely monitor the ever-changing needs of their consumers.

Many clothing items, especially private-label (store brand) merchandise, are actually designed by *product developers*. Product developers, rather than creating original design ideas, modify successful and popular designs to meet a specific customer niche. For example, a product developer may create a simpler version of a popular design using less expensive materials so that it can be sold by mass retailers at a low price point.

Apparel Production

Models skimming down Paris runways, celebrities viewing new fashions from front-row seats, lights, cameras, and beautiful avant-garde fashions—these are the images most people conjure up when the apparel design and manufacturing industry is mentioned. Producing fashion garments seems like an unattainable dream to many—one that is beyond the scope of reality. Although Paris haute couture (high fashion) does represent a small segment of the fashion industry, most apparel manufacturers create the clothing that people wear every day. From jeans to sweatshirts, prom dresses to back-to-school skirts, and business suits to outdoor wear, most designers and manufacturers create fashions for "ordinary" people of varied ages and income levels.

Fashion is always changing, and the clothing that was worn by teens last year is unlikely be the trend this year. Other markets may change trends less quickly, but most consumer markets do succumb to design trends. Clothing is one of the quickest changing design products. It involves the lowest monetary investment when compared to other design products, such as those used in interiors, appliances, transportation, and housing. Apparel designers and manufacturers are always looking ahead, forecasting fashions that will appeal to consumers, and creating trends that reflect the changing values, moods, and ideologies of society.

Apparel Production Management

After a garment is designed, it must be produced. Skilled workers who specialize in cutting and marking fabric, pattern drafting, sewing, and quality control all form the team to produce apparel products. Apparel production forms the largest segment of the fashion industry worldwide, and most developed countries have some apparel manufacturing industry. *Apparel production management* involves the administration of all aspects of the apparel manufacturing process from start to finish. Apparel production management includes skilled supervisors, plant managers, and general managers of manufacturing plants. In the case of overseas production, it involves the management and coordination of contract manufacturers, a job that is similar to a general contractor in the building construction industry. Apparel production managers must know the ins and outs of the entire production process. For example, if a man's shirt is to be made, they must understand and orchestrate its production from sourcing fabric through cutting, sewing, and final pressing. They strive to produce high-quality, cost-effective, timely apparel.

Managers are savvy in problem solving, communication techniques, technical knowledge, manufacturing systems, and personnel issues. Because apparel production processes rely heavily on technology, managers must be knowledgeable about manufacturing machinery and computer software. They must also understand and apply economic and marketing principles to consumer and industry issues in the global economy.

Wholesale and Manufacturing Merchandisers

Fashion merchandisers in the wholesale and/or manufacturing field are involved in every stage of the apparel manufacturing process. They begin by researching fashion trends, studying the needs and specifications of retail buyers, and communicating with designers about their source of inspiration. They advise apparel designers on trends, secure fabric samples, and assist in securing design samples. They follow the production process through from beginning to end and are responsible for making sure merchandise is delivered to retailers in a timely fashion.

Fashion merchandisers may also be independent of any manufacturing company. For example, wholesale representatives carry one or more lines of clothing and sell them to retail buyers. Generally, they specialize in a fashion category such as children's sportswear. *Wholesale representatives* attend trade shows and fashion markets, and they sell their lines one-on-one. Independent sales representatives are often self-employed and manufacturers pay them a sales commission.

Wholesale merchandising is a fast-paced, demanding career that offers great variety and flexibility. It demands great organizational skills and an ability to sell. Fashion merchandisers must possess both the heart (passion) and the mind (business skills) of the fashion industry.

Retail Marketing and Promotion

After clothing is made, it must be sold. Retail marketing and promotion concerns itself with the marketing, distribution, and selling of clothing. Without this component of the fashion industry, apparel would sit in warehouses gathering dust. Traditionally, clothing manufacturers sold to retailer stores who, in turn, sold to customers. This is still the way the majority of apparel is sold. Today, however, online retailing, outlet stores, catalog shopping, and television shopping also play a major role in the marketing, distribution, and promotion of fashion apparel. In this section, major categories of retail marketing and promotion are highlighted. It should be noted, however, that a variety of career opportunities exist in fashion marketing and promotion outside the realm of the traditional retail store.

Fashion Merchandising

Earlier in this chapter, we began with the notion that a good idea only goes so far. The idea must become a tangible product that can be sold to consumers. Between the designer and the consumer, however, *fashion merchandisers* perform the duties of marketing and selling the product. *Fashion merchandising* is the umbrella term used for the business side of fashion. It involves the buying and selling of fashion, product development, retail management, and fashion marketing. Fashion merchandising is a fast-paced, energetic, and ever-changing field that offers many opportunities to hard-working, creative individuals who have a good business sense.

Retail fashion merchandisers are the point persons for ensuring the right apparel products are in the right store at the right time. They know which trends are coming and how much of an impact a design trend may have on potential sales. Will it be a short fad or a long-term

---

Issues in the News
Retail Trends

Shopping. Some people love it. Some people hate it. Fashion is trendy, timely, and constantly changing. Consumer spending drives the economy. Being aware of trends in consumer spending can help pinpoint areas of growth in the industry, where jobs may be most plentiful.

Methods of getting goods to consumers have changed in many ways during the past several decades. First, smaller and more traditional retailers have been replaced or threatened by the large mass merchandisers. Large discount stores and large specialty retailers have made it difficult for smaller stores and traditional department stores to compete against these dominant retailers. Second, since electronic retailing became available to consumers in the 1990s, sales through this medium have risen at astronomical rates. Although many traditional retailers also offer online shopping services, the electronic trend has continued to jeopardize the sales of traditional retailers.

In the early days of electronic commerce, sales of clothing lagged behind other product categories. Potential buyers wanted to try on items for fit because there is no standard sizing in the industry. Some e-tailers responded to this concern by providing free return shipping. Additionally, new advances in body-scanning technology are making it easier for customers to order the correct size. A consumer can now step into a booth at a shopping mall and have her or his body scanned with radio waves. In just 10 minutes, the consumer receives a printout identifying her or his size in several different brands. The service, supported by the brands, is free to customers. A similar technology is being used to create customized sewing patterns for the home sewer.

Electronic retailing has expanded to reach consumers through mobile devices and social networking sites. A customer can take a picture of a scannable code on a print advertisement or store shelf and be linked to the company's website for information and

fashion direction? How much inventory should be devoted to each product category and within each category? How much floor space and money should be designated toward basic apparel items, and how much should be designated toward trendy items? Merchandisers plan inventory stock levels and monitor the sales performance of clothing lines and even individual items. They decide where money should be spent and how many lines should be purchased. They monitor the delivery and distribution of stock. If inventory arrives early, the merchandiser must decide where to store it and when it should appear on the store's sales floor. If inventory is delivered late, the merchandiser must problem-solve with the supplier. Sometimes this involves negotiating discount rates. When a particular item does not sell well, the fashion merchandiser may choose to mark down the retail price in order to move the merchandise off the retail floor. Retail fashion merchandisers are always thinking of the bottom line—how to maximize profits.

Retail Buying

Are retail buyers just professional shoppers? Yes and no. Retail buyers do shop for their target customer niche, but they do more than just pick out fashionable clothing. *Retail buyers* work with fashion merchandisers to select fashion apparel that will meet the needs of their target customer base, establish an image identity for their department or store, and most importantly, increase revenue. To do so, they must select apparel their customers will want to purchase.

services. Retailers use Facebook and other networking sites as a cost-effective strategy to communicate with customers (Stall-Meadows, 2011). Technology has also created a demand for new fashion products, such as cell phone cases, e-reader covers, and laptop sleeves.

Another area where consumer demand is growing is in the plus-size market. Two-thirds of Americans are overweight or obese, and the numbers are expected to increase (Dor, Ferguson, Langwith, & Tan, 2010). Overweight individuals face many challenges, including finding fashionable clothing that fits.

The growth of private-label merchandise, also known as *store-brand merchandise*, is another trend. Consumers like to buy brand names they recognize. Brand recognition has always enhanced traditional retail sales. Discount and mass retailers have found, however, that buying brand-name products can be expensive. To counteract costs, retailers at all price levels began developing their own branded merchandise. The store-brand merchandise is advantageous to both the consumer and retailer. For the consumer, store-brand merchandise can offer the same quality as national brands at a lower cost. For retailers, it can offer a higher profit margin. As a result, store brands continue to grow.

People are becoming more conscious of the effects of their purchases on the environment and on other species. This awareness has led to increased demands for a variety of green or vegan products, such as better synthetic furs, clothing made from unbleached fibers, vegan shoes, and reduced or recyclable packaging.

Changes in technology, demographics, and customer values will continue to influence the future of retailing, and retailers must continue to find ways to meet consumer needs in a changing business climate.

Retail buyers work within the parameters established by the retail fashion merchandiser. This is called a merchandise plan. The retail buyer selects and purchases apparel goods from manufacturing sales representatives. Retail buyers must work within an established budget and must be prepared for unexpected changes in the market. For example, an unexpected heat wave may greatly increase the demand for swimwear. An unexpected fall in employment may make it difficult to move career clothing or, in the case of widespread unemployment, any clothing at all that is not considered a necessity. A description of the types, sizes, prices, and quantities of merchandise that will be selected is called a *buying plan*. Math and analytical skills are very important along with a strong sense of fashion. They must also have knowledge of textile product serviceability, know product quality indicators, and be very familiar with the likes and dislikes of their target customers.

Retail Management

"Who is minding the store?" This has become a common phrase in everyday English language. The phrase stems from the idea that every business needs one person to be responsible for the daily business activities of that organization. It means, "Who's paying attention?" or

---

Professional Profile

Co-Founder and Chief Executive Officer, Retired

Joe Boldan
ExOfficio, Inc.

How did you get into your line of work?

How many people dream of owning an apparel company? I have learned many people may have this dream, but that they also believe it is not possible or at least a very unlikely dream to materialize. In college, I never fathomed that I would one day work in the apparel business, but here I am today, the retired co-founder and CEO of a successful company that designs, manufactures, and markets outdoor and adventure travel apparel to retailers throughout the United States and internationally.

After I graduated from college, I followed two former college roommates to San Francisco. One was pursuing a law degree, while the other worked for a major clothing retailer. The latter friend encouraged me to apply for employment where he worked. Since I had no retail experience, he counseled me to be enthusiastic about retailing being a "fast-paced, ever-changing, and people-oriented business." When I interviewed for a position in the executive training program, I told my interviewer exactly that. Plus, I finished my interview with an enthusiastic "and I am a people person!" Thus began my career in fashion.

I definitely enjoyed my years in the fashion industry. I moved from retail sales and management to retail merchandising as a young men's fashion buyer. My experience varied from large corporate department stores to small manufacturing and wholesale. In the mid-1980s, I decided I was ready to start my own company. In 1989, my business partner and I were asked to knock off a fly-fishing shirt. We quickly noticed there was a void in outdoor

"Who knows what is going on?" In most retail stores around the world, there is at least one manager who runs the store.

The retail industry provides fashion goods and services directly to customers. Managers are needed to ensure customers get prompt service and quality goods. This means they have total responsibility over all aspects of the daily functioning of the store. This includes managing stock, reviewing inventory and sales records, developing merchandising plans, and coordinating sales promotions. On a larger scale, they manage the physical facilities of the store, security and loss prevention programs, and general operating procedures. They handle customer complaints and inquiries. They also supervise employees and are responsible for hiring, interviewing, training, and staffing. In larger stores, they manage supervisors and department managers. In short, *retail managers* are responsible for the entire operation of their store.

Managers are needed at all levels of the retail fashion industry, from department managers to regional and division managers. At all levels, managers are responsible for the daily functioning as well as the long-range planning of their group. Most importantly, the manager is ultimately responsible for the sales profit margin.

apparel for people who were willing to spend a lot of money on fly-fishing and outdoor travel adventures. We recognized a niche in the marketplace, a "reason for being," and the ExOfficio Company was born.

What did your "typical" day entail?

As the CEO of a growing company, I spent the majority of my time helping to build the authenticity of our brand, making sure all aspects of the company were legally protected, developing plans to fund our company's rapid growth, and dealing with situations that would come up on a moment's notice.

Looking back at our company, I'm most proud of the business culture my partner and I created. Our goal was to create a culture of respect. My role as an employer was also that of a teacher. In order for our associates to be passionate about what they did, we needed to treat them with respect and instill genuine passion for the product we offered to consumers.

Running a company certainly doesn't come without mistakes. Once I retired, one of the most important things I learned was how to understand the difference between passion and emotion. Emotion drives us and comes from a negative, insecure environment within ourselves. Passion is something we drive and it is almost entirely secure and positive in nature!

How do you fulfill the mission of family and consumer sciences—that is, how does your work improve people's quality of life?

As a CEO, my work directly affected the quality of the life of my associates and customers. Our job was to provide the very best product that met the needs of our customers. It did not matter whether or not the clothing fit my "personal style," but whether we were offering an authentic product to the customer we served. It was also important the company extolled the values of our associates. For example, ExOfficio helps humanitarian agencies by donating clothing every year to people in need. The company also outfits medical relief teams that provide medical and dental aid throughout the world. In addition, the company donates product for annual fundraising events for several organizations. Through product sales that meet our customer needs and humanitarian aid, the fashion industry can improve quality of life for families and individuals.

Visual Merchandising

For every store mannequin, display rack, or window dressing that captures your eye, a successful visual merchandiser is behind it. *Visual merchandisers* work to put the merchandise in front of consumers, capturing the consumer's attention through skillful manipulation of color, texture, light, sound, and styles. They promote retail sales through visual means and are responsible for the overall "look" of the store. This is done in collaboration with the retail fashion merchandisers, the buyers, and store management.

Visual merchandising includes window and interior store displays, placement of posters, signage on clothing racks and rounders, wall displays, seasonal store displays, and media used to capture attention. For example, in juniors and young men's departments, videos are often used to showcase merchandise or to create a desired atmosphere. Visual merchandisers are always thinking and planning ahead to upcoming seasons and promotional events. They must be very artistic and conceptual. They must also have well-honed communication skills so their artistic vision is conveyed to those who will implement it.

Professional Profile

Merchandise/Store Planner

Jessica Plutt
Dots, LLC

How did you get into your line of work?

While in high school, I spent my evenings and weekends working in a local jewelry store. This first experience in retail left me wanting to learn more about the business, which led me to major in merchandising in college. While taking merchandising classes, I learned about the options available to graduates. It seemed as if I was destined to be a buyer. It was not until I came across a position describing many of the concepts that I learned in my coursework, such as creating assortment plans, forecasting sales, and positioning product in stores, that I knew I was meant to be a planner. A role in the world of planning and allocation would allow me to be close to the product, which I love, but also allowed me to utilize my analytical skills in order to drive sales. Beginning as an allocator, I learned more about the business and how to position product by store. This led to a role as store planner, which built on my strengths of analyzing the business at the store level. I have now been given the opportunity to learn the business from the product perspective as a merchandise/store planner. Not only am I able to evaluate store-level performance, but I am also able to review product selling in order to deliver the best-selling styles to the stores.

What did your "typical" day entail?

One great aspect of working in retail is the fact that each day is different. Every day has its own challenges and rewards; however, there are specific tasks that must be accomplished in order to drive the business, which is the main priority of a merchandise planner, store planner, or allocator. Much of my role requires significant interaction with the merchant team. A typical day

Fashion Forecasting

Have you ever wondered who decides which new fashions are around the corner? People often refer to an anonymous group of people—*"they* have decided olive green will be in next year"—that decides the next fashion trend. Fashion forecasters are the "they" who *forecast,* not dictate, the upcoming fashion trends. They are the eyes and ears of the fashion industry. Which colors and fabrics will attract consumers' attention next year? What styles will interest them? Fashion forecasters answer these questions for the textile and apparel manufacturing industry.

Fashion forecasters review significant social developments, political events, economic trends, and weather changes to determine what consumers will demand in clothing in the future. They convey trends through forecasting publications, subscription websites, and training seminars. In making predictions, fashion forecasters take a risk. Effective fashion forecasters provide an extremely valuable service to textile manufacturers, apparel producers, and retailers. Manufacturers and retailers put a considerable investment into decisions, and if a forecaster can help them to invest in the right trends, there is potential for a lucrative financial payoff.

begins by analyzing the prior day's sales. I then complete the total weekly sales projections for my specific product category. These actions allow me to determine opportunity or risk in each product category, which I can then relay to the buyer to take further action. In addition, we decide and plan the product promotions that take place throughout the year, such as a back-to-school sale or a holiday sale in December. All areas of opportunity and risk as well as promotions are then entered into the financial plan to be reviewed in a monthly meeting.

I also plan the sales and inventory levels for all stores within my product category. These store forecasts are used by the allocators to place product by store in order to support the store's sales volume. These forecasts are also used to create assortment plans. These outline the choices that the buyers can purchase each month for their product category. Once a month, the buyers and planners meet to discuss the choices and make the final choices for the stores.

Another part of the product life cycle is markdowns. I determine which products should be marked down in order to allow for new product to take its place on the sales floor. These decisions are based on product sell-through, sales turn, and timing. All markdowns must be in compliance with a monthly markdown budget.

How do you fulfill the mission of family and consumer sciences—that is, how does your work improve people's quality of life?

By planning and allocating the appropriate assortment by store, I help women easily obtain fashion at a reasonable price. In the past, women would become disappointed and feel defeated because they were unable to locate the styling they prefer in their size. Because part of my role involves analyzing size selling, we are able to provide the appropriate assortment by size, so that the women shopping will have a more enjoyable shopping experience. Advances in planning have allowed better placement of product by size in order to improve customer satisfaction

Fashion Journalism

What are the latest shoe styles for the season? Are pants going to be straight-legged or flared? What is the "must have" color? Which colors are out of fashion? Consumers want to know the trends in fashion. In fact, browsing the Internet or a magazine stand may lead you to believe Americans, in particular, are obsessed with knowing about fashion trends. They want to see it, read about it, and get it for themselves. *Fashion journalists* disseminate information about beauty and fashion trends for consumers. Since fashion is an artifact of societal trends, fashion journalists act, in a sense, as "contemporary archaeologists." They tell us what is in, what is out, what to expect, and what is appropriate or not appropriate in beauty and fashion.

Traditionally, fashion journalists wrote articles for beauty magazines and newspapers such as *Glamour, InStyle, Essence, GQ, People, Seventeen, YM, Women's Wear Daily (WWD)*, and *Vogue*. Today, the possible media for fashion journalists has exploded. Internet articles, blogs, and websites, e-mail and e-bulletins, tweets, podcasts, television, and videos are all used to relay fashion and beauty trends and advice. Media forms are blending. For example, a "magalogue" is a website that is part catalogue and part fashion magazine, allowing the consumer to read about fashion news and buy items from the same site.

Fashion journalists have many titles. Editors plan publications and assign stories. Market editors are responsible for communicating the latest information about a particular fashion segment, such as accessories or beauty. Sittings editors coordinate the fashion photography for a story, booking the models and photographers. Editors are a major influence on what becomes popular. Copywriters create material for catalogs, Internet shopping sites, and other forms of advertising.

Fashion Styling

A *stylist* chooses clothing and accessories to create a desired image. Fashion stylists may have different titles, depending on the work setting. A celebrity stylist helps clients dress to communicate an image in the media. An image consultant is similar to a stylist. An image consultant, however, may work with a client only once to facilitate a wardrobe makeover. Image consultants also work with noncelebrity clients, such as business executives who need to select appropriate clothing to advance their careers. Personal shoppers at major fashion retailers perform similar functions for their regular clients, keeping track of their wardrobes and helping them select clothing for each new season, event, or travel destination.

Stylists may also choose the clothing and accessories for characters in television shows, advertisements, or films. The fashion editor at a magazine is the publication's chief stylist, creating the visual image. A retailer may use the term *artistic director* or *creative director* to describe the person responsible for the overall "look" of the store's merchandise. *Fashion publicists*, who may work for design houses or public relations firms, try to influence celebrities to wear their clients' new designs. Stylists and publicists often have a background in fashion journalism, and there is a recent trend of stylists evolving into designers.

Historic Costume Preservation

Although fashion is forward-thinking, it can also give tremendous insight into the present and the past. As an artifact, clothing offers tangible clues about the wearer and the society in which he or she lived. Thus, preservation of historic clothing is important for maintaining a useful and valuable historic record. *Historic costume preservationists* care for antique textiles and clothing so they can be maintained for years of enjoyment in exhibitions, museums, libraries, and other historic or educational institutions. Conservation staffs work to eliminate factors that cause damage such as light, chemicals, pests, temperature extremes, and humidity. They clean, store, and display clothing in an appropriate manner. Research and classification are also important tasks for proper preservation of historic items.

Professional Profile

Fashion Blogger and Author

Jessica Quirk
What I Wore: The Blog
(http://whatiwore.tumblr.com)

How did you get into your line of work?

I work as a personal style and fashion blogger and author. I've always applied my interest in personal style and fashion design to getting dressed each day. Eventually I studied Apparel Merchandising and Costume Construction at Indiana University, where I graduated in 2005. After that, I moved to New York City to work as a fashion designer. I did a lot of traveling for that job, and while on a trip to Hong Kong, I discovered an online community where people were photographing their daily outfits. I had been writing a personal blog for a couple years at that point and decided to start documenting my daily outfits as well. Simply put, I took a photo of my outfit each day and wrote a short description of when, what, where, and why I wore it. What began as a hobby quickly became a full-time job!

Last year I also published my first book—an illustrated style guide for women called *What I Wore: Four Seasons, One Closet, Endless Recipes for Personal Style.*

What does your "typical" day entail?

Although each day is different, my standard routine is to get up and pick out an outfit for the day, get ready, then scout a location where my husband takes my photos. We take upwards of 200 photos that get edited down into five to 10 that make the post. Some days I work from home, but most days I go into a shared studio space in downtown Bloomington. I usually get in between 9 a.m. and 9:30 a.m. and then start to check e-mails and updates on my key social media outlets (Tumblr, Twitter, Facebook and Pinterest). My first post usually goes up at 10 a.m., and I'll promote that before starting to edit the new batch of photos. I stay at the office until 1 p.m. and then return home to work on sewing, do-it-yourself, or illustration projects.

How do you fulfill the mission of family and consumer sciences— that is, how does your work improve people's quality of life?

What we wear each day might seem superficial, but I know the power that clothing has to make us look and feel great. "What I Wore" gives women the inspiration and tools to make the most of the wardrobe they already have and to become smarter shoppers.

Preparing to Enter the Apparel Industry

The apparel industry demands workers who are creative and savvy, fashion-oriented, good problem solvers, and business-minded. They must be passionate about the product they are marketing. All fashion industry professionals, whether designing textiles or selling on a retail floor, must consider the needs of the end-user, the consumer. Since fashion is always changing, the field requires the ability to explore and apply new ideas and concepts. Consider the academic training needs and working conditions discussed in the following sections and compare them to your own academic and work environment interests. Professional organizations can provide insight into the textile and apparel field. Several professional organizations, their websites, and descriptions are listed in **Figure 8-2.**

Trade and Professional Organizations Supporting the Textiles and Apparel Industry		
Trade and Professional Organization	**Web Address**	**Description**
American Apparel and Footwear Association	wewear.org	A national trade association that represents apparel, footwear, and other sewn apparel products companies and suppliers. The association actively participates in public policy and international trade arenas that affect the sewn product industry and offers legislative and trade news updates to members.
American Association of Textile Chemists and Colorists	aatcc.org	A trade organization focused on expanding practical working knowledge for professionals in the textile industry working specifically with the application of dyes and chemicals. Educational opportunities, publications, and student activities enhance the sharing of knowledge.
American Fiber Manufacturers Association	fibersource.com	A trade association that represents all U.S. fiber producers and advocates for members on a broad range of regulatory and international trade issues.
American Sheep Industry Association (ASI)	sheepusa.org	A trade organization that works to improve the international development, production, and sales of wool fiber. The American Wool Council is a division of ASI.
The Costume Society of America	costumesocietyamerica.com	Focusing on dress and appearance, this scholarly group offers its members several forums for learning and disseminating information related to the field of costume.

Figure 8-2 Check out the websites of these professional textiles and apparel organizations.

(Continued)

Trade and Professional Organizations Supporting the Textiles and Apparel Industry		
Council of Fashion Designers of America	cfda.com	A nonprofit trade association of more than 400 American designers of women's wear, menswear, accessories, and jewelry. It supports scholarships for fashion design students and provides professional development and recognition for designers.
Fashion Group International	fgi.org	A worldwide association of fashion professionals that works to help fashion professionals advance in their field and to recognize their achievements. It provides networking opportunities, educational forums, and trend data. The group has chapters in most states within the United States.
International Textile & Apparel Association	itaaonline.org	A professional and educational association that includes professionals, researchers, educators, and students in the textile, apparel, and merchandising disciplines in higher education. The purpose of the organization is to expand and disseminate knowledge, exchange ideas, and provide educational opportunities through meetings, special events, and publications.
[TC]^2	tc2.com	A professional organization that assists companies in the apparel and soft goods industries. A demonstration center in North Carolina educates members on leading edge technologies and supports research for new technologies and business processes.
The Textile Institute	texi.org	An international organization headquartered in England that focuses on the global fashion industry.

Figure 8-2 Continued

What Kind of Training Is Needed?

Many aspects of the apparel industry require professionals who possess a creative flair combined with business skills. Are people born with creativity and business sense, or can these traits be learned? The answer is yes and no. A creative flair and good business sense can get you started, but in today's highly competitive market, a college or university degree combined with natural talent and industry experience create an unbeatable combination. The specific training needed depends on the job. Dozens of potential career tracks exist in the fashion industry, and each has its own requirements for training and experience. Computer skills have become essential. For creative positions, ability to use computer-aided design software is important. For more business-oriented careers, proficiency with word-processing and spreadsheet programs is expected.

Many colleges and universities around the world offer programs in textiles and apparel, apparel design, fashion merchandising, retail management, textile production and technology, textile design, historic preservation, and visual merchandising. Students learn technical skills, textile knowledge, and business skills, and they hone their creative skills. All the schools are connected to their local or regional fashion industry. Many of these college and university programs require a portfolio or an internship experience. Opportunities for international experiences are common and valued as global awareness is an important part of the fashion industry. For this reason, ability to speak a foreign language is an asset.

In general, the apparel industry requires no licensure or particular specialized degree. However, due to the diverse and complex nature of the industry, strong technical skills, problem-solving and analytical skills, and industry knowledge are needed to effectively compete. As the global fashion industry becomes more reliant on technology and more complex problems are addressed, a solid education, a college degree, and experience will be desired by employers. While a student, you can gain valuable experience by working part-time in the industry, volunteering to help with charity fashion shows, writing about fashion for your college newspaper, or entering design competitions.

What Are the Working Conditions?

The fashion industry is fast-paced, creative, dynamic, and demanding. With each change in technology and with each new trend, new opportunities arise in the research, production, design, and dissemination of clothing products. New markets form, new methods produce new products, and consumers keep chasing the newest fads. The fashion cycle is truly a cycle that never ends.

The fashion industry is known for both its teamwork among coworkers and its fierce rivalry among industry competitors. It demands creative, forward-thinking people who are not afraid to take a risk. It is an industry known for long working hours that vary by season. For example, November and December are months notorious for long, frantic working hours due to the increase in sales around the holiday season. Likewise, apparel manufacturers face pre-season peak demands during which long working hours are expected.

The fashion industry continually offers new opportunities and new ideas, and the creative nature of the environment is stimulating. People who thrive in this environment are attracted to the pace and energy. Industry professionals are always on the lookout for fresh, new recruits who can breathe new life into an ever-changing industry.

Summary

Apparel is one of the basic needs of families and individuals. However, clothing goes far beyond providing warmth and protection. In developed societies, apparel is fashion, an ever-evolving artifact of societal trends. The fashion industry is a multimillion dollar global industry that provides fashion products to meet the social, psychological, and physical needs of people. It is a fast-paced, dynamic, and creative industry.

A variety of career opportunities exist in the fashion industry. There are careers in design, production, and sales of fashion products in the textile industry, the apparel manufacturing industry, and the retail and marketing segments of the industry. How can you know if a career in the fashion industry is right for you? Evaluate your strengths, weaknesses, skills, and interests in the fashion industry. If you are considering a career in the industry, contemplate increasing your knowledge of the profession.

Pursuing a Career in Fashion

1. **Interview a professional.** The fashion industry can seem very appealing. To get

a perspective of daily work in the apparel industry, interview a fashion industry professional. If there are few in your local area, consider interviewing by phone or e-mail. There are many opportunities, such as interviewing an apparel designer, a fashion buyer, a merchandiser, or a store manager. Ask the person how he or she entered the field, what the advantages and disadvantages are, and what a typical day entails. Be sure to solicit advice for your career decision making. What personal qualities are needed to be successful in the field?

2. **Evaluate your fashion awareness.** Fashion awareness is important for apparel industry professionals. How much fashion savvy do you have? Can you predict the upcoming fashions? Test your fashion awareness by choosing an apparel category and making a prediction of trends for the next season. Consider possible social, economic, and technological influences. Evaluate your success by checking websites of prominent retailers or designers.

3. **Shadow a professional.** Seek permission to spend a few hours or a day job shadowing a fashion industry professional. Often, you can arrange this through your university. The more you observe, the more you will become familiar with the diverse and complex apparel industry. Observations could range from a few hours to several days. Internships, part-time and summer employment, and volunteer experiences will help you decide if this is the field for you.

4. **Become acquainted with professional organizations.** Since their mission is to educate and support professionals, professional organizations provide a wealth of industry information. They also provide relevant industry research and review innovations. Many professional organizations include job banks for prospective employers and employees. Generally, they do not try to sell anything to members. Look up each of the websites listed in Figure 8-2. Do they provide opportunities to students, such as student memberships, internships, scholarships, or competitions?

Questions for Thought

1. Access the United States Department of Labor, Bureau of Labor Statistics website. Choose two related career profiles listed here and report on the career description, typical working conditions, job outlook, and expected earnings:
   - fashion designers
   - marketing managers
   - wholesale and retail buyers
   - first line managers/supervisors of retail sales workers
   - merchandise displayers
   - apparel sales representatives
   - sales managers

2. Identify three fashion trends for college students today. What factors influenced these trends? Will the trends be sustained over several seasons, or are they short-run fads?

3. Which fashion designers will define this decade? Why? How will future fashion historians describe this decade?

4. Which retailers are the most popular among college students today? Do you predict their popularity with this generation and with future students will be sustained over the next decade? Why or why not?

5. Consider the population profile of the United States and the groups expected to be larger. How will the fashion industry look in 5 years? In 10 years? What changes may occur? How will it remain the same?

6. Much of the labor-intensive components of United States textile and apparel manufacturing have moved overseas. Research and design has continued its presence in the United States, however. How could a student best prepare for the increasingly global fashion marketplace?

References and Resources

Aliva, A., & Angeletti, N. (2006). *In Vogue: The illustrated history of the world's most famous fashion magazine.* New York: Rizzoli.

Badia, Enrique. (2009). *Zara and her sisters: The story of the world's largest clothing retailer.* Basingstoke: Palgrave Macmillan.

Baudot, F. (2006). *Fashion: The twentieth century.* New York: Universe.

Beker, J. (2008). *Passion for fashion: Careers in style.* Toronto: Tundra Books.

Boucher, F. (1987). *20,000 years of fashion.* New York: Abrams.

Brown, C. (2010). *Fashion & textiles: The essential careers guide.* London: Laurence King Publishing Ltd.

Burns, L.D., Bryant, N.O., & Mullet, K.K. (2011) *The business of fashion: Designing, manufacturing, and marketing* (4th ed.). New York: Fairchild.

Clarke, S.E.B., & O'Mahony, M. (2007). *Techno textiles 2: Revolutionary fabrics for fashion and design* (revised ed.). London: Thames and Hudson.

Cohen, A.C., & Johnson, I. (2012). *J.J.Pizzuto's fabric science* (10th ed.). New York: Fairchild Books.

Csikszentmihaly, M., & Rochberg Hulton, E. (1981). *The meaning of things: Domestic symbols and the self.* Cambridge, MA: Cambridge University Press.

Diamond, J., & Diamond, E. (2008). *The world of fashion* (4th ed.). New York: Fairchild Books.

Dor, A., Ferguson, C., Langwith, C., & Tan, E. (2010). *A heavy burden: The individual costs of being overweight and obese in the United States.* [Research Report]. The George Washington University, School of Public Health and Health Services, Department of Health Policy. Retrieved from http://www.gwumc.gwu.edu/sphhs/departments/healthpolicy/dhp_publications/pub_uploads/dhpPublication_35308C47-5056-9D20-3DB157B39AC53093.pdf

Engle, J. (2008). *How to open & operate a financially successful fashion design business.* Ocala, FL: Atlantic Publishing Group.

Frings, G. S. (2008). *Fashion: From concept to consumer* (9th ed.). Upper Saddle River, NJ: Pearson Prentice Hall.

Gehlhar, M. (2008). *The fashion designer survival guide: Start and run your own fashion business.* New York: Kaplan.

Goworek, H. (2007). *Fashion buying* (2nd ed.). Ames, IA: Blackwell Pub. Ltd.

Granger, M. (2007). *Fashion: The industry and its careers.* New York: Fairchild Publications, Inc.

Granger, M. (2010). *The fashion intern* (2nd ed.) New York: Fairchild Books.

Granger, M.M., & Sterling, T.M. (2012). *Fashion entrepreneurship: Retail business planning.* (2nd ed.). New York: Fairchild Books.

Hartsog, D. (2007). *Creative careers in fashion: 30 ways to make a living in the world of couture.* New York: Allworth Press.

Henly, N. M. (1977). *Body politics: Power, sex and nonverbal communication.* Englewood Cliffs, NJ: Prentice Hall.

Institute for Career Research. (2008). *Careers in fashion merchandising.* Chicago: Institute for Career Research.

Johnson, M. J., & Moore, E.C. (2001). *Apparel product development.* New York: Prentice Hall.

Kunz, G.I., & Glock, R.E. (2004). *Apparel manufacturing: Sewn product analysis* (4th ed.). New York: Prentice Hall.

Lupton, E. (2002). *Skin.* New York: Princeton Architectural Press.

Mikaelsen, D. (2008). *FabJob guide to become a boutique owner.* Calgary: FabJob.

Mower, S. (2007). *Stylist: The interpreters of fashion.* New York: Style.com in association with Rizzoli.

Peiss, K. L. (1999). *Hope in a jar: The making of America's beauty culture.* New York: Henry Holt.

Riegleman, N. (2007). *Nine heads: A guide to drawing fashion* (3rd ed.). New York: Prentice Hall.

San Martin, M. (2009). *Field guide: How to be a fashion designer.* Beverly, MA: Rockport Publishing.

Scranton, P. (2001). *Beauty and business: Commerce, gender, and culture in modern America.* New York: Routledge.

Stall-Meadows, C. (2011). *Fashion now: A global perspective.* New York: Prentice Hall.

Steele, V. (2006). *Encyclopedia of clothing and fashion.* Farmington Hills, MI: Charles Scribner's Sons.

Swanson, K.K., & Everett, J.C. (2008). *Writing for the fashion business.* New York: Fairchild.

Vescia, M. (2011). *Career launcher: Fashion.* New York: Infobase Publishing, Inc.

Vogt, P. (2007). *Career opportunities in the fashion industry* (2nd ed.). New York: Ferguson.

Wolbers, M.F. (2009). *Uncovering fashion: Fashion communications across the media.* New York: Fairchild Books.

World Trade Organization. (2012). *What is the WTO?* Retrieved from http://www.wto.org/english/thewto_e/whatis_e/whatis_e.htm

Yates, J., & Gustavsen, D. (2011). *The fashion careers guidebook: A guide to every career in the fashion industry and how to get it.* Hauppauge, NY: Barron's Educational Series.

Professional Journals and Trade Publications

Clothing and Textiles Research Journal

Dress: The Journal of the Costume Society of America

Fashion Theory: The Journal of Dress, Body, and Culture

Journal of Fashion Marketing and Management

Women's Wear Daily (wwd.com)

On the Internet

http://www.pantone.com—Pantone is an authority on color and provider of color systems and leading technology for the selection and accurate communication of color across a variety of industries.

http://www.ecofashionworld.com—Eco Fashion World is a resource to sustainable designer brands and online eco fashion stores.

http://www.apparelsearch.com—Apparel Search is a fashion industry directory that provides members of the international fashion community with educational information regarding virtually every aspect of the apparel and textile market.

Chapter 9

Careers in Interior Design and Housing

After studying this chapter, you will be able to:

- discuss the current state of the interior design and housing fields.
- discuss career opportunities in interior design and housing.
- explain what academic training is needed to work in the interior design and housing field.
- describe working conditions in interior design and housing.

Imagine sitting in a restaurant and enjoying a relaxing meal with friends while palm trees sway, the sun sets, and exotic birds chirp in the background. Now imagine this restaurant is in Anchorage, Alaska. Better yet, imagine getting paid for being the one who designed the tropical paradise interior of the restaurant. Or, imagine creating giant boulders to be used as tables and chairs in the lobby of a Stone Age-themed theater. I do not have to imagine. I have done both. I am a commercial interior designer who specializes in fantasy-themed commercial spaces for hospitality.

How did I get into this line of work? My story dates back to high school. I have always been fascinated with building and construction. My father is a builder. He encouraged me to become an architect so that we could work together. In high school I followed a local architect around for a day as part of a "job shadow" program in my family and consumer sciences class. Although it was interesting, it did not quite capture my curiosity. I was more interested in the inside of a building than the building as a whole. I wanted to create the interior environment of buildings.

In college I earned a degree in interior design. I had the opportunity to do an internship with a commercial interior design firm. This gave me some experience to put on my résumé when I applied for a position after graduation. I have been working my way toward specialization in fantasy-themed commercial spaces for the past ten years. Today, I really have the best of both worlds as I work closely with architects and builders. I speak their language and understand building codes, but I focus on my passion, the interior.

If you think my job sounds like a lot of fun, you are right. It is. My team of designers works with our client to create a total fantasy environment through lighting, color, interior space planning, texture, carpet, furniture, drapery and fabric, and a myriad of other highly inventive materials. As far as creativity goes, the sky is the limit. However, just like any other designer, I am bound by financial, safety, functional, and building code requirements. This makes the design process complex and challenging. This is the way I like it.

Today will be an interesting day because I meet with my new client for the first time. I will be leading a design team to renovate the interior of a restaurant at a large urban zoo. I enjoy this part of the design process because I get to really talk to my clients. I am fully aware that the process of successful design involves an in-depth understanding of the client's requirements and cultural values. A design must not only look great, it needs to work great, too.

Don't get me wrong. I can't completely hold back and wait to hear from the clients before I am treading down the creative road to "zoo land." In fact, my mind is brimming with zoo animals and safari-inspired colors and textures. Will there be animated monkeys and zebras surprising diners through a leafy partition? Will there be different sections that look like a South American rain forest, an African savannah, or a North American tundra? Everywhere I turn, I see something that inspires me. I even found myself losing my train of thought at the grocery store when my eyes focused on an amazing color combination in the produce aisle! It is hard to rein back the onslaught of ideas at this early stage. It is part of the appeal of a new project. But I remind myself that I am not designing my fantasy, but my client's and their customers' fantasy.

This morning I will start the discussion with senior management, but I won't stop there. I want to hear from everyone who will use this space. I will start by asking them what their goals are, which hopefully they will be forthright and clear in revealing. Next, I need to know what they need in the space to achieve those goals. For employees, I want to know what their job functions are, how they interact with other people, and how they hope the space will function. I also want to talk with families who will use this space. I will suggest putting together a small focus group of restaurant customers to solicit their ideas.

I know my clients are counting on me to create an environment that surpasses their expectations. Of course, that does not mean that I will forget about efficiency. After all, a restaurant is a busy, working space. Once I fully understand my client's goals and what they need to work toward them, I will then come up with strategies for moving people through the space efficiently, creating a desirable room for dining, conserving space where possible, finding multiple uses of space and making better use of the building's exterior. I want to "think outside the box" and not create another theme restaurant where all interior components are in their expected locations.

By taking the time to really listen to my client and their constituents, I'm confident we'll implement an interior renovation that will provide the best visual and functional design solution within the parameters established. I want to create a space that is fun, inviting, interactive, functional, and really makes my client say "wow!"

I know the ideas will come. Through working with the architect and builder, continuing conversations with the client, space planning, drawings and renderings, and taking in the world around me, it will all come together.

There will be times in the upcoming months when I will struggle to focus on anything but the project, as I will be so engulfed in the creative process. As we implement the design concept, I will work long hours overseeing the process. I want to make sure everything is done right. Sometimes it will overwhelm me as deadlines quickly approach, materials do not arrive as scheduled, disagreements come up, or installation problems arise. However, in the end, there will be a fantastic new zoo-themed restaurant for people of all ages to enjoy. It is difficult to articulate how invigorating it will be when the restaurant opens and our ideas come to fruition. I will enjoy it for a moment, take a deep breath, and start the process again just as excited for the next project as I am for this one. How can I not be? After all, it's a fantasy.

Throughout history, people have constructed buildings as shelter to keep out the natural elements. Buildings provide protection from heat, cold, rain, sun, and any creatures that could cause harm. However, when people lose their shelter, whether it is their home, community building, or a commercial space, it is more than loss of protection from the elements. Buildings, whether private or public, hold symbolic meaning. Probably the most famous description of the impact of buildings on people came from former British Prime Minister Winston Churchill when he said, "First we shape our buildings; thereafter, they shape us" ("Famous Quotations," n.d.). In explaining the symbolic importance of buildings, there is no better example than the importance of home.

There really is no place like home. *Home* is a place where people reside during nonwork hours, that stores material goods, and that is a reflection of their values, interests, and personalities. There is evidence from the earliest recorded history that people have always personalized their living spaces. It is the things that people put in their living spaces and how they organize the space that make it feel like home.

Before the Industrial Revolution in the latter half of the 1800s, home furnishings were made by hand. For common people, home furnishings were primarily functional, but they were also pleasing to the eye. Because of the relatively high price of furniture, most people considered it a solid investment. Furniture was handed down through generations and was often a carefully planned purchase or custom made. Furniture was generally kept throughout a person's lifetime, and trendy changes were not considered. After the Industrial Revolution, mass-produced home furnishings were created. Designs were simplified and function was emphasized. More products were made easily available to consumers. Except for a brief backlash period when the art and craft of furniture making was esteemed, form was considered an afterthought to function (Clark, 1986; Mason, 1982).

After World War I, consumers became more interested in trendy, quick-changing, and relatively inexpensive home furnishings. The world had opened up to the United States during the war, and in the decade that followed, the influence of modernism and international styles forever changed the home furnishings market. The Great Depression of the 1930s slowed design trends in the United States, and the onset of World War II brought new home furnishings design to a standstill. Design, whether in automobiles, home appliances, clothing, or home furnishings was utilitarian and practical. After World War II, mass-produced furniture, new materials such as plastics, and an emphasis on the growing youth population resulted in new home furnishings products that were modern, hip, and readily available. Beanbag chairs, modular furniture, and futons flooded the market as consumers looked for quick-change items to decorate their homes (Clark, 1986; Mason, 1982).

In the decades that followed, furniture and home furnishings became more affordable. Warehouse and discount stores began offering inexpensive, trendy home furnishings. Home-improvement projects that could be done on a budget and in a short time frame were touted in the media along with showcases of how the rich and famous live. The home furnishings field expanded rapidly into a trendy, fashionable, and status-seeking industry that appeals to every possible consumer niche market. Warehouse stores, low-price to high-price retailers, and international aesthetics have made more types of products available to more people.

Today, interior design and housing is a multi-billion dollar industry. Television programs focus on interior design and renovation. The availability of home furnishings through Internet shopping, discount stores, design trade shows, and markets that are open to consumers as well as professionals has contributed to the expansion of the interior design and housing industry. Also, increases in disposable income have supported the growth of the interior design and housing industry.

The Structure of the Interior Design and Housing Fields

Cicero, the ancient Roman orator, philosopher, and writer once asked, "What is more agreeable than one's home?" ("Marcus Tullius," 1999–2006). Some 2,000 years later, Frank L. Baum, the author of *The Wizard of Oz*, wrote, "There's no place like home, there's no place like home, there's no place like home" (Baum, 1900/1960). Housing exerts a powerful cultural, psychological, and economic influence on societies. Housing provides shelter and a sense of "place." While the exterior of a building may be its most prominent visible aspect, or its "public face," its interior can be even more important in conveying social and psychological meaning for inhabitants or users. Although distinct from each other, strong markets and many career opportunities exist in both interior design and in housing.

Interior Design

Interior design is the process of shaping the experience of interior space through the manipulation of the space, the application of the elements and principles of design, and the use of materials. An *interior designer* is responsible for the design, functionality, safety, performance, and aesthetic image of a client's residential or business space. There are a variety of career paths a person can take within the interior design profession. However, the field of interior design is generally broken down into the two large categories of residential and commercial interior design. *Residential interior design* includes single-family houses, multifamily houses such as duplexes, apartments, and condominiums, and any other form of residence. *Commercial interior design* encompasses all kinds of nonresidential interior spaces; for example, offices, restaurants, religious facilities, recreational and community centers, health care facilities, schools, libraries, museums, and retail spaces. No matter which career path a person pursues, an interior designer needs skills that go above and beyond just selecting colors, finish materials, and furniture.

Housing

Housing is a basic need of individuals and families. The *housing industry* focuses on the behavioral, social, economic, functional, and aesthetic aspects of housing, interiors, and other built environments. The housing industry includes diverse careers in community development and policy, housing technology, management and finance, construction, and real estate.

Career Opportunities in Interior Design and Housing

From securing housing for low-income families to designing the interiors of high-end residences, the interior design and housing field provides a wealth of job opportunities. In the following section, the opportunities in housing and interior design are explored. Some of these career opportunities represent large segments of the industry, while others highlight smaller specialty areas. Typical careers in the interior design and housing field are listed in **Figure 9-1**.

Residential Interior Design

There is a saying that home is where the heart is. From space planning to selecting fabrics, flooring, and paint color to designing lighting and electrical plans, the job of the residential interior designer is to create environments that are safe, functional, aesthetically pleasing, and that feel like home.

Residential interior designers focus on the design needs of individuals and families in their

Sample Careers in Interior Design and Housing		
Housing	**Interior Design**	**Interiors Sales and Marketing**
Fair housing agent	Color consultant	Journalist
Housing planner	Commercial interior designer	Retail buyer
Housing specialist	Exhibit designer	Retail design consultant
Property manager	Home furnishings designer	Retail manager
Relocation consultant	Home stylist	Retail merchandiser
Residence hall coordinator	Kitchen and bath designer	Retail sales
Resort manager	Lighting designer	Textile sales representative
Retirement complex administrator	Residential interior designer	Wholesale representative

Figure 9-1 The interior design and housing field offers a variety of careers.

Professional Profile

Interior Designer

Lisa Blanchard, ASID
NCIDQ Certified Interior Designer
Lisa Blanchard Design, Inc.

How did you get into your line of work?

Born into a family of architects and contractors, I was surrounded by creative people designing and building beautiful, functional spaces, primarily homes, churches, and schools. My father designed our home in the early 50s to last a lifetime and meet the needs of his growing family and his aging parents. Although it did not have a label, this was my first introduction to universal design. Throughout the years I observed this family home accommodate the needs of a range of ages and abilities, from toddlers to the elderly. Through the halls and walkways of this space, strollers and mobility equipment have traveled; young and old have lived without barriers.

After graduating from high school, I enrolled in a local college and graduated with a degree in health science. After having a family, I returned to school, following my true passion of design. I received a B.S. in interior design while working in the San Francisco Design Center. During this time our daughter, a teenager, had a debilitating snowboarding injury. I examined the difficulties and challenges of living in a space while using a wheelchair and began the journey of training and researching universal and accessible design. My background in the health industry made this a comfortable transition. I then purchased a company that specialized in ADA consulting and accessible design. I incorporated this existing company into my residential design business, which included the practice of universal design. I focused on universal and accessible design while volunteering for Guide Dogs for the Blind and the community of people living with disabilities and while expanding and developing my business. My goal was and is to design beautiful, functional homes for people with disabilities because of disease or injury.

What does your "typical" day entail?

With the advent of the Internet and electronic communication, much of my workday begins at the computer in my office. I begin by communicating via e-mail or phone. Following up in a timely manner with clients, vendors, manufacturers, and contractors is a priority for keeping a job on track and must be accomplished daily.

home living environment. That environment may be a single-family home or a multifamily residence such as an apartment, condominium, or townhouse. Newly built housing develop- ments employ residential designers to cre- ate model interiors for showing homes during sales. In the planning stage, residential interior designers create space lighting and electrical

I also spend a significant amount of time on paperwork and tracking project progress. This includes accounting and bookkeeping practices and requires that I keep accurate records and understand accounting practices. This often requires daily communication with my accountant. Ethical practices of a transparent business model dominate my bookkeeping and accounting procedures and require a virtual paper trail to accurately and efficiently follow progress on projects and my business goals.

Each day can include the following: design and execution of plans, meeting with contractors for review of drawings and specifications, and working with clients to discuss the scope of the project or for selection and approval of materials.

Often a day or portion of it is used for the study and research of new materials and practices and inclusion of continuing education seminars.

The scope of every project is as unique and challenging as an individual client. Each day has a consistency and rhythm, but they are rarely the same.

How do you fulfill the mission of family and consumer sciences— that is, how does your work improve people's quality of life?

As a residential interior designer, my profession calls me to enhance the lives of clients by designing safe, functional homes that meet their needs and desires. By way of example, a recent project I worked on was for an 18-year-old client with a spinal cord injury who could not return home after his accident until I designed an accessible dwelling by converting the current garage. He was living in a rehab hospital because he could not enter the existing home, maneuver his wheelchair, or use the bathroom or kitchen. I was able to create a home for him that he could live in independently and continue his young life. Each person deserves to be given opportunity to care for him- or herself.

My goal is to incorporate functional, accessible features in the homes of people with disabilities to allow them independence, safety, comfort, and beauty throughout their lifetimes. I believe each and every human being is valuable and should never be marginalized because of a physical or mental disability. It is with this belief that I practice interior design, honoring each individual for who they are, no matter their abilities, strengths, or weaknesses, giving them the opportunity to live a full and productive life without barriers. My goal is to create spaces that are not institutional but maintain the character and beauty of individual homes, creating built environments that enhance and meet the needs of their occupants.

plans and select kitchen surfaces and equipment, bathroom fixtures, wall treatments, flooring, and window treatments. In the sales stage, residential interior designers "set the stage," making a home looked lived in and inspiring potential homeowners or renters to imagine living in the space. Residential interior designers are also employed during renovations to select furniture, colors, textures, and materials that make the renovated interior feel like home and perform functionally for the user.

Commercial Interior Design

If you were to design an interior of a new coffee shop, what would it look like? You would need to consider how to make the space function properly so that employees could efficiently and easily serve customers. The design should allow customers to move easily in and out of the space. Customers should also feel relaxed, comfortable, and safe. Perhaps they would want to sit down and stay awhile. Lighting, traffic patterns, food service and storage features, seating arrangements, accessibility, convenience, signage, and the general aesthetic atmosphere would all need to be considered.

Did you know that certain colors make you hungry? For a fast-food restaurant, using colors to create an appetite and the desire to eat quickly is advantageous. Did you know that other colors make you relax and even heal faster? For hospitals, interior spaces that relax patients and their families and promote healing are highly desired. Colors are symbols that create both an emotional and physical response. Hotel rooms and lobbies, hospital wings, airport lounges, museums, religious facilities, restaurants, schools, and government buildings are just a few of the commercial spaces that require the talents and skills of a commercial interior designer.

Commercial interior designers focus on creating safe, efficient, functional, and aesthetically pleasing interior spaces used for commercial uses. Commercial design has the same purpose and incorporates the same components as residential design; that is, the creation of safe, efficient, functional, and aesthetically pleasing interior spaces. These spaces are not meant for living but for conducting business. Although aesthetics are just as important as in residential interior design, the commercial designer must design for the functional needs of many users, rather than focusing on one individual or family. Commercial interiors differ from residential

interiors in the level of safety regulations and the end use. For example, fire safety is of utmost importance in commercial spaces. Strict flammability standards exist for carpets, draperies, and mattresses used in commercial spaces. Commercial interiors must be accessible to people with varying physical abilities.

Commercial designers tend to specialize in one area. For example, one commercial designer may concentrate on upscale retail stores for the youth market. Office spaces, hotels, restaurants, places of worship, department stores, libraries, educational facilities, medical facilities, and government buildings are just a few of the many commercial design specialties.

Real Estate

The real estate field involves the buying and selling of homes and commercial properties. Real estate transactions involve people in many professions. For example, *real estate agents* list property for sale and facilitate the offer and acceptance process. *Mortgage lenders* provide the funding for the purchase. *Escrow officers* coordinate the transfer of property ownership. (Attorneys and accountants are involved in more complex transactions.) *Inspectors* look for physical problems with the property. *Insurance agents* provide insurance coverage through the transfer process, while *appraisers* determine the relative value of the property.

Money for the purchase is often obtained through various lending sources. Banks and credit unions are classic sources of funds, and they employ loan officers to work with buyers. *Mortgage brokers* serve as sales and marketing agents for loan sources, but they do not provide funds themselves. They gather data from the buyer and connect the buyer with lenders. *Loan officers* work with a team of support personnel who do credit checks and process the large amount of paperwork required to qualify a buyer to obtain a loan. Some loan companies represent many different sources of loans; some offer only those products that their institution originates. Loan officers must be able to juggle

Professional Profile

Interior Designer

Keith Miller, ASID
Miller and Associates Interior Consultants

How did you get into your line of work?

My older sister was enrolled in college when I was in junior high. She discovered the interior design program at her university and insisted it suited me perfectly. I went through high school keeping this idea in mind. However, thinking it more fitting for a male career, I enrolled in an architectural drafting course. It became very evident that I had a calling to meticulous artistic details. When I turned in my interpretation of the house elevation assignment, it showed the technical basics—windows, doors, roof, and walls—but also included embellishments that gave the elevation life and character.

As I matured, I was continually drawn out from the mere technical prowess of an artistic expression and to the uniqueness of shaping spaces with personality that connected with real people. I enrolled at the local university in my city, completed a four-year undergraduate degree in housing and interior design, and accepted my first job as an interior designer. I was a student intern and was hired after I received my degree. My specialization in this position was designing offices and conference areas on military bases and designing modular cabinetry for the health care industry. After less than a year, I left the position to pursue my own business, specializing in residential design. Networking with other professionals provided the catalyst for my career move.

What does your "typical" day entail?

When my day begins, I spend time making phone calls and using e-mail to set up appointments and to follow up on project progression. During the day, I meet with clients to evaluate their needs and discuss values. I communicate appropriate design solutions through research, budgeting, creative thinking, experimentation, sketching, computer drafting, accurate record keeping, consulting specialists, and creating detailed specification forms for ordering products and services. These tasks are repeated again each day, but they never seem repetitive because no days, no clients, and no projects are ever the same. I love the independence and constant change of owning my own business. I meet and work with all kinds of people.

How do you fulfill the mission of family and consumer sciences— that is, how does your work improve people's quality of life?

My work funnels itself into a practical end: to make beauty usable by people. When I am able to take the elements and principles of design and shape them into a beautiful environment, I offer the user personal solace and well-being. Good design must be functional and responsible. Residential design, in particular, has led me to unravel the mystery of each client and to weave together the most appropriate expression for every single client.

many tasks at one time. Several loans may be at different stages of application and qualification, and the loan officer must keep them all progressing to provide a timely closing. People who work in real estate must have financial knowledge so that they can explain to clients what attributes of a loan are most suitable. The position requires a service-oriented "people person" who can work with all kinds of people to provide the best mortgage solution.

Property Management

Imagine that you have just bought a new condominium. It was a huge financial investment and one that you were willing to make at the expense of spending money on short-term desires such as vacations or clothing. You will carefully maintain your new home. Your hope is that the home will keep its value or, better yet, increase in value over time.

Issues in the News
Affordable Housing

Even in the prosperous United States, finding affordable housing is difficult, if not impossible, for some people, especially low- and moderate-wage earners, despite the fact that the majority of jobs in the United States pay low to moderate wages. Currently approximately 65 to 70 percent of Americans own homes. This is an impressive figure, and credit is often given to favorable interest rates, despite rising home values, and government policies that favor home ownership. However, for millions of people in the United States, the goal of home ownership is out of their reach, and they rent the housing units in which they live.

Although both households that rent and households that own experience affordability problems, the most difficulty is experienced by low-wage earners in metropolitan areas. Their incomes are too low to afford market-rate rental housing. And the supply of low-cost units is insufficient to meet the demand for these units. The gap between the cost to rent and incomes is widening at an alarming rate. There simply are not enough housing units available that are affordable to people earning in the low-income categories. They may have to pay excessive amounts of their income for housing, crowd in with other people to pool resources, or live in substandard housing. Nonmarket rate housing provided by the government and nonprofit developers helps to fill the gap, but it, too, is insufficient to meet the demand.

Government at the local, state, and federal level is involved in housing, with the goal of creating policies that support the development of more affordable housing. This is achieved either by decreasing the cost of housing to producers or consumers or by increasing the resources of low- or no-wage households. Efforts are in place both to create more affordable housing and to preserve the existing affordable housing units in all communities. It is beneficial to individuals, households, and communities to have workers living close to where they work. Recently emphasis has been placed on studying housing availability and affordability for police officers, teachers, firefighters, and retail workers. Both individuals and communities benefit when these key workers live and work in the communities they serve. Benefits include decreasing commute time, decreasing traffic congestion and pollution, providing employees for local employers, and supporting participation in the local community. Decent, affordable housing is important to the quality of life for individuals and households and for the health and vitality of communities.

Now imagine that you own not only the condominium in which you live but also the entire condominium complex of 200 units. Across town, you own another, similar property. Can you imagine carefully maintaining all of your real estate holdings? Real estate property can be a source of income to owners if properly managed to preserve and enhance property values.

Many real estate investors rely on property managers to care for and maintain their properties. A *property manager* oversees the overall performance of income-producing commercial or residential properties. Sometimes, real estate investors or owners may hire a *community association manager* to oversee the common property in multifamily residences such as apartment or condominium complexes. The common property could include gardens, health or fitness areas, swimming pools, or other spaces shared by residents. Community association managers hire landscape, janitorial, waste disposal, and maintenance services to maintain common areas. They may secure bids from contractors to perform these services. They often help to enforce community homeowners' association regulations and help homeowners make group decisions on maintenance issues. Sometimes community association managers are hired by the volunteer board of directors of the association rather than the property investor.

Asset property managers oversee the financial status of properties and report relevant information such as occupancy rates, the status of leases, and other financial matters to property owners. For example, an asset property manager of a shopping mall would oversee and report on store vacancies, payment of monthly leases, and adherence to mall regulations. This person would also solicit and secure merchants that will financially increase the property values of the mall. In residential rental properties, asset property managers collect rent and make sure that all financial responsibilities, such as insurance payments and taxes, are met.

The forecasted growth of the older adult population is expected to increase job opportunities in the property management field because various types of new housing will be needed. For example, retirement communities will flourish, and assisted-living facilities will expand to meet the growing demand. As long as development and construction of new commercial and residential buildings continues, property managers will be needed.

Housing Specialist

Housing specialists have expertise in serving special populations with unique housing needs. For example, a special populations housing specialist may work with families who have children with developmental disabilities and help the families overcome obstacles to securing appropriate housing. Another housing specialist may counsel older adults who are exploring housing options. Housing specialists provide technical assistance and consultation to mortgage lenders, real estate agents, property developers, and property management companies. Government housing specialists may provide community resource information or pretrial mediation in landlord/tenant cases. The housing field draws from the social and behavioral sciences, economics, public policy, planning, design, and technology.

A housing specialist may help homeless individuals find temporary shelter, transitional housing, or permanent housing. The specialist may also help them navigate the complex requirements of a government work program, act as their advocate in dealing with public housing authorities, or help them line up subsidized child care, as well as provide critical emotional support and counseling. Housing specialists may also help military families find housing during relocation or deployment. Others specialize in group homes for people with special needs, assist people going through home foreclosure, or manage leased housing.

The following is an example of how a housing specialist helped a family:

Rebecca had worked hard over the past 10 months to define goals and clear up debt so she could find financial stability for herself and her children. Today was the day that she would finally be able to place her new house key on the empty key ring she had been carrying for several months. A housing specialist helped Rebecca and her two young children move from the temporary shelter to which she escaped after fleeing an abusive relationship. Today, she and her children are moving into a new government-subsidized townhouse where they will stay indefinitely.

Housing specialists plan, organize, and direct activities relating to affordable and market housing. They often consult with and solicit the cooperation of community groups, government and nonprofit agencies, developers, and the public in identifying county and regional housing needs and objectives. They then formulate plans to meet the identified needs of their community and constituents. Often, they coordinate and develop partnerships with private

Issues in the News
Universal Design

Every house does not accommodate every person. It is not just a matter of aesthetics but a matter of function. The nature of disability has changed. More people are living with disabilities and finding it difficult, if not impossible, to access some buildings and interiors, including housing. Also, life expectancy is increasing and the United States population is aging. As a result, designers have become more intentional about designing products and environments that are usable by more people over longer periods of time.

Universal design is an approach to design that recognizes and accommodates the changes that people experience over their lifespan. Formally, it is the "design of products and environments to be usable by all people, to the greatest extent possible, without the need for adaptation or specialized design" (Mace, 1988). Universal design

"evolved from the changing demographics of age and disability, as well as the barrier-free design, assistive technology, and architectural accessibility movements, and also legislative activities in the late 20th century" (Hartje, 2006, p. 196). Those legislative activities included the Architectural Barriers Act of 1968, The Fair Housing Amendments Act of 1988, and the Americans with Disabilities Act of 1990 (ADA).

Seven principles of universal design were developed in the 1990s. For each of those principles, design features related to housing were identified. Creating access is an important part of universal design. A few of the typical universal design features include a zero step entrance, wider than traditional hallways and doorways, electrical outlets and wall switches that can be accessed

easily by standing or sitting, and color contrast between countertops and flooring. It's important to acknowledge that a house that contains some universal design features is not necessarily a universally designed house. Rather, the more universal design features, the more usable the house. "Incorporating universal design features and products during the design and construction phase of housing results in easy-to-use, flexible, and safe housing that is emotionally supportive, integrated in design, and cost effective" (Hartje, 2006, p 207). The concept promotes designing furnishings, products, and buildings so they are useable by more people over longer periods of time. Hopefully, universal design will become the standard for how houses are designed and built, rather than the exception, and universal design will be the standard for good design.

sector, nonprofit, and public agencies to meet the needs of the community. (Housing specialists often work in the family services field, which is discussed in more depth in Chapter 11.)

Space Planner

Imagine that you have just been assigned the task of designing the seating and traffic flow arrangement for a 1,000-seat concert hall. The space must have easy to locate entrances and exits that promote the smooth and orderly flow of traffic. The space must feel both intimate and comfortable to patrons. It must be accessible and conform to safety regulations. All seats must have a good view of the concert hall stage and great sound. Where do you begin?

Space planners creatively solve complex problems that involve the organization and layout of interior spaces. Typically they work closely with architects and interior designers. Their work is highly specialized, and they most often work in the commercial design field. Many specialize in lighting design within a certain genre of commercial space planning; for example, retail boutiques, places of worship, amusement parks, or community buildings such as senior service centers.

Space planners are concerned about space efficiency and function, about making the space the most usable for end users. Continuing education is important in order to keep up with the ever-changing standards and regulations for commercial spaces. Space planners use technology such as computer-aided design software rather than depending on manual drawings or sketches.

Kitchen and Bath Designer

A kitchen is often described as the heart of the home. It is the place where people gather, visit, and, of course, prepare meals. Bathrooms are often the most private areas of the home. Because of their heavy use, kitchens and bathrooms are the common focus of both new construction and building renovations. Since

function is of utmost importance in these rooms, they are also the most costly and often the most complex rooms to design.

Kitchen and bath designers specialize in kitchens and bathrooms. Many factors make kitchen and bathroom design complex. New technology offers continual improvement of kitchen and bathroom features. Quicker, more efficient, or easier to maintain kitchen appliances, bathroom fixtures, countertop materials, flooring, lighting, windows, plumbing, and storage are always being introduced. Utilizing these new technologies requires training and continuing education to create safe, comfortable kitchen and bathroom spaces.

Space is generally at a premium in kitchens and bathrooms. Necessary features such as bathroom fixtures, kitchen appliances, and work or grooming areas require specialized knowledge of installation, electrical wiring, lighting, plumbing, and control systems. Certification in kitchen and bath design is available in some academic programs or through advanced training after graduation.

Exhibit Designer

Have you ever attended a home show, a car show, an electronics show, a garden show, a college fair, or some other kind of trade show? If so, you may have been overwhelmed by sights, sounds, and information that were presented to you. Vibrant colors, extroverted salespeople, videos, music, models, displays, brochures, and free merchandise all competed to grab your attention. Each of these features was designed to stimulate your senses and focus your interest on the product or service being sold. It is likely that each exhibit was created by a designer who specializes in trade show exhibits. Trade show exhibits are often designed to be temporary and moved and reset in another location.

Exhibit designers may also create permanent, semi-permanent, or temporary exhibits that have nothing to do with sales. For example, exhibits created for a museum may focus on education. *Museum exhibit designers* create displays that showcase artifacts or works of art in a way that is pleasing, emphasizes the object, keeps it safe, and preserves it. They work closely with museum curators in the design and installation of the cabinets or display cases and the lighting.

Exhibit designers must know their client's customers. Are they looking for a product, service, or idea? The designers need to know what will capture customer attention and what will make the interaction between the customer and the exhibit meaningful.

Lighting Designer

Imagine a softly lit dining room that appears elegant and sophisticated, a brightly lit deli that

Issues in the News
Green Design

Lowered heating and cooling costs, more natural light, less expensive recycled and composite materials—who doesn't like to save money on living expenses? Amidst the energy crisis of the 1970s, many energy-saving features were designed into homes and commercial buildings. Insulated windows, efficient heating and cooling systems, improved roofing, and increased insulation were just a few of the features that became commonplace. People discovered that saving energy was good for the environment but—even closer to home—it was good for the family budget.

Since the 1980s, designers, architects, business owners, and government officials have become interested in design that goes beyond just being efficient and good looking. They want buildings that have a positive effect on people and the environment. Sustainable (or green) design trends emerged. *Green design* attempts to diminish the impact of new

buildings on the environment. It evaluates the design, materials, and methods used in construction as well as the maintenance features and use of the building over time. Green design is a component of the broader concept of sustainability, which includes environmental, social, and economic sustainability.

Green design is accomplished by creating buildings and interiors that are healthier for people and enhance productivity. For example, natural light and vegetation are frequently incorporated into designs. Green design tends to minimize use of fossil fuels, conserve energy, and lower the output of pollution. Less use of fossil fuels saves on operating costs. Green design incorporates waste management systems and reduces the impact on land. In addition, green design minimizes the use of environmentally adverse building materials.

Since the 1990s, green design standards have been

established and promoted. These voluntary standards promote the development of high-performance, sustainable buildings and interiors. The standards are known as LEED (Leadership in Energy and Environmental Design). They include a rating system, and certification is bestowed on buildings according to the number of rating credits they achieve. Sustainable or green design standards may also have been developed by state or local governments.

Does green design cost significantly more than traditional methods of building construction? At this point, the answer is yes. However, this calculation uses initial building costs and does not consider operating cost savings over time. Even so, green design is one of the fastest growing segments of the interior design and housing industry as builders and designers come to recognize the long-term effects of environmentally friendly design.

appears clean and trendy, or a warmly lit coffeehouse that invites conversation and encourages you to sit and relax. Creating spaces with a particular ambience is not just about choosing the right colors, textures, and furniture; it also involves effectively lighting the space. Lighting is a critical design component for creating interior spaces that are functional, aesthetic, and safe.

Lighting involves much more than choosing the desired style of lighting fixture. It is a highly technical area. *Lighting designers* know how to combine light intensities and how to direct and use different light colors to create a functional, pleasing environment. They understand architectural needs, electrical codes, energy issues, maintenance concerns, and the latest technological advancements in lighting and control systems. Some lighting designers specialize further in a particular commercial design genre such as theaters, concert halls, libraries, places of worship, or other facilities with unique lighting needs. Not all lighting designers are interior designers, but most interior designers must possess a basic level of knowledge and skill related to lighting.

New lighting technology is continually introduced in the marketplace. Lighting designers must keep up with the products of hundreds of manufacturers and evaluate and select the right lighting for the space. Lighting professionals can stay current in this fast-moving industry by joining professional lighting designer organizations, taking continuing education courses, and reading and contributing to trade publications.

Home Furnishings Sales and Marketing

From dishes and table linens to bookshelves and computer desks, the home furnishings industry presents a broad scope of career paths and specializations. Look through the Sunday newspaper and you will be bombarded with home furnishing advertisements from budget and discount stores to expensive designer brand goods. Switch on the television and you will see a variety of programming that focuses on home improvement and renovation. Many television programs highlight specific retailers and brand names of home furnishing products. The media offer ideas for home furnishing products that will individualize living space and make it feel like home.

The *home furnishings* industry includes many segments that focus on very specific niche markets. In fact, it is difficult to convey the number of career opportunities available in the home furnishings and housing. As in the field of apparel, home furnishings sales and marketing is the segment of the industry that focuses on getting products to consumers. Home furnishing products are sold first to wholesalers or retailers. They are then merchandised and sold to consumers.

Many of the same characteristics exist in home furnishings sales and marketing that are found in apparel sales and marketing. They are both fashion products, and both industries share similar career opportunities, including production management, buying and merchandising, retail management, and visual merchandising. Because home furnishings are fashion-oriented products, advertising and promotion play a large part in sales. The home furnishings industry offers career opportunities in broadcast media, journalism, home and trade shows, and other promotional marketing. Retail stores often employ interior designers as consultants for their consumers, especially when selling high-end home furnishings.

Preparing to Enter the Interior and Housing Industry

The interior design and housing industry deals with complex issues that focus on providing housing for all individuals and families. This field involves much more than changing the color of your bath towels, adding a shelf for

Issues in the News
Planned Growth

As the population grows, not only is affordable housing needed, but also land is needed on which to build affordable housing. Affordable housing and efficient land use go hand-in-hand. Growth needs to be planned. Land needs to be used responsibly. Builders and designers as well as community and national leaders are looking for ways to develop land in a responsible manner while providing enough housing to meet the needs of people at all economic levels.

Clean air, wetlands preservation, and land-use density are all issues that must be balanced against providing adequate housing for a growing and diverse population. Housing is not the only consideration with land-use issues, however. Land use must also accommodate industrial and commercial needs of the community and provide open spaces for recreation. Much of planned growth encompasses the idea that not only should people be able to afford housing, but they also should be able to live close to work, thus reducing the stress and pollution of commuting. Planned growth also lowers the number of major highways and roads needed for commuting. Schools, recreational facilities, places of worship, and government facilities must also be planned. Planners must decide how and where to preserve meaningful open spaces for recreation and, most importantly, how to protect environmentally sensitive areas.

books in your bedroom, or investing in fragrant candles for your dining room. Current issues include the need for housing a growing population, the impact of the interior environment on human health, and the lack of affordable housing. In addition, the population of older adults who have unique housing needs is increasing. Other concerns include sustainable or green design, smart growth, and universal design.

Because the interior design and housing field deals with complex issues, workers must demonstrate creativity as well as problem-solving and technical skills. The field requires the ability to explore and apply new ideas and concepts. Consider the academic training needs and working conditions discussed in the following sections and compare them to your own academic and work environment interests. Professional organizations can provide insight into the interior design and housing field. Several professional organizations, their websites, and descriptions are given in **Figure 9-2**.

What Training Is Needed?

The interior design industry requires professionals who possess a creative flair combined with scientific knowledge and business and technical skills. In Chapter 8, the following question was posed: Are people born with creativity and business sense, or can these traits be learned? Again, the answer is yes and no. A creative flair and good business sense can get you started, but in today's highly competitive market, a college or university degree combined with natural talent and industry experience are an important and valued combination. An abundance of potential career tracks exists in the interior design and housing industry, and each has its own requirements for training and experience.

Is an interior decorator the same as an interior designer? No. Although people often use the terms interchangeably, they do not mean the same thing. An *interior decorator* is someone who focuses on the aesthetic aspects of interior

Professional Organizations Supporting the Interior Design and Housing Industry		
Professional Organization	**Web Address**	**Description**
American Institute of Architects (AIA)	aia.org	A 150-year-old organization that supports the work of architects and designers through education, publications, and conferences.
American Society of Interior Designers (ASID)	asid.org	The comprehensive professional organization for interior designers that offers educational opportunities, advocacy, outreach opportunities, and networking for interior designers and students aspiring toward careers in the field. Local chapters exist in most states, and many colleges and universities support student chapters.
Council for Interior Design Accreditation (CIDA)	accredit-id.org	An independent nonprofit organization that accredits U.S. and Canadian interior design education programs at colleges and universities through a process of program self-evaluation and peer review. Accreditation is referred to as FIDER accreditation based on the organization's former name, Foundation for Interior Design Education Research.
Interior Design Educators Council (IDEC)	idec.org	IDEC seeks to advance interior design education, scholarship, and service.
Interior Design Society	interiordesignsociety.org	A professional organization that focuses specifically on residential interior design. Membership status is based on years of experience in the field and education. Corporations may also join.
International Association of Lighting Designers (IALD)	iald.org	A professional lighting designers' organization that provides education and networking for architectural lighting designers.
International Furnishing and Design Association (IFDA)	ifda.com	An interior design organization that focuses on the interior furnishings industry. Members are executives from corporations within this specific industry.
International Interior Design Association	iida.com	An organization that merged several previous groups, this global network provides opportunities for members to connect with designers around the world on issues related to the impact of design.
Manufactured Housing Institute (MHI)	manufacturedhousing.org	A trade organization that offers support, education, networking, and advocacy for members who are actively engaged in any aspect of the factory-built housing industry.
National Council for Interior Design Qualification (NCIDQ)	ncidq.org	An organization that serves to certify interior designers through the NCIDQ examination, which focuses on health and safety aspects of interior design, including materials used and construction techniques.
National Kitchen and Bath Association (NKBA)	nkba.org	A trade organization that provides education and training, networking opportunities, and three levels of internationally recognized certification in kitchen and bathroom design, among a variety of other services.

Figure 9-2 Check out the websites of these professional interior design and housing organizations.

furnishings with the intent of making the space pleasing. Interior decorators help people choose colors, textures, flooring, window coverings, furniture, and other home furnishings. Becoming an interior decorator does not require formal training or experience.

An interior designer, on the other hand, is defined by the American Society of Interior Designers (ASID) as a professional who is trained to create functional, quality environments. An interior designer is qualified through education, training, experience, and professional examination. Interior designers focus on more than just aesthetics. They are trained to create an environment that is comfortable, safe, healthy, and efficient as well as aesthetically pleasing. In order to accomplish this, interior designers must learn about the unique needs of their clients and understand space planning and function, accessible or universal design, building construction, lighting and electrical specifications, and building and home furnishing materials. Interior designers consider the movement of people around and through a space, noise and sound transmission, maintenance, and safety requirements. In essence, interior design is the art and science of creating an interior environment for the people who live or work in the space.

In some states, interior designers are required to be licensed or registered. They may be required to have an NCIDQ certificate, which is earned after meeting education and experience requirements and passing an exam. (NCIDQ stands for National Council for Interior Design Qualification.) The housing field is very different from the interior design field. Housing specialists work in business or family services careers. (See Chapter 11.) A bachelor's degree in housing, family services, business or public administration, finance, economics, or a related field is needed for a career as a housing specialist. Housing specialists need knowledge of housing laws, regulations, ordinances, programs, and resources. They must understand current social and economic issues and practices affecting housing and community development. A combination of educational background and experience provides the best preparation for a career in this field.

What Are the Working Conditions?

While some interior designers are employed by small to large architectural and interior design firms, others own a business and are self-employed. They may be part of an architectural and design team or may work independently. The work is creative, but it also requires a knowledge of business practices and technical knowledge of building materials and specifications. Just like the fashion industry, the interior design industry is fast-paced and dynamic. With each change in technology and with each new trend, new opportunities arise in the research, production, design, and sales of home furnishing products. It is an industry in which new markets form quickly, new methods produce new products, and consumers keep chasing the newest trends. Home furnishing fashions may not change as quickly as clothing fashions, but they are always changing.

Another similarity to the fashion industry is the creative work environment. Like the fashion industry, interior design is known for teamwork among coworkers and rivalry among competitors. It demands professionals who are creative, forward-thinking, and not afraid to take a risk. It is an industry known for long and variable working hours. Some parts of a project may require more personal involvement and a greater time commitment than others. For example, when a project is being implemented and installation takes place, a higher level of activity and longer work hours are often required.

The interior design industry continually offers new opportunities and new ideas. The creative nature of the environment is stimulating. People who thrive in this environment are attracted to the pace and energy. The creative process stimulates them.

Professionals in the area of housing work in a variety of settings including affordable housing communities, group homes, retirement communities, real estate offices, military support services, construction and development companies, utility companies, college and university campuses, and federal and state government agencies. They work with program participants to identify affordable housing that meets the needs of their clients. For those who enjoy working closely with people, careers in the housing field are ideal because job duties revolve around the development of personal and professional relationships with others. There are significant intangible rewards in helping people secure housing.

Housing careers promote collaborative working teams that share a common purpose. Working with like-minded colleagues in a collaborative effort is gratifying. In this environment, there is often room for creative problem solving. In addition, housing careers offer interactions with people from diverse socio-economic, ethnic, and cultural backgrounds.

Summary

Just like food, apparel, and nurturance, housing is one of the basic needs of individuals and families. It provides shelter from the elements. It also provides psychological and emotional stability and a sense of "home." The industry has two distinct segments: interior design and housing.

The field of interior design focuses on creating attractive and functional interior spaces that meet the needs of their users. There are many career paths within the interior design field, which is organized into two broad categories: residential and commercial interior design. Residential interior design focuses on the design of the inside of homes, while commercial interior design encompasses nonresidential interior spaces such as work environments, health care facilities, educational facilities, retail stores, and community spaces.

The housing segment deals with providing appropriate and affordable housing to individuals and families. This includes the family service and government agencies that provide housing assistance to low-income families. It also includes the business sector of real estate, mortgage lending, and relocation services and nonprofit housing developers.

How can you know if a career in interior design or housing is right for you? Start with these ideas.

Even if you decide that it is not an appropriate career path for you, the activities will give you an appreciation for the importance of housing and interior design in meeting people's basic needs.

Pursuing a Career in Interior Design and Housing

1. **Interview a professional.** The interior design and housing fields offer a wide array of professional opportunities. To explore career possibilities in interior design, refer to the American Society of Interior Designers website at asid.org. To understand career paths in the interior design and housing industries, refer to Figure 9-1. To get a practical view of the daily work of an interior designer, interview a professional in your chosen field. For example, you could interview a residential interior designer, the housing director at your university, an architect, a commercial interior designer, or an interior design or housing educator. Ask the person how he or she entered the field, what the advantages and disadvantages are, and what a typical day entails. Be sure to solicit advice for your career decision making.

2. **Shadow a professional.** Seek permission to spend time job shadowing an industry professional. Often, you can arrange this through your college or university. The more you observe, the more you will become familiar with the diverse and complex industry of interior design and housing. Observations could range from a few hours to several days. Also, internships, part-time and summer employment, and volunteer experiences will help you decide if this is the field for you.

3. **Train your eye for design.** If you are interested in interior design, you probably already have artistic aptitude. Train your eye to recognize good design by using the skills of observation and evaluation. Flip through architectural and design magazines, visit model homes or trade shows, and attend open houses in neighborhoods. Walk through furniture showrooms and if possible, visit

design markets where buyers purchase home furnishing goods and services. Visit art galleries, office buildings, and in general, become aware of the design world around you. Visit stores that sell flooring, home appliances, upholstery fabrics, and other materials used in interiors. Begin experimenting with paint and textures in your living environment. Experiment with the effect of light on the perception of color. Experiment with traffic patterns and furniture arrangement. File advertisements, photographs, magazine pictures, and articles relating to interior design in a notebook for easy reference.

4. **Know the issues.** Housing involves many issues. Attend a public hearing on community development for residential housing. Study the request for input related to environmental impact, affordability, and neighborhood issues. Acquire information about energy and water savings and policy from utility companies and cities. Explore how these affect housing and design.

5. **Become acquainted with professional organizations.** Professional organizations provide a wealth of information regarding housing and interior design careers since their mission is to educate and support professionals. They also cover relevant industry research and review new developments. Many professional organizations include job banks/listings of open positions for prospective employers and employees. Generally, they do not try to sell anything to members. Look up each of the websites listed in Figure 9-2.

Questions for Thought

1. Access the United States Department of Labor, Bureau of Labor Statistics website. Choose two related career profiles listed here and report on the career description, typical working conditions, job outlook, and expected earnings:
   - interior designers
   - housing program administrators
   - appraisers and assessors of real estate
   - real estate brokers
   - real estate sales agents
   - property, real estate, and community association managers
   - retail salespeople
   - eligibility interviewers, government programs

2. As you look back on interior design trends over the past several decades, it is easy to distinguish between eras. For example, the 1970s are remembered for the colors (harvest gold, avocado green, burnt orange) and textures (shag carpet, printed velvets, fake fur). The 1980s are remembered for the colors (dusty rose, light blue, grey) and textures (sleek, metallic, smooth). The 1990s are known for bland color palates (taupe, sage green) and natural textures. Which interior design trends will define this decade? How will this decade be described by future design historians?

3. Which home furnishing retailers are the most popular among college students today? What are the most prominent trends in interior furnishings in student housing? Do you predict that their popularity will be sustained over the next decade? Why or why not?

4. In Chapter 5 you read about forecasted changes that will affect the family. These changes will affect every aspect of how people live and work. Based on what you have read in previous chapters, how do you predict communities will look in 10 years? Will affordable housing remain an issue? Will the quest for universal design continue or is it a fad? Will sustainable, or green, design become a legislated building requirement? For each question, explain your answer with specific information.

5. Architecture is an expression or symbol of current events. For example, ornate Victorian homes of the 1800s were a reaction to the Industrial Revolution and the quickly changing society. Simple and uncluttered homes of the 1950s were a response to the need for housing for baby boomers and a reflection on the appeal of Modernism. How does residential architectural and interior design today reflect the values of current society?

References and Resources

Ackerman, J. S. (1990). *The villa.* Cambridge, MA: Princeton University Press.

Apgar, W. C. (1991). *Housing in America: 1970-2000: The nation's housing needs for the balance of the 20th century.* Cambridge, MA: Joint Center for Housing Studies, Harvard University.

Baker, J. M. (1994). *American house styles.* New York: Norton.

Baum, F. (1960). *The wonderful wizard of oz.* New York: Dover. (Original work published 1900)

Bauman, J. F., Biles, R., & Szylvian, K. M. (Eds.). (2000). *From tenements to the Taylor homes: In search of an urban housing policy in twentieth-century America.* University Park, PA: Pennsylvania State University Press.

Bonda, P., Sosnowchik, K. (2007). *Sustainable commercial interiors.* Hoboken, NJ: Wiley.

Branson, G. B. (1991). *The complete guide to barrier-free housing: Convenient living for the elderly and the physically handicapped.* Whitehall, VA: Betterway Publications.

Burden, E. (1998). *Building facades.* New York: McGraw Hill.

Clark, C. E. (1986). *The American family home.* Chapel Hill: The University of North Carolina Press.

Craven, J. (2003). *The healthy home: Beautiful interiors that enhance the environment and your well-being.* Gloucester, MA: Rockport.

Davis, S. (2004). *Designing for the homeless: Architecture that works.* Berkeley, CA: University of California Press.

Famous quotations/stories of Winston Churchill. (n.d.). Retrieved from http://www.winstonchurchill.org/i4a/pages/index.cfm?pageid=388

Hartje, S., Tremblay, K., & Birdsong, C. (2006). Universal design in housing. In The Housing Education and Research Association (Ed.), *Introduction to housing* (pp. 191-224). Upper Saddle River, NJ: Prentice Hall.

Hays, R. A. (1995). *The federal government and urban housing: Ideology and change in public policy.* Albany: State University of New York Press.

Imrie, R. (1996). *Disability and the city: International perspectives.* London: Paul Chapman Publishing.

Knackstedt, M. (2002). *The interior design business handbook: A complete guide to profitability.* New York: Wiley.

Mace, R. (1988). *Universal design: Housing for the lifespan of all people.* Washington, DC: U.S. Department of Housing and Urban Development.

Marcus Tullius Cicero quotes. (1999–2006). Retrieved from http://thinkexist.com/quotes/marcus_tullius_cicero

Mason, J. B. (1982). *History of housing in the U.S., 1930-1980.* Houston: Gulf Publishing Co., Book Division.

Moe, R., & Wilkie, C. (1997). *Changing places.* New York: Holt.

Peloquin, A. A. (1994). *Barrier-free residential design.* New York: McGraw-Hill.

Pirkl, J. J. (1994). *Transgenerational design: Products for an aging population.* Florence, KY: Van Nostrand Reinhold.

Schwartz, P. C. (1983). *What style is it?* New York: Wiley.

Sorenson, R. J. (1979). *Design for accessibility.* New York: McGraw-Hill.

Urbanelli, E. (1996). *Modern American houses.* New York: McGraw-Hill.

You never can tell. (March 23, 2007). In Wikipedia, The Free Encyclopedia. Retrieved from http://en.wikipedia.org/wiki/You_Never_Can_Tell

Chapter 10

Careers in Family and Consumer Sciences Education and Extension

After studying this chapter, you will be able to:

- analyze opportunities, issues, and trends in family and consumer sciences education and extension.

- discuss career opportunities in family and consumer sciences education and extension.

- explain what academic training is needed to become a family and consumer sciences teacher or extension agent.

- describe working conditions of a typical family and consumer sciences teacher or family and consumer sciences extension educator.

Terry Carnahan laid the stack of student papers on her desk, sat down, and put her feet up. It was a typical spring day. Windows were open to let in fresh air, and the school year was still in full swing. A feeling of satisfaction flooded her mind. As was her daily habit, she spent a few minutes reviewing her day before she left for home. She realized that the day had been a success. She had reasonable focus in the classroom, and there were no major skirmishes between students. She even had time to have a couple of one-on-one conversations with students about personal matters. As she regrouped, her thoughts turned toward her guest speaking engagement tonight at her college alma mater. Her task was to talk to students about the field of education. She had only been a family and consumer sciences high school teacher for two years, which caused her to wonder how she could possibly articulate all she had learned in these past two years. She wanted to share an honest account of what it was like to be a teacher—both the highs and the lows. As her thoughts went back to when she first decided to be a teacher, the words she would say tonight took shape:

I decided to become a teacher. Not because of a lifetime dream and not because my mother was a teacher. I didn't have a favorite teacher whom I wanted to emulate. I became a teacher because I was told that I couldn't.

I was quite confident of my decision to major in family studies with the intent of going to graduate school to become a therapist. To expand my volunteer experience for graduate school admissions, I decided to volunteer as a tutor at the local high school. The first day I walked in, I realized I was walking into a whole new world. Sure, I had been in high school just a few years before, but my experience was nothing like this one. The suburban, ethnically homogeneous, upper-middle-class school I attended was very different from the ethnic, social, and economic diversity I found in this large urban high school. At the end of the first day, I was frustrated and ready to quit.

I walked into the principal's office and told her I had experienced enough chaos. She asked me what I was studying in college and I told her of my dream of counseling teens. After a rather discouraging conversation with the "worldly-wise" principal, I sat wondering why she would dissuade me from working with teens just because of my upper-middle-class, suburban upbringing. I left the office, still frustrated, and shortly thereafter, decided to really "get in the trenches." I decided to become a teacher simply to prove her wrong.

At that time, I thought being a teacher meant having summers off and short workdays, and that anyone could be a good teacher. I was going to touch young lives and be everyone's favorite teacher. Students would come to me and share their darkest secrets. I would prepare and execute brilliant and inspiring lessons that would change lives. In the summers, I would travel the world. No one told me what teaching was really going to be like. These are the things I never knew.

I never knew that I would spend infinite evenings planning lessons that would be met by rolling eyes, groans, and complete apathy. I never knew that in the rare case that a new lesson went off brilliantly and without a hitch, an unexpected fire alarm would sound and the rest of the class time would be lost forever. I never knew that my homework assignments would be ignored and threats of failing grades would fall on deaf ears. I didn't know that I would often feel more stress over giving a failing grade to a student than the student who received it would. I didn't know that students wouldn't always give me the respect I thought all teachers deserved (even though I was known for my silly teacher impersonations and attitude when I was in high school).

Two years later, I now know the exhilaration of creating a lesson that leaves teenagers buzzing as they leave the room and how it feels to work in a collegiate atmosphere with other intelligent and like-minded people who pull together and help one another. Back then, I didn't know how astonished I would be when a holiday card was laid on my desk or when a "thank you" escaped a smiling face. I didn't know how I would learn to laugh at myself and to not take myself so seriously when I tripped over an electrical cord in front of 30 sixteen-year-olds or innocently used a phrase that had a whole different (and vulgar!) meaning than what I intended.

No one told me I would be haunted at night by a conversation with one of my many students who have traumatic home lives. Take Carl, for example. His mother, trying to make ends meet but struggling with a drug addiction, finally came to the end of her resources. She and Carl ended up living on the streets to avoid staying with an overbearing uncle. Of course, I didn't find out about Carl's situation right away, but through circumstantial evidence, it became apparent over time. Despite my desire, I know I can't give my students a family life like I was fortunate

enough to have, where I never worried about food on the table or needed to hide out in my own bedroom. For some, I just wanted to give them a home. Although I've learned how to access multiple social service resources, I have also learned when contacting authorities can make a potentially volatile situation downright dangerous. I'm learning when to help and when to just listen. I've learned to live my own life through worrisome holidays and school vacations when I wonder how "my kids" are faring.

Most of all, I didn't know that I would feel so needed. I've discovered that teaching happens in one-on-one relationships. By just seeking out a student and asking how she is, I'm teaching her that someone really cares. Often, I'm teaching life can be better by offering ideas and resources for solving problems that my students encounter. This is where my expertise in family and consumer sciences comes into play.

I never knew how practical and important family and consumer sciences content and skills are for high school students until I began relating the content I learned in college to their teenage lives. Every day I help students gain practical knowledge about the important things of life—human growth and development; personal behavior; housing and environment; food and nutrition; apparel and textiles; and personal resource management—that everyone needs in order to make sound decisions that contribute to a healthy, productive, and fulfilling life. In the hour I spend every day with each student, including Carl, I try to open options for them to improve their quality of life for years to come. Everywhere I look I'm inspired with a new teaching strategy. Every day I have new encounters and new breakthroughs.

My life is so varied. No two days are the same. No two students are the same. My days are filled with grading assignments, planning lessons, purchasing supplies, following through on discipline issues, and keeping up on individual student needs. Sometimes I'm so busy living each day in the fast pace of adolescence that I forget I am a teacher because I crave cultivating minds and spirits.

Each semester I face a whole new group of students and I see another group moving on. In each group there are a few students who have finally discovered their ability to succeed and have come to understand they can improve their own quality of life. There aren't many people who get to witness these profound changes in people on a daily basis.

Suddenly, Terry realized that an hour had passed and she would now have to grab a quick dinner before she drove to her alma mater. As she got into her car, she paused and sighed. She thought about how full her life was. All things considered, teaching was a lifestyle and a career choice that was right for her.

Issues in the News
The Future of Family and Consumer Sciences in Public Schools

Why aren't family and consumer sciences courses required in all districts and states? Why are some districts and states actually cutting back on family and consumer sciences programs? Is there a future for family and consumer sciences education? These are questions that plague many family and consumer sciences professionals. What are the answers? The answers are unknown, but it is known that quality and perception of need play a large part.

Family and consumer sciences classes are based on the premise that everyone needs preparation in basic life skills for career and family success. Parenting, budgeting, and nutritional meal planning are some of the life skills taught in family and consumer sciences. Critical thinking is an important part of all family and consumer sciences courses. In some districts and states, family and consumer sciences courses are required for graduation. For example, in Washington State, personal health and wellness is a graduation requirement. In many districts in Washington State, these courses are taught by family and consumer sciences teachers.

Family and consumer sciences classes are very popular with students because they often include practical learning experiences such as observations, in-house preschools, internships at local food service establishments or at apparel or interiors firms, classroom visits of infants and young children, or field trips. Some students earn service-learning credits. Many students make career decisions based on these class experiences. Generally speaking, many students report that their family and consumer sciences experiences have had a major impact on them and will continue to do so in future years, both personally and professionally.

Unfortunately, far too few students are able to participate in family and consumer sciences courses. Why? A commonly held misconception is that these courses are not important for college-bound students. Yet, learning life skills prepares both college-bound and non-college-bound students for life. Since many school administrators, parents, politicians, and students place high value on college preparation courses, many opt out of courses that are perceived as superfluous to reaching the goal of college admission. Government officials respond to what they hear when making budget decisions. If family and consumer sciences advocates are not making their voices heard, family and consumer sciences curriculum could be cut from educational budgets.

What can you do? Encourage students to take family and consumer sciences courses and talk about the skills you gained from the courses you have taken. Also, advocate for family and consumer sciences programs through letters or testimony to your school boards, legislators, and State Department of Education.

From helping people to understand mortgage rates and food labels to providing parenting information, the family and consumer sciences discipline focuses on family relationships and meeting the basic needs of food, clothing, shelter, and nurturance. According to the mission of family and consumer sciences, meeting family needs is done through empowerment. This means individuals and families are taught how to meet their own needs—a process that comes about through education and resource availability. The many roles of the family and consumer sciences teacher, from preschool through corporate training, will be discussed in this chapter. Also, basic questions such as what a teacher's typical day involves and what their working conditions are like will be answered.

The Field of Family and Consumer Sciences Education and Extension

Today's classroom teachers are members of a vital and rewarding profession. Will there be jobs by the time you have the proper training? For the most part, the answer is yes. According to the U.S. Bureau of Labor Statistics, there were approximately 4.1 million teaching jobs in 2013. Of those, roughly 1.1 million taught high school, and approximately 2 million were elementary or middle school teachers (U.S. Department of Labor, Bureau of Labor Statistics, 2013).

Today's family and consumer sciences classes are relevant for everyone. Focusing on all ages of the lifespan, they include classes on subjects such as life careers, nutrition and wellness, interpersonal relationships, child development and parenting, and age-related roles and responsibilities. Family and consumer sciences educators, whether in the private or community sector, need in-depth knowledge in child and family studies as well as an understanding of nutrition, consumer education, textiles, and interior design. Many states now mandate consumer education or financial literacy. This subject matter may be taught by family and consumer sciences teachers.

Career Opportunities in Family and Consumer Sciences Education and Extension

Traditional teaching in public or private schools is one of the most visible career paths in education. Many teachers wish to pursue additional education in order to serve as a school counselor, school or district administrator, or college or university professor. Other opportunities that utilize teaching skills include extension, corporate training, research, textbook publishing and sales, government positions, and curriculum and test development. Typical careers in the family and consumer sciences education and extension field are listed in **Figure 10-1**.

Sample Career Areas in Family and Consumer Sciences Education and Extension		
Adult education teacher	**Corporate trainer**	**Researcher**
After-school program supervisor	Curator	School administrator
Career counselor	Curriculum developer	Secondary school teacher
College/university professor	Government affairs specialist	Technical writer
Community educator	Legislation lobbyist	Teenage parenting educator
Cooperative extension specialist	Marketing specialist	Textbook editor

Figure 10-1 A variety of careers are available in family and consumer sciences education and extension.

Middle School and Secondary School Education

Family and consumer sciences teachers help students know how to function independently in the home, school, workplace, and in the community. The focus of middle school and high school programs is different from that in elementary school teaching because there is a more direct focus on educating individuals and families to take action for the well-being of self and others in the home, community, and workplace. Middle school and high school family and consumer sciences programs help students learn to balance their family life and work life.

Middle and high school teachers help students delve more deeply into family and consumer sciences subjects introduced in elementary school and expose them to more information about the world around them. High school teachers specialize in a specific subject within family and consumer sciences such as personal finance, personal decision making, ethics, marriage and family relationships, child development, apparel construction, textiles, interior design, food science, nutrition, and cultural foods, among others. These courses are often career-oriented and are part of the school's career education program. Family and consumer sciences high school teachers focus on the following topics (Association for Career and Technical Education, 2007):

- balancing personal, home, family, and work lives
- communicating and interacting effectively as a spouse and parent
- strengthening the well-being of individuals and families across the lifespan
- promoting optimal nutrition and wellness across the lifespan
- functioning effectively as providers and consumers of goods and services, including food, clothing, and shelter
- managing limited resources to meet the needs of family members
- becoming responsible citizens and leaders in family, community, and work settings

The *National Standards*, developed by thousands of family and consumer sciences educators and other professionals, offer specific guidelines and communicate direction for family and consumer sciences curriculum across the United States. The boxed feature *Issues in the News: National Education Standards and Guidelines* in this chapter has more information about the National Standards. For example, family and consumer sciences high school teachers often use critical and creative thinking skills to address problems in diverse family, community, and work environments.

Family and consumer sciences teachers integrate content from many basic disciplines into their curriculum, including English, history, social studies, and psychology. Science, technology, mathematics, and even engineering principles are often included in family and consumer sciences courses such as food science, child development, and interior design. Science, technology, engineering, and mathematics are often referred to as STEM disciplines.

Family and consumer sciences career education teachers instruct and train students for life management and to work in a wide variety of fields. Family and consumer sciences teachers teach early childhood development, food production and hospitality management, and apparel and interior design. They often teach courses that are in high demand by area employers, who may provide input into the curriculum and offer internships to students.

Secondary school teachers' responsibilities are often more varied than at the elementary school level. Secondary teachers may have structured responsibilities outside the family and consumer sciences classroom such as monitoring study halls, advising school clubs, chaperoning events, or coaching. Teachers will occasionally assist students in choosing courses, colleges, and careers. Unstructured activities may include counseling students or assisting them with personal issues.

Many high school classes are becoming less structured, with many more application activities and collaborative group learning. Students

Professional Profile

High School Teacher— Family and Consumer Sciences

Tami Brewer

How did you get into your line of work?

As I look back on my life, I think that my earliest career influence was my mother. She is a teacher. I grew up "helping out" around the school. I would clean the classroom, cut out art projects, take down or put up bulletin boards, and run errands. Eventually, I would correct papers, enter grades, design bulletin boards, tutor kids after school, make copies, or anything else my mom would let me do. People would always ask me what I wanted to be when I grew up and I swore I would never be a teacher. I knew it was a lot of work and much of it was not very glamorous. What I did not realize was that, in my heart, I was a teacher. I am not sure if this was inherited, learned, or both, but I admit that it is a big part of who I am. It took me until my junior year of college to finally realize that teaching was for me. It energizes me. In fact, I enjoy each year more than the last as I work to improve my teaching and adjust to changing times.

What does your "typical" day entail?

What "typical" day? One thing is for certain, teaching is never boring! I teach subjects that I love and relate to life—Family Health (a ninth-grade state requirement), Independent Living, Family Psychology/Relationships, and Honors Psychology.

There are a few tasks that I prefer not to do (grading is one of them), but for the most part, I am "always on my toes." Most days include prepping materials, talking to students, communicating with many colleagues and parents by e-mail, answering questions, finding resources, assessing student progress, problem solving, motivating the unmotivated, behavior management, supervising the halls, leading classroom discussions or labs, planning/designing lessons, research (I am always learning new things), and most of all having fun with my students. (A sense of humor is a must!)

How do you fulfill the mission of family and consumer sciences— that is, how does your work improve people's quality of life?

Fulfilling the mission of family and consumer sciences involves classroom instruction that focuses on skill building, critical thinking, self-reflection, leadership development, and community involvement. However, I believe that who I am as a role model is just as important as what I teach in the classroom. Students can sense if you truly "practice what you preach." This means that I must have good self-care too! My students will not benefit from a haggard, exhausted teacher. I am only able to give my best in the classroom when I am in balance. I am not sure if I can claim to actually improve people's quality of life, but I may point them in a new direction, teach them a skill, motivate them to action, increase their awareness, connect them to community resources, or cause them to rethink their behavior so that they can improve their own quality of life.

Issues in the News
National Education Standards and Guidelines

The educational standards movement has gained much public visibility. Educational standards have been the basis of many political platforms and the subject of countless news broadcasts, newspaper and magazine articles, and the controversial topic of conversation among teachers and parents.

Rigorous educational standards have been strongly supported by many people, both in and outside the education field. Why and how did educational standards become such a hot topic? Most people credit the now infamous report *A Nation at Risk* (National Commission on Excellence in Education, 1983) as the initiating event of the contemporary standards movement. An often-quoted line from the report announced: "The educational foundations of our society are presently being eroded by a rising tide of mediocrity that threatens our very future as a nation and a people."

After this report was widely distributed, then President George Bush and the nation's governors called an Education Summit in Charlottesville in September, 1989. At this summit, they established six educational goals to be reached by the year 2000. These goals were outlined in the State of the Union address of 1990. The next year, congress established the National Council on Education Standards and Testing (NCEST). This group began asking questions such as: What should be studied? How should learning be measured? What standards of performance should be set?

These efforts had an impact on national subject-matter organizations, such as family and consumer sciences educators, who sought to establish voluntary standards or guidelines in their respective areas. The family and consumer sciences national education standards were established

with the input of thousands of family and consumer sciences educators, business and industry people, and other family and consumer sciences professionals. These 16 standards define and give common direction to the discipline of family and consumer sciences and serve as guidelines throughout the country to ensure comprehensive quality programs. They were specially designed to align with academic standards in math, science, and language arts. The standards include program competencies and objectives, along with suggested teaching methodologies. The 16 standards are listed here.

Standard 1: **Career, Community, and Family Connections:** Integrate multiple life roles and responsibilities in family, work, and community settings.

Standard 2: **Consumer and Family Resources:** Evaluate management practices related to the human, economic, and environmental resources.

often work in groups to discuss and solve problems. For example, family and consumer sciences teachers may teach course content using child development laboratories, food preparation kitchens, or computer simulations. Student groups complete exercises that require them to apply knowledge, interact with others, adapt to new technology, and logically think through

problems. *Family, Career and Community Leaders of America (FCCLA)* is a nonprofit student organization that promotes application of family and consumer sciences content in schools, at home, and in the community. The FCCLA goal is to improve the quality of life for students and their families and to prepare students for the adult world.

Standard 3: **Consumer Services:** Integrate knowledge, skills, and practices needed for a career in consumer services.

Standard 4: **Education and Early Childhood:** Integrate knowledge, skills, and practices required for careers in early childhood, education, and services.

Standard 5: **Facilities Management and Maintenance:** Integrate knowledge, skills, and practices required for careers in facilities management and maintenance.

Standard 6: **Family:** Evaluate the significance of family and its effects on the well-being of individuals and society.

Standard 7: **Family and Community Services:** Synthesize knowledge, skills, and practices required for careers in family and community services.

Standard 8: **Food Production and Services:** Integrate knowledge, skills, and practices required for careers in food production and services.

Standard 9: **Food Science, Dietetics, and Nutrition:** Integrate knowledge, skills, and practices required for careers in food science, food technology, dietetics, and nutrition.

Standard 10: **Hospitality, Tourism, and Recreation:** Synthesize knowledge, skills, and practices required for careers in hospitality, tourism, and recreation.

Standard 11: **Housing and Interior Design:** Integrate knowledge, skills, and practices required for careers in housing and interior design.

Standard 12: **Human Development:** Analyze factors that influence human growth and development.

Standard 13: **Interpersonal Relationships:** Demonstrate respectful and caring relationships in the family, workplace, and community.

Standard 14: **Nutrition and Wellness:** Demonstrate nutrition and wellness practices that enhance individual and family well-being.

Standard 15: **Parenting:** Evaluate the effects of parenting roles and responsibilities on strengthening the well-being of individuals and families.

Standard 16: **Textiles, Fashion, and Apparel:** Integrate knowledge, skills, and practices required for careers in textiles and apparel.

Establishing national educational standards has not been without controversy. Many people question whether the standards should be mandatory or voluntary. Others question whether the right people are establishing the standards. Still others question whether standards and guidelines should be established at the state or local rather than the national level. The most widely questioned issue, however, deals with the concern that standards and guidelines may lead to teaching toward standardized exams or other assessment outcomes.

Developed by the National Association of State Administrators of Family and Consumer Sciences (NASAFACS).

College and University Teaching and Research

College and university professors generally specialize in one specific discipline such as family and consumer sciences, textiles, interior design, or nutrition. Most colleges and universities require a doctoral degree, although some hire teachers with a master's degree for part-time teaching or instruction of lower division classes for freshman and sophomore students. Two-year colleges and community colleges generally require a master's degree. Higher education is becoming more competitive, however, and colleges and universities are becoming more selective in their hiring process, making it more difficult for those with a master's degree to secure employment.

It usually takes three or more years of full-time study to complete a doctoral program. Some graduate programs require completion of a master's degree (2–3 years) before acceptance into a doctoral program, while others combine the master's and doctoral degrees. Graduate programs include required coursework, comprehensive examinations, and a dissertation or research project at the doctoral level.

Higher education provides many benefits for faculty members. It offers many of the same benefits of K through 12 education but is generally more flexible—allowing opportunities for international teacher exchanges, research, professional development, travel, student advising, assignments to conduct in-depth research projects and writing, and fewer discipline issues.

Professional Profile

Retired Secondary Family and Consumer Sciences Teacher, Part-Time College Professor

Kathleen Wilson

How did you get into your line of work?

From an early age, I have had a love for learning new things. So many subject areas interested me. I received my degree in food, nutrition, and education. In college, I was very involved in the student preprofessional section of the American Home Economics Association, now the American Association of Family and Consumer Sciences. This gave me the chance to hone my leadership skills as well as make many contacts in the field of education. I became a public high school teacher. After a couple of years of teaching, I completed my master's degree in consumer economics and education. Later I completed graduate work in hospitality and restaurant management.

Being a teacher has given me the opportunity to explore my many varied interests. Early in my teaching career I was nominated to serve on President Nixon's White House conference on Children and Youth. Many other opportunities became available, including serving as a Cooperative Extension Agent, local television appearances on consumer issues, and being selected as a state finalist for the Teacher in Space program, National Aeronautics and Space Administration.

Most of my teaching career has involved developing, directing, and acting as a chef instructor for the culinary arts and commercial foods program for a public school district. Today, I teach in a university-level family and consumer sciences program that prepares students to become effective family and consumer sciences educators.

Adult Education

Adult education offers instruction for adults outside the traditional degree-seeking programs of colleges and universities. Generally administered through state and community agencies, adult education may include literacy programs, workforce development programs, technical training, high school degree equivalency programs, English as a second language (ESL) programs, or basic academic skill development in math, science, or computers.

Adult educators plan, deliver, and evaluate educational programs. Their roles are similar to those of elementary, middle school, high school, and college educators, but their audience is different. Like their counterparts in other educational fields, they use lecture, practical learning, group work, and projects to teach the course content. They must stay informed and current

What does your "typical" day entail?

As a high school teacher running a high school culinary arts program, my day progressed much like a restaurant owner or manager. However, adding extra complexity to the day was working with teens as students rather than employees. Each new term, I had new students. The exciting part was seeing students learn new food service skills, develop interpersonal skills, and grow in confidence. I mentored and encouraged all those with whom I came in contact. I tried to give them a chance to succeed.

The field of education can be a strong base for many career fields. It is versatile and adaptable. Teaching and running a high school culinary arts program is a good example. This can also be a disadvantage, however. As a high school family and consumer sciences teacher, I often had to be a "jack of all trades." The field changes constantly, with new technology, new scientific advances, and societal and professional progressions. This can be

How do you fulfill the mission of family and consumer sciences— that is, how does your work improve people's quality of life?

Every day, I encourage, teach, and mentor others to use technology, resources, personal energy, and developing skills to improve their quality of life. I have always believed in the saying, "You can give people fish to eat, but you can help them more by teaching them how to fish." My joy is seeing others become successful.

Over my career, I have worked with many special needs students and their families. I have helped them see possibilities and have aided them in helping themselves to adapt for successful living. I usually did not dwell on the problem, but helped them find solutions. My major goal in living has been, and still is, to help those with whom I come in contact to live to their full potential.

Professional Profile

Professor, Apparel and Textiles

Jaeil Lee, Ph.D.

How did you get into your line of work?

To become a professor has been my dream since I was a little girl. I grew up in Korea and finished college there. While I was working on my undergraduate degree, I had a professor who inspired me to reach for my dreams. I admired her work, her lifestyle, and her love for learning. She mentored me and advised me to go to graduate school in the United States. Although it was a big leap, I chose and applied to a large university in America that is known for its excellent graduate programs. I moved to the United States and completed both my master's degree and Ph.D. It was not easy to move to a foreign culture and to complete graduate work in my second language. However, it was a challenge I am glad I took. After graduation, I worked as a technical designer at Abercrombie & Fitch. I enjoyed my work immensely but still had the lifelong dream of being a college professor. I took a risk and made a career switch from industry to higher education. It is a perfect fit for me. The working and teaching experiences I had equipped me to teach hands-on experience as well as industry standards to students.

What does your "typical" day entail?

Although my days vary, each day focuses around three basic tasks. These include class preparation and teaching, advising students, and working on academic projects. I usually teach three courses per term. This means I spend a number of hours in the classroom each week. I enjoy working with students immensely, but each class period takes preparation. I want my students to learn what they need to know to be competitive in their chosen field. Teaching involves preparing lectures and demonstrations, setting up field trips and guest speakers, preparing syllabi and class projects, writing exams, and of course, grading all the work I have assigned. Fashion is an ever-changing field and, thus, my courses have to reflect this constant change.

I also spend a significant part of the week advising students. I help them with course selections and registration, help them to secure internship sites and supervise their experiences, and generally serve as a sounding board or guide. One of the most gratifying experiences is helping students secure employment. When I know a student well, I can help match him or her with the right employer.

Lastly, I spend time working on my academic pursuits. This includes doing research, writing journal articles and textbooks, and sometimes submitting creative projects to juried conferences. Although I never seem to have enough time to pursue all of the projects in which I am interested, my academic pursuits provide for a highly creative outlet.

How do you fulfill the mission of family and consumer sciences— that is, how does your work improve people's quality of life?

In my job, I see people grow and change as they learn new skills, have new experiences, and are faced with challenges that require critical thinking. I help people prepare for and find rewarding careers in the fashion industry. Clothing is one of the essential items related to each individual's well-being. Clothing is a moveable environment; thus comfortable clothing is important to a person's physical as well as psychological well-being. Therefore, designing functional as well as aesthetically pleasing clothing is essential to improve people's quality of life.

in their teaching. As in all teaching, personal interaction between students and the instructor is important.

Adult education programs are often government-funded or supported, although they may be privately funded and for profit. Community colleges and universities may also provide adult education through non-degree programs. Because the field is so varied, career opportunities run the gamut from one-course contractual agreements to full-time teaching positions. Adult education teachers can also be found in corporate training departments, job training centers, community centers, hospitals, churches, or any environment where training and educational programs have been implemented.

Family and consumer sciences educators should be well prepared to seek career opportunities in adult education. First, they understand adult learners from a human development perspective, including cognitive, emotional, and social needs in a learning environment. Second, they are trained to take research-based knowledge and apply it to practical daily living. Adult education programs provide instruction in a wide variety of subjects that students take for personal enrichment or self-improvement such as cooking, personal finance, and time management classes. Third, family and consumer sciences educators are equipped with skills to plan curriculum, choose appropriate teaching strategies for different learners, and to assess learning.

Cooperative Extension Agent/Educator

The *cooperative extension service*, also known as the Extension Service of the United States Department of Agriculture (USDA), provides nonformal educational programs designed to help people use research-based knowledge to improve their lives. These programs are primarily administered through thousands of county and regional extension offices that are federally funded and connected to land-grant universities in each state.

Cooperative extension agents, or educators, provide educational programs in family and consumer sciences, 4-H youth development, agriculture, and community and rural development. They act as community resource people, spokespeople, and community educators in all areas of family and consumer sciences. For example, they answer questions posed by community members pertaining to parenting, family budget matters, and consumer concerns by giving specific information and technical assistance. It is common for cooperative extension agents to coordinate youth 4-H activities and to recruit, train, and develop community lay leaders. They are professional employees of state land-grant universities and are supported by the federal government. Their job duties are varied and include offering formal and informal educational outreach opportunities to individuals and families. On a day-to-day level, agents may teach courses, consult with the public, plan programs based on current and future needs, consult with experts, or seek outside funding grants or collaborative opportunities. Their work is practical and people-oriented.

Corporate Training

Corporate trainers design, conduct, and supervise development programs for company employees or members of organizations. Classes and workshops offered by corporate trainers can focus on technical or physical skills, but most often they are focused on people skills such as motivation, effective communication, leadership, or team building. These are often referred to as "soft skills."

This is a natural role for family and consumer sciences educators since corporate training often centers on managing work and family life—a subject family and consumer sciences educators are well prepared to teach. Increasingly, employers recognize that support in family/work issues enhances employee productivity and quality of work and builds loyalty to the firm. Family and consumer sciences gives corporate trainers a unique understanding of their clients as individuals and as participants in families and communities.

Some corporate trainers are self-employed and work on a consulting basis. Others are employed within a human resources division of an organization or work for a company that specializes in providing corporate training.

Preparing to Enter the Family and Consumer Sciences Education and Extension Field

What does it take to be a good teacher? Most of us can name a favorite teacher from our past. What was it about this person that made him or her successful as a teacher? Good teachers may be outgoing and dramatic, soft-spoken and caring, articulate and intimidating, or "out of the box" in their approach to life. Although teachers may vary, good teaching requires a common set of skills and aptitudes. The most obvious skill, of course, is a talent for working with people of all ages. Educators must also be equipped with organizational, administrative, communication, and recordkeeping knowledge and skills. In their educational program and field experiences, they must develop the ability to influence, motivate, and train others utilizing patience and creativity. Teachers also need solid knowledge of content. The ability to understand, assess, and address learner needs is also very important.

There is always a need for talented teachers. Education, training, and library occupations are anticipated to add more than 1.4 million jobs over the next ten years in the education, training, and library field. This represents about a 15 percent increase in jobs and many of these will be in elementary/middle school and postsecondary education (U.S. Department of Labor, Bureau of Labor Statistics, 2013).

Several factors play into the increased need, including a desire for smaller class sizes, a large number of retiring teachers, and an increase in

the youth population. The education of America's children has become a political issue, and decision-makers are looking for ways to improve the educational system. Many people believe better-trained and more qualified teachers will solve many problems in the United States.

What kinds of teachers will be needed? It depends. Some geographic locations are predicted to experience larger population increases when compared to other areas. In addition to fast-growing suburban areas, many positions are available in inner city schools and rural communities where limited financial resources make recruiting and retaining teachers more challenging. Also, school districts may have difficulty finding qualified teachers in subject areas such as mathematics and science. Depending on teacher preparation programs and teacher retirements, family and consumer sciences teachers may also be difficult to find. For example, in Washington, California, Kansas, and other states, there were more family and consumer sciences high school teaching positions available than there were candidates to fill them (U.S. Department of Labor, Bureau of Labor Statistics, 2006). Most of the openings are not in major urban areas, so teachers who are mobile have an advantage over those who are not. Some districts offer incentives such as loan forgiveness and assistance in home-buying to attract teachers to the more rural and high cost-of-living areas.

Family and consumer sciences education is a vital component of private and public education and is relevant for everyone. Family and consumer sciences education includes classes for people at all levels of the lifespan on such topics as careers, nutrition and wellness, financial management, consumer decision-making, interpersonal relationships, child development and parenting, and age-related roles and responsibilities.

How can you know if the teaching profession is right for you? You can evaluate your strengths, weaknesses, skills, and interests in teaching family life and consumer knowledge and skills. If you are considering teaching

Professional Profile

Director of MESA (Math, Engineering, and Science Achievement)

Rashanah Botley

How did you get into your line of work?

I had an amazing experience as a family and consumer sciences major. Being a part of this major gave me the opportunity to study a topic that I am extremely passionate about: how to nurture healthy human development. The interdisciplinary nature of this major allowed me to capture a holistic snapshot of the many areas that are critical to development. As the product of a family that put an emphasis on the importance of education, I found myself focusing on how education plays a role in development, particularly for minorities. I did not plan on this exact line of work but the opportunity arose when I did my job search after graduation.

The knowledge I gained as a family and consumer sciences major prepared me to step into my current role as Director of MESA (Math, Engineering, and Science Achievement) at our local community college. The MESA program is designed to guide, support, and promote academic and career success among low-income community college students. The program is particularly concerned with providing underrepresented student populations, such as women and minorities, an opportunity to excel in these areas of study. My knowledge of development, social services, and education that I gained as a family and consumer sciences major has prepared me to nurture and respond to my students' needs holistically and with confidence.

What does your "typical" day entail?

My days involve working directly with students and interacting with colleagues and college administrators. It is a vibrant environment full of opportunities and challenges. Each day is different. Although I do spend considerable time doing paper work and planning, the majority of my time is in relationship. Whether talking in person or on the phone, e-mailing, or using social media, my job is about connections.

How do you fulfill the mission of family and consumer sciences— that is, how does your work improve people's quality of life?

I help people set and meet their educational goals to better their lives. While I have been blessed to find a great career, I plan to go to graduate school to further my knowledge. I plan to return to school to pursue a master's degree that will allow me to study the connection between education and culture and how this connection can be used to promote education among minorities. After completing my master's degree, I intend to pursue a doctoral degree. It is my ultimate dream to become a respected voice and advocate for minority education; I want to engage the culture and change the world one diploma at a time. I will forever be grateful for my experience as a family and consumer sciences major for planting the seeds of my dream.

family and consumer sciences, you may wish to increase your knowledge of the profession by observing teachers or attending a professional conference. Professional organizations can give you insight into the education and extension field. Several professional organizations, their websites, and descriptions are given in **Figure 10-2**.

What Training Is Needed?

Teaching is a career that offers the variety, challenge, and reward you would expect from a graduate-entry job. Teacher preparation standards vary by state and by the level of teaching. For example, teacher preparation varies greatly between high school and university-level teaching.

For a high school graduate, the usual route to becoming a teacher is to enroll in a four-year college or university program that includes student/practice teaching. Some states may require a four-year undergraduate degree followed by one or two years of education courses, including an internship or student/practice teaching. Other states offer four-year programs that

Professional Organizations Supporting Family and Consumer Sciences Education		
Professional Organization	**Web Address**	**Description**
American Association of Family and Consumer Sciences	aafcs.org	The premier and comprehensive professional organization dedicated to family and consumer sciences. Educational opportunities, certification, public policy support, and other resources are offered to professionals and students.
American Federation of Teachers	aft.org	An educators' labor union that sets standards and advocates for teachers in public policy arenas.
Association for Career and Technical Education	acteonline.org	A professional organization for educators in the career and workplace preparation field (sometimes referred to as vocational education). The organization provides member resources and advocates for funding of career and technical education programs.
Family, Career and Community Leaders of America (FCCLA)	fcclainc.org	A national career and technical organization aimed at students in family and consumer sciences in public and private schools in the U.S. Leadership skill development is emphasized.
National Association of Teachers of Family and Consumer Sciences	natefacs.org	An affiliate of the Association for Career and Technical Education. Its purpose is to improve and strengthen teacher education in family and consumer sciences. Other affiliated groups include the National Association of State Administrators of Family and Consumer Sciences and the National Association of Teacher Educators for Family and Consumer Sciences.
National Education Association	nea.org	The largest national professional organization for educators in the U.S. All levels of public education are supported, from early childhood through adult education.
National Extension Association of Family and Consumer Sciences	neafcs.org	A professional organization that provides education, leadership, networking, and scholarship opportunities for extension professionals.

Figure 10-2 These professional organizations support family and consumer sciences education and extension.

include all requirements for certification, including a student teaching experience. Teacher education programs are usually coordinated with state requirements for certification or licensure.

All 50 states require public school teachers to be licensed, but licensure is not usually required for teachers in private K through 12 schools, although individual schools may require a credential. State boards of education grant teaching licenses for the state the board represents. Teachers may be licensed to teach at the early childhood level, the elementary grades, the middle grades, a secondary education subject area, or in a specific subject area such as family and consumer sciences.

Some colleges and universities require students to wait until their junior year to apply for admission to a teacher education program. Entrance requirements often include personal interviews, arts and sciences prerequisite courses, a minimum grade point average, and proficiency tests in language arts and mathematics. For both elementary and secondary school education credentials, students take professional education courses such as philosophy of education along with courses that focus on teaching in specific subject areas. Many states also require that teachers work toward or obtain a master's degree, such as a Master of Education (M.Ed.).

Because many districts and states are finding it difficult to secure well-qualified teachers, many are offering alternative routes to teaching. For example, some states offer provisional teacher certification to college graduates who lack teacher education training but have expertise in subject areas where teachers are needed. Teachers who have provisional certificates are given a specified time to complete all requirements. If there are not enough certified teachers available, many states will issue emergency credentials to college graduates who want to teach but who have not met the state's minimum requirements. There are also special courses for graduates who want to make rapid progress in their careers. To find the best route into teaching for you, it is best to contact the advisor for the family and consumer sciences education program or a professor of education at a university that offers teaching programs and credentials.

What Are the Working Conditions?

Many experienced teachers will tell you that teaching is inspiring, challenging, and as unique as each student is. It's a career that does make a difference in the world, even though you might not feel it on a daily basis. Because learning takes time, the rewards tend to be long-term rather than instantaneous.

Most of a teacher's day is spent designing and delivering classroom learning experiences and managing activities that foster learning by meeting student needs and acknowledging their abilities. As time permits and depending on class size and teacher ratios, they may also work with students individually. Teachers plan, assign, and evaluate lessons; prepare, administer, and grade assignments; and maintain classroom discipline. They observe and evaluate student performance and potential, and increasingly they are asked to use new assessment methods. In many states, the use of standardized testing is increasing. In some schools, teachers are responsible for helping students organize personal portfolios. Teachers prepare report cards and meet with parents and school staff to discuss students' academic progress or personal problems.

In addition to classroom activities, teachers coordinate and communicate with other specialists, including reading consultants, speech therapists, and counselors. They identify physical or mental problems and refer students to the proper resource or agency for diagnosis and treatment. They may supervise extracurricular activities and accompany students on field trips. Teachers also participate in educational conferences and workshops.

Teachers have traditionally been autonomous decision-makers. Although teachers are frequently isolated from their colleagues because they work in a classroom of students,

Issues in the News
Teacher Pay and Recruitment

Beginning teacher salaries are improving in response to the nationwide teacher shortage. Experienced teachers, especially those with master's degrees or special certifications, make considerably higher salaries, especially in large urban areas. Individual teacher salaries vary greatly by district and state, too. Connecticut, Massachusetts, California, New Jersey, and New York have led in average teacher salaries over the past few years while South Dakota, North Carolina, Oklahoma, and Mississippi have offered some of the lowest teacher salaries. For some states, such as California, higher salaries reflect the state's effort to reduce class size and hire more teachers. According to the American Federation of Teachers, salaries for nonteaching personnel varied widely, too.

Teachers have a variety of ways to increase their base pay. There are often coaching and club advisor positions available along with various other extracurricular activities. Teaching summer school, securing grants for extra work, and serving as a mentor teacher are some other ways to boost pay. For teachers who complete a master's degree or national certification, there is often a subsequent increase in pay.

Teacher shortages are prevalent across the country. Public and private schools are determined in their pursuit to find the right person for the right classroom. Most states are brainstorming ways to attract and keep good teachers by raising teacher salaries and offering other incentives. Although public schools provide benefits that vary by district, most offer the following additional benefits: health insurance, paid and unpaid leave of absence, retirement savings plans, and various other benefits. Some public school districts, in an effort to entice top teaching candidates, offer additional incentives such as signing bonuses, mortgage assistance, and tax breaks

some schools are encouraging teachers to work in teams to promote more creative thinking and set standards. It is becoming more common for two or more teachers to work as a team that is jointly responsible for a group of students. Some schools have teachers who specialize and teach only one subject, such as music, art, reading, science, arithmetic, or physical education. Other schools use the "one-room schoolhouse" approach that requires teachers to instruct multilevel classrooms, with students at several different learning levels. In multilevel classrooms, students learn at their own pace and ability level.

In recent years, site-based management, which encourages teachers and parents to participate actively in management decisions, has gained respect. In many schools, teachers work together cooperatively with fellow teachers and administrators to make decisions regarding budget, personnel, textbook choices, curriculum design, and teaching methods.

Most teachers agree seeing students develop new skills and knowledge can be very rewarding. However, teaching may be frustrating when classroom management or discipline is an issue. Dealing with unmotivated or disrespectful students is often cited as one of the displeasures of teaching. Increasingly, teachers cope with unruly behavior and violence in the schools. Teachers may experience stress when dealing with large classes, students from backgrounds different from their own, and heavy workloads. Schools, particularly in inner cities, may be run-down and lack the amenities of schools in wealthier communities. Because education has come into the national spotlight, many of these problems are receiving careful analysis with the goal of making schools safer and more positive for both teachers and students.

A teacher's assigned hours may be shorter than the typical eight-hour workday, but because of additional responsibilities and class preparation, many teachers work more than 40 hours a week. Teaching can be flexible and job-sharing or part-time opportunities exist. Most teachers work the traditional 10-month school year with a 2-month vacation during the summer. During the vacation break, those on the 10-month schedule may teach summer school, work other jobs, travel, or pursue other interests. Many teachers enroll in college courses or workshops to continue their education, especially if the state in which they teach requires additional education credits. Teachers in states or districts with a year-round schedule typically work eight weeks, are on vacation for one week, and have a five-week midwinter and summer break. Preschool teachers outside the K through 12 systems often work year round.

The classroom can be stimulating for the teacher as well as students. There is an old saying that if you really want to know a subject well, try teaching it to someone else. The classroom environment is constantly changing with innovations in technology and new ideologies. It is also stimulating for its diversity as teachers often work with students and coworkers from varied ethnic, racial, and religious backgrounds. With growing minority populations in many parts of the country, it is important for teachers to establish rapport with a diverse student population and their families. For many teachers, diversity skills must be developed. For this reason, some schools offer training to help teachers enhance their awareness and understanding of different cultures. Training frequently includes ideas for including multicultural programs in the curriculum to address the needs of all students.

Adult educators work in a variety of settings, including hospitals, religious facilities, colleges, community centers, and libraries. Their work can be contracted by each course taught, or they may work for an organization or agency such as a social service agency. Depending on the topic, adult education can take place in a variety of settings, including traditional classrooms, on cruise ships, or outdoors. These educators' work environments are as varied as the setting in which they teach.

Extension agents generally work in an office setting as their home base. Extension offices can be found in rural, suburban, and urban areas. Sometimes extension agents work at university campuses. Even though extension agents operate out of an office, they spend considerable time in the community in settings similar to those used by adult educators.

Corporate trainers usually work in clean, pleasant, and comfortable office settings. They usually work a standard 35- to 40-hour week. Although most work in an office, some travel extensively. For example, corporate trainers may travel to attend professional meetings or to the client's site chosen for training.

Summary

It has been said that education is the backbone of civilization. Why? Educators help people learn how to function in society. In family and consumer sciences, educators help youth and adults learn life skills and prepare them to meet the needs of their families in order to improve the quality of life for themselves and serve individuals and families in their community.

The field of family and consumer sciences education offers many career opportunities. Traditional classroom teaching opportunities exist in public and private middle and high schools. These teachers work with children and teens in a structured setting.

Many career opportunities also exist for those interested in educating and training adults, including teaching careers in colleges and universities, community classes, corporate training, and cooperative extension. Educators usually specialize in one area of family and consumer sciences when working with adults. For example, a college professor may focus on one specific area. Many adult educators work in less structured environments and may even be self-employed.

There is always a need for talented teachers. The kinds and number of teachers needed varies by location. Teacher preparation standards vary by state and by the level of teaching. Licensing requirements also vary by state.

Classroom teachers spend most of their day designing and delivering learning experiences and managing activities, though they also have duties and responsibilities outside regular class hours. Adult educators work in a variety of settings, including hospitals, religious facilities, colleges, community centers, and libraries. Extension agents are generally based in an office but spend considerable time in community settings. Although most corporate trainers work in an office, some travel extensively.

Education is essential to all societies, and career opportunities in family and consumer sciences education will always exist. Today's classroom teachers are members of a vital and rewarding profession. How can you know if the teaching profession is right for you? Start with these ideas. Even if you decide that it is not a career track for you, the following activities/exercises will increase your knowledge of the profession.

Pursuing a Career in Education

1. **Interview a teacher.** Although being a student may have drawn you to teaching, being on the "other side of the desk" may be a far different reality than your experience as a student. Make contact with a teacher. Prepare questions you would like answered and interview teachers and school administrators.

2. **Conduct classroom observations.** Seek permission to spend a few hours or a day job shadowing teachers at the grade level or in the curricular areas in which you aspire to teach. Often, you can arrange this through your university. The more you observe, the more you will become familiar with diverse teaching and learning styles. Sometimes school principals or family and consumer sciences teachers can be helpful in arranging

such experiences. Your college academic advisor may also be helpful in scheduling a classroom observation. Most schools do not allow guests on campus without prior arrangements, so be sure to obtain official approval before you begin. Observations could range from a few hours to several days. Internships, part-time and summer employment, and volunteer experiences where you work with children in your content area will help you decide if teaching is for you.

3. **Seek a teaching mentor.** As you observe different teachers, look for those who could serve as mentors and positive role models as you explore teaching as a career. Consider relatives in the education profession, former teachers, or college and university professors when seeking a mentor. Prepare a list of questions and ask for advice.

4. **Evaluate your skills to teach.** There is not just one right way to be a good teacher. If you were to ask a group of people to describe their favorite teacher, their list of characteristics would not be the same. However, most successful teachers are known for respecting their students, cherishing the discipline that they teach, having high expectations for themselves and their students, and having the ability to adapt to change.

5. **Volunteer.** You can volunteer as a tutor for children in the community where you are attending college. Most colleges and universities have organized centers for community engagement. Regular experiences with children in after-school programs or community organizations such as Boys and Girls Clubs provide a way to test your interest in working with various age levels and help you to develop leadership skills.

Questions for Thought

1. What characteristics make a good teacher?

2. Which teacher in your past influenced you the most? How and in what ways were you influenced?

3. Why should family and consumer sciences be taught in public schools?

4. Which basic family life skills are most important for elementary school children today? middle school children? high school students? adults?

5. Family and consumer sciences responds to changing societal needs and as a result, life skills that were taught in classrooms in the 1950s are very different than those taught in the decades that followed. What life skills will family and consumer sciences teachers teach in five years? in 10 years?

6. Access the U.S. Department of Labor's Occupational Outlook Handbook website. Choose two related career profiles from the following list and report on the career description, typical working conditions, job outlook, and expected earnings:
   - child care workers
   - teachers—adult literacy
   - teachers—preschool
   - teachers—kindergarten
   - teachers—elementary
   - teachers—middle school
   - teachers—high school
   - teachers—special education

References and Resources

Armstrong, T. (2006). *The best schools: How human development research should inform educational practice.* Alexandria, VA: Association for Supervision and Curriculum Development.

Association for Career and Technical Education. (2007). *Family and consumer sciences education.* Retrieved April 18, 2007, from http://www.acteonline.org/about/division/facs.cfm

Bolger, D.A. (Nov./Dec. 2008). Integrating CTE and Academics: One Teacher's Account—Deborah Ann Bolger, a family and consumer sciences teacher, describes how she integrates math, science, social studies and geography in her FACS program. *Techniques, 83*(8), 44.

Bruner, J. (1996). *The culture of education.* Cambridge, MA: Harvard University Press.

Bureau of Labor Statistics, U.S. Department of Labor. *Occupational Outlook Handbook, 2012-13 Edition.* Projections Overview. Retrieved from http://www.bls.gov/ooh/about/projections-overview.htm

Campbell, C. (2006). *The comprehensive public high school: Historical perspectives.* New York: Palgrave Macmillan.

Delpit, L. (1995). *Other people's children: Cultural conflicts in the classroom.* New York: The New Press.

Fine, G. A. (1987). *With the boys: Little league baseball and preadolescent culture.* Chicago: University of Chicago Press.

Fine, J. (2005). *Opportunities in Teaching Careers.* New York: McGraw-Hill.

Gilligan, C. (1977). In a different voice: Women's conceptions of self and morality. *Harvard Educational Review, 47,* 481-516.

Gisler, M. M. (2002). *101 Career alternatives for teachers: Exciting job opportunities for teachers outside the teaching profession.* New York: Three Rivers Press.

Gutek, G. (2006). *American education in a global society: International and comparative perspectives.* Long Grove, IL: Waveland Press.

Hirsch, E. D. (1996). *The schools we need.* New York: Doubleday.

Hitch, E. J., & Youatt, J. P. (2002). *Communicating family and consumer sciences: A guidebook for professionals.* Tinley Park, IL: Goodheart-Willcox.

Howson, J. (2005). *Taking control of your teaching career.* New York: Routledge Falmer.

Leicester, M. (2006). *Early year's stories for the foundation stage: Ideas and inspiration for active learning.* New York: Routledge.

National Association of State Administrators of Family and Consumer Sciences. (n.d.). *National Standards & Competencies.* Retrieved from http://www.nasafacs.org/national-standards--competencies.html

National Commission on Excellence in Education. (1983, April). *A nation at risk: the imperative for educational reform.* Retrieved February 7, 2007, from http://www.ed.gov/pubs/NatAtRisk/title.html

National Education Association. (February 22, 2013). *Rankings & Estimates.* Retrieved from http://www.nea.org/home/54597.htm

Reese, S. (March 01, 2004). Family and Consumer Sciences Education: The Compassionate Curriculum. *Techniques, 79*(3), 18-21.

Ryan, K. (Ed.). (1992*). The Roller coaster years: Essays by and for beginning teachers.* New York: Harper Collins.

Smith, S. (2003). *Do you think teaching is easy?: How to relate, facilitate, and survive your way through a fabulous teaching career.* Bloomington, IN: Authorhouse.

Turner, J. (2005). *High school reform: Focusing on rigor, relevance, and relationships.* Arlington, VA: Educational Research Service.

United States Department of Agriculture. (2007). *Cooperative state research, education, and extension service.* Retrieved from http://csrees.usda.gov

Chapter 11

Careers in Family and Community Services

After studying this chapter, you will be able to:

- analyze opportunities, issues, and trends in the field of family and community services.

- discuss career opportunities in child, family, and community services.

- explain what academic training is needed to become a family and community services professional.

- describe working conditions of family and community services professionals.

People are drawn to family and community services careers for different reasons. Like most, watching the effects of a hurricane hitting the shores of a country already struggling with rampant poverty profoundly affected Carissa. She can trace her passion for helping people back to that time. Carissa was home from school nursing a stubborn sore throat on the day that the storm hit the coast. With not much to do or to keep her interest, she turned on the television in an attempt to find something entertaining to watch. On every major television network, news reports flashed photographs of the devastation and loss. In the days that followed, the somber news coverage focused on the many families who had lost loved ones and all of their material possessions. Watching the families mourn and the desperate search for loved ones by those who had not yet heard that their loved ones had perished, Carissa was especially moved by the stories of children who lost one or both of their parents. It was in watching these stories that Carissa's passion grew for helping displaced children.

Sometimes it takes a big event like a natural disaster to jolt a person into meaningful life choices. Sometimes it is a gradual realization that helping others is what gives meaning to life. For Carissa, helping others means helping foster kids find safe temporary homes. Personally, Carissa had no experience with foster care. She had been reared in a privileged urban home. During her adolescence, she lived with her mother after her parents divorced. Even so, she maintained a strong relationship with both of her parents. Education was highly esteemed in her family, and she had many strong role models. She was considered a high achiever throughout high school and college both in academics and in extracurricular leadership activities. Family services proved to be the career track that allowed her to combine her drive for excellence and her leadership skills with her passion to make a difference in the world.

When Carissa walked into her cold, dark apartment in the very early morning, she finally had time to catch up on messages received on her phone and Facebook. It was comforting to see what her friends were doing. Some had posted cute photographs with friends and family. Others complained about their funny foibles throughout the day. It always helped her to get a sense of what was going on in the lives of her family and friends before trying to sleep. It had been a much longer day than usual, but the sense of satisfaction she felt from getting two-year-old Mikey placed with a secure foster care family was well worth the time and energy it took to make it happen.

Carissa had learned about Mikey several months ago. When neighbors reported concerns about his safety, the state's child protective services became involved. He had not been physically abused, but it appeared that he was often left without proper supervision. Neglect is hard to prove, and it took several months to build a case for removing Mikey from his home and placing him in foster care. Carissa was sure that Mikey's mother had a desire to care for him, but her lack of family support and long-term struggle with substance abuse made it difficult, if not impossible, to provide proper care for him. Still, Carissa and her colleagues at the foster care agency hoped to provide enough emotional support for Mikey's mother that she would rise to the occasion and get her life under control so that she could properly care for him. Mikey was found alone, hungry, and dirty this afternoon. When his mother could not be found, the local police stepped in. Later that evening, a social worker placed Mikey in the care of the agency Carissa worked for. As the family services case manager, Carissa had to quickly find a place for him to live.

It was 11:30 p.m. before the legal paperwork was completed and Mikey was ready for temporary placement. Carissa called a foster care family that she had relied on several times before when emergency or short-notice foster care was needed. These foster care parents were the type of people who were always willing to provide a safe, nurturing environment—even at a moment's notice. Carissa pulled up to the foster home with Mikey in the back seat. He was already asleep when she carried him into the quiet, gently lit house. Carissa handed Mikey, wrapped in a blanket, over to his new foster mother. Carissa wondered whether he would sleep through the night or wake up frightened. She knew he would be well taken care of. Her highest hopes were that his mother would be able to stop her substance abuse and that she and Mikey would be reunited. But for now, Carissa would rest easy. Tomorrow would hold a new day for Mikey and his foster parents. It could be filled with fear, grief and loss, and dismay. She hoped it would also hold a sense of warmth and stability for Mikey.

Family and community services professionals serve the needs of people at all stages of life development. They may provide housing assistance for low-income individuals, offer financial education and assistance to single parents, or supervise after-school activities for teens. They may provide care for the elderly, nutrition advice for young parents, or temporary housing for people in transition. In fact, for every identified family need there is usually a family and community services professional who can provide resources for meeting the need. In this chapter, basic questions about pay, working conditions, and employment potential in the family and community services field will be explored.

The Family and Community Services Field

Jobs in family and community services today are many and varied. Because families exist in every culture and every community, the skills of family service professionals are greatly needed. The environments in which families exist are always changing. As a result, use of new knowledge and technology must be combined with an age-old concern for improving the lives of those in the community. As the world's population continues to grow, so will the need for family and community services workers. There will continue to be a need for family and community services professionals as long as there are people and families. The family and consumer sciences discipline offers a strong knowledge base for family and community services professionals.

Career Opportunities in Family and Community Services

As discussed previously, there are many positions in the family service field. Some are called family and community services careers, some are referred to as human services careers, and others go by entirely different names depending on the region, the agency, and the source of funding. Sometimes this makes it difficult to track statistics about specific career opportunities. In this section, broad employment categories will be discussed. Keep in mind that hundreds of job titles exist that cannot begin to be covered in this chapter. The exercises/activities at the end of the chapter will help you explore some of the possible career paths in family and community services.

Family service agencies vary greatly, and each type of agency works with diverse clients including infants, children, adolescents and young adults, the elderly, homeless, addicts, mentally ill, and individuals who are disabled. Because of this, it is difficult to distinguish specific job title categories. Family and community services careers can be found in government agencies, nonprofit community organizations, churches and religious organizations, and foundations serving very diverse segments of the population. Job titles and daily tasks of family and community services careers may also be very different. Agencies provide client services that are carried out in offices, clinics or hospitals, day treatment programs, correctional institutions, group homes, shelters, and clients' homes. Common family service careers include case managers, counselors, therapists, and social workers, but this is just a beginning list of opportunities in family and community services. On the administrative level, program directors, development directors, and executive directors lead family and community services agencies. Typical careers in the family and community services area are listed in **Figure 11-1**.

Family and Community Services Paraprofessionals

Family and community services paraprofessionals work directly with all populations. For example, in a foster care agency, they work with foster children, their parents or other family members, and foster parents and their families. They also collaborate with staff of other organizations in the community who provide family support services, resources, and information regarding legal issues. Family services paraprofessionals typically spend most of their time providing relevant information to clients, supervising care programs, and monitoring the therapeutic environment.

Other family and community services career opportunities include child and youth care workers, crisis intervention personnel, residential managers, mental health care aides, life skills counselors, and gerontology care aides. People in these and other related positions assist people in applying for welfare grants, food vouchers, and other benefits by assessing client financial records and physical/mental health status. They may help people secure affordable housing or find emergency housing. They work in hospitals, prisons, halfway houses, residential care facilities, rehabilitation centers, social service agencies, and

Family and Community Services Careers		
Adult day care worker	Marriage and family therapist	Recreation worker
Career counselor	Mental health aide	Residential advisor
Child abuse caseworker	Mental health counselor	School counselor
Child and family social worker	Mental health/ substance abuse social worker	Social and community services manager
Disability counselor	Personal financial advisor/planner	Social services worker
Employment specialist	Personal home care aide	
Gerontology aide	Probation officer	

Figure 11-1 The family and community services field offers a variety of careers.

Issues in the News
Family Trends for Tomorrow

Family and consumer sciences professionals must understand the changing environment in order to meet family needs and to forecast career trends. In Chapter 4, environmental trends and forecasts were explored. Specifically, these trends include the aging population, increasing population diversity, the global economy, digital technology, and work-life issues.

The individual and/or family are the center of the human ecosystem model. The human-constructed, human behavioral, and natural environments surround the individual and family and create the context for which decisions are made and resources are used. In response to environmental changes, the family and consumer sciences profession adapts to meet the changing needs of the family.

In a highly populated and diverse world, it is difficult to make global predictions regarding family structure and change. As discussed in Chapter 4, however, there are universal global trends related to population and aging. The world population is growing and aging. However, marriage, divorce, childbirth rates, household size, and family roles are highly dependent on culture.

In the United States, families have undergone dramatic change in the past 50 years. Birth rates have dropped and most women have given birth later in life.

Fewer people married, and those who did, married later in life. Divorce rates increased, peaking during the 1970s and 1980s. Even so, marriage remained the majority lifestyle for adult Americans. Marriage took the form of serial monogamy. In other words, marriages were usually monogamous, but marriage often did not last a lifetime. Divorce and remarriage were common. More women earned college degrees than ever before. Subsequently, women entered the workforce in droves. These are changes all Americans have seen and experienced in the past 50 years (Huston, 2001).

What will happen to the family in the next 50 years? It is easy to look back and see trends of the past, but looking ahead is more difficult. Economic, social, environmental, political, and technological changes may occur that are beyond forecasters' comprehension. Despite the difficulty of forecasting, current trends point to several potential changes in the family unit in upcoming decades. These include changes in the institution of marriage, divorce rate, birthrate, single-parent families, and family roles (Huston, 2001). Each of these areas is briefly discussed here.

Changes in Marriage

Changes in marriage are predicted over the next several decades. These may entail the definition and meaning of marriage, the number of marriages, the age at first marriage, and the rate of divorce. In some states, the definition of marriage as the legal union between a man and a woman has changed to include unions between two individuals of the same sex. Should marriage only be between a man and a woman? Should two women be allowed to be married? should two men? City by city, county by county, and state by state, these questions are being asked. The questions address the definition of marriage; the rights, responsibilities, and benefits of marriage; and the moral and practical function of the marriage institution.

Many futurists believe that marriage will continue as the majority lifestyle for adult Americans. Nonmarital cohabitation has become so prevalent in the past few decades, however, that it will still be a chosen lifestyle for many. The rate of cohabitation may remain steady rather than increasing, as the initial climb and peak have already occurred. Whether through marriage relationships or cohabitation, serial monogamous relationships will most likely remain prevalent due to continued concerns over sexually transmitted diseases, including HIV-AIDS. Some futurists predict that the millennial generation (generation Y) will be more interested in monogamous long-term stable relationships than the generation before them.

Over the past few decades, the average age of first marriage in the United States has steadily increased for both men and women. The pursuit of advanced education and training, the desire to remain single for a longer period of life, personal economics, and more open attitudes toward sexual activity outside of marriage have been dominant factors in this trend. In the last few years, the upward trend has leveled off and in some segments of society; the average age of first marriage has begun to decline slightly. Many forecasters predict that this trend will continue, albeit very slightly, over the next few decades. It is difficult to predict if this trend may be peculiar to the millennial generation who are just beginning to come of age or if the trend will continue into the next generation as well. It does appear that relationships are important to the current younger generation and that they seek more stability in their relationships than recent past generations.

Divorce Rates

As stated earlier, the divorce rate in America peaked in the latter 1970s and early 1980s and has since been on a slow decline. Divorce is still prevalent, however, and the decline in divorce rates has not been sharp. Whether divorce rates will continue to decrease depends in large part on public policy (Fields, 2004). For example, government

regulations and laws can make it easier or more difficult to obtain a divorce. The issues are complex and include human rights issues, economic issues, and moral issues.

Birthrates

The United States is expected to follow the global trend with slightly decreased birthrates. As a result of fewer children being born, households will be smaller. Because the current birthrate is less than two children per family, it is likely that this rate will fall only slightly and may plateau (Darling, 2005). In the past several decades, families at lower socio-economic levels tended to have more children. There may be a new trend toward having more children among some politically conservative, higher socio-economic levels. For many, home schooling has been combined with the decision to have more children. Since these families tend to be middle to upper class, the availability of one parent at home is often an option. As United States citizens live longer than before, there is more time to have children. This is especially true for men since they have more reproductive years than women.

Single-Parent Families

In the past 20 years, the fastest growth among family types has been single-parent families with children. The number of male single parents has especially grown at a rapid rate (Fields, 2004). Male single parents tend to be older than their female

counterparts, although single mothers far outnumber single fathers as heads of households (Fields, 2004). Separation and divorce were the chief causes for single-parenting. Will this trend continue? Single parents are certainly more accepted in society than they were 50 years ago. As discussed earlier, early indications of attitudes and values of generation Y point toward valuing stable, long-term relationships. Many in this generation have lived as children of single parents and have strong opinions about the benefits and disadvantages of this family structure. Generational attitudes combined with public policy will affect the trend toward more or fewer single-parent family structures.

Changing Family Roles

When divorce and remarriage, single-parent families, an aging population, and birthrate trends are considered, changing family roles emerge. For example, with fewer children born, there will be fewer caregivers for elderly family members. If the divorce rates remain high, family lines will blur, and the responsibility of elder care may not be as clearly defined. At the same time, more grandparents are raising their own grandchildren. More families may need to relocate further from family members for employment reasons. This, too, will affect family roles as fewer family care givers will be available for the large elderly population (Ervin, 2000).

Professional Profile

Clinical Psychologist, Executive Director of Programs

Karen Bergstrom, Ph.D.

How did you get into your line of work?

My career journey began in my undergraduate studies. I majored in human services because I knew I wanted to work with people–specifically with youth. After graduation, I accepted a job as a child care worker. I supervised children who were dependents of the court system and children at risk. I knew I wanted to expand my responsibilities and so I began to pursue a master's degree. Over 3,000 hours of clinical work were required to finish my degree, most of it working with emotionally disturbed youth in residential centers.

Over time, I realized that my passion was not just working with youth but also in impacting the community on a larger scale. I decided to pursue my Ph.D. Today, I am the director of staff training and program development for a residential foster care organization that places at-risk children in safe, nurturing homes. I train counselors, child care workers, and foster families as well as design programs that will best benefit the youth we serve.

What does your "typical" day entail?

Every day is different, but each day involves working with people. This was my goal from the earliest days of my career, and my training and experience have given me more diverse ways of doing so as my career has progressed. Today, my days are filled with meetings with staff, state agencies, families, and community leaders. I try to build/foster collaboration among all participants. I work with state agencies to generate funds to support our efforts and educate others about the needs of families and children. My job is to see the "big picture" and give leadership to the organization. Although my job is largely administrative, my role is to make it possible for the "front line" to do their work.

How do you fulfill the mission of family and consumer sciences— that is, how does your work improve people's quality of life?

I hear stories every day about children in need, and our agency finds ways to meet their needs. We want to give children a chance at succeeding in life. Each child is unique and his/her situation requires a unique approach. I know that we are making a difference. In fact, over 300 children are helped through our agency each year. These relationships are not short-term, either. Some of our former foster children are still using our support services in mid-adulthood. Why? Because many came from such broken childhoods, their needs continue into adulthood. It is now acknowledged that a high number of adults who went through foster care as children will struggle through life without continued support that extended families generally offer. Our goal is to serve as their extended family by providing support, a listening ear, or even financial help as they transition from youth into adulthood.

detoxification centers. Their job is to help people help themselves by providing support services and finding helpful resources. They often act as mediators between their clients and community resources or government agencies.

For managerial or decision-making positions in family and community services, a four-year college degree is needed. A four-year degree also offers the opportunity for advancement in caseload size and supervisory responsibilities. For example, a person may take on more of a supervisory role by becoming a *case manager* (sometimes called a case coordinator or case worker). Case managers work directly with clients from all representative populations. They are responsible for developing appropriate case plans as well as helping direct care managers develop specific plans. Case managers are more involved in assessing client cases and supervising caseloads.

Case managers are experienced in working with community resources to meet individual client needs. Therapeutic counselors depend on case managers to implement treatment plans. Family and community services professionals do not provide therapeutic care or counseling, however, unless they have the required education, experience, and licensure. Family and community services professionals make certain that the directives of the clinical staff are carried out. They generally report directly to the agency director.

Counselors

Counselors and therapists offer psychological evaluation and care to their clients. They help people solve personal problems and find the resources they need to live a healthy and safe life. For the most part, counseling is an unregulated field. Many people choose to call themselves counselors because they offer advice and provide support services. Therapeutic counselors, such as marriage and family therapists, psychologists, and substance abuse counselors, however, are required to hold some form of licensure or certification to practice in all but a few states. School counselors must be certified in all states.

A master's or doctoral degree is often required to be certified or licensed as a counselor.

Counselors often specialize in a specific area such as eating disorders, child development, mental health, substance abuse, life skills, or family relationships. *Marriage and family therapists* help individuals, couples, family groups, or organizations resolve conflicts. As they work with clients, marriage and family therapists help them modify perceptions and behavior. They also teach people how to enhance communication and understanding among all family members. For example, a marriage and family therapist may help families establish goals, help teens communicate with their parents, or help couples come to terms with health issues.

Rehabilitation counselors help people deal with the effects of disabilities, including the personal, social, physical, and vocational ramifications. One example is a young person recently diagnosed with HIV-AIDS. As health issues arise, a rehabilitation counselor helps the person and his family deal with the psychological, personal, social, and physical ramifications of the disease. The counselor also helps the individual consider changes in employment and appropriate care options if needed. A rehabilitation counselor would help the individual come to terms with the disease as a part of his life.

Mental health counselors help people assess, address, and treat mental and emotional disorders. They often work closely with psychologists and psychiatrists. After diagnosis of a mental health issue, counselors often provide a variety of therapeutic techniques to help their clients regain optimum mental health. Likewise, substance abuse counselors help people who have problems with alcohol, drugs, or other substances. They also assist people with other behavioral disorders such as gambling or eating disorders.

Vocational counselors assist people with finding employment. They also help people to assess their skills, talents, personality, job history, experience, and interests in order to find a good match between jobs and individuals. Some vocational counselors work in educational settings, such as college and university career centers and

Professional Profile

Hospital Child Life Specialist

Madeline Caryl Wion

How did you get into your line of work?

I learned about the career of a child life specialist through one of my classmates in family and consumer sciences. As she described the career field, I felt like it would be a great fit for me. I researched the field and learned that to become a child life specialist you must have your bachelor's degree and at least 480 hours of child life internship training in order to sit for the certification exam. In my senior year I applied to eight internship programs around the country to work toward becoming a child life specialist. I was accepted into a program at the University of California, Davis Children's Hospital in Sacramento, California. After graduation I moved to Sacramento and completed over 600 hours of child life internship. I learned about the medical field and hospital environment as well as how to work with sick children and their families. After my internship I was hired as a child life specialist fellow for 6 months. This opportunity gave me paid child life experience as well as more hours to help me to be a better candidate for future employment. After completing this fellowship, I took and passed the certification exam, and I am proud to say that I am now a certified child life specialist.

What does your "typical" day entail?

Every morning our staff gets a census that has the name, age, diagnosis, and additional psychosocial and medical information necessary to work with the patient and family. My job revolves around family-centered care. This means that we do not only treat the patient but the whole family.

trade schools. They can also be found in secondary schools, where they help students decide whether to pursue higher education, vocational education, trade school, or apprenticeship programs. Others work in organizations that cater to a specific clientele outside of school settings, such as private career counseling services or government job placement agencies.

Counselors assist people with personal, family, substance abuse, mental health, educational, and vocational decisions. They offer help in one-on-one meetings as well as in group settings. Counselors must be good communicators who possess high mental and physical energy to cope with the daily stresses of working with people in difficult situations. They must be compassionate since a counselor's job is to help people help themselves.

Social Workers

Social workers coordinate and plan programs and activities to meet the social and emotional needs of their clients. Typically, they work with their clients to utilize community resources to meet individualized needs. Most social workers are advocates for people who cannot or do not know how to help themselves. Many social workers provide services for mentally

I prioritize my patients for the day and work accordingly. Procedures, such as surgeries and IV placement, and new diagnoses often take priority in the day.

My job is to prepare children for procedures and medical care in order to reduce stress and anxiety in the hospital environment. Preparation can come in many forms but typically involves teaching children about what is going to happen in developmentally appropriate terms. I often describe things in terms of senses: what they will smell, see, feel, hear, and taste. I also work with the children and families to discover and implement coping skills that would be beneficial throughout the procedure, illness, and hospital stay.

How do you fulfill the mission of family and consumer sciences— that is, how does your work improve people's quality of life?

In the PICU (pediatric intensive care unit), I work with kids and their families in very high-stress situations. Much of my work in the PICU deals with end-of-life issues, which means that the child is actively dying. We focus on preparing siblings and parents for what to expect and how to cope. I also do "memory making" for the family to have hand/footprints and molds as well as a clipping of hair and other mementos to aid in the grieving process. I believe that it is a great honor when a family allows you to be involved in their child's end-of-life process.

I love being a child life specialist! Although it can be emotionally taxing at times, I believe there is so much reward in helping a child and family in the hospital. Sickness is the reality for many families. My goal is to help to reduce the stress and fear as much as possible.

---

ill or educationally disadvantaged families coping with poverty. Other social workers support family members during a time of chronic or critical illness. A social worker interviews clients and their family members to determine needs, provides counseling, helps families access support services, leads support groups, consults with other health professionals, and prepares a treatment plan for care, rehabilitation, or treatment of a client and his or her family. For example, when a child is removed from an abusive home, a social worker is responsible for placing the child with a foster care agency and establishing a plan for rehabilitation with the parent(s).

They often work with clients and family members, monitoring progress toward goals set in the treatment plan.

The problems that social workers encounter are often complex with many "layers." Sometimes, social workers do not have the luxury of time to solve complex issues, but they intervene on behalf of clients to resolve emergency problems or conflicts. For example, if an elderly person enters a hospital with no known immediate family members, with evidence of abuse, without a known address, or when life-or-death medical decisions must be made, the social worker must uncover the layers of the problem at hand. A master's degree in social work, more commonly referred to as an MSW, is required for a career as a social worker.

Social workers are employed by government agencies, schools, private social service agencies, and health care organizations such as hospitals and treatment centers. Health care organizations represent one of the largest employment segments for social workers. School social workers help clients and their families utilize home, school, and community assets to meet the needs of students. For example, a social worker may collaborate with family members, school personnel, and community resources such as a local Boys and Girls Club to help a child overcome social and personal problems. To qualify as school social workers, individuals must generally possess a master's degree in social work (MSW), have had two years of supervised social work experience, and have received a passing score on the social work component of the National Teaching Examination. Some social workers continue their education by completing a Ph.D. in social work. Additional coursework includes extensive knowledge in welfare policies and politics, human development, abnormal behaviors, and research methodology. Advanced training prepares social workers to handle more complex, responsible assignments or administrative positions.

Administrative Careers in Family and Community Services

Careers in family and community services offer many opportunities for promotion, especially for people with an advanced degree, specialized training, and experience. Program directors, development directors, and executive directors oversee agency operations and supervise personnel. They see the "big picture" and move the agency forward in meeting its goals. Each plays a distinct role in the family and community services agency.

A *program director* oversees the mission, goals, and programs of an organization. This involves development of programs, implementation, and evaluation of whether programs meet the needs of clients and the objectives of the organization. This is a supervisory position that requires a combination of education and experience. Most program directors spend a considerable amount of time working with state and federal agencies to secure grants, maintaining compliance with regulations, and staying up to date with current developments. Program directors usually report to the agency's executive director.

Development directors implement strategies for securing funding to meet program goals and objectives. Development directors write and help others to write grant proposals, cultivate relationships with potential donors, and interface with auxiliary support groups. The development director oversees fundraising events, such as charitable auctions or other entertainment. The development director is usually part of the senior staff, reporting directly to the executive director. A development director in a larger organization generally supervises several grant writers and assistants. Development work can be creative and involves event planning as well as grant writing skills.

The *executive director* is responsible for the overall management and leadership of an organization. He or she oversees day-to-day operations and acts as a liaison between the organization and the governing board. Successful executive directors are active in their community, serving as the "face" of the organization. The executive director must have a vision for the future, while leading the agency to meet its mission and goals on a daily basis. Also, the executive director must be skilled at working with opposing constituencies to inspire collaboration.

Preparing to Enter the Family and Community Services Field

Family and community services professionals help others improve their quality of life at all stages of life development from childhood through the phases of adulthood. They help family members better communicate with each other and those around them. They help individuals and families to find, secure, and use available resources. Overall, family and consumer sciences family and community services professionals focus on improving the quality of life for families through meeting the basic needs of food, clothing, and shelter. Professional organizations can provide insight into the family and community services area. Several professional organizations, their websites, and descriptions are given in **Figure 11-2**.

Where Are Family and Community Services Professionals Employed?

Family and community services careers are difficult to describe because of the myriad of titles used for specific jobs. The same position may have a different title depending on geographic location, type of agency, and source of funding for the position. A variety of entry-level positions in family and community services can be found in residential care, correctional facilities, homeless shelters and food banks, substance

Professional Organizations Supporting the Family and Community Services		
Profession	**Web Address**	**Description**
American Academy of Child and Adolescent Psychiatry	aacap.org	A professional medical association dedicated to families and children dealing with mental illness issues.
American Association for Marriage and Family Therapy	aamft.org	A professional association for the field of marriage and family therapy that facilitates research, theory development, and education. It develops standards for graduate education and training, clinical supervision, professional ethics, and clinical practice.
Annie E. Casey Foundation	aecf.org	A private family foundation that focuses on providing financial support for foster care and other issues related to children in need.
Federal Interagency Forum on Child and Family Statistics	childstats.gov	A collection of 20 United States federal agencies that collaborate to provide current data on children and families. Data is used to inform policy makers with the intent to improve the status of children.
National Center for Children in Poverty	nccp.org	A public policy forum that promotes the health and well-being of children and families in need.
National Council on Family Relations	ncfr.org	A professional organization that supports family educators, practitioners, and researchers through educational conferences and journals, public policy advocacy, and networking. It provides the Certified Family Life Educator (CFLE) program.
National Institutes of Health	nih.gov	Part of the U.S. Department of Health and Human Services, the NIH includes 27 institutes and centers focusing on research into topics such as aging, child health and human development, and mental health issues affecting families.
U.S. Department of Health and Human Services	hhs.gov	The United States government's principal agency for providing essential human services. Services include Medicare, Head Start preschool programs, immunizations, and abuse prevention programs, among others.

Figure 11-2 Check out the websites of these professional family and community services organizations.

abuse programs, elder care, organizations that find resources for at-risk children and families, employment services, mental health agencies, and domestic violence prevention programs.

For example, suppose a recent family and consumer sciences graduate secures an entry-level position with a private foster care agency. This agency finds homes for children who are considered hard to place, specializing in finding quality foster homes, providing support services to children and foster families, and aiding reconciliation among biological family members. As in most entry-level positions, the job responsibilities would include helping others obtain services, monitoring and keeping records, organizing or leading group activities, assisting clients in mastering everyday living skills, and modeling healthy behaviors for residents or clients. For this recent graduate, the possibilities and opportunities for helping foster care children and families through this agency are endless.

Family and community services careers are many and varied as you can see in **Figure 11-1.** Each has specific requirements for education and training. Some require undergraduate degrees, while others require graduate work and licensure. The United States government provides extensive information about each of these careers, including general responsibilities, wage and employment trends, and career videos of interviews with practicing professionals. This information can be accessed on the America's Job Bank website.

What Do Family and Community Services Professionals Need to Know?

Although there are many career titles in family and community services, a common base of knowledge is essential. This knowledge base includes expertise in human behavior and developmental stages, counseling principles and methods, customer service principles and processes, group behavior, societal trends, and competence in the primary spoken language of clients.

Family and community services professionals work with people of all ages. Thus, it is critical to have a thorough understanding of how humans develop and change throughout their lifespan. Physical, emotional, social, cognitive, and spiritual awareness is essential to work effectively with people. You have probably observed how the needs of a 30-year-old are different from those of a 60-year-old or an 80-year-old. Although they are all adults, their needs and values are very different. Their motivations are different and, subsequently, their behaviors are different. At the same time, all humans need social interaction, emotional support, cognitive stimulation, and physical activity. Family and community services professionals work within the boundaries of appropriate human development by providing services that are age-appropriate. They appreciate human diversity and understand that people learn differently and are motivated by different values.

Depending on the requirements of the specific job, some knowledge of behavioral and affective disorders may also be desirable. To meet the needs of their clients, family and community services professionals need basic knowledge of the principles, methods, and procedures for diagnosis, treatment, and rehabilitation of physical and mental disorders. This knowledge is used for initial screenings, assessment, and referrals to the proper resources that can help people meet their needs. Vocational counselors also need knowledge about career counseling and guidance. For example, they need to know how to help people assess their marketable career skills, how to prepare a résumé, how to conduct a job search, and how to interview for a job. In today's information-based society, vocational and guidance counselors must be versed in employment trends, essential skills, wages, and sources for obtaining job information.

Family and community services professionals also need expertise in the principles and processes for providing customer and personal service. The perceived care that clients receive is important to their effective utilization of services offered. Customer service is also essential to building trust between service providers and

Professional Profile

Licensed Mental Health Counselor in Private Practice

Jenae Kronbach, MA, LMHC
Seattle, Washington

How did you get into your line of work?

From design to cuisine to finances to body image, the FCS program prepared me to advance well into the next season of my life. I am grateful for all that I studied and where it has brought me in my personal and occupational life.

Throughout my coursework in the family and consumer sciences department, I found myself constantly curious. How did my experiences combined with my temperament give me a unique encounter with the world, and how was this similar or different from my classmates? How could I begin to know myself more and appreciate the variety of voices and stories around me? I was encouraged and challenged by my professors and classmates on both a personal and cultural level throughout my studies.

Family and consumer sciences encompasses the study of psychology, sociology, anthropology, and art in a way that no other program does. It provides a catalyst to pursue specialized careers while also gaining knowledge in broad areas of daily life. It marries the practical with the existential and the individual with the global. It was the interconnected approach to the curriculum that broadened my horizons while helping me locate my passions. Inspired by these newfound passions, I chose to pursue a graduate degree in counseling psychology. I went on to obtain my master of arts degree in marriage and family therapy and opened a private practice here in my campus neighborhood because I wanted to remain connected to the first neighborhood that I called "home." In my practice, I counsel clients through the many stages and challenges of life.

My undergraduate degree in family and consumer sciences reaffirmed what I believe to be essential to human existence: relationships. We are constantly driven to connect with each other and with our surroundings. The relationships we form both help us survive and bring an incredible sense of meaning to our lives.

---

clients. Family and community services professionals often deal with sensitive topics related to family life, so trust is needed to maintain honesty, open communication, disclosure, and confidentiality. Knowledge of group behavior, diverse cultural norms, and societal trends and influences is an important part of customer or personal service to clients. Thus, good communication skills are very important. A working knowledge of the primary spoken language is needed, including well-developed speaking, writing, and listening skills.

Specific knowledge in family and consumer sciences can help family and community services professionals provide resources for families to meet their basic needs of food, clothing, and shelter. For example, family service professionals with family and consumer sciences knowledge can teach people budgeting, how to prepare healthy food, and other daily living activities. They also teach communication and conflict resolution skills. They may organize or lead discussion groups for pregnant teens or AIDS patients or support work in food banks and housing assistance programs.

Family service organizations often provide rich cultural ethnic and racial diversity among coworkers and clients. Just as everyone has different boundaries, many people have different lifestyles and values that become more apparent when working with intimate family issues. These differences can lead to challenges. Family and community services workers realize that each individual should be helped within the context of his or her values system. Family service professionals must learn to help others without being judgmental about education, income, culture, and values.

What Training Is Needed?

The type of training needed in family and community services is highly dependent on the specific position. For example, most paraprofessionals do not hold baccalaureate, clinical, or medical degrees. However, paraprofessionals comprise the largest part of the team and are considered the front line of the profession. Most family and community services paraprofessionals interact with children and families on a daily basis and are the first people that new clients encounter. Family and community services professionals, on the other hand, include social workers, counselors, therapists, psychologists, and physicians. They also work closely with clients, but often after initial interaction with family and community services paraprofessionals. Teamwork is essential for the organization to be effective, and all members must contribute to the team.

Professional positions in family and community services require a college degree, and nearly all of them require internships and/or specialized training. Career advancement to supervisory positions often requires an advanced degree or several years of experience. Positions that include therapeutic counseling require both an advanced degree and licensure. For entry-level professional positions, an undergraduate degree in a field such as family and consumer sciences is often required. Many college graduates are hired as a result of a successful college internship experience. Although internships are not required prior to employment, they often help job seekers contact the "right" people and give them the opportunity to demonstrate competency to potential employers. Employers find there is little risk in hiring a former intern since he or she has been observed in the role.

Family and community services workers must continue training and education to stay current in their professions because legal regulations, therapeutic measures, and demographics constantly change. Seminars, workshops, and government training are important parts of the career development of most family service workers. Those who are licensed must take courses to keep their certification current. The National Council on Family Relations (NCFR) sponsors a program to certify family life educators. The *Certified Family Life Educator (CFLE)* designation recognizes the educational, preventive, and enriching nature of the work of family life educators.

Some employers invest in educating employees or provide advanced training on the job. Experience is another important source of training for family and community services professionals.

What Are the Working Conditions?

Family and community services professionals are as diverse as the agencies for which they work and as the people they serve. Family and consumer sciences professionals who work with families focus on helping others find safety, health, or success within their own lives. Most workers report that they find their family and community services careers to be personally gratifying–often their motivation for entering the field in the first place. For those who enjoy working closely with people, careers in the field are ideal because job duties revolve around the development of personal and professional relationships with children, teens, or adults.

There are significant intangible rewards from helping people improve their lives. First, people who are drawn to family and community services have a vision of a better community and tend to be compassionate toward others. Thus, those who are civic-minded are often drawn to the field. They can accomplish personal goals through their vocation. Second, family and community services careers promote collaborative working teams that share a common purpose. Working with like-minded colleagues is extremely gratifying. In this environment there is often a need for creative problem solving. Third, family and community services careers offer diversity in interactions with people from various socioeconomic, ethnic, and cultural backgrounds.

Despite the rewards, there are challenges for those working in family and community services. Most family service workers find that one of the biggest challenges upon entering the field is finding the right balance between personal and professional roles. Establishing appropriate personal boundaries is paramount to long-term success in the field. Experienced professionals know this, and supervisors often mentor those who are new to the field to help them establish how much personal information is appropriate to share in the workplace.

Daily activities in family and community services include interviewing clients and family members to assess their needs, determining if clients are eligible for benefits and services, and helping clients fill out forms to receive benefits and services such as supplemental nutrition assistance (food stamps) and medical care. Other activities include arranging transportation for elderly clients, telephoning or visiting homes of clients, helping to provide emotional support, monitoring and maintaining case records, advising clients on budgeting and shopping, and leading support groups. The daily tasks of family and community services professionals are different depending on the specific professional role, the people served, and the type of organization from which services are rendered. However, tasks and activities of family and community services professionals can be generalized into five distinct groups: interpersonal tasks, legal tasks, family-related tasks, data and information collection tasks, and business tasks. See **Figure 11-3.**

Typical Daily Tasks of Family and Community Services Professionals				
Interpersonal	**Legal**	**Family/People**	**Data/Information**	**Business**
Utilize group dynamics and collaborate with others	Compile evidence for court actions	Apply theories of child development	Utilize research methodology	Utilize business principles
Counsel clients	Identify legal/safety issues	Hold parent conferences	Compile social services data	Develop policies
Establish trust and maintain confidentiality	Apply local, state, federal laws	Identify abuse	Manage case details	Supervise staff
Empathize with others	Understand legal process	Refer clients to resources	Obtain information from clients, coworkers	Prepare reports

Figure 11-3 These are just some of the tasks that family and community services professionals must have the skills to perform.

After experience in jobs in family and community services, many family and consumer sciences graduates work as staff or lobbyists for organizations that promote public policy changes in areas such as health care coverage and child care policies. This area of concentration is called *family policy.* The purpose of family policy is to improve programs and legislation to specifically benefit individuals and families.

Voicing criticism or support for current programs and policies that affect families is one of the best ways for family and community services professionals to invoke change. Working to educate others on the implications of current or proposed public policy is another way to be involved. Family and community services professionals can facilitate discussions and explain points of view of various constituents, helping decision makers sort through the details and data that support or dispute a particular stance.

family life is a constant, the environment in which families exist is always changing. As a result, the use of new knowledge and technology must be combined with concern for improving the lives of those in the community. As the world's population continues to grow, so will the need for family and community services workers. There will be a need for family and community services professionals as long as there are people and families. The family and consumer sciences discipline offers a strong knowledge base for family and community services professionals.

How can you know if a career in this field is right for you? Evaluate your strengths, weaknesses, skills, and interests in the field of family and community services. If you are considering a career in the field, contemplate increasing your knowledge of the profession. Even if you decide that family and community services is not a career track for you, the exercises will give you a better idea of the services that are available in your community.

Summary

Family service professionals serve the needs of people at all stages of life. For example, they provide foster care for children needing homes, substance abuse counseling, financial education, or after-school activities for young teens. They work with people in all stages of life from the young to the elderly. Family and community services professionals support all basic needs—including food, clothing, shelter, and relationships—to help people achieve quality of life. They do this through counseling, services, education, or other resource distribution with the goal of individual and family empowerment and self-management.

The field of family and community services offers many career opportunities. Family service agencies also vary greatly, and each type of agency works with diverse clients including young children to older adults, people of varying income levels, addicts, the mentally ill, and the disabled. Job titles and daily tasks may also be very different, but they all focus on meeting the needs of people.

Families exist in every culture and community, so the skills held by family service professionals are greatly needed and very marketable. Although

Pursuing a Career in Family and Community Services

1. **Interview a family and community services specialist.** Specialists in family and community services play a variety of roles depending on the type or age of the clients. Choose one of the career paths listed. (You may add to this list). Arrange an interview with someone in the field. Find out what this person's job entails, the advantages and disadvantages of the position, and what an "average" day involves, and ask for advice about your education and career path.
   - child care provider or consultant
   - adult educator in a community program
   - foster care caseworker
   - latchkey program director
   - community-based organization activity coordinator
   - homeless shelter director
   - recreational specialist at youth club
   - health and welfare aide
   - family life educator
   - youth program director
   - senior citizen program director

- child care center director
- elder care center director
- independent living facilities director

2. **Conduct a mock job search.** Choose one of the family service employers listed (or one of your own) and find three different job descriptions for each employer. The description should include the job title, a brief description, job duties, location, a description of the agency and whom it serves, and salary range and benefits. Job descriptions may be found in newspapers or online.
   - AARP
   - child care centers
   - children's homes
   - civic groups
   - community health centers
   - correctional facilities
   - cooperative extension agency
   - consumer credit counseling agency
   - crisis center
   - Opportunity Corps
   - Supplemental Nutrition Assistance Program (SNAP)
   - halfway houses
   - hospitals
   - neighborhood youth corps
   - nursing homes
   - Peace Corps
   - Planned Parenthood
   - Project Head Start
   - religious organizations
   - Social Security offices
   - YMCA/YWCA

3. **Seek an internship.** If you feel that the family and community services field is a career path you would like to pursue, it may be wise to invest time in an internship. (Because of the sensitive and personal nature of family and community services interactions, it may not be possible to do a short-term or one-time observation in an agency setting.) A formal internship not only provides insight into the day-to-day work of a family service agency but also provides valuable professional contacts for job seeking and getting established in the field. Internships can be found by working with your college placement office, your professors, and through newspaper and online postings.

American Job Center at jobcenter.usa.gov, an online employment service offered by the United States government, lists thousands of internships and jobs. Many other online databases can also give valuable leads to family and community services positions.

4. **Evaluate your skills.** Family service specialists need knowledge of family resource and development combined with interpersonal and creative problem-solving skills. Experience and information technology skills further strengthen qualifications. Family and community services specialists are the liaison between clients, their extended families, government entities, and other agencies. They spend their days giving much of themselves to others. In return, there is a great amount of personal satisfaction that comes from helping others live a better life. Contact your university career center to utilize the resources available to assess your skills and interests.

5. **Volunteer.** You can volunteer at a food bank, crisis center, or homeless shelter in the community where you are attending college. This would provide a way to test your interest in working with families and communities.

6. **Become acquainted with professional organizations.** Since their mission is to educate and support professionals, professional organizations provide a wealth of information. Many professional organizations include job banks for prospective employers and employees. Look up each of the websites listed in Figure 11-2.

Questions for Thought

1. The U.S. Census Bureau's site factfinder2.census.gov provides statistics about population, income, households, etc., in American communities. Look up your community—or another—on this site. What can you learn about the current state of families in the community? What trends are indicated by the data?

2. Locate the following family and community services in your community and identify the

target audience served, resources made available, and methods of accessing the programs and services:

- a food bank
- a nonprofit consumer credit counseling service
- legal help for low-income families
- clothing assistance
- low-income housing assistance
- a homeless shelter
- a battered women's shelter or safe house
- domestic violence counseling
- church aid
- job search assistance
- welfare information
- hospice care
- marriage counseling
- a youth center
- a senior center
- a community center

3. Access the United States Department of Labor, Bureau of Labor Statistics website. Choose two related career profiles listed here and report on the career description, typical working conditions, job outlook, and expected earnings:

- child care workers
- child protection services
- child welfare
- family and community services
- family therapy
- teachers—adult literacy
- disability counselor

References and Resources

Barber, J. G. (1994). *Social work with addictions.* New York: New York University Press.

Barth, R. P., & Ramler, M. (1993). Toward more effective and efficient programs for drug- and AIDS-affected families. In R. P. Barth, J. Pietrzak, & M. Ramler (Eds.), *Families living with drugs and HIV: Intervention and treatment strategies* (pp. 272-295). New York: Guilford Press.

Cherlin, A. (2004). The deinstitutionalization of American marriage. *Journal of Marriage and the Family, 66*(4), 848-862.

Coles, R. (2005). *Race and family.* Thousand Oaks, CA: Sage.

Collison, B. (1996). *Careers in counseling and human services.* Washington, DC: Hemisphere.

Corey, G. (2007). *Issues and ethics in the helping professions.* Pacific Grove, CA: Brooks/Cole/ Thomson Learning.

Crane, D. (2005). *Handbook of families and health.* Thousand Oaks, CA: Sage.

Darling, C. (2005, January). Changes and challenges: Families in a diverse culture. *Journal of Family and Consumer Sciences, 97*(1), 8-13.

Dortch, S. (1995). The future of kinship. *American Demographics, 17*(9), 2-4.

Emener, W. (1991). *Career explorations in human services.* Oxford: Oxford Press.

Erera, P. (2002). *Family diversity: Continuity and change in the contemporary family.* Thousand Oaks, CA: Sage.

Ervin, S. (2000, November/December). Fourteen forecasts for an aging society. *The Futurist,* 24-28.

Fields, J. (2004). *America's families and living arrangements: 2003.* Retrieved December 12, 2006, from http://www.census.gov/ prod/2004pubs/p20-553.pdf

Floyd, K. (2005). *Widening the family circle.* Thousand Oaks, CA: Sage.

Frey, W. (2003). Married with children. *American demographics, 25*(2), 17-20.

Haupt, A., & Kane, T. (2004). *Population handbook.* Washington, DC: Population Reference Bureau.

Huston, P. (2001). *Families as we are.* New York: City University.

Ingoldsby, B. (2005). *Families in global and multicultural perspective.* Thousand Oaks, CA: Sage.

Littrell, J. (2005). *Portrait and model of a school counselor.* Boston: Lahaska Press/Houghton Mifflin.

Malley-Morrison, K. (2004). *Family violence in a cultural perspective: Defining, understanding, and combating abuse.* Thousand Oaks, CA: Sage.

Moffat, C. T. (2011, December 7). Helping those in need: Human service workers. *Occupational Outlook Quarterly, 55*(3), 22-32.

Neisuler, S. (2003). *Justice at the city gate: Social policy, social services, and the law.* New York: Writer's Advantage.

Rose, S. R. (1998). *Group work with children and adolescents: Prevention and intervention in school and community systems.* Thousand Oaks, CA: Sage.

Rotgers, F., Keller, D. S., & Morgenstern, J. (Eds.). (1996). *Treating substance abuse: Theory and technique.* New York: Guilford Press.

Sutton, C. (2006). *Helping families with troubled children: A preventive approach.* Hoboken, NJ: John Wiley & Sons.

Wormer, K. S. van. (1995). *Alcoholism treatment: A social work perspective.* Chicago: Nelson-Hall.

Zimmerman, S. (1992). *Family policies and family well-being.* Thousand Oaks, CA: Sage.

Zimmerman, S. (1995). *Understanding family policy.* Thousand Oaks, CA: Sage.

Zimmerman, S. (2001). *Family policy.* Thousand Oaks, CA: Sage.

Chapter 12

Careers in Human Development: Early Childhood through Older Adulthood

After studying this chapter, you will be able to:

- identify factors influencing opportunities in human development occupations.
- describe various career opportunities in the human development field.
- explain what academic training and credentials are needed to work in human development professions.
- describe working conditions in the human development field.

Louise Hawkins plopped down on the adult chair in the reading corner of the Rainbow Room at Pine Hills Preschool. "Wow! What a morning!" the preschool teacher thought as the last of the three-year-olds went out the door with their mothers or fathers. Only three hours ago, she had felt so organized for the day. What happened?

To begin with, Will's mother, Christine, who was the parent volunteer on Thursdays, had to cancel because Will's baby brother had a fever. That meant there were only two adults in the room, Louise and her aide Selena Rivera, for the 12 lively preschoolers. Louise had planned to have Christine stationed near the water table while Selena kept an eye on the blocks and the role-play corner. She didn't want to move Selena from the block area because lately a couple of the boys had been pretending that some of the blocks were guns, and they were "blasting" each other. She needed someone there to redirect them.

Louise decided she would monitor the water table while also conducting an assessment with Brandon. She couldn't put off the assessment because she was meeting with his parents and a psychologist later in the afternoon. Keeping Brandon focused on the assessment tasks distracted Louise from watching the water table, and before she knew it, Mia and Kelsey had splashed water all over themselves and the floor.

Selena left the block area to take the girls to the bathroom to change into their spare sets of clothes. While she was gone, Trevor and Alex resumed their gun battle with the blocks. "Bang-bang, you're dead!" cried Alex. "Am not!" retorted Trevor, who threw a block at Alex, and both boys began to cry. Louise intervened to ask the boys, "What's the rule about throwing? No more blocks today. Put them back on the shelf, and then I need you to help Mrs. Rivera get the snack ready. Can you do that?" That task appealed to the boys; they stopped sniffling and went to find Selena.

Louise looked across the room and saw Viola trying to fit into the doll stroller. When she reached her, she saw that Viola had wet her pants again and had her thumb in her mouth. Viola had a three-month-old baby brother at home. Before his birth she had been dry during the day for six months and had stopped sucking her thumb. Louise and Viola's parents had discussed her regression and agreed to ignore the thumb sucking and treat the toilet accidents very nonchalantly. They were also trying to provide Viola with lots of cuddles and attention at school and home. When Selena brought in the snack, Louise took Viola to the bathroom to change her pants.

At least there were some bright spots in the day, Louise thought. Circle time went better than she expected. She usually placed the parent volunteer and the aide next to the children who had the most difficulty sitting still, and she was minus one person. One of those fidgety children was Andrew, the youngest child in the class. Yesterday he had spotted a caterpillar on the patio and watched it for almost all of the outdoor playtime, so Louise had decided to read The Very Hungry Caterpillar today. He listened the entire time, and later she saw him "reading" the book himself.

And Lauren and Lee were absorbed for quite some time with paper and crayons at the art table. They had discovered that the beginnings of their names looked the same, and they were covering sheet after sheet of paper with crooked L letters in different colors. Louise traced some Ls with glue and gave them glitter to shake on top.

She was also happily surprised to see Brandon give up the dump truck to Will when he asked for a turn. Brandon had a lot of trouble sharing, and Will usually grabbed for a toy instead of asking, so they had frequent tussles over toys. She had been working with them on sharing and asking for months, and it looked as if they might be getting the idea. Finally!

Louise began to think about the next day. She would add lots of cars, trucks, and other vehicles to the block area. Perhaps the children would get so interested in building roads, bridges, and garages that they would forget about pretending the blocks were guns. And it would fit with the transportation unit she was starting. They were going to have a visit from a fire truck tomorrow. Where is that toy fire truck?, she wondered.

Just as she got up to look for the fire truck, a little face peeked around the door. It was Lauren, still clutching her paper of glittery Ls. Her mother soon appeared in the doorway as well and explained, "She insisted on coming back to give you a good-bye hug." Louise laughed and embraced Lauren, who whispered in her ear, "I love you, Mrs. Hawkins." Louise whispered back, "I love you too, sweetie" and thought to herself, "and I love this profession."

The Field of Human Development

Like Louise Hawkins in the vignette just described, many family and consumer sciences professionals work in fields that require a deep understanding of human development. This chapter provides an overview of careers serving individuals at different stages of the lifespan, from infant and toddler day care services to geriatric care managers. Typical career opportunities in the field of human development are listed in **Figure 12-1.**

Career Opportunities in Early Childhood Development

Career opportunities in working with young children are increasing because of several factors.

Sample Career Titles in the Human Development Field		
Activities director	Executive director	Outreach worker
Adult day care manager	Family coordinator	Parent educator
Adult protective services investigator	Family life educator	Preschool teacher
Case manager	Family preservation worker	Probation/parole counselor
Child development specialist	Family services representative	Program director
Child life specialist	Family support worker	Recreation specialist
Child welfare specialist	Geriatric care manager	Residence supervisor
Day care administrator	Group home manager	Service coordinator
Day care licensing specialist	Home/school liaison	Therapeutic behavior specialist
Diversion specialist	Life coach	Truancy prevention program manager
Early intervention specialist	Life skills instructor	Volunteer coordinator
Eligibility specialist	Long-term care ombudsman	Youth services coordinator

Figure 12-1 The field of human development offers interesting career opportunities.

Early Childhood Mental Health Consultant

Marci Masters, Q.M.H.P.
D & E Counseling Center

How did you get into your line of work?

I enrolled in college with the intent to obtain an associate's degree in pre-kindergarten education. I am a mother of three children, and I have always loved being around children and wanted a career helping them develop. Through my studies, I realized that there are many facets of child development, not just academics, and that parents and teachers have a tremendous impact on the lives of children.

After obtaining my associate's degree, I spent some time in the early childhood field getting first-hand experience with children, teaching, observing, documenting, planning for, and evaluating their progress. Through my experience and conversations with colleagues, I realized that the foundations of learning are social and emotional in nature, rather than solely intellectual, and that there is a need for teachers to obtain help with children who use challenging behaviors.

I decided to continue my education and pursue a degree in family and consumer studies with a concentration on early childhood and a minor in psychology. I found a love for psychology and statistics and a desire to apply that knowledge to improve the lives of children in my community. As a senior, I did an internship for the summer with the Early Childhood Department at the D & E Counseling Center. After completing the internship, I was hired as the Early Childhood Mental Health Consultant.

What does your "typical" day entail?

During a typical workday, I make two or three visits to preschools. I work with children 3-5 years of age who have been referred for social, emotional, or behavior issues. During the visits I will be discussing with teachers the child's challenging behavior and possible reasons for it. I may administer or share results of social and emotional assessments. The day might include meetings with parents and teachers in which we devise behavior plans for the child, and I provide resources on social and emotional development. I will also play with the child and conduct role plays so that I can facilitate the use of appropriate skills and build relationships with the child. I model desired teaching skills and advise teachers on adaptations to lesson plans and teaching practices.

The consultation process takes an average of 14 visits, and each visit is about an hour. When I receive a referral for a child, I contact the teacher, get an informed consent signed by the parent or guardian, and schedule an initial visit. During the first two visits, my focus is on building relationships with the administrator, teacher, and child. I also observe the classroom environment, the teacher's strategies and teaching practices, the child, and the reactions of the other children to the child; and I document my observations. I will ask the teacher and parent to complete a strength-based social and emotional assessment of the child, and I'll have the teacher use several checklists to reflect upon teaching practices and how they impact the child's behaviors. After scoring and analyzing the assessments, the teacher, parent, and I will meet. I will share the assessment results, and we will collaborate on devising a behavior plan to decrease the child's use of the challenging behavior.

During the next visits, I aid the teacher in developing and using the skills needed by modeling, role-playing, and providing resources. I help the child to develop proactive social and emotional skills and help the other children in the class respond appropriately to my client. I provide the parent support and resources necessary for the interventions to be used at home, as well. At the conclusion of the consultation, I will administer a post-assessment so that the child's progress can be documented.

After the visits are completed for the day, I return to my office so that I can file the documentation I've gathered, complete online data entry, score assessments, analyze the data that have been generated, and contact parents and teachers to make future visits and discuss the child's progress. My supervisor and I discuss each client's progress and address any concerns or difficulties that may arise.

How do you fulfill the mission of family and consumer sciences— that is, how does your work improve people's quality of life?

This career allows me to impact the lives of community members directly every day. The quality of the preschool teachers' lives is improved by helping them develop positive, proactive skills they can use in their classroom. This improves their effectiveness at work, and the positive environment is more enjoyable and reduces work-related stress. Preschool administrators are directly impacted by employing teachers who are committed to furthering their education, which results in more highly qualified teachers employed at their school and may generate higher enrollment numbers. Also, teachers who are more satisfied with their jobs will decrease turnover rates at that preschool center.

Children's lives are improved because they are developing positive social and emotional skills that increase their opportunity for academic success, making friends, and participating in meaningful ways in their classroom community. Children who receive this service improve the quality of attachments they form with adults and peers in their lives, develop more self-control, and appropriate initiative at school and home.

Benefits to parents include children who are more prosocial, use challenging behaviors less frequently, respond appropriately to their parents, and engage in positive family interactions. Parents learn more effective and proactive parenting skills, which may reduce stress in the home. Also, the quality of the community is improved by helping young children develop the skills needed to become productive members of the community in which they live.

The number of preschool age children has been growing; most mothers and fathers of young children are employed outside the home; and society has recognized the critical importance of the early years in human development. Research indicates that high-quality early childhood programs do make a difference in outcomes for children, and well-educated personnel are essential to quality (Galinsky, 2006). Federal and state policies, such as publicly funded preschool programs and services for children with special needs, have created employment opportunities for those with knowledge of child development and early childhood education. Career opportunities include early intervention, early childhood education, and child life services.

Early Intervention

The goal of early intervention programs is to improve the life prospects for children who may be at risk because of poverty, low birth weight, disabilities, or other factors that may hinder their development. Research has shown the critical importance of environmental factors in brain development during the first three years of life. Children born into families where there is abuse, neglect, domestic violence, or substance abuse may never realize their full potential without additional support.

Early intervention programs may begin during the mother's pregnancy, in infancy, or the early childhood years. They often seek to serve economically disadvantaged families because of the destructive effects of poverty on children or to reach out to teen parents who may lack parenting skills as well as resources.

The oldest and most well-known intervention program is Head Start, which serves children from low-income families. More recently, the Individuals with Disabilities Education Act mandated states to provide services to infants and toddlers with disabilities.

Early intervention specialists usually conduct home visits. They do developmental screenings, provide referrals and information to parents, and link families to needed services. They often work with parents to improve their parenting skills or teach them how to use developmentally appropriate educational activities and toys. Facilitating parent support groups or supervising paraprofessional staff may be part of the job.

Professionals in this field may also be called *case managers*, *service coordinators*, or *home visitors*. Whatever the title, they need a strong knowledge base in child development and the ability to conduct assessments. They must be respectful of the parents' authority and cultural heritage. Working in early intervention requires flexibility and being comfortable with families whose values and attitudes may be quite different from your own.

Early Childhood Education

Early childhood is generally defined as birth through age eight, and there are a variety of programs to serve this age group, including infant and toddler programs, day care centers, preschools, kindergartens, and elementary schools. Becoming a *preschool teacher* is the goal of many students who are studying child development or early childhood education. Preschool teachers generally work with children aged three to five.

Traditional preschools follow a typical nine-month school calendar, and children may attend two, three, or more days a week for half-day sessions. However, because so many parents need child care services, many preschool programs today are embedded in day care programs where children are present for a much longer time. Whether employed in a traditional preschool or in a day care center, preschool teachers are responsible for providing a developmentally appropriate curriculum. They promote the healthy development of the whole child (social, emotional, cognitive, and physical) through creative learning activities. The uninformed observer may think the children are "just playing," when in fact the teacher has carefully planned the play to promote social interaction, language development, or fine motor skills. Preschool teachers introduce literacy, math, and science concepts. They must also be skilled observers of the child's behavior to build on the child's interests and to note any problems that need attention. These early childhood educators build relationships with parents and involve them as partners in their child's education.

Child care centers may provide services for a wider age range of children than preschools. They may offer infant and toddler programs and after-school care for elementary-age children. Early childhood educators who work in day care settings often have responsibilities for the physical care of children that are not part of the typical preschool teacher's job. For example, those who care for infants change diapers and bottle-feed them while also providing mental stimulation and emotional security. These teachers partner with parents to promote their toddlers' mastering of developmental skills of walking, toilet training, and eating with utensils. Day care personnel supervise naps and oversee health routines such as brushing teeth. Children in day care may eat more meals at the center than at home, so knowledge of nutrition, food safety, and how to introduce healthy food to children is extremely important.

Family day care home providers care for a limited number of children in their own homes. This is a particularly appealing career option for those who would like to be at home with their own small children. They can use their professional skills to meet the needs of families who prefer a more intimate environment for their children.

After gaining experience in the early childhood field, some individuals become *preschool* or *child care center directors*. Directors are responsible for the operation of the entire program, although they may report to an owner or board with ultimate authority. As administrator of a preschool or day care center, you would hire, train, evaluate, schedule, and supervise staff. Another responsibility is making sure the facility complies with licensing rules, fire and health codes, and if the program receives public funding, state or federal guidelines. Planning budgets, collecting fees, and overseeing payroll and purchases are part of the job. The center director leads development of policies, procedures, and curriculum. He or she communicates with parents and involves them in the activities of the school. An administrator's day can include tasks as varied as checking to see that the bathrooms are clean, reviewing lunch menus, meeting with parents, making referrals to community agencies, writing a grant, or resolving concerns of staff members.

Child Life Services

Imagine that you are three years old, in the hospital, very sick, and undergoing sometimes painful procedures. Your parents are allowed to visit you for only short periods of time, and your siblings not at all. Fortunately, times have changed. Hospitals practice family-centered care, and the child life profession was instrumental in bringing about this change. *Child life specialists* help children and their families deal with the stress of hospitalization and traumatic events such as injury, chronic illness, health care procedures, or the death of a loved one. *Child life assistants* work under the direction of child life specialists and have less education.

Child life specialists use play therapy to help children cope with their anxieties. They prepare their young patients for medical procedures by carefully explaining what is going to happen. If you had a scheduled surgery or procedure as a child, you may remember going to the hospital for a pre-admission tour. During procedures, child life workers distract children and help them relax with a variety of techniques such as music and toys. The child life department also plans activities and special events to make a hospital stay more pleasant. When children are hospitalized for long periods of time, child life specialists help with arrangements for keeping up with school work.

Parents can obtain information, resources, and guidance from the child life staff. These professionals also are sensitive to the needs of the young patient's siblings and help them with their concerns. When a family loses a child, child life specialists are there to provide understanding and comfort. Occasionally child life specialists work with children who are facing the illness or death of a parent.

Preparing to Enter the Early Childhood Development Field

Successful professionals in the early childhood field have certain personal characteristics. Perhaps the most important is passion to make a difference in the lives of young children. You will also need high energy, a sense of humor, patience, flexibility, and creativity. Early childhood professionals must be willing advocates for children and their families. Being authentic, respecting families, and valuing diversity are essential for creating a caring atmosphere where children can develop to their fullest potential (Colker, 2008). In addition, directors of preschools, day care centers, or child life departments need especially good leadership skills to train, motivate, and supervise staff. They must be able to communicate effectively, not only with children but also with parents and other professionals.

Issues in the News
Child and Elder Abuse and Neglect

A Kansas City woman was recently charged with assault, child abuse, and endangering the welfare of a child after police found her 10-year-old daughter locked in a closet. The little girl weighed only 32 pounds and told police that she was not allowed out of the closet for days at a time. Neighbors had no idea the child existed (Lupkin, 2012). A 92-year-old man was abandoned by his son along an Arizona highway. The son admitted to police that he had tried to kill his father. An elderly blind woman had $52,000 stolen from her bank account by a son who used it to buy a motorcycle, take a trip to Hawaii, change his name, and make arrangements to move to another state (Cole, 2012). Media outlets report

cases of neglect and abuse of children and the elderly almost every day.

The family, the source of love and support for most people, is a place where some are victimized. How common are neglect and abuse? The Children's Bureau of the U.S. Department of Health and Human Services estimates that child protective agencies found 695,000 children in the United States to have been abused or neglected in 2010. The most common form of maltreatment was neglect, but 17.6 percent suffered physical abuse, and tragically 1,560 children died from abuse and/or neglect (Child Welfare Information Gateway, 2012). Many additional cases went unreported.

The prevalence of elder abuse is more difficult to determine because there is no national reporting system, and definitions of elder abuse are not uniform. Nevertheless, based on a review of available data, the National Center on Elder Abuse (2005) believes that between 1 and 2 million Americans over 65 have been mistreated by someone they depended upon for care. Mistreatment can take many forms, such as failure to provide food, heat, clothing, or medical care, or physical abuse. One of the fastest growing crimes against the elderly may be financial exploitation (Cole, 2012).

You can play a significant role in preventing and reporting abuse. Professionals in

What Training Is Needed?

Until fairly recently, many states did not license teachers for working with children below kindergarten. Teachers were generally licensed to teach the elementary grades. Educational qualifications for early childhood occupations have been increasing, but the requirements vary widely from state to state. As of 2013, Head Start programs across the country began requiring at least half of their preschool staff to hold baccalaureate degrees. Preschool teachers employed by public schools usually must have a bachelor's degree and teaching licensure in early childhood. Some states offer paraprofessional or associate teaching licenses to holders of associate degrees in the field.

Staff and administrators must meet certain minimum requirements for facilities to be licensed. Check with your state child care licensing office for the specific regulations in your location. Training in first aid, child abuse recognition and reporting, and communicable disease management are typical requirements. Generally, educational requirements for administrators are higher than for staff. Although state requirements may be minimal, with some states requiring only a high school diploma, many employers look for individuals with an associate degree or higher.

---

education, social services, law enforcement, and health care report over half of the suspected child abuse and neglect cases that are investigated. In most states, if you have a professional position working with children, you are required by law to report suspected abuse. Learn the symptoms and find out how to report concerns in your state. The U.S. Department of Health and Human Services provides information and reporting procedures through the Child Welfare Information Gateway website.

Careers in early childhood and human development provide many opportunities to prevent child abuse and neglect. Facilitate friendships among the parents you serve; parents with strong social support networks are less prone to abuse. Strengthen parenting skills through parent education; parents who understand typical child development are not as likely to abuse. Respond to family crises, and connect families to the services they need. Build children's social and emotional competence; children with challenging behaviors are at higher risk for abuse. Specific ways to implement these strategies can be found in "Strengthening Families," a series of publications available on the Center for the Study of Social Policy website.

There are also systems in place to help prevent and deal with abuse of the elderly. Adult Protective Services workers investigate allegations of abuse and neglect. This may include self-neglect when individuals are not able to care for themselves. The National Adult Protective Services Resource Center, funded by the U.S. Administration on Aging, provides information on its website. The Older Americans Act requires states to have ombudsman programs to investigate complaints regarding the treatment of residents of long-term care facilities. Information about professional and volunteer opportunities can be found on the National Long-Term Care Ombudsman Resource Center website.

Professional Profile

Assistant Program Director

Jennifer Lyszaz
Girard Multi-Generational Center

How did you get into your line of work?

My interest in working with senior citizens started in eighth grade when my church class visited a nursing home and we were paired with a senior to visit every Sunday. This lasted for a few months, but after class had ended for the year, I continued to visit my senior because I had grown so attached to her. She had a severe case of Alzheimer's, so I am not sure she realized why I was there, but I knew she enjoyed the company. Local newspapers did stories about me because they thought my willingness to give up my free time for our visits and the relationship between a junior high student and an elderly woman was interesting. It was then that I realized what I wanted to do in life.

I began college in the medical field because I had such a growing interest in helping people, but soon learned that it just was not for me. I then met a professor who introduced me to a major in family and consumer studies. When it was time to do my internship, I found a place that would soon change my life forever, the Girard Multi-Generational Center, a local community center. This is how I obtained my current position, Assistant Program Director.

What does your "typical" day entail?

A typical day for me can vary because of the purpose of the center. What is unique about the center is that we carry no boundaries and serve anyone and everyone. My work each day is based on who needs help and what their particular needs are. Although senior citizens are a big part of our clientele, we do provide many services and programs to enhance the

---

Although certification to work in child life is not mandated by law, many employers do require it. Individuals interested in becoming Certified Child Life Specialists (CCLS) must complete a bachelor's or master's degree program that includes at least ten courses in relevant subject matter, such as medical terminology and child psychology. Degrees can come from a variety of fields, such as child/human development, family studies, early childhood education, or psychology. Candidates must also complete a clinical experience of 480 hours under the supervision of a CCLS to be eligible to take the qualifying exam. Potential child life specialists study

the impact of injury, illness, and the health care experience on children and their families. They learn how to conduct therapeutic play, prepare children emotionally for health care procedures, and provide support to parents and siblings (Child Life Council, 2012).

Early intervention workers also have diverse preparation, including degrees in early childhood, child development, special education, family studies, and social work. You can gain valuable preparation for early childhood careers through volunteer experiences and part-time work with children, such as being a babysitter or camp counselor. Most hospitals have volunteer

lives of people and children of all ages. A day for me involves items such as data collection and planning programs which support our center's mission: "to promote interaction between generations through education, health, fitness, and socialization for the purpose of preserving and enhancing our community." I work side by side with a licensed social worker and registered nurse providing services such as fitness education/recreation, supportive services, medical assessments, information and referrals, socialization, and volunteer services. I assist clients with Medicare education and prescription assistance. In some situations I simply lend an ear to someone who is at the end of their rope and just needs someone to talk to. I also have a certification as an Ohio Benefit Bank Counselor, which allows me to help people with government programs, for example, food stamps and home energy assistance. A great deal of my job is being an advocate for senior citizens in making sure they are understood and their voice is being heard.

How do you fulfill the mission of family and consumer sciences— that is, how does your work improve people's quality of life?

I still remember my college program mission statement: "To enhance the human condition through education, service, and research related to basic human needs for food, clothing, and shelter and the well-being of children, families, consumers, and communities." Every aspect of my career, and the relationships that I gain along the way, come back to the contents of this mission statement. Improving the quality of people's lives is providing them with a safe haven, someplace to go that they can feel safe and get help. Being a part of the staff of the Girard Multi-Generational Center, a place where the community has placed confidence and trust, enables me to assist with the daily and unexpected needs of many diverse individuals, families, and the community itself. I have learned to put the needs of others before my own. I personally feel that I fulfill the mission of family and consumer sciences to improve people's lives by adhering to the foundational values of the field.

---

programs where potential child life specialists could learn about the hospital environment.

What Are the Working Conditions?

Day care centers, child life departments, and preschools are fast-paced. Although preschools may follow a school calendar, closing during holidays and summers, day care centers are open year-round. They may open very early in the morning and close late in the evening. There are even some that care for children overnight. Administrators often work more than 40 hours a week to handle their multiple responsibilities.

Most child life specialists work in hospitals as part of a multidisciplinary health care team. Large pediatric hospitals usually have a child life department, as do many smaller hospitals. However, there are also opportunities in outpatient facilities, doctors' offices, hospice care, special camps, and funeral homes. Part-time work and flexible hours are available. Working with sick children can be very stressful. Child life specialists must be able to handle their own emotions when faced with tragic events, including death.

Career Opportunities in Youth Development

Youth development programs aim to help young people develop their potential and become responsible adults. They range from single-focus programs, such as a youth sports camp, to multifaceted national organizations such as Boys & Girls Clubs, Boy Scouts, Girl Scouts, and Camp Fire. Parks, museums, libraries, community organizations, and churches may sponsor youth development programs. Organizations that also serve adults, e.g., the YWCA or YMCA, also offer programs for youth. There are more than 8,000 nonprofit youth development programs (Krasna, 2010). These organizations provide enriching experiences, a safe place to be after school, and interactions with caring people.

Youth development programs often rely heavily on volunteers but usually have leadership from paid staff. The member organizations of the National Collaboration for Youth have more than 100,000 paid staff members and 6 million volunteers to serve over 40 million youth (National Collaboration for Youth, n.d.). Youth development professionals may provide direct service to youth, design programs, or manage programs. Youth workers must be able to foster a youth-centered atmosphere, provide individual attention, and give adolescents choices and responsibilities. They communicate high expectations and enforce rules while engaging youth in challenging activities. They plan programs where youth can explore their interests, learn new skills, demonstrate leadership, and receive recognition. Depending upon the organization's focus, they may involve the youth in cultural activities, recreation, community service, or mentoring programs. Professionals in youth development may also provide training to parents, other staff, and volunteers.

Some youth development programs may be targeted to divert adolescents from dropping out of school or becoming involved with gangs or other criminal activity. Other programs may be focused on preventing drug abuse, violence, bullying, or teen pregnancy. Juvenile courts may employ youth workers in programs to redirect young people who have come to the attention of the court because of truancy, running away from home, or other violations. Job titles in the youth development field include *program director, executive director, life skills counselor, youth leader,* and *recreation worker.*

One of the oldest and best known youth development programs is the 4-H program offered by the Cooperative Extension Service, which is available in most counties throughout the United States. Information about the Extension Service can be found in Chapter 10.

Preparing to Enter the Youth Development Field

Chances are that you participated in a youth development program at some time in your life. What do you remember about the adults who have been significant in your life? What characteristics did they have? The National Collaboration for Youth has identified competencies for frontline youth workers. These include understanding child and adolescent development, the ability to develop positive relationships with youth, and skill in creating age-appropriate activities. Youth development workers must respect cultural and human diversity, work as part of a team, and show professionalism. They serve as positive role models while engaging youth in program planning and building on their strengths.

The factors that enable youth workers to be successful can be divided into two categories: (1) knowledge and skills and (2) characteristics and beliefs. Knowledge includes an understanding of relevant theories (such as the human ecosystem model) and current trends affecting youth. Professionals in this field need the ability to create and maintain relationships not only with youth but also with families and community organizations. Designing positive learning experiences and safe environments where youth can assume significant responsibilities are other important skills (Yohalem, 2003).

Youth development professionals are more successful if they hold certain beliefs, including viewing youth as contributors or potential contributors to society rather than problems. They must be consistent, following through on promises and providing structure that young people can rely on. On the other hand, they need to be flexible to adapt to the needs of the clientele. Perhaps most of all, they must be committed to youth and passionate about their work (Yohalem, 2003).

What Training Is Needed?

No specific degree is required for entering the youth development field. However, some family studies/human development programs include specific courses or options aimed at preparing youth development workers. Relevant courses include subjects such as adolescent development, youth in families, cultural diversity, contemporary youth issues, policy development, program planning and evaluation, research, grant writing, and program administration. Family and consumer sciences education, discussed in Chapter 10, is also excellent preparation for working with youth outside of the classroom setting. Many opportunities for college students to gain experience in this field are available in part-time and summer employment or through internships.

What Are the Working Conditions?

Programs for youth are usually offered by nonprofit organizations and therefore dependent upon donations and grants for a majority of their funding. They tend to have few paid staff and rely a great deal upon volunteers. This can be stressful for those who manage the programs. Federally funded programs, such as the 21st Century Community Learning Centers, also employ youth workers. Individuals who work in publicly funded programs must be careful to comply with the program and/or grant regulations. Professionals in youth-serving organizations may spend a great deal of time, not directly with the youth but working in the community to advocate for programs and policies to better serve young people.

The culture of workplaces in youth development will vary depending upon the target population and the sponsoring organization. A church-sponsored program to attract urban youth away from gangs will offer different challenges and satisfactions than a nonprofit organization that offers camping and outdoor experiences for young people with physical disabilities.

Career Opportunities in Adult Development and Aging

Students of human development sometimes have long-term goals of becoming licensed counselors or marriage and family therapists. These professions generally require graduate school. A degree in human development, child development, or family studies can also prepare you to become a parent educator or family life educator. See Chapters 10 and 11 for more information about these possibilities. This section explores other careers for professionals with education in human development who wish to work with adults.

Life Coaching

Life coaching is the practice of assisting clients to determine and achieve personal goals. A *life coach* partners with clients to help them create fulfilling results in their personal and professional lives. This includes solving personal and work life issues including confidence and self-esteem, communication skills, relationship skills, parenting skills, executive training, health and fitness, time management, and goal setting and achievement. Through the process, life coaches help clients deepen their learning about themselves and their situation, improve their performance, and ultimately, enhance their quality of life. Life coaches do not target psychological illness. They are not therapists, although some therapists may do life coaching.

Most life coaches tend to specialize in a particular area, such as career coaching. Life coaches may work with groups of people through giving speeches, holding workshops, and writing books or content for a web page or magazine.

Working with Older Adults

As discussed in Chapter 4, the population of the United States and the world is aging. For this reason, occupations that serve the needs of the elderly and their families are growing. Career opportunities can be found in senior centers; retirement communities and assisted living residences; health care and long-term care facilities; local, state, and federal government agencies; and community and religious organizations. Some professionals work directly with the elderly, while others conduct research, plan and/or evaluate programs and services, or develop public policies.

Care management helps older adults remain in their homes through coordination of services. A *geriatric care manager* consults clients and their families, assesses client needs, and provides resource and referral services, education, and support to families. He or she may connect clients with a variety of service providers, such as companion services, chore services, and home health care. Management of nonmedical in-home care services (e.g., housekeeping, meals, companionship, assistance with dressing and bathing, errands, shopping) is another career possibility for those who want to improve the quality of life for senior citizens.

Families, friends, and volunteers provide most of the direct care that elderly individuals receive. Caregiving can be stressful, but there are services to support the caregiver. *Caregiver specialists* provide information and resource and referral services. Their duties may include organizing support groups, providing training for family caregivers, and counseling. They typically work for government agencies, such as an Area Agency on Aging. Many family caregivers are employed and cannot provide round-the-clock attention. Adult day care services are needed for the elderly who may not require skilled nursing care but cannot be left alone. To meet this need, there are more than 4,600 adult day care centers in the United States where one might find employment (Metropolitan Life Insurance Company, 2010).

Activity directors and *activity assistants* meet leisure and educational needs of the elderly. They work in adult day care programs, retirement communities, senior citizen centers, hospices, and assisted living or long-term care facilities. Their clients may also include individuals of any age who have disabilities.

Preparing to Enter the Adult Development and Aging Field

Gerontology is an interdisciplinary field, so professionals may come from a variety of backgrounds. Because geriatric care managers work in a holistic way with families, a background in the broad field of family and consumer sciences can be an advantage. To most effectively serve their clients, professionals need to apply knowledge of human growth and development; family resource management; and nutrition, clothing, and housing needs across the lifespan.

Advocacy and professional organizations can provide insight into the human development field. Several advocacy and professional organizations, their websites, and descriptions are given in **Figure 12-2**.

What Training Is Needed?

Individuals can enter the activity professional field from a variety of educational backgrounds, such as human development,

Professional Organizations Serving the Human Development Field		
Professional Organization	**Web Address**	**Description**
Association for Childhood Education International	acei.org	Promotes education and well-being of children worldwide.
Child Life Council	childlife.org	Provides professional development, resources, and certification for those who work in the child life field.
International Coach Federation	coachfederation.org	A professional development organization that provides independent certification, education, and networking opportunities in life coaching.
National Adult Day Services Association	nadsa.org	Provides advocacy, research, and education to serve the adult day services community.
National Association for the Education of Young Children	naeyc.org	A nonprofit association for those who work with or on behalf of children, birth through age 8.
National Association of Professional Geriatric Care Managers	caremanager.org	A professional development organization to advance the field of geriatric care through education, collaboration, and leadership.
National Certification Council for Activity Professionals	nccap.org	Sets standards for certification and provides education.
National Council on Family Relations	ncfr.org	A multidisciplinary organization focused on family research, education, and practice.
National Organization for Human Services	nationalhumanservices.org	Provides professional development and advocacy for those who work in the human services field.
The Gerontological Society of America	geron.org	Interdisciplinary organization for professionals in research, education, and practice related to aging.

Figure 12-2 Check out the websites of these human development organizations.

gerontology, education, family studies, or recreation. Three levels of certification are available once the person has gained some experience: Activity Assistant Certified, Activity Director Certified, and Activity Consultant Certified. Each level requires a combination of academic background, experience, and continuing education. Certified Activity Directors and Consultants must pass a national exam. Activity professionals need to understand human development and aging, including biological, sociological, psychological, and spiritual aspects. They also must be able to plan appropriate leisure and therapeutic activities and to work cooperatively with other staff members. Knowledge of basic first aid and CPR is important.

Life coaches come from a number of disciplines, including family and consumer sciences, business management, sociology, psychology, career counseling, and numerous other types of counseling. Life coaching is a difficult career path to define as there is no governed education or training standard established at this time (Carr, 2004). However, certification programs are available from the International Coach Federation, which has identified core competencies for the field.

What Are the Working Conditions?

Human development professionals who focus on adults may work in many settings. These include the public, nonprofit, health care, and business sectors.

Life coaches and geriatric care managers are often self-employed and work out of their own homes and in the homes of clients. These self-employed professionals must be able to market their services and manage the business aspects of their jobs as well as meet the needs of their clients. Travel, at least local travel, is often part of the job.

Summary

How can you know if a career in this field is right for you? Evaluate your strengths, weaknesses, skills, and interests in working with people at different stages of the lifespan. If you are considering a career in the field, contemplate increasing your knowledge of the profession by observing people in their work environment or by studying opportunities in the field. Even if you decide it is not a career path for you, the exercises/activities will give you an appreciation for the importance of professions working with children, youth, and the elderly.

Pursuing Careers in Human Development

1. **Interview a professional.** To get a perspective of daily work in the human development field, interview a professional. There are many opportunities, such as interviewing a preschool teacher, day care center manager, youth counselor, or activities director in an assisted living facility. Ask the person how he or she entered the field, what the advantages and disadvantages are, and what a typical day entails. Be sure to solicit advice for your career decision making. What personal qualities are needed to be successful in the field?

2. **Shadow a professional.** Seek permission to shadow a professional in the field in which you are interested. Often, you can arrange this through your university. If you are unsure about the age group with which you wish to work, you might shadow different professionals working with different age groups, such as a preschool teacher, youth counselor, or gerontologist. Observations

could range from a few hours to several days. Internships, part-time and summer employment, and volunteer experiences will also help you decide if this is the field for you.

3. **Become acquainted with professional organizations.** Since their mission is to educate and support professionals, the professional organizations provide a wealth of information. Many professional organizations include job banks for prospective employers and employees. Look up each of the websites listed in Figure 12-2. What is their mission? Do they provide opportunities to students, such as student memberships, internships, scholarships, or competitions?

4. **Become acquainted with professional publications.** Review some recent issues of journals in the field (see list at the end of the chapter). What are current topics of interest in human development? How can these publications be useful to you as a student and in the future?

Questions for Thought

1. Access the United States Department of Labor, Bureau of Labor Statistics website. Choose two related career profiles listed here and report on the career description, typical working conditions, job outlook, and expected earnings:
   - preschool and child care center directors
   - preschool teachers
   - probation officers
   - recreation workers
   - social service managers

2. Review major trends that are described in Chapter 4. How do you predict these changes will affect the work of professionals in early childhood and human development?

3. Children and the elderly are two groups served by day care services. Imagine that you are designing a multigenerational day care that would serve children and the elderly as well as individuals with disabilities of any age. What would it be like? In what ways would their needs be the same and how would they differ?

4. Have you ever suspected that a child or adult was abused? Did you report it? How is abuse reported in your state? Who is required to report?

5. Did you participate in any youth development activities (such as those offered by Family, Career and Community Leaders of America, Boys & Girls Clubs of America, Boy Scouts, 4-H, and Camp Fire) as you were growing up? What were the benefits? What were the characteristics of the adults involved?

References and Resources

Ballard, S.M., Jenkins, C., Savut, N.Y., McKinnon, W.H., Carroll, K.E., & Escott-Stump, S. (2011). Innovative and complementary approaches to aging in place. *Journal of Family and Consumer Sciences, 103*(2), 24-34.

Carr, R. A. (2004). *Peer resources: A guide to coach credentials.* Retrieved March 3, 2007, from http://www.peer.ca/credentials05.html

Center for the Study of Social Policy. (n.d.). *Strengthening families: A protective factors framework.* Retrieved from http://www.strengtheningfamilies.net

Child Life Council. (2012). *Certification.* Retrieved from http://www.childlife.org/Certification

Child Welfare Information Gateway. (2012). *Child maltreatment 2010: Summary of key findings.* Retrieved from http://www.childwelfare.gov/pubs/factsheets/canstats.cfm

Cole, C. (2012, June 24). Elder abuse: The silent scandal. *Arizona Daily Sun.* Retrieved from http://azdailysun.com.

Colker, L.J. (2008). Twelve characteristics of effective early childhood teachers. *Young Children, 63*(2), 68-73.

Eckenrole, J., Izzo, C., & Campa-Muller, M. (2003). Early intervention and family support programs. (Ch. 7). In F. Jacobs, D. Wertlieb, & R.M. Lerner (Eds.), *Handbook of applied developmental science: Vol. 2: Enhancing the life chances of youth and families* (pp. 161-195). Thousand Oaks, CA: Sage.

Feeney, S., Moravcik, E., & Nolte, S. (2013). *Who am I in the lives of children?: An introduction to early childhood education* (9th ed.). Boston: Pearson.

Galinksy, E. (2006). *Economics benefits of early childhood programs: What makes the difference?* Report of the Families and Work Institute. Retrieved from http://www.familiesandwork.org/site/research/reports/main.html

Institute for Career Research. (2009). *Career as a certified child life specialist.* Chicago: Institute for Career Research.

Krasna, H. (2010). *Jobs that matter: Find a stable, fulfilling career in public service.* Indianapolis, IN: JIST Publishing.

Leslie, C.A., & Makela, C.J. (2008). Aging as a process: Interconnectedness of the generations. *Journal of Family and Consumer Sciences, 100*(1), 6-13.

Lupkin, S. (2012, June 24). *Police rescue malnourished girl from closet in Kansas City.* Retrieved from http://abcnews.go.com

Metropolitan Life Insurance Co. (2010). *The MetLife National Study of Adult Day Services.* Retrieved from http://www.MatureMarketInstitute.com

National Center on Elder Abuse. (2005). *Elder abuse prevalence and incidence: Fact sheet.* Retrieved from http://www.ncea.aoa.gov

National Certification Council for Activity Professionals. (2011). *Certification standards.* Retrieved from http://www.nccap.org/certification/NCAP_Certification_Standards.pdf

National Collaboration for Youth. (n.d.). *Helping youth reach their full potential.* Retrieved from http://www.collab4youth.org/Default.aspx

Roth, J.L., & Brooks-Gunn, J. (2003). What is a youth development program? Identification of defining principles. (Ch. 8). In F. Jacobs, D. Wertlieb, & R.M. Lerner (Eds.), *Handbook of applied developmental science: Vol. 2: Enhancing the life chances of youth and families* (pp. 197-223). Thousand Oaks, CA: Sage.

Schwarts, R.G. (2003). Juvenile justice and positive youth development. (Ch. 19). In

F. Jacobs, D. Wertlieb, & R.M. Lerner (Eds.), *Handbook of applied developmental science: Vol. 2: Enhancing the life chances of youth and families* (pp. 421-443). Thousand Oaks, CA: Sage.

Yohalem, N. (2003). Adults who make a difference: Identifying the skills and characteristics of successful youth workers. In F.A. Villarruel, D.F. Perkins, L.M. Borden, & J.G. Keith (Eds.), *Community youth development: Programs, policies, and practices.* Thousand Oaks, CA: Sage.

Professional Journals and Trade Publications

Child Abuse and Neglect

Child and Youth Care Forum

Child Development

Community, Work, and Family

Day Care and Early Education

Family Relations

Generations

Human Relations

Journal of Aging and Social Policy

Journal of Family Issues

Journal of Marriage and the Family

Teaching Young Children

Young Children

On The Internet

http://www.nifa.usda.gov/nea/family/family.cfm—provides links to cooperative extension service resources to strengthen families, youth, and communities

http://www.nncc.org—provides over 1,000 reviewed and research-based articles about child care

http://www.futureofchildren.org—a collaboration of the Woodrow Wilson School of Public and International Affairs at Princeton University and the Brookings Institution provides free online journals and policy briefs related to the well-being of children

http://www.idealist.org—provides links to jobs, internships, volunteer opportunities, and nonprofit organizations throughout the world

Chapter 13

Careers in Family and Consumer Resource Management

After studying this chapter, you will be able to:

- describe the field of family and consumer resource management.
- identify the various career opportunities in the family and consumer resource management field.
- explain specific academic training that is needed to work in various family and consumer resource management careers.
- describe working conditions and career paths in the family and consumer resource management field.

The five years since I graduated from college have flown by. I chose family finance (personal financial planning) as a major because I had personally experienced the heart-wrenching decisions that come with declaring personal bankruptcy brought on by overused high-interest credit cards and overspending. As a single divorced mom of two school-age children, it was not easy going back to school in my mid-forties. My goal was to help others who, like me, have struggled financially.

Since graduating from college with a degree in family finance, I have learned two things about the field. One, there are more jobs available in this field than I ever imagined. Two, an economic downturn situation can lead to more job opportunities as individuals and families in the community struggle to find ways to make limited resources cover their expenses. My first job ended up being closer than I imagined. I was hired, and am still employed, in the human resources area of my university as a personal finance advisor.

What does it mean to be a personal finance advisor? I counsel university staff and faculty in all areas of personal finance. I do not make decisions for them but educate them on options and help them make their own informed decisions. First, I counsel my clients on their income allocations. Together we look at where their money comes from and where it goes. For example, we first look at their fixed expenses, their savings and investments, and their variable expenses. Next, we discuss possible risks that could financially devastate them. These tie directly to insurance planning. Third, we look at ways to accumulate wealth for the future by setting specific goals for making informed decisions. Tax planning is also important. Next, we talk about retirement and how savings and investments can make a difference in later years of life. Lastly, I talk with my clients about how they would like to pass on their financial resources after their death.

My days are filled with one-on-one meetings with clients, collaborative meetings with colleagues, and training with vendors to keep me up to date on available services and changing regulations. I love what I do. It is a perfect blend of working with people and desk work. There is no doubt in my mind that I am helping people make informed decisions to improve their quality of life.

As you begin to think about careers in resource management, some important questions come to mind. Does money really make the world go around? Why do so many Americans cite a lack of time and energy despite the many conveniences that technology offers? Is life becoming more frantic than in generations past? Many individuals and families today face a shortage of time, money, and other resources, yet we are in a nation that enjoys a high standard of living. Does it matter? Of course. In families today, the number one source of stress among married couples is finances (Olson & DeFrain, 2006).

Managing personal and business resources is no easy task. For example, in the last several decades, Americans have had savings rates much lower and household debt much higher than historical averages. In fact, savings rates are the lowest since the Great Depression of the 1930s (Garrett, 2007). Both personal and business bankruptcy filings have tripled over the past 20 years (United States Bankruptcy Courts, n.d.). Without adequate income or savings, many individuals and organizations have too little money to face their current financial needs, let alone think about the future. Without adequate financial resources, businesses lose people. Without people, it is difficult to meet goals. People, money, and time are three critical resources for individuals, families, and communities to survive.

The Family and Consumer Resource Management Field

In the past several decades, sweeping changes have occurred in the U.S. and global economic systems. For example, with an increase in female workforce participation, traditional gender roles have changed. Technology has transformed both the workplace and home. Personal, family, and corporate debt has increased while fewer families save. All of this means that family and consumer resource management professionals are needed now more than ever.

Family and consumer resource management professionals help individuals and families adopt financial management behaviors that lead to more secure financial situations. The field of family and consumer resource management examines decision making regarding credit and debt, insurance, savings, investments, retirement and estate planning, and daily consumer choices. It is an applied field where quantitative analysis and economic principles are combined to understand decision making at the individual, family, community, and organizational levels. The principles of family resource management are grounded in economics and decision making, and they are applied to decisions about food, housing, apparel, and other resources in the context of families and public policies.

Areas of employment in the family and consumer resource management field vary from opportunities in management, marketing, administration, and research to education, consulting, and regulatory activities. These opportunities can be found in many sectors of the financial services industry, such as financial institutions, insurance companies, financial planning, consumer affairs, customer service, and investment firms. Professionals in the field understand the basic tools of economic theory, quantitative analysis, and our economic system and apply those theories to everyday life. Family and consumer resource management professionals might also work with private nonprofit agencies, such as the Consumer Credit Counseling Services and the Better Business Bureau, or with government agencies.

Career Opportunities in the Family and Consumer Resource Management Field

From advocating for consumer rights to influencing the financial decisions and well-being of families, the family and consumer resource management field provides a wealth of job opportunities. Some opportunities involve working with individuals and the family unit, while others are related to businesses or organizations. Still others focus on the rights and responsibilities of consumers in general. In the following section, the opportunities in the family and consumer resource management field are explored. Some of these career opportunities represent large segments of the industry, whereas others highlight smaller specialty areas. Typical careers in the family and consumer resource management field are listed in **Figure 13-1.** Cooperative extension educators and specialists as well as family and consumer sciences teachers at all levels also help individuals and families manage their financial and other resources. These careers are described in Chapter 10.

Financial Management

If money is at the root of all business decisions, it needs to be managed with care. To make clear, concise, and effective financial decisions, finance specialists facilitate budget planning and identify the financial implications of all decisions made. This is where financial managers come into play.

Financial managers are responsible for providing financial guidance to their clients. They oversee the preparation of financial reports, execute cash management strategies, and guide investment activities. Although *financial manager* is a generic term, specific titles such as controller, credit manager, cash manager, treasurer, or finance officer are also used, depending on the specific job tasks. *Controllers* prepare financial reports for an organization and prepare documentation for regulatory agencies such as the Internal Revenue Service. *Credit managers* typically oversee the use of credit and monitor credit accounts, whereas *cash managers* oversee the cash flow. *Treasurers* and *finance officers* prepare financial budgets, goals, and objectives while overseeing investment strategies. Other titles include *budget analysts* or *business analysts*.

The overall goal of financial managers is to provide financial advice and support to their clients in order to make sound business decisions. Many organizations employ several financial managers, with each one responsible for a particular division or function.

Consumer Credit Counseling

Money has meaning at many levels for individuals and families, including lifestyle, power, status, entertainment, and securing goods. Graduates of family and consumer resource management programs understand these multiple meanings and are well equipped to help consumers understand the complexity of spending and debt.

The lure of easy credit is difficult to pass up, and temptations abound for consumers to increase personal debt beyond their means to repay it. *Consumer credit counselors* work with consumers by educating them on ways to avoid and reduce personal debt. They focus on both debt repayment and credit education.

Sample Careers in Family and Consumer Resource Management		
Account manager	Corporate trainer	Move manager
Claims representative	Credit manager	Office organizer
Communications coordinator	Customer service representative	Patient representative
Consumer affairs specialist	Financial planner	Personal financial advisor
Consumer banker	Home organizer	Personal planner
Consumer reporter	Human resources manager	Time management consultant
Consumer researcher	Investment consultant	Work and family manager

Figure 13-1 The family and consumer resource management field offers a variety of careers.

Issues in the News
The Lure of Easy Credit

The lure of easy credit is difficult to pass up, especially when being bombarded by many sources of easy money and desirable products. Credit card offers abound for anyone with a mailbox. You hear messages on television and the radio: "no payments for two years," "zero down," and "no interest." Who wouldn't want to have that car, furniture, or clothing?

The future earning potential of college students is a target for especially aggressive marketing by those who want to lend money. College students are often bombarded with offers of credit cards as soon as they hit the college campus. For many students, this is the first credit card they have ever had. These cards can offer what appear to be very attractive payment plans—as little as one percent of the balance per month. Most students think they will have no problem paying the minimum balance. But the interest rates quickly add cost to using the cards. It's possible to make payments for several years on that pizza you bought!

The ability to borrow money should be viewed as a privilege and carefully guarded and nurtured. Each person has a "credit rating" or "credit score." A high score can provide you with easy loans at favorable rates, while a low score can prevent you from obtaining a loan or getting a good rate. A low score can also make it more difficult to find employment. Employers, particularly in the financial area, sometimes check the credit rating of job applicants. Missing just one payment on your credit card quickly shows up on your credit report, adversely affecting your credit rating. Review your credit rating regularly. In addition, make sure that erroneous information or identity theft is not adversely affecting your score. For information on obtaining a free credit report, visit the Federal Trade Commission website and search "free credit report."

The ever-increasing cost of education also contributes to a higher debt load. Although college loans may have low rates, finishing school with tens or hundreds of thousands of dollars of debts can put a heavy burden on recent graduates.

The weight of increasing debt can create a seemingly impossible financial situation to solve. Credit counseling services exist to help people establish workable plans of repayment, but more people look to bankruptcy as a solution. Bankruptcy can only be considered a last resort since the repercussions and negative credit ratings last for many years after filing, and many assets can be taken away from the filer.

The key to successfully managing credit and debt is to use credit only when necessary and for short periods of time if possible. Create and adhere to realistic personal budgets. Finally, know the cost and terms of assuming debt.

Consumer credit counselors usually begin by establishing a budget that matches the income and debt responsibilities of a client. They may assist clients in negotiating with creditors to establish a plan to repay creditors. Plans sometimes include negotiated payments, fees, and interest rates that are reduced, making it possible for consumers with out-of-control debt to repay it. These are called *debt management plans.*

These plans are controversial. While debt management plans are sometimes considered a good alternative to bankruptcy (since more creditors are repaid and the credit rating and self-esteem of the consumer are protected), sometimes consumers with these plans are questioned or denied when they apply for new loans.

Consumer credit counselors may work for nonprofit family service agencies located in government county offices, or they may work at for-profit debt management agencies. Nonprofit family service agency counselors typically help consumers prepare a budget and devise a plan for repaying debt. For example, American Consumer Credit Counseling (ACCC) is a nonprofit organization offering confidential credit counseling and financial management education to consumers. Other similar nonprofit consumer credit counseling agencies can be found through the Association of Independent Consumer Credit Counseling Agencies.

For-profit agencies generally collect a monthly fee for services and in exchange for managing multiple payments and due dates. Even with paying the monthly fee, many consumers recover from debt more quickly than they would without help from credit counselors. The for-profit consumer credit counseling industry is relatively new and unregulated. The Federal Trade Commission has filed lawsuits against several credit counseling agencies and continues to urge caution in choosing a credit counseling agency until more regulations are instituted and enforced.

Issues in the News
Identity Theft

We often hear of people's identities being stolen. What exactly does this mean? *Identity theft* is defined by the U.S. Department of Justice as "crimes in which someone wrongfully obtains and uses another individual's personal data in a way that involves fraud or deception, often for economic gain" (U.S. Department of Justice, 2011). Today, identity theft is the fastest growing crime in the country. In fact, the means by which a person's identity can be stolen are increasing faster than measures to prevent identity theft can be enacted.

In the not-so-distant past, the most prevalent form of identity theft was someone illicitly applying for a copy of a birth certificate from a deceased person and taking that person's identity. Today, daily activities using electronic banking, the Internet, ATMs, credit cards, e-mail, and e-commerce create an endless number of ways for personal information to be intercepted for illegal use. Surprisingly, stealing a person's identification or financial information may not be a crime in and of itself. Within certain legal jurisdictions, identity theft is not a crime until the information is used in an illegal way.

What can be done about identity theft? The best defense is prevention. Create "consumer alerts" with the credit reporting agencies to limit who can obtain credit information and flag any illicit applications. Use a shredder to dispose of anything that has financial information on it. Watch for "shoulder surfers" at ATMs, and be careful with whom you share credit card information. Use a post office box (PO Box) or locking mailbox. Do not give out your Social Security number to anyone. Instead, use another form of identification when possible. Only enter credit card information on known secure websites. Never reply with personal information to e-mails that you receive, even if they appear to come from legitimate sources. Finally, review your credit reports regularly.

What if you're a victim of identity theft? The U.S. Federal Trade Commission provides information and a procedure to follow through their website. File a complaint with the FTC, take a copy of the FTC Affidavit to the police, and get a copy of the police report.

Personal Financial Planning

Like financial managers, personal financial planners are responsible for providing financial advice and support to their clients. However, their clients are individuals and families rather than business organizations. *Personal financial planners* provide guidance to individuals to help them with their budgeting, spending, income, insurance, credit, and other financial decisions.

They assess the overall financial needs of their clients and offer them a wide range of financial options based on their financial goals and objectives. Depending on their expertise, they may also assess the economic performance of investments and advise their clients on investment decisions. Personal financial planners may specialize in one or more specific areas, such as retirement savings, real estate, insurance, or equity trading.

Professional Profile

Retired President

JoElla Weybright
Gilmore Research Group

How did you get into your line of work?

After graduating from college, I went to work in the research labs of a large food company in Chicago. My job was to manage the small expert-panel taste testing that went on every day, enabling food scientists to determine what impact various experiments and formulations had on the taste and texture of products. I found it fascinating that a scientific approach to training people, preparing and presenting food samples, and analyzing the end data could provide guidance on making sound decisions for quality products.

Upon moving to Seattle, I found a small market research firm looking to offer new services to clients, including several local food manufacturers. The taste test work I had done with small trained panels enabled me to design studies that presented test food products/formulations to consumers to determine which were preferred and why. Some of these studies involved finding qualified people to come to central locations for the test, and others required that we place products in homes for "real-life" trial. This new service, called "NW Taste Test," provided information about consumer opinion of such things as flavors, packaging, and pricing that could be used to make sound business decisions about products. Over the years, the consumer opinion research broadened to include many industries in addition to food, and surveys about many issues in addition to acceptance of consumer products. As the company grew from 5 to over 45 professionals, I learned applied statistics, sampling, and survey design on the job. I also learned a great deal about managing people and working in a team environment.

I was with the company close to 40 years. As president, I had responsibility for setting and oversight of company policies, goals, and profitability. I came to this position through many years of working "in the

Personal financial planners must understand their clients' specific family needs. For example, clients may be interested in spending money on their first home, college savings plans, high-growth investments, or retirement savings. Guidance and financial advice should vary by the client's stage of life, too. Younger clients may be more interested in higher risk investments than those who are nearing retirement. Overall, personal financial planners play an important objective role in personal financial decision making.

Consumer Affairs

Have you ever purchased a product that did not live up to its advertising? Have you ever had a frustrating dispute with a landlord? Where can you go for help? Professionals in the consumer affairs field collect data about consumers,

trenches," building operational systems, designing questionnaires, analyzing data, writing reports, and presenting findings. It is unusual today to find people who stay with one company for 40 years, but it really feels as if I have been in multiple jobs over the years as the company grew and changed.

What does your "typical" day entail?

I come to work at 7 a.m. for an hour of quiet time and e-mail reading; meet with operational staff regarding active projects (are any new resources needed to get projects completed?); meet with the executive committee regarding company policies, financial issues, etc.; review a proposal going out; have lunch with a potential client who wants to discuss our services; edit the summary of a report that will help a client understand what the study findings mean and how they can be applied to his business; sit in on a pretest of a telephone survey to help the project manager fine-tune the draft questions; laugh with colleagues and have a great time. Throughout my time at Gilmore Research Group, I particularly enjoyed working closely with clients in a wide variety of industries to determine their needs and design the appropriate type of study to answer their questions.

How do you fulfill the mission of family and consumer sciences— that is, how does your work improve people's quality of life?

Market and opinion research provides vital information for decision making. Often the information that is needed about a product or service does not exist in any library or database. I have to get it directly from the person who has the experience or who will be impacted by changes, new features, or prices. Businesses, government agencies, educational institutions, and nonprofits all want to better understand what their constituents—their "customers"—want and need. Using data from well-planned and executed research can reduce the risk of making poor decisions, whether it is the preferred design for a new cell phone, the advertising message that is most effective in helping reduce teen smoking, or the planning for a new transit route near your home. People use a wide variety of products and services every day that help make their lives better, easier, happier, and more fulfilling. It is gratifying that research plays an important role in making those products and services possible.

educate consumers, and advocate for consumer rights. For example, *consumer researchers* collect and disseminate data about consumer decision making, spending, savings, and values. *Consumer affairs specialists* advocate for consumer rights and mediate between interested parties. They investigate consumer complaints about false advertising, misrepresentation of services or products, unethical practices, and

violations against established laws or regulations. They help consumers find the resources needed to solve their consumer problems.

Advocating for consumers can take place in the form of mediation, educational journalism, television or radio media spots, government support, or any number of resource formats. Consumer affairs specialists work for governmental agencies, media, business groups, and

Professional Profile

National Program Leader Family and Consumer Economics

Susan S. Shockey, Ph.D, CFCS, CPFFE

United States Department of Agriculture, National Institute of Food and Agriculture (USDA/NIFA)

How did you get into your line of work?

Throughout my childhood I was engaged with my mother's and aunt's work as high school home economics teachers by listening and participating in meaningful discussions about the important role of home economics in society. These family members whom I admired were unwavering believers in what home economics could offer families through the application of science to home and family problems. Consequently, home economics (now family and consumer sciences) education was my choice as a profession.

At the beginning of my career I taught high school family and consumer sciences for two years. Those two years in the classroom helped me realize the importance of critical thinking and its relationship to family resource management. The ability to think critically affects decision-making processes and personal financial management. Later I moved from the public school classroom to work for the Ohio State University Extension as an extension educator and leader in family resource management. When I entered a doctoral program, my interests in money management and critical thinking led me to write my Ph.D. dissertation *Low-Wealth Adults' Financial Literacy, Money Management Behaviors, and Associated Factors, Including Critical Thinking.*

Currently I serve at the United States Department of Agriculture, National Institute of Food and Agriculture, Division of Family and Consumer Sciences, as the National Program Leader, Family and Consumer

community organizations. Much of their work is preventative. Consumer affairs specialists seek to educate consumers not only on their rights but also on their responsibilities. To do this, they must first collect and analyze data. In essence, they are problem solvers, advocating for consumers and businesses. This can result in fair business practices and high standards among all parties.

Customer Service

Whom do you call when you need to directly communicate with a specific company or organization? Most companies and organizations employ a customer service specialist or manager. *Customer service representatives* are employed to serve as the direct contact between the company and the customer. They serve as

Economics. My professional goal is to teach people to be resourceful and live an enriched life by understanding money management and to be aware of their attitudes and behaviors.

What does your "typical" day entail?

I wake up early, determined to make a difference, with a keen focus on what is important. Each day is different and varies depending on requests from my federal and state colleagues. I work with USDA/NIFA Partnerships, including the 105 land-grant colleges and universities. We collaborate with cooperative extension specialists and educators to reach individuals and families living within the 3,000 counties and territories throughout the United States. Nationwide the Family and Consumer Economics programs foster three dimensions of financial capability: (1) financial knowledge and understanding, (2) financial skills and competence, and (3) financial responsibility. My role is to provide leadership for research, extension, and education functions. This involves overseeing educational messages delivered through the USDA/NIFA education and cooperative extension systems and ensuring that program evaluations measure the impacts of participation in financial education.

How do you fulfill the mission of family and consumer sciences— that is, how does your work improve people's quality of life?

The family serves as the economic foundation for our society. I believe that the purpose of the family is to enhance the pursuit of happiness of its individual members and thereby preserve its human, intellectual, and financial capital. To do this each family must determine its purpose and define its personal core values and assets.

USDA/NIFA Division of Family and Consumer Sciences strengthens families, farms, communities, and the economy. We do this by establishing educational and research priorities related to the economic well-being of individuals and families. Our priority issues include financial instability across the lifespan, helping rural and urban individuals and families maintain economic stability in a changing economy, and supporting community development in increasingly complex and diverse environments.

company resources before, during, and after a customer purchase. They listen to complaints, answer questions, address concerns, and help customers find the resources they need, make purchasing decisions, and complete transactions. They assess the quality and seriousness of complaints and inquiries and direct them to the appropriate person. If customers are dissatisfied with their purchase, they help them return it, exchange it, or receive credit. They also help customers understand company policies. Although some interaction takes place face-to-face, many customer service representatives interact with customers exclusively by phone or via computer. Many companies have found that good-quality customer service can create loyal customers and differentiate their company from rivals. Another place where customer service representatives are being employed is in hospitals. The title is usually *patient liaison* or *patient representative*.

Account Management

Many one-time business transactions are done through customer service representatives. When there are more complex sales and support issues, and relationships to foster between supplier and customer, an account manager is often assigned. *Account managers* are responsible for the overall satisfaction of a major client or customer. In addition to selling products or services, this person must be skilled at understanding the desires, needs, and problems of individuals within the client company. He or she will often deal with issues that arise—late deliveries, quality problems, pricing—and handle all aspects of the supplier/customer relationship. Interpersonal skills are a must, as are organizational and problem-solving abilities.

Human Resources

When thinking about resources, it is common to focus on financial resources. *Human resources* focus on people as important organizational resources. Human resources include employees, volunteers, and other constituents.

Human resources specialists deal with hiring, firing, training, benefits, and other personnel issues within an organization.

A *human resources manager* oversees and administrates overall human resources activities within an organization, including hiring, firing, training, benefits, and lifestyle enrichment programs. In smaller organizations, a *human resources generalist* handles all areas associated with human resources. In large organizations, a *human resources director* oversees several specialized areas of human resources. A director may have many human resources specialists working for him or her and may be part of the top executive management group within the organization. Human resources directors participate in strategic planning including policymaking.

Large organizations often have specialized human resources managers. For example, a *benefits counselor* manages the company's employee benefits program. This may include medical and dental insurance, child care, and pension plans. A *labor relations manager* prepares information for management to use during collective bargaining agreement negotiations. This requires expert knowledge in economics, wage data and trends, labor law, and collective bargaining trends. *Recruiting specialists* focus on finding, hiring, and securing qualified employees. In the process, they screen, interview, and match potential employees to positions within the organization. Because companies must be in compliance with governmental employment regulations, larger organizations employ *Equal Employment Opportunity specialists* who investigate and resolve grievances regarding federal equal employment opportunity policies, regulations, and practices. They operate as company "watchdogs" to maintain regulatory compliance and submit statistical reports to support their findings to the *Equal Employment Opportunity Commission (EEOC)*. Other specialists include *compensation managers* who establish and maintain an organization's pay system and *corporate training and development managers*, as described in Chapter 10.

Family and consumer sciences graduates may be especially interested in the position of *work and family program manager,* also known as *work/life program managers.* They design and oversee programs that help employees balance their work and personal lives, such as flextime, job-sharing, telecommuting, or on-site child care. They may manage resource and referral services that connect employees with counseling, elder care, or other community services.

Professional Organizing and Life Coaching

An education in family resource management is excellent preparation for careers in life coaching and professional organizing. Just as financial counselors help individuals manage their money, professional organizers help people manage their physical resources and time. Professional organizers may specialize in organizing homes or business offices.

The *home organizer,* consultant, or organizational entrepreneur analyzes storage areas, home offices, and other home environments that accumulate clutter and can become inefficient. This professional develops and implements a plan to organize the area. Professional organizers may also help individuals develop systems for handling paperwork, filing, maintaining financial records, and organizing computer files. Organizing professionals who work with businesses can increase productivity by improving work flow and office design and can teach organizational and time-management skills to employees.

Some organizers also manage household moves for busy people. A related specialty is the growing field of senior move management. *Senior move managers* apply their organizational skills to help older adults transition to more suitable living quarters or reorganize their homes for aging in place. They can coordinate the "downsizing" process by facilitating the sorting and disposal of items, arranging for movers, overseeing packing and storage, and setting up the new home. Other organizers specialize in working with the chronically disorganized, hoarders, or people with attention deficit

disorder. For a description of life coaching as a career, see Chapter 12.

A new career area that blends financial management and organizing skills is the *daily money manager.* These individuals manage day-to-day financial activities, such as paying bills and banking, for individuals who cannot manage these tasks themselves. Clients include senior citizens, individuals with disabilities, busy executives, and people who are ill, travel frequently, or are out of the country.

Preparing to Enter the Family and Consumer Resource Management Field

The family and consumer resource management field deals with complex issues that involve finances as well as other resources such as people and time. Many of the current concerns in the resource management field have grown out of the effect of the Internet on consumer decisions, credit, and personal identity. Consumers are oversaturated with information. On the other side of the counter, businesses must compete on a global scale. Technologies often support wise consumer decisions, but they complicate others. With an increasing number of financial and consumer transactions on the Internet, there are issues regarding identity, security and privacy, and consumer protection.

Because the field deals with complex issues, professionals must demonstrate interpersonal, problem-solving, and analytical skills. The field requires the ability to work with people and to apply ideas and concepts to actual problems. Consider the academic training needs and working conditions discussed in the following sections and compare them to your own academic and work interests. Professional organizations can provide insight into the family and consumer resource management field. Several professional organizations, their websites, and descriptions are given in **Figure 13-2.**

Professional Organizations Supporting the Family and Consumer Resource Management Field		
Professional Organization	**Web Address**	**Description**
American Association of Daily Money Managers	aadmm.com	An association that provides professional development and credentialing for daily money managers.
American Bankers Association	aba.com	A professional organization that represents banks and holding companies, savings associations, trust companies, and savings banks on national issues that affect both financial institutions and their customers.
American Consumer Credit Counseling	consumercredit.com	A nonprofit organization, founded in 1991, that offers confidential credit counseling and financial management education to consumers.
American Council on Consumer Interests	consumerinterests.org	An organization for professionals involved in consumer advocacy, education, policy development, and research.
Association for Financial Counseling and Planning Education	afcpe.org	A professional organization dedicated to educating, training, and certifying financial counselors and educators.
Association of Independent Consumer Credit Counseling Agencies (AICCCA)	aiccca.org	A national membership organization established to promote quality and consistent delivery of nonprofit credit counseling services through service standards of conduct.
Financial Management Association International	fma.org	A professional organization that promotes research and education about financial management.
International Society of Certified Employee Benefit Specialists	iscebs.org	A professional organization that represents professionals who have earned the Certified Employee Benefit Specialist (CEBS), Group Benefits Associate (GBA), Retirement Plans Associate (RPA), or Compensation Management Specialist (CMS) designations through educational resources and networking opportunities.
National Association of Credit Management	nacm.org	A professional organization that provides networking, education, and advocacy for business credit and financial management professionals.
National Association of Personal Financial Advisors	napfa.org	A professional organization for personal financial advisors that provides educational opportunities, a code of standards, and networking opportunities for members.
National Association of Professional Organizers	napo.net	A nonprofit educational association whose members include organizing consultants, speakers, trainers, authors, and manufacturers of organizing products.
National Association of Senior Move Managers	nasmm.org	A trade association for businesses that assist older adults and their families with the emotional and physical aspects of relocation or aging in place.

Figure 13-2 Check out the websites of these professional family and consumer resource management organizations.

(Continued)

Professional Organizations Supporting the Family and Consumer Resource Management Field		
Society for Human Resource Management	shrm.org	An organization for human resources professionals to share expertise and create innovative solutions to people management challenges.
Society of Consumer Affairs Professionals	socap.org	A professional organization whose core purpose is to advance customer care through education and networking.

Figure 13-2 Continued.

What Training Is Needed?

There are several training routes to careers in the family and consumer resource management field. The level of expertise and education credentials required depends on the type of work. For example, personal financial advisors should have a credential from a professional organization. A *certified financial planner* is a financial planning expert who has been credentialed by the Certified Financial Planner Board of Standards. The Association for Financial Counseling and Planning Education awards the *Accredited Financial Counselor* designation, and individuals who pass the required exam may receive the *Certified Personal and Family Finance Educator* credential from the American Association of Family and Consumer Sciences. Additional certifications in specialized areas may also be required for specialized work in particular industries.

Most careers in the family and consumer resource management field require a four-year college degree. Family and consumer sciences programs offer many degrees that appropriately prepare graduates to work in the field. Specific degree programs include consumer economics, family economics, personal financial planning, family resource management, and consumer issues, among others. Some organizations require a degree in a specific area such as these. Others require a degree in business administration or finance. Overall, preparation and knowledge are needed in family systems, economics, finance, business management, and communication. Because of the wide diversity in educational requirements and desired experience and training, it is wise to seek advice from professionals in the field you wish to enter to determine the most desirable preparation and education path. Fluency in languages in addition to English is increasingly important as the United States becomes more diverse and new residents often need assistance in family and consumer resource management.

What Are the Working Conditions?

The working conditions of individual professionals in the family and consumer resource management field are as different and varied as each individual, family, community, or organization with which he or she works. However, due to the nature of the field, there are common personal characteristics that are desirable. Whether working as a customer service representative, a public relations specialist, or a consumer researcher, those in the family and consumer resource management field should be calm, flexible, and able to work through complex issues to ensure the well-being of their clients. Working conditions may be stressful, so professionals must be able to work with a variety of people and have good interpersonal and helping skills. Since they act as resource people, they must be confident in their knowledge and able to apply it to different settings.

Family and consumer resource management professionals also need expertise in the principles and processes for providing excellent customer and personal service. The field is very practical, and the perceived care that clients receive is important to their effective utilization of services offered. Good customer service is also essential to building trust between the service provider and client. Family and consumer resource management professionals are often dealing with sensitive topics related to family life, and trust is needed to maintain honesty, open communication, and full disclosure. Knowledge of group behavior, cultural norms, and societal trends and influences is also an important part of customer or personal service to clients. A good working knowledge of the primary spoken language and well-developed speaking, writing, and listening skills are essential. A recent survey of consumer affairs employers indicated that success in the field requires an understanding of ethics, audience needs, and technology; respect for workplace diversity, culture, and structure; and skills in conflict management, collaboration, leadership, and management (Morrison, Saboe-Wounded Head, & Cho, 2012).

Summary

Effectively managing resources is critical to the health and well-being of individuals, families, organizations, and communities. Many complex issues have emerged in the past few years in the family and consumer resource management field. These include the move toward globalization, changing lifestyle trends, and safety and security concerns. Specific factors that have caused changes in the family and consumer resource management field include overextended credit, identity theft, and unethical business practices. In addition, changes in the family economic system and consumer orientation to the marketplace have left many without necessary skills to manage their resources. As a result of the changes and transition, professionals in the family and consumer resource management field who understand these family and societal changes and can relate them to families, education, the business world, and the public sector are needed more than ever.

As the field of family and consumer resource management focuses on effective utilization of resources, there are several career paths a person can take within the field. All of these paths deal with the effective allocation and use of resources, including time, people, and finances.

How can you decide if a career in family and consumer resource management is right for you? Start with these ideas. Even if you decide that it is not a career track for you, the exercises will give you an appreciation for the importance of responsible resource management in people's lives.

Pursuing a Career in the Family and Consumer Resource Management Field

1. **Interview a professional.** The family and consumer resource management field offers a vast array of professional opportunities. However, due to the sheer number of possibilities, finding a career path can be overwhelming. You can get a view of the field by interviewing a professional. For example, you could interview a financial advisor, customer service representative, or professional organizer. Ask the person how he or she entered the field, what the advantages and disadvantages are, and what a typical day entails. Be sure to solicit any advice for your career decision making. What personal qualities are needed to be successful in the field?

2. **Shadow a professional.** Seek permission to spend a few hours or a day job-shadowing with a family and consumer resource management professional. Often, you can arrange this through your university. The more you observe, the more you will become familiar with this diverse and complex industry. Observations could range from a few hours to several days. Internships, part-time employment, summer employment, and volunteer experiences will also help you decide if this is the field for you.

3. **Become acquainted with professional organizations.** Since their mission is to educate and support professionals, professional organizations provide a wealth of industry information. They also provide relevant industry research and review innovations. Many professional organizations include job banks for prospective employers and employees. Generally, they do not try to sell anything to members. Look up each of the websites listed in Figure 13-2.

4. **Become acquainted with professional publications.** Review some recent issues of journals in the field. What are current topics of interest in family and consumer resource management? How can these publications be useful to you as a student and in the future?

Questions for Thought

1. Access the United States Department of Labor, Bureau of Labor Statistics website. Choose two related career profiles listed here and report on the career descriptions, typical working conditions, job outlooks, and expected earnings:
   - human resources specialists
   - personal financial advisors
   - customer service representatives
   - financial analysts

2. What are college students spending their money on today? Identify three consumer spending trends for college students. What factors influenced these trends? Will the trends be sustained over several seasons, or are they short-term fads? How will these trends affect future interests, fads, and ultimately careers?

3. What are college students spending their time on today? Many students are employed while in college. Is this expenditure of time to gain experience or to have a certain lifestyle? Does it erode their focus on academics?

4. Which family resource trends will define this decade (child care, elder care, leisure time, etc.)? How will this decade be described by future historians regarding family resources? What new jobs may emerge from these trends?

5. Look through a magazine and find two advertisements that seem to support competing beliefs about time, money (spending, saving), gender, and power. What concept of the relationships between economics and culture do the advertisements suggest? Are they both realistic? Do they conflict?

6. The effects of overspending can be financially devastating to individuals and families. Yet, messages that encourage overspending and extended credit abound. For some families, overspending and extended credit result from lack of education. For many, they stem from a lack of financial resources or desire for a specific lifestyle. What can and should various sectors of society do to combat overspending and debt? Consider the role of government agencies, schools, community groups, and the public sector.

References and Resources

American Association of Family and Consumer Sciences. (2012). *Certified Personal and Family Finance Educator (CPFFE)*. Retrieved from http://www.aafcs.org/CredentialingCenter/CPFFE.asp

Budd, J., & Scoville, J. (Eds.). (2005). *The ethics of human resources and industrial relations.* Champaign: University of Illinois at Urbana-Champaign, Labor and Employment Relations Association.

Careers in credit management: Credit analyst, loan officer, credit counseling. (2010). Chicago: Institute for Career Research.

Careers in financial planning: Personal financial advisors. (2006). Chicago: Institute for Career Research.

Careers in focus: Financial services (4th ed.). (2012). New York: Ferguson's.

Certified Financial Planner Board of Standards, Inc. (2012). *Financial services credentials.* Retrieved from http://www.cfp.net/learn/knowledgebase.asp?id=15

Fitch, T.P. (2007). *Career opportunities in banking, finance, and insurance* (2nd ed.). New York: Checkmark Books.

Garrett, T. (2007). The rise in personal bankruptcies: The eighth Federal Reserve district and beyond. *Federal Reserve Bank of St. Louis Review, 89*(1), 15-37.

Hersey, P., Blanchard, K.H., & Johnson, D.E. (2008). *Management of organizational behavior: Leading human resources.* Upper Saddle River, NJ: Prentice Hall.

Morrison, K., Saboe-Wounded Head, L., & Cho, S.H. (2012). Undergraduate consumer affairs program needs: Employers' perspectives. *Journal of Family and Consumer Sciences, 104*(1), 29-33.

National Association of Professional Organizers. (n.d.). *Our profession.* Retrieved from https://www.napo.net/ourprofession/

National Association of Senior Move Managers. (2012). *Senior move managers FAQs.* Retrieved from http://www.nasmm.org/faqs/index.cfm

Olson, D. H., & DeFrain, J. (2006). *Marriages and families: Intimacy, diversity, and strengths.* New York: McGraw-Hill.

Reis, D., Pena, L., & Lopes, P. (2003). Customer satisfaction: The historical perspective. *Management Decision, 41*, 195-198.

Spector, R., & McCarthy, P. (2005). *The Nordstrom way to customer service excellence.* New York: Wiley.

Trager, A., & Collins, N. (2006). Professional organizing: FCS preparation ideal for emerging career field. *Journal of Family and Consumer Sciences, 98*(3), 75-77.

United States Department of Agriculture. (2012). *Financial security.* Retrieved from http://www.nifa.usda.gov/ProgViewOverview.cfm?prnum=18447

United States Department of Justice. (2011). *OJP fact sheet: Identify theft.* Retrieved from http://www.ojp.usdoj.gov/newsroom/factsheets/ojpfs_idtheft.html

Professional Journals and Trade Publications

Economic Inquiry

Financial Counseling and Planning

International Journal of Consumer Studies

Journal of Consumer Affairs

Journal of Family and Economic Issues

Journal of Personal Finance

Review of Economics of the Household

The Wall Street Journal

On the Internet

http://www.ftc.gov—the Federal Trade Commission offers comprehensive consumer protection information

http://www.jumpstart.org—the Jump$tart Coalition for Personal Financial Literacy hosts an online library of free financial education materials

http://www.nefe.org—the National Endowment for Financial Education provides resources for teaching money management

http://www.nifa.usda.gov/financialsecurity.cfm—the U. S. Department of Agriculture Family and Consumer Economics program website provides research, news, and links to other financial security resources

http://www.extension.org/personal_finance—links the reader to personal finance education from extension, a partnership of 74 universities

Unit Three

Launching a Career in Family and Consumer Sciences

In this unit, you will begin planning your own career path and strategies for educational and professional development. The process starts with looking inward using self-assessment exercises that will help you to further understand your motivations, skills, interests, and needs. A variety of exercises and questions will help you look inward. Next, you will begin looking outward by researching career opportunities that exist in family and consumer sciences today. You will be encouraged to use your self-assessment as a basis for exploring a major and career that will best suit you as an individual. This foundation will provide you with the personal and professional knowledge and resources to begin making connections with people in your chosen career field and, ultimately, to find the career that is right for you. You will focus on making connections by setting personal and career objectives and goals. This unit will also offer numerous career-building tips and resources.

Lastly, you will understand how you, as a future family and consumer sciences professional, can make an impact on the world by incorporating the ideals, goals, and mission of family and consumer sciences in your own personal and professional life.

Chapter 14

Looking Inward: Self-Assessment

After studying this chapter, you will be able to:

- explain why self-assessment and planning are key factors that lead to life and career success.
- conduct a comprehensive assessment of your personality, interests, and values; knowledge and skills; learning needs; and self-employment potential.
- describe your personal attributes and limitations as they relate to career and life goals.
- set personal and professional goals.

I suppose it must have been inevitable. From my rural Southern upbringing to my current life in a West Coast urban setting, I have always been drawn to working with disadvantaged kids. Perhaps this should have been clear to me sooner, but a series of life events did not allow much downtime for me to focus on what I wanted to do with my life. Growing up economically disadvantaged—one of seven siblings and the son of a hardworking single mother—I always believed I was a great example of a kid who was "raised by a village." So many people were involved with my upbringing—coaches, teachers, clergy, family, and friends. I always did well in school and when I was 14, I was chosen as a scholarship recipient for an esteemed private high school. People told me I was a gifted basketball player, so after high school graduation, I decided to pursue the game by playing at a community college on the West Coast. After two years of

playing, I was recruited by a four-year university in the Pacific Northwest. Far from home, family, and friends, my life revolved around basketball. What I missed most was the time to talk with those who knew me best. It made me start thinking about my past and how it has influenced my present and future.

Growing up, I always got a lot of attention from playing basketball. It was as if I didn't have to try hard in school, but when I did—my mom wouldn't let me get away with anything else—people made a big deal about it. So much so it seemed awkward, especially since others worked at least as hard as I did. I got used to being held up as the "minority kid who had potential."

I often thought nobody, especially a kid, should have to live with that pressure. People should be appreciated for who they are. So, when I went away to college, I felt like I had to give a big dream answer to those who asked me what I was going to do with my life. I started to say I was going to be a doctor, perhaps a pediatrician. This seemed to get everyone around me excited. I was the hope of the small town. The thing was, I took my first premed course in chemistry my freshman year and I got an F. I was not remotely prepared for being so far away from home, living in a dorm, and trying to juggle a demanding basketball schedule. I was struggling to keep my athletic eligibility. The next quarter, my counselor signed me up for easy courses. I raised my grade point average to an acceptable level, but I felt like I was wasting my time. By the middle of my sophomore year, I knew something had to change.

I went to the college placement center and saw an opening for a public relations internship position at a kid's summer basketball camp in Los Angeles County. I'm not a city kid, and I really wanted to get a taste of what life was like for kids living in the city. Well, the internship paid off. First, because I had a great time with a lot of great kids who needed someone who cared. Second, because one thing led to another, and I ended up connected to a basketball recruiter for a four-year university. I make it sound like it was my goal. Actually, I am pretty focused, but at that point, I thought, "I can play this game. My plan is to go back home, but if my tuition is paid, I'll play basketball as long as they want me to."

The great thing about this move was that I now had a coach and an academic counselor who really wanted to help me find a career path. As I talked to my counselor, he suggested several courses that matched my interests. One course in particular really intrigued me—human development. I am a pretty opinionated person, but I had gotten in the habit of not contributing a lot in classes. In this class it was pretty hard to keep my mouth closed. I was intrigued from the beginning to the end. I did not know that three-year-olds could make peer friendships very similar to adult friendships. I did not know that teenagers actually did need more sleep than adults or that their brains were not fully developed. What surprised me the most was that adults went through stages of development throughout their lifetime. People have always fascinated me, and this class gave me some insight to the people around me.

As an athlete and student, the pressure was on for Michael to retain his grade point average and to choose a major course of study. Between the team's travel schedule and the part-time work he did at the local Boys & Girls Club, he simply had no time to think of what major he wanted to study or what type of career he might want to pursue. The content of several courses had intrigued him, but he was not sure which path to pursue. At the advice of his academic counselor, Michael enrolled in a course that helped him think about who he was and what he had going for him.

Playwright William Shakespeare in *Hamlet, Prince of Denmark* (1602/1992) wrote, "This above all, to thine own self be true; and it must follow, as the night the day, thou canst not then be false to any man." Effective career planning requires three types of data: inward self-assessment, outward environmental assessment, and information that helps you make connections between the inward and outward. This chapter will help you begin the process of self-assessment. *Self-assessment* is an ongoing lifetime process that helps you reflect on and identify your personal values, needs, wants or desires, resources, and abilities. It is an inward look at who you are.

Getting Started

Self-assessment is often hard to initiate. In a busy lifestyle, there is often little time to reflect on your personal values, skills, accomplishments, and resources. Yet, you operate on these every day. Because it is often difficult to begin, you may want to devote a half hour each day for a couple of weeks to beginning the process. Investing time at regular intervals over a period of time will help you focus more clearly and complete a more meaningful thought process. Use a checklist similar to the one in **Figure 14-10** to track your self-assessment progress.

Creating a Notebook

As you read through this chapter, keep a notebook nearby. A loose-leaf binder that allows you to add and subtract paper works best because it is more flexible. It takes away the pressure to write a "permanent" response. View your notebook as a working document. Take notes and record any insights you have as you reflect on yourself. Include the results of any self-assessment tests you have taken, career advice you have been given, comments you receive from others, and any other data that might be useful in self-assessment. Date each entry so you can record your thought process. It is your self-assessment, so choose a method of organization that makes sense to you. Even the way you organize and move through this process will give you better insights.

Using Self-Assessment Tests or Surveys

Career or vocational tests or surveys are often used to help people determine their interests. They also help people find out what their relational style is, what types of problems they solve best, the type of career that best matches their skills, and a myriad of other things. How helpful are tests or surveys in guiding your career decisions? It all depends. They can be very useful if they are viewed critically. Typical types of self-assessments include:

- aptitude and ability tests
- interest inventories
- values assessments
- career development assessments
- personality or management style inventories

There are several considerations you should make when selecting career surveys or aptitude tests. First, avoid the tendency to be pigeonholed or categorized by test results. Everyone is unique. If a test describes you as a "rabbit," implying that you are quick, impulsive, and decisive, do not generalize these characteristics in other areas such as personality or communication style. Tests and surveys measure very specific characteristics. If you take one test or survey, be sure you understand what it means and do not generalize the results to other areas of your life.

Second, utilize many tests and surveys instead of relying on just one. Each different test and survey measures a unique aspect of being you. Some formats will appeal to you more than others. For example, some people prefer forced-choice tests. Others prefer responding to open-ended (essay) questions. There is no one test or survey that everyone agrees is the best. Taking multiple tests and surveys will help paint an accurate picture of you because similarities will surface.

Lastly, the process of completing tests and surveys and the thoughtful self-evaluation of the results are often more valuable than analysis by a career counselor. Some people might be surprised at the results, but it doesn't mean the results are wrong. Talk to friends and relatives about results. Ask them if they agree with the analysis. The most important benefit of career or vocational tests or surveys is that they get you thinking.

How can you find good career or vocational tests and surveys? The best place to start is in your college or university career center. Career center staff and career counselors are trained to help you select the most appropriate assessments and to help you interpret the results. They can direct you toward tests and surveys that are the most reliable and relevant. Frequently, tests and surveys for students are available at no cost or at a discount price. College is a great time to take advantage of these readily available services. Some frequently used assessment tests and surveys include:

- Strong-Campbell Interest Inventory
- Myers-Briggs Type Indicator®
- Princeton Review Career Quiz
- Career Key™

From the tests and surveys described in this book and others provided by your instructor, choose at least two tests or surveys to complete. After completing them, write a brief description of the experience in your notebook. What did the tests or surveys measure? What did the results indicate about you? Do you believe these results accurately describe you? Why or why not?

Getting to Know Yourself

As you do your self-assessment, you will focus on general experiences or accomplishments and personality characteristics. Understanding your experiences and the characteristics of your personality and attitudes will help you find career and lifestyle choices that match you as an individual and will help guide your decision regarding a major or minor degree program. In this section, you will identify accomplishments throughout your life, identify key traits of your personality, and compose a personal statement.

Key Accomplishments

A good place to begin your self-assessment is identifying and focusing on experiences from your past that have been positive. These experiences are your *key accomplishments*. Generally, these are achievements in which you take pride. Accomplishments can include achievements such as being an employee of the month, earning a high grade on a school project, being elected as a leader of an organization, or receiving an award. They may also be experiences that did not receive commendation from others but were important to you. If you recall your earliest memories, these are experiences where you said, "I did it myself!" In later years, these may be experiences where you did something you thought you could not do or exceeded your personal best record. Here are some examples of personal accomplishments:

- sought employment and was hired
- helped an elderly neighbor by setting up a neighborhood gardening service
- learned to skateboard at age 7 and competed in local tournaments
- raised $500 for a cancer society walk
- redecorated my bedroom
- taught myself how to play the guitar
- coached at a children's summer camp
- created a website
- earned $1000 to go on a Spanish language trip to Spain with my high school class
- read through my local library's list of "must-read classics" over one summer
- planned a surprise birthday party and family reunion for my mother

Begin your list of accomplishments by using a chart similar to the one shown in **Figure 14-1.** Fill in your accomplishments by age category and

area of life. For example, were the accomplishments related to school, work, family, friends, or to your personal hobbies and interests? If one area or age category is less represented, you may wish to reflect on ideas for these underrepresented categories.

Think about all areas of your life—school, sports and exercise, volunteering, religious activities, family roles, cooking, or even pet ownership. Consider both long-term and short-term achievements. After you have developed a list of at least 25–30 items, prioritize them into your top five achievements. Base your ranking on the level of joy, pride, energy, or happiness in recalling the achievement. Rank these five achievements and record them in **Figure 14-2.** The five achievements you have chosen will be used to explore your personality characteristics, values, and wants or desires.

Your next step is to write a descriptive paragraph about each of these achievements. In the paragraph, describe exactly what you did, how you did it, and what you enjoyed about it. This is a time to be honest, not a time for modesty. Use clear language and provide details as if you were describing the achievement to someone unfamiliar with the situation. For example, if one of your achievements was beginning college and finding an apartment in a new town, you probably have clear memories of what it took to achieve this. Instead of writing, "I found an apartment I could afford in a new town," write: "I scoured newspaper classified ads, the university housing website, and postings in the university housing office. Then I made a list of the places that met my criteria for price, distance from campus, safety and security, bus access, and design features of the apartment. I had to figure out my finances and how rental agreements worked by including first and last month's rent, security deposits, utilities, and lease length. When I could not find an apartment in my price range, I found a two-bedroom apartment I could afford with a roommate. Then I searched for a roommate. Since I didn't know anyone in the town, I relied on my good judgment, instinct, and references to select a roommate. This was

Achievements				
Age	School	Work	Family and friends	Hobbies and personal interests
0–5				
6–11				
12–15				
16–18				
19–21				
22–25				
26–40+				

Figure 14-1 Think about your achievements. Create a chart similar to this one in your notebook.

Achievement Ranking	
#1 Achievement	
#2 Achievement	
#3 Achievement	
#4 Achievement	
#5 Achievement	

Figure 14-2 Rank your achievements in order of their importance to you. Create a list similar to this in your notebook.

the first truly independent decision I have made. It was sometimes scary and overwhelming, but I was proud of myself for following it through. I think it was the first time I felt 'grown up.' I have a great apartment that meets all of my criteria and a wonderful roommate who has become a dear friend."

Write each of your paragraphs in your notebook. If you are having trouble getting started, get together with three or four of your friends and share stories verbally before writing your stories. Again, be specific and include details. Tell how you felt (happy, sad, disappointed, frustrated, confused, etc.) and/or what you observed.

Personality Characteristics

Writing about your accomplishments can be a window into what makes you "tick." Your personality and personal characteristics are evident in your key achievements. Experiences that you define as key achievements are those that bring you happiness and joy and through which you have experienced success. Read through your paragraphs again. As you do so, write down characteristics that were demonstrated in your stories. The table in **Figure 14-3** lists characteristics, and you should add your own traits to the list. Be honest. Don't overstate or be too modest. If you have

trouble identifying your personal characteristics, ask a close friend or family member to help you. Do this with each of your top five key achievement stories. Take note of the characteristics that received multiple tallies.

Writing a Personal Statement

Your last activity in this section will involve writing a one-page *personal statement* about yourself. This statement should be written as a biography or as a promotional piece about you. It should introduce who you are as a person to a future employer. It should be an upbeat statement that captures the reader's attention from the start. Begin with an interest-capturing title or opening and follow with a few key personality traits. Starting your personal statement by saying "My name is" or "I was born on" will not capture the reader's attention.

Give examples to support your statements. For example, if you state that you are resourceful, give an example of your resourcefulness. In the story example given, the writer might focus on the many resources used to find an apartment. After you write your first draft, ask yourself the following questions about your personal statement:

Personality Characteristics				
Accurate	Creative	Helpful	Outspoken	Reticent
Adaptable	Cultured	Idealistic	Patient	Rugged
Adventurous	Curious	Imaginative	Peaceful	Satisfied
Ambitious	Daring	Impulsive	Perfectionist	Scheduled
Analytical	Deep	Independent	Permissive	Self-reliant
Animated	Delightful	Insecure	Persistent	Self-sacrificing
Assertive	Demonstrative	Insightful	Persuasive	Sensitive
Athletic	Dependable	Inspiring	Pessimistic	Shy
Balanced	Detailed	Intellectual	Planner	Sociable
Bashful	Diplomatic	Intuitive	Playful	Spirited
Behaved	Disciplined	Inventive	Pleasant	Spontaneous
Bold	Down-to-earth	Kind	Popular	Stable
Bossy	Driving	Leader	Positive	Strong-willed
Bouncy	Efficient	Listener	Powerful	Stubborn
Calm	Emotional	Lively	Practical	Submissive
Careful	Empathetic	Logical	Precise	Sure
Cheerful	Energetic	Loyal	Productive	Sympathetic
Competitive	Enthusiastic	Mediator	Promoter	Tactful
Confident	Expressive	Mixes easily	Proud	Talkative
Conforming	Faithful	Mover	Refreshing	Thoughtful
Considerate	Flexible	Musical	Repetitious	Tolerant
Consistent	Forceful	Nonchalant	Resentful	Understanding
Contented	Forgiving	Obliging	Reserved	
Controlled	Frank	Optimistic	Resistant	
Convincing	Friendly	Orderly	Resourceful	
Cooperative	Funny	Original	Respectful	

Figure 14-3 These are typical personality characteristics. You may think of others that are not on the list.

- Does it convey an overall sense of who I am?
- Is it well-organized?
- Does the first paragraph give an overall summary of me?
- Does it convey positive energy?
- Are there parts that are unnecessary?
- Is it too personal?

Revise your draft and write it in final form. This will be a valuable introduction that can be used and adapted for many purposes, such as scholarship applications, applications to a school or major, cover letters, or portfolios. When you have completed the personal statement, you are ready to move on to assessing your values and wants or desires.

What Motivates You?

What motivates you to try new things? pursue goals? make decisions? organize your time? Many choices you make are based on what is important to you. These are your values and wants or desires.

Values are your beliefs that certain behaviors, attitudes, and actions are preferable to others. Values are what you hold important. They are the guideposts in your life. They are what motivate you and the basis upon which you evaluate experiences. Even though values are basic to your functioning in the world, they are often difficult to identify and articulate.

If you analyze the stories of famous people, it is easy to identify the values of these people based upon their actions. For example, Ellen Swallow Richards, the founder of family and consumer sciences, was motivated by her belief in the importance of education, intellectual inquiry, and her desire to improve the quality of life through the application of scientific knowledge.

Many of your values are probably very evident to you. Others may be more difficult to identify. Your wants are based on your values. *Wants* are the psychological requirements that give you satisfaction in life. Personal wants may include status, belonging, respect, love, or other psychological benefits.

In this section, values and wants will be explored. Your family, friends, and mentors play important roles in the formation of your values and desires. These, too, will be investigated.

Identifying Personal Values

How should you treat an obstinate customer? Where will you eat lunch today? How much time will you devote to studying for an upcoming exam? Each day you are faced with life situations that call for thoughtful reflection, opinion formation, decision making, and action. Each opinion, decision, and action is based on your values. Values and motivations are intertwined, as values drive motivation to tackle or complete a task. Because values are often difficult to define, understanding your motivations can sometimes get you started on defining your personal values.

Personal values create beliefs, actions, and behaviors that are important in your personal life. Most values remain constant over one's lifetime, but may alter somewhat in response to experiences. Read over the list of values in **Figure 14-4.** In your notebook, write down the values that you consider ideal for your life. Decide how important each personal value is to you by writing one of the following descriptors next to each. (Try not to give "always important" to too many values. Try to limit your list of most important values to 10 or fewer, and then rank order these top values.)

- always important
- often important
- sometimes important

Identifying Work Values

Personal values are related to *work values* but may not be exactly the same. For example, you may have a personal value to serve the poor. You may not have the opportunity to serve the poor in your work life, but a related work life value might be to work in a supportive environment with your coworkers, customers, or clients.

Consider the values listed in **Figure 14-4.** In your notebook, write down those values you consider important in your work environment. Decide how important each work value is to you by writing one of the following descriptors next to each. (Try not to give "always important" to too many values. Try to limit your list of most important values to 10 or fewer. Lastly, rank order these top work environment values.)

- always important
- often important
- sometimes important

Although this exercise is not easy, it will help you clarify those values that are most important to you in future work or career environments. It

Personal and Work Values				
Accomplishment	Decisiveness	Gratitude	Personal growth	Service
Accountability	Democracy	Happiness	Physical activity	Simplicity
Accuracy	Detail work	Hard work	Pleasure	Sincerity
Achievement	Determination	Harmony	Positive attitude	Skill
Advancement	Discipline	Health	Power	Speed
Adventure	Discovery	Helping	Prosperity	Spirituality
Aesthetics	Diversity	History	Punctuality	Stability
Aspiration	Education	Honesty	Purity	Standardization
Balance	Efficiency	Honor	Rationality	Status
Beauty	Equality	Independence	Recognition	Strength
Calm	Excellence	Inner peace	Regularity	Style
Challenge	Excitement	Integrity	Reliability	Success
Change	Fairness	Joy	Resourcefulness	Systemization
Cleanliness	Faith	Knowledge	Respect	Teamwork
Collaboration	Family	Leadership	Responsibility	Timeliness
Commitment	Fast pace	Learning	Results	Tolerance
Communication	Flair	Location	Risk	Tradition
Competence	Freedom	Management	Rules	Tranquility
Competition	Friendship	Money	Safety	Truth
Concern	Fun	Moral fulfillment	Security	Unity
Cooperation	Generosity	Optimism	Self-reliance	Wealth
Coordination	Global view	Orderliness	Selflessness	
Creativity	Goodness	Patriotism	Seriousness	

Figure 14-4 Which of these describe your personal and work values?

will also give you a reference point for making trade-offs among your values.

Psychological Wants or Desires

What wants or desires do you have that must be met? Do you want to live in a certain geographic location due to family issues? Do you desire creative expression? Wants and desires are closely related to values. When you hold something important (a value), having it in your life can become a want or desire. Physical and environmental wants, such as health and workplace environment, will be discussed later in this chapter. In this section, you will explore your psychological wants and desires.

Psychological wants are the fundamental desires you have that lead to personal well-being and self-satisfaction. Your wants are not the same as those of others. For example, you may feel satisfied when you have the opportunity to lead a group in accomplishing a project. Another person may feel more satisfaction from working as a member of the team accomplishing the task. Many psychological wants overlap, and in the above example, both people may have the desire to lead and to work collaboratively. For the first person, however, the desire to lead is stronger than the desire to collaborate.

Review the list of basic psychological wants or desires in **Figure 14-5.** Select the top wants or desires that are the most important for you. Write each of the wants or desires you have selected in your notebook. Next to each want or desire, write a short description of what this means in your life. For example, if you chose the want or desire "to have status," you might explain that having a career that is respected, appreciated, or highly regarded is important to you.

Decide how important each identified want or desire is to you by writing one of the following descriptors next to each: (Try not to give "always important" to too many wants or desires. Try to limit your list of most important wants or desires to five or fewer.)

• always important

• often important

• sometimes important

Lastly, select the one want or desire you must have fulfilled. Go back and review your key accomplishments and top values. This top want or desire will be the one that shows up in almost every choice you have made. It also affects almost every way you interact with people. This most important want or desire is the foundation of your life purpose.

Family Influences

Your family has a powerful influence on who you are and how you view the world. Family members are often motivators who shape your values and wants or desires over time. If you think back over the past few years, you can probably identify your family's influence on your motivation to attend college, your college choice, your academic interests, and lifestyle choices. This does not mean that your family has always positively influenced you toward the choices you have made. In fact, the exact opposite may be true. Your family may have equipped you with a set of "shoulds" or "oughts," both positive and negative. Nevertheless, family plays a major role in the life decisions of many people.

Families impart both prescriptive and prohibitive words of advice and messages. *Prescriptive advice* encourages you toward a certain decision or life path. *Prohibitive advice* warns against a certain decision or life path. Look at the following pieces of advice and distinguish between prescriptive and prohibitive messages:

• A college degree costs too much money for the long-term payback.

• A college degree is the only way to get a high-paying job.

• A college degree does more than prepare you for a career.

Basic Psychological Wants or Desires	
To achieve	To earn a living
To be alone	To ease boredom
To be competent	To follow
To be dependent	To gain approval
To be expressive	To gain power
To be free	To have an identity
To be in unity	To have balance
To be independent	To have security
To be responsible	To have stability
To be social	To have status
To be useful	To have structure
To be with people	To have variety
To belong	To influence
To build	To lead
To compete	To learn, grow
To contribute	To participate
To cooperate	To serve
To create	To work hard

Figure 14-5 Which of these psychological wants or desires guide your decisions?

- Choose a major that will lead to a high-demand career.
- Choose a major that you are passionate about, and the financial rewards will follow.

Think about the positive messages your family has imparted to you. Make a list of these positive messages. Next, make a list of the negative messages you have received from your family. It is not always easy to determine whether messages are positive or negative. For example, "you should go into the family business" could be seen as positive or negative depending on your interpretation and your life goals.

Friends and Mentors

Friends and mentors are people you choose to have in your life. You may not consciously choose them and it may be difficult to trace their entrance into your life, but something attracted you to them. Friends and mentors have characteristics you admire and value. Because you selected them, reflecting on friends and mentors can give you valuable insight into your own personal characteristics and values.

Friends are often similar to you in one or more ways. These are the characteristics you have in common. Identify people you call friends. Your friends may fall into different categories, such as school friends, childhood friends, family friends, work friends, or friends from other experiences.

- How did you become friends?
- Was there an initial attraction to this person? If so, what attracted you?
- Did the friendship develop over time?
- What did you discover about this person that drew you to him or her?
- What activities, values, attitudes, or goals do you have in common?
- How do you benefit from this friendship? Why is this important to you?

Mentors are people you learn from and admire. Of course friends can be one type of

mentor. Older adult friends, relatives, teachers, employers, and coworkers can be mentors. People your own age may also be mentors if they have had experiences that give them perspective that can be used to advise others. These are often referred to as *peer mentors*.

Who are the people you respect most in this world? Are they people you know and interact with daily? people you admire from afar? people you have only read about? Identifying the people you admire is a helpful exercise in assessing your values and wants or desires.

Perhaps you have had people in your life who have served as "official" (or formal) mentors. These people have guided you, modeled appropriate behaviors or attitudes, and have taken an active role in your development over time. More likely, you have had a number of people in your life who have served as "unofficial" (or informal) mentors. These are people you admire and aspire to be like, even if they do not know it. For some reason, you have been drawn to them. Why? Only you can answer that question. Take a few minutes to compile a list of both your role models and friends as well as informal and formal mentors.

Why is it important to identify mentors? In compiling a list, you may find a need for more mentors. Mentors can have a huge impact on you and your career path decisions. They can serve as guideposts for navigating your way in life (Ensher & Murphy, 2005). They can serve as role models, sponsors, or even as your advocates when needed. Many colleges and universities offer formal mentoring programs comprised of alumni and others in the community.

What Are Your Assets and Skills?

In this section, your attention will be drawn toward tangible assets and skills you possess. These are what you have to offer to others in exchange for something you want. This exchange could result in a healthy relationship with a family member or friend, employment wages, status, or another form of personal satisfaction. Knowing what your personal assets and skills are will help you make informed choices. It will also help you to determine the types of skills you need or want to develop.

Assets

Your *assets* are all the characteristics and experiences that are strengths. They include your personal characteristics, experiences, resources, education, and skills. Take a few minutes to identify your assets. Do not limit your list. Brainstorm and make the list as long as possible. For example, you may have ready access to a computer, have citizenship in a country that offers great personal freedoms, own or have access to a car or public transportation, have completed some college, or have an abundance of energy. Personal assets are collected through life experiences over time, just the same as you accumulate financial assets. Assets can be developed over time through education, life, and career experiences. For example, professionalism is a characteristic that evolves throughout a career.

Skills

A *skill* is the ability to do something well. You are not born with skills, but you learn them over time, through experience, practice, or instruction. In the labor market, skills are presented as a form of currency. Employers inquire about your skills. The Partnership for 21st Century Skills (2009) has identified the following skills needed for success in life and work: critical thinking and problem solving, creativity and innovation, information and media literacy, digital and technology literacy, communication skills, leadership and responsibility, collaboration, social and cross-cultural skills, flexibility and adaptability, initiative and self-direction, and productivity and accountability. How many of these skills have you developed?

Most people possess hundreds of skills. Because skill analysis often focuses on career skills, many people do not easily identify their full skill repertoire, and if they do, they may be modest in promoting it.

Your family can teach you skills. What skills have you learned from family members? organizational skills? stress management skills? Perhaps you have learned hands-on skills such as automobile repair or cooking. Make a list of skills you have learned from your family. You may also want to compose a list of skills you would like to learn from family members in the future. Skills learned from family members are often overlooked, but they are an important part of your personal skill set.

Next, think about the skills you have learned in your work experience, at school, from friends and mentors, and through recreational activities. Remember to not be modest. Write down all of the skills that come to mind. Lastly, review the key accomplishments you identified earlier in the chapter. Add any skills you overlooked to your skills list. Remember to include technology skills, leadership skills, communication skills, and any other skills you can identify.

Technology Skills

Technological literacy is the ability to choose appropriate technology tools and applications and use them effectively. However, as discussed in Chapter 4, technology is changing at an incredible speed. The specific skills needed to be technologically literate will continue to change over your lifetime. Individuals with up-to-date *technology skills* can access, organize, and communicate information using digital technology. They are also aware of the ethical issues related to accessing and sharing information (Mosenson & Fox, 2011). In this section, you will identify your basic technology skills. Review the list of technology skills in **Figure 14-6.** Place a check by the skills you currently possess. Make a separate list of those skills you need to develop. These are basic technology literacy skills. Add skills you possess that go beyond these basic skills, such as building a webpage or writing a blog.

Technology Skills	
General Computer Knowledge and Skills	Can you launch a specific program and navigate between programs? Do you understand the basic function of computer hardware components, such as the central processing unit, monitor, keyboard, printer, and disk? Can you save your work on a hard drive? on removable storage? Can you use software for word processing, presentations, and spreadsheets? When buying a computer, do you know what features to look for and compare? Can you describe the advantages and disadvantages of wireless communications? Do you know how to protect against spyware, viruses, and malware?
Telephone and Tablet Knowledge and Skills	Do you know the advantages and disadvantages of Voice over IP, cell phones, and landline phones? Can you text message? Do you know how to choose the best cell phone provider for you? Can you name which features are important in choosing a wireless phone? a tablet or e-reader? Can you download an application to a smartphone or tablet?
Hardware Knowledge	What type of personal computer, tablet, and/or smartphone do you have? What type of operating system (OS) does each device use? What type of CPU does each device have? What is the storage capacity of each device?
Internet Knowledge and Skills	How do you choose an Internet provider? Do you have a choice of cable, DSL, satellite, or other broadband provider? What is your connection speed? Which web browser and what browser version are you using? Can you identify the advantages and disadvantages of different browsers? Can you find a book or a journal through an online library catalog or database? Can you browse a website (utilize links, move forward and backward)? Can you bookmark or save a site for future reference? Can you do an Internet search using a search engine such as Google or Yahoo? Can you download and install browser plug-ins such as Media Player or Acrobat Reader? Can you instant message or chat in a chatroom? Can you create a page on a social media site and establish privacy settings? Can you read, send, reply to, forward, delete, and save e-mail messages? Can you send e-mail attachments? Can you open an attachment that was sent to you?

Figure 14-6 Which technology skills do you possess or want to develop? Can you think of others?

Leadership Skills

You have probably heard the term *born leader*. It is true that some people have personality characteristics and temperaments that make others want to follow, but leadership skills can be learned, practiced, and improved. Many books and articles have been written about leadership. Most *leadership skills* fall into one of two categories: people-oriented leadership skills and task-oriented leadership skills. Both are valued and needed. Review the list of leadership skills in **Figure 14-7.** As you answer the questions in the chart, make two lists. In one list, compile a record of your leadership skills. In the second list, compile an inventory of the leadership skills you would like to develop. Add the lists to your notebook.

Communication Skills

Communicating with others is an essential skill in business, families, friendships, and virtually any relationship. In fact, in many employer surveys, *communication skills* are listed as the top criteria that employers desire in employees. How well do you communicate with people? What skills do you possess? A list of communication

Leadership Skills	
People-Oriented Leadership Skills	Can you... build personal and business relationships on mutual trust and respect? deal with conflicts and disagreements with others quickly? debate, clarify, and enunciate your values and beliefs? draw out information and ideas by asking open-ended questions? encourage dreaming and thinking the unthinkable? facilitate interpersonal and group relationships? fuel, inspire, and guard the shared vision? keep agreements and commitments made to others? help groups maintain discipline and direction toward achievement? listen actively to colleagues? maintain an open, warm relationship with others? mediate for others? mentor, coach, and develop others, including those who do not work directly with you? motivate others? provide others with clear feedback? recognize the creative and innovative ideas of others? show others respect, regardless of their status or rank?
Task-Oriented Leadership Skills	Can you... achieve goals and objectives within budget and on time? anticipate future consequences or implications of current situations or events? communicate ideas effectively? coordinate ideas, activities, and relationships? develop and implement action plans? diagnose the sources of difficulties? elaborate on ideas, using examples and definitions? engage in goal-setting? evaluate progress, process, and products? identify fresh and innovative approaches to existing situations? initiate ideas, actions, solutions, and procedures? make decisions under time pressure and with limited information? manage by planning and delegating tasks? quickly find relationships and connections between seemingly unrelated facts and events? recognize and cope well with the realities of organizational politics? sort out the relevant and important facts and information? update your skills and professional knowledge on a regular basis?

Figure 14-7 Which leadership skills do you have or want to develop? Can you think of others?

skills is given in **Figure 14-8.** Think about each skill. Rate your ability by giving yourself a score for each skill:

- 0 = no ability
- 1 = minimal ability
- 2 = some ability
- 3 = strong ability

In your notebook, write a narrative summary of both your strongest and weakest communication skills. Think of situations or experiences that could help you hone your weaker communication skills.

Remember, you have hundreds of skills. Most of your skills have not been listed or addressed in the previous sections because they are unique to you. They may include artistic skills, physical skills, or data management skills. You probably can't list all of your skills in one sitting, so carry a notepad with you and jot down your skills when they occur to you.

Communication Skills	
Rating	**Communication Skill**
	Asserting opinion
	Being sensitive
	Confronting others
	Conveying feelings
	Cooperating
	Counseling
	Delegating with respect
	Describing feelings
	Developing rapport
	Editing
	Expressing ideas
	Facilitating group discussion
	Influencing attitudes
	Instructing
	Interviewing
	Listening attentively
	Mediating conflicts
	Motivating
	Negotiating
	Perceiving feelings, situations
	Perceiving nonverbal messages
	Persuading
	Providing appropriate feedback
	Providing support for others
	Reporting information
	Sharing credit
	Socializing
	Speaking effectively
	Supervising others
	Understanding people and their behavior
	Writing concisely

Figure 14-8 Which of these communication skills do you have or want to develop? Can you think of others?

Health, Physical Ability, and Activity Level Preferences

Every career and individual job has its own physical requirements and general activity level. For example, teaching kindergarten requires more than a love for young children. It requires physical stamina to bend over, kneel, hug, and move with the children. On the other hand, teaching college students requires far less physical stamina. Some jobs require walking, lifting, reaching, and stacking, whereas others require hours of "chair time."

How much physical activity do you desire? It is not just a matter of physical ability; it is also a matter of preference. In other words, sometimes physical ability and general health play a part, but more often than not, your activity level preference overrides your ability. Matching your physical abilities, activity level preference, and general health to your work is important to achieve a good match between physical needs and preferences and your work environment. Your general health should also be assessed. Only you can determine your capabilities, abilities, and preferences.

Can you change your physical ability and activity level preferences? For many people, the answer is yes. Increased physical activity and training can prepare you for a job that is more physically demanding than your current capabilities allow. The perception of health and activity can also play a part.

To begin your assessment of physical activity abilities and preferences, answer the following questions and record your responses in your self-assessment notebook:

- What type of activities do you do to relax and have fun?

- In what type of physical activities do you participate each week?

- If you had one day completely schedule-free and money was not a concern, with what type of activities would you fill your day?

- Do you prefer to walk, run, or generally move throughout your day, or are you comfortable sitting and working on a project? for how long?

- Do you do your best work when you are involved in physical activity or when you are in a state of repose?

- How do you describe your overall health?

- Do you have any concerns or limitations in regard to physical activity, activity level, or your general health?

- How do you describe your stamina level in comparison with other people of your age and gender? people of other ages?

- How many hours can you work at your peak performance level? Do you prefer one long working session or several short sessions?

What conclusions can you draw about your physical ability and activity level preferences? Record your conclusions in your notebook.

Task Preferences

What motivates you to complete a task? Your answer probably changes depending on the situation. You may be highly motivated in some situations and with some tasks and hardly ever motivated to do other tasks no matter what the situation. Reflecting on the tasks that you are interested in pursuing and motivated to complete can give you interesting data about yourself. Think of a task you are usually motivated to do no matter what the situation. Many times, it is an activity that brings you pleasure. If not, it may be a task that will reap pleasurable rewards, such as allowing you more time to pursue a hobby or spend time with friends. Once you have identified a task you are highly motivated to do, answer the following questions:

- What draws you to this task?

- Do you enjoy the process of the task or activity itself?

- Are you motivated by the end result more than the process of doing the task?

- Will completing the task or activity result in a by-product that motivates you?

- Are there other, similar tasks or activities you enjoy? What do the tasks have in common?

- Is the activity or task solo or does it involve people? Does it involve working with a few people or many?

- Does the task or activity involve organizational skills or pure chance?

- Does the task or activity involve collaboration, leadership, or dependence on others to complete their tasks?

- Are you motivated by money, status, the chance to socialize with others, or a purpose?

Different people are drawn to different types of tasks and activities. The type of task or activity to which a person is drawn is based on what the person holds dear, in other words, what the person values. Determining what attracts and motivates you to certain types of tasks will help you to understand the type of values upon which you base your beliefs, actions, and behaviors. In the following sections, you will have the opportunity to reflect and assess your personal values and work values.

Life Satisfaction

Previous sections in this chapter focused on the sum of your parts, giving you a good idea of who you are, what is important to you, and what you have to offer. This section deals with identifying and turning your dreams into reality.

Dreaming About the Future

What are your dreams and goals for life? Where do you dream about living? What type of lifestyle do you want? What would you like your future family and friendship circle to look like? What type of work will you be doing? What will be your hobbies? Everyone has dreams. However, life events, time constraints, and financial challenges can keep you from letting yourself dream. For many people, it is easier to look back on dreams you used to have and evaluate their relevance to your current life before dreaming about the future. To help you formulate goals for your life, think back to the life dreams you had as a child. Make a chart with three columns. Label the columns with the following questions:

- When you think back as far as you can remember, what did you dream of doing/ being when you were a child?
- Why did this appeal to you?
- What does this reveal about you that still holds true today?

For each childhood dream you identify, fill in the corresponding responses in your chart. An example is shown in **Figure 14-9.**

Next, take some time to dream about your future. You have already identified your values, psychological wants or desires, and skills. Now figure out what you want for your future. If you value and need creative expression, what do you want specifically? Figuring out what your wants specifically look like will greatly improve your odds of achieving these wants in your life.

This is not an exercise to complete in a few minutes. If you are unable to take a few days to focus on your goals and aspirations, take a few hours instead. For many people, physical activities such as walking, running, or biking offer solitude and time to contemplate their dreams. For others, spending time with a close friend or relative sharing their aspirations can help identify a

Dreaming About the Future				
When I think back as far as I can remember, what did I dream of doing/being when I was a child?	Singing rodeo star (age 4)	Paleontologist (age 6)	Professional soccer player (ages 7 to10)	A professional basketball player, basketball coach, celebrity (ages 10 through about my sophomore year of high school)
Why did this appeal to me?	My cousin wanted to be a rodeo star and I wanted to sing country songs. So when we were about six, we decided to combine the two (singing rodeo stars!).	I was obsessed with dinosaurs!	I wanted to be a star athlete!	Hmmmm... because basketball was my life?
What does this reveal about me that still holds true today?	I like to work with other people. Some of my best ideas still come from being with friends. I'm not much of a performer or a singer today, though.	I've always liked to find out as much as possible about my interests. I'm good at understanding scientific concepts, but I like people better than dinosaurs.	Obviously, I've always been athletic. I do like to be recognized for my ability. I guess I still like to be a star.	I do like teamwork. I also admire people who take the time to teach others and develop relationships with them as my coaches did.

Figure 14-9 This example shows how childhood dreams can be used to help formulate goals for life. Create a chart similar to this one in your notebook.

desired future. Use the following thoughts to get your ideas flowing:

- Where would you like to live?
- What type of lifestyle would you like to have?
- What would you like your future family and friendship circle to look like?
- What type of work will you be doing?
- What will be your hobbies?
- What would you like to accomplish?
- For what would you like to be known?

When you are finished dreaming, make a list of the things you hope will be a part of your future. This list can include events, activities, people, values, experiences, or any variety of items you desire to have in your future.

Personal Essentials

Life is about choices, unplanned events and circumstances, and continual change. In this section, you will identify values, needs, and wants that are critical to you. These are your *personal essentials*. They are the things you are not willing to sacrifice. This exercise takes hard work and concentrated effort.

Begin by reviewing your notebook from start to finish. It is best if you can do this in one sitting. Highlight or mark items or thoughts that appear frequently. When you have finished, complete the following statement in your notebook.

To feel happy and successful, the following are absolutely essential in my personal life and career:

- Values:
- Goals:
- Needs:
- People:
- Experiences:
- Other (specify):

Life Goals

Dreams rely on chance, whereas goals take concerted effort. However, life dreams can become life goals. So how do you change your dreams into feasible goals? Begin by reviewing your list of dreams. Are some more important to you than others? Do any conflict with each other? Are some of your life dreams most appropriate for a certain stage of life? Rank the top three most important dreams in your life. Remember, to become a goal, your dream should meet the following criteria:

- It should be important to you personally.
- It has to be feasible and reasonable.
- It has to be clearly defined.
- It requires a specific plan of action.
- It has to be something that you have a reasonable chance of achieving.

Goals can be long-term and take years to accomplish or they can be short-term, requiring only a few weeks or months for completion. Both long-term and short-term goals require the same method for goal achievement, however.

1. Define your goal. Write down exactly what you want to accomplish. Be specific. Describe how you will feel when you accomplish this goal. Think about how you will evaluate whether or not you have achieved your goal. In other words, how will you measure goal attainment? For example, if your goal is to spend more time studying, how will you judge success? Will you use improved grades as a measure? Will you measure it by less anxiety before exams? Will you log hours spent studying? How you evaluate success is up to you.

2. Outline the steps you will take to achieve the goal. Consider the example of increasing study time. Will you buy a day planner or calendar? Will you remove yourself from distractions? Will you spend less time working or in leisure pursuits? Will you set aside certain blocks of time? Will you turn off your cell phone during certain hours?

Consider possible roadblocks or challenges to meeting your goal. How can you deal with these?

3. Set deadlines for achieving your goal. Once again, be specific. Set up a system of reminders. This may be asking a friend to check on your progress or posting reminders in your daily planner.

For this exercise, choose two goals that can be completed in the next one to three months. Choose a goal for each of the following categories:

- your academic or career life

- your personal life

Follow the three steps outlined above for planning and achieving your goals. Report on your progress in your notebook during the process and when your goals are achieved. Completion of the two goals is the last item in the self-assessment checklist in **Figure 14-10.**

Summary

Throughout this chapter, you have focused on many ways of getting to know yourself better. You evaluated your strengths, determined what motivates you, and decided what you value and what you want or desire. You identified key accomplishments in your life. You have also described your personality traits, preferences, general health, and physical abilities. Family, friends, mentors, and experiences work together to form your personal and work values, needs, and wants. These are the things you hold important and necessary in your life.

You also identified your assets and skills. These are your resources and abilities. You emphasized skills that are learned, such as technology, leadership, and communication skills. Lastly, you thought about life dreams, both past and present. Dreams become reality when they are made into goals. For dreams to become goals, they must be important to you personally, be feasible and reasonable, be clearly defined,

Self-Assessment Checklist			
Assessment/Exercise	**Completed**	**Assessment/Exercise**	**Completed**
Self-assessment test		Assets list	
Key accomplishments chart		Skills list	
Key accomplishments ranking		Skills to develop list	
Key accomplishments descriptive paragraphs		Communication skills ranking	
Personality characteristics		Physical and health assessment	
Personal statement		General work habits/strengths	
Personal values list and rankings		Task preferences	
Work values list and rankings		Dreams chart	
Wants/desires descriptions and ratings		Your dreams about the future	
Family influences		Your personal essentials	
Friends and mentors analysis		Two goals	

Figure 14-10 Use this checklist to help track your self-assessment progress.

be based on a specific plan, and have a realistic chance of being achieved.

Self-assessment can be arduous and cumbersome, especially when life is full of other tasks and responsibilities. Making plans for your future can also be difficult during times of change. On the other hand, times of change may be the most opportune time to shift gears and adopt new plans for the future. Self-assessment pays off in the long run as you make choices that take you further away from or closer to your dreams.

Questions for Thought

1. Complete the activities in this chapter. Summarize what you learned about yourself overall. Did you learn anything new about yourself? What are the areas that need further investigation?

2. Visit a career center at a college or university. Make a list of the events and resources that are relevant to your educational, career, and life goals. Which resources would most benefit you? Why?

3. Take standardized career assessment tests or surveys. Review the results with a trained counselor. What were the tests or surveys attempting to measure? Were the results an accurate assessment of you?

References and Resources

Barkley, N., & Sandburg, E. (1995). *Taking charge of your career*. New York: Workman Publishing.

Blanchard, K., & Miller, M. (2012). *Great leaders grow*. San Francisco: Berrett-Koehler Publishers.

Bolles, R. (2012). *What color is your parachute? 2012: A practical manual for job-hunters and career-changers*. New York: Ten Speed Press.

Buckingham, M., & Clifton, D. (2001). *Now, discover your strengths*. New York: Free Press.

Covey, S. (2004). *The seven habits of highly effective people*. New York: Free Press.

Edwards, P., & Edwards, S. (2003). *Finding your perfect work: The new career guide to making a living, creating a life*. New York: J.P. Tarcher/Putnam.

Embree, M. (2003). *Self-managing your career: An interactive career workbook*. Victoria, British Columbia: Trafford.

Ensher, E., & Murphy, S. (2005). *Power mentoring: How successful mentors and protégés get the most out of their relationships*. San Francisco: John Wiley & Sons.

Harkness, H. (1997). *The career chase*. Palo Alto, CA: Davies-Black.

Holderness, G. (2001). *Career and calling: A guide for counselors, youth, and young adults*. Louisville, KY: Geneva Press.

Holmes, O. (1992). *The complete poetical works of Oliver Wendell Holmes*. Cambridge, MA: Reprint Services, Cambridge edition.

Howard, E. (2004). *Career pathways: Preparing students for life*. Thousand Oaks, CA: Corwin Press.

Johnson, S. (1998). *Who moved my cheese?* New York: Putnam.

Keirsey, D. (1998). *Please understand me II*. Del Mar, CA: Prometheus Nemesis Press.

Krumboltz, J. D., & Levin, A. S. (2004). *Luck is no accident: Making the most of happenstance in your life and career*. Atascadero, CA: Impact.

Lore, N. (1998). *The pathfinder*. New York: Simon and Schuster.

Martriner, M., McAllister, B., & Gebhard, N. (2005). *Finding the open road: A guide to self-construction rather than mass production*. Berkeley, CA: Ten Speed Press.

Moen, P. (2005). *The career mystique: Cracks in the American dream*. Lanham, MD: Rowman & Littlefield.

Mosenson, A.G., & Fox, W.S. (2011), Teaching 21st century process skills to strengthen and enhance family and consumer sciences education. *Journal of Family and Consumer Sciences, 103*(1), 63-69.

Oldham, J., & Morris, L. (1990). *The personality self-portrait*. New York: Bantam Books.

Partnership for 21st Century Skills. (2009). *P21 framework definitions*. Retrieved from http://www.p21.org

Patterson, T. (1998). *Living the life you were meant to live*. Nashville, TN: Thomas Nelson.

Shakespeare, W. (1992). *Hamlet, Prince of Denmark*. Dover, MA: Dover. (Original work published 1602)

Sher, B., & Gottleib, A. (2004). *Wishcraft: How to get what you really want*. New York: Ballantine Books.

Tieger, P. D., & Barron, B. (2007). *Do what you are: Discover the perfect career for you through the secrets of personality type* (4th ed.). New York: Little, Brown.

Van Oech, R. (1986). *A kick in the seat of the pants*. New York: Harper and Row.

On the Internet

http://www.careeronestop.org—sponsored by the U.S. Department of Labor, includes several online self-assessment tools

Chapter 15

Looking Outward: Researching Career Opportunities

After studying this chapter, you will be able to:

- apply practical reasoning in making career decisions.

- choose an academic major.

- research a specific career field in business, industry, government, education, or another area of employment.

- describe sources of career and job market information.

- explore options for gaining career experience while you are a student.

Through self-assessment exercises (described in Chapter 14), Michael discovered many things about himself. For example, he discovered he prefers to work on projects where there is a definite goal. In fact, he derives immense satisfaction from reaching goals. He also realized he needs to be around people, especially young, energetic people, as much as possible. He prefers to be in a leadership position. He does not mind the responsibility that goes with leadership and thoroughly enjoys being the decision maker and motivator in groups. He still loves basketball but is not sure he has an interest in combining his athletic skills and abilities with a future career. Overall, he believes he has a pretty good idea what his interests, values, and needs are. What he does not know is how he will move from self-assessment to choosing a major and a career.

Making Life and Career Decisions

Usually, it takes more than the flip of a coin to make a decision. Daily decisions, such as what you are going to eat for lunch and which route you will take to get to class, generally take little time and energy. There is little perceived risk in these decisions. Other decisions, such as choosing a college to attend, selecting a major or career field to pursue, and deciding where to live, require considerably more time and effort. To some, the task of choosing a major seems overwhelming. Picturing themselves in a career seems impossible. Why is that? For most people, it is the realization that this one decision could bring many consequences to life. They operate under the assumption that if the "wrong" career path is chosen, they may end up living a totally unfulfilling life. Of course, this assumption may not be true, because people often change careers throughout their lifetime.

Choosing a major or a career is an example of a *practical problem*. Practical problems are questions about what is best to do. They do not have easy, clear-cut solutions. There may be different solutions to the same problem depending on the context. Practical problems are complicated because they involve consequences, not only for you but usually for others as well. Acceptable solutions depend upon one's values, which may conflict. Some people experience almost a mental paralysis when it comes to making these decisions. Fortunately, you can learn to solve such complicated problems through *practical reasoning*. Practical reasoning is one of the philosophical foundations of the family and consumer sciences field (Laster, 2008; Roofe, n.d.). There are many components of practical reasoning, including:

- recognizing and clarifying the problem
- identifying relevant personal factors, such as values and goals
- examining facts relevant to the situation (contextual factors)
- finding and evaluating information needed to solve the problem
- generating possible alternative solutions
- analyzing consequences of different solutions for yourself and others
- selecting the best choice according to your criteria
- making and implementing a plan of action
- reflecting on the results

The first step of practical reasoning is to understand the problem clearly. What exactly is the problem? Who else is involved? What factors in this situation will affect the decision about what to do? This chapter deals with two common problems: What major should I choose? What career should I pursue? If you learn to apply practical reasoning to these questions, you will become a better problem solver in other areas of your life.

Practical reasoning involves clarifying your values and goals. This step is sometimes referred to as an internal search. In Chapter 14, you spent considerable time and effort looking inward. You should know yourself better than when you began or, at least, be better able to describe yourself. You also considered some of the relevant situational factors, such as family influences. Based on your self-assessment research, you are now ready to begin exploring college majors and career areas that best fit your interests, skills, values and personal preferences, gifts, and passions.

In this chapter, the focus will be outward on finding current and credible information needed to choose a major and a career field. Looking outward means you are observing and deciphering the conditions that are present in your environment. Looking outward is not passive, however. It involves seeing, experiencing, and analyzing yourself in the context of the environment.

Chapters 6 through 13 introduced you to many career alternatives in family and consumer sciences. The next step is thinking about the consequences of choosing one of those career fields or a related area. For example, what are the job prospects? Are jobs available throughout the country or only in large metropolitan areas? Consider the consequences for others in your life as well. Will this career accommodate your plans for family and personal life?

After you have done research on one or more career possibilities, use your self-assessment as a basis for choosing a major and career path that will best suit you as an individual. How well does the career you are considering match with the personal essentials you identified while reading Chapter 14? These are your criteria for evaluating your alternatives.

Once you have formed a tentative career decision, make a plan for successfully completing your major and obtaining relevant experience. As you implement your plan, you will have the opportunity to reflect upon your decisions. Would you make the same choices again? Perhaps not. Remember, you change and develop over time. So will your career interests. You can modify your career path by returning to the same reasoning process throughout your lifespan. In this chapter, you will learn how to choose an academic major, what considerations help in choosing a career field, how to find information about a career field, and what opportunities exist for gaining experience in your chosen field.

How to Choose a Major

From anthropology to zoology, there are hundreds of different majors offered in colleges and universities. How do you know which one is right for you? This decision is enough to cause the most relaxed person to panic. Advice on choosing the right major abounds, yet many students change their majors several times during their college years. Many college students express high levels of anxiety and pressure over choosing a major. Much of this pressure is fueled by commonly held myths. This section will explore these myths. It will also encourage you to take action in planning your major and academic career so you gain the most you possibly can from your college experience. You will be encouraged to make a plan for completing required courses to obtain a degree and learn about recommended tasks for transitioning into a career.

Selecting the Right Major

Choosing a major is one of the first concerns of college students. Even so, most studies report at least one-half of college freshmen have no idea about what their major will be.

Choosing a major can be a difficult and bewildering process. Many students feel the decision to major in a certain subject area will guide their entire career and the rest of their lives. You may believe the sooner you decide on a major, the better. This is not necessarily true. Studies show that even when college freshmen know what their majors are, the chances are high they will change their majors at least once before they complete their degree. There are a few credit-heavy majors that require early planning. These tend to be in the natural sciences, in professional fields such as medicine and education, and in applied sciences such as engineering. However, most specialized courses in majors do not require much more than two years to complete. (Keep in mind that the prerequisite courses for these courses need to be taken in previous years.)

The idea that career planning is a passive process and the right major will be revealed to you is generally erroneous. Choosing a major takes thoughtful consideration, and there are many factors to consider. However, it does not

have to be stressful. The best way to begin the process of choosing a major is to relax.

Why relax? Given time and thoughtful consideration, you will find a major. It is important to remember that choosing a major is not always the same as choosing a career. Numerous examples exist of famous and not-so-famous people who majored in one area but enjoyed an unrelated and personally satisfying career in another area. At a minimum, your college education offers you several things. These include the opportunity to demonstrate you can begin and complete a goal, an education of many disciplines and fields, and opportunities to develop critical thinking, written and oral communication skills, and interpersonal skills. These skills, such as the ability to orally express an idea, are called *transferable skills* because they can be transferred from one situation to another. In addition, you develop peer relationships that can aid you throughout life.

After you have taken a deep breath and relaxed about choosing a major, try these four steps:

- Think about what you enjoy studying.
- Gather information.
- Evaluate the information you have collected and make a decision.
- Take action.

You may be thinking, "Did I not just spend an entire chapter assessing myself?" Absolutely. The work you have completed is valuable in selecting a major that is right for you. The more you understand yourself, the easier your decision will be.

What Do You Enjoy Studying?

Determining what you enjoy studying is a valuable exercise in choosing a major. This exercise includes reflection on past experiences and evaluation of current experiences. First, think back to elementary, middle, and high school. What were your favorite subjects? What was it that you enjoyed about these subjects? Was it the content? the way your teacher taught the subject matter? Was it the way you participated in the learning process through practical projects, complex problem solving, taking exams, completing labs, or through creative expression? Did these subjects come easily to you, or did you enjoy the challenge they presented? People often see lifetime similarities between favorite school subjects and career pursuits. Although you may not want a career in your favorite school subject, something about the mode of learning or the type of content may have appealed to you.

To what general subject areas are you most drawn? Are you drawn to fine arts, business, the natural sciences, the mathematical sciences, humanities, or combinations of these areas? Which do you enjoy studying more, people or data? Do you enjoy numbers or words? Remember, you are basing your responses on experience. There are many subject areas and subspecialties you have not yet experienced. At this point, try to think in broad terms. For example, if you are drawn to fine arts, you may be drawn to apparel design, interior design, fashion merchandising, graphic design, or any of the applied arts. Your values relate strongly to your propensity toward a subject area.

Next, think about the methods you use to learn today. Do you enjoy discussing ideas, writing about your ideas, or expressing your ideas through artistic mediums such as music, dance, or art? Do you like complex problems that have no single right answer, or do you prefer concrete, indisputable outcomes? You are likely more comfortable dealing with certain types of issues more than others. What you are drawn to depends on your past experiences, your natural abilities and gifts, and opportunities to hone new skills.

Gathering Information and Exploring Options

There are many ways you can gather information and explore options. Reading, talking, and surfing the Internet are great ways to begin exploring your options. First, read the materials available to you. Your college or university catalog is a good place to start. Read books about your fields of interest. Introductory books, like this one, are a good source of information. If a major interests you, read the descriptions of courses that are required in the major. Read about the faculty and their educational backgrounds. Libraries offer bibliographies on selected topics—including majors. Lastly, visit your bookstore or an Internet site. Browse offerings in majors in which you are interested. These are the books you will purchase and read if the major is selected. Are you interested?

Next, talk to people. Ask students who are friends or acquaintances what they are majoring in, what they like about it, what they do not like about it, and what they are learning. Ask them if there are particular challenges or opportunities of which you should be aware. Talk to faculty and advisors in the major you are researching. Ask them what you will learn, the types of problems you will solve, the mode of learning that will take place, and typical career pursuits of graduates. Ask faculty and advisors about prerequisites, recommended course sequencing, and courses that are challenging.

Surf the Internet. There are many resources available online that can help you narrow your choice. Colleges and universities usually provide resources for choosing a major on their website. The Internet also provides valuable resources for researching the career opportunities in a chosen field. You can find information about wages, employment trends, and necessary knowledge, skills, abilities, education, and training. Accessing this information will be discussed later in this chapter.

After you have gathered information about potential major areas of study, narrow your choices. One way to do this is to take a class in a major you are considering using your elective credits. Taking a course will give you information about testing procedures, types of projects that are typical to the major, and what types of skills you will gain. If you do not have very many elective courses, you may wish to "audit" a course without earning credit.

Making a Decision and Choosing Your Major

After you have explored your options and gathered information, it is time to make a decision on an academic major. Weigh the pros and cons of the majors you are considering. Narrow your choices to two or three potential majors. If you can't decide between two majors, consider majoring in one area and minoring in another. Also, some students are seeking a double major to increase their employment opportunities and increase their qualifications. For example, many employers are looking for job candidates who are fluent in more than one language since so many businesses are international in scope.

If you are still having difficulty making a decision, consider the following commonly held myths about choosing a major:

- **Myth:** Choosing a major will determine your career opportunities. **Fact:** A few careers require a certain major and a certain degree. However, the vast majority of careers do not require a particular major. A college education offers more than specific content knowledge. It offers you an opportunity to learn communication and critical thinking skills and to demonstrate your ability to persevere and complete a goal.

- **Myth:** Once a major is chosen, there is no turning back. **Fact:** Most students change their major at least once during their college careers. Many students change their majors several times before graduation. People even change their careers an average of three times during their lifetime and change their jobs seven to ten times.

- **Myth:** Job markets should determine major choices. **Fact:** Looking at economic and employment trends can be helpful, but if you are not passionate about a field, do not force yourself to study the major. Choose an area for which you have a passion. Many career counselors support the idea that your major choice should be a combination of economic feasibility and personal passion.

Taking Action

Once you have decided on a major, find out all you can about it. This involves going back to the information you collected when researching your options and looking at a deeper level. First, review your program of study in the course catalog. You will be amazed at the wealth of information that is included about all the academic majors, including course descriptions and specialty tracks as well as faculty qualifications and unique experiences such as study tours. Review the list of graduation requirements. Which courses are required? Are there course substitutions? Are internship, clinical, or practical experiences required? Who are the faculty? What is their educational background? All of this information is in your college catalog.

Your professors are a great source of information about your selected major. After you narrow your preferred majors, find out if there is a separate admission process for the majors in which you are most interested. Meet with an academic advisor in your area of interest and ask questions about the major. For example, should courses be taken in a particular order? How long does it take most students to complete the degree program? Be sure to meet and talk with advisors in person. If you avoid developing an exclusively online relationship, you will be more likely to have the support of your advisor when you transfer from college to career. It is wise to make sure an advisor and faculty members know you as a person, not just as an e-mail address.

Next, if there is an introductory course, take it. You will learn about the history, philosophy, and theories relating to your major. You learned about the history, philosophy, mission, and theoretical model of family and consumer sciences in Chapters 1 through 3 of this book. If you are interested in a major within the family and consumer sciences field, learn more about it. For example, if you are interested in nutrition, read further about the history of the field. Explore some of the suggested learning experiences at the end of Chapter 6.

Other good sources of information about a major are current students, alumni, guest speakers, family, and friends. Upperclass students can act as mentors and resource people. They have a recent memory of courses, internship experiences, and other information about your major. Ask for advice. They will probably recommend course groupings that work together and steer you away from groupings that do not work together. For example, they can advise you on how to balance heavy lab courses with heavy writing courses. Likewise, alumni can act as valuable resources. If you have guest speakers, take the time to greet them, introduce yourself, and ask questions. If you are fortunate to have family or friends with insights and information about your major, be sure to tap this resource, too.

Your college career center and library offer invaluable resources on your major, and both offer a variety of resources on-site and via the Internet.

The Course Planner and Four-Year Plan

Planning the remaining terms you have to complete your degree is one of the best ways to set and achieve your educational goals. Do not rely on your academic advisor to make a plan. Chart out a *course planner* or course of study yourself. Working through it will give you a better understanding of how courses work together and will help you learn how to develop plans and schedules over a period of time. Chart the courses, the times and days they are offered, and any other relevant information you need to know. After you complete a degree plan, it is wise to make an appointment with your academic advisor and review your plan. An advisor often has good ideas about ways to expedite degree completion and can make suggestions about special courses and other experiences that will enrich your educational experiences.

Many people view their college education as an exercise in checking off required courses when completed. Avoid this narrow view of your education. Instead, use each year of your education as an opportunity to transition to your career and to develop as a person. Suggestions for making the most of your college experience are given in **Figure 15-1.**

What Do You Need to Know When Choosing a Career?

Imagine you have chosen the "perfect" academic major. You understand and value the subject matter, the mode of learning, and the types of issues and questions faced. However, does understanding and valuing the subject mean you will enjoy working in the field? For example, if you study families and children, will you be successful working with families and children? It is important to make the distinction between being interested in the field and wanting to perform the job. How can you know if a career in your chosen major is one you will enjoy? To identify your work passion, it is critical to discover if you enjoy the work itself.

It is important to carefully research areas of interest to learn more about career realities, desired skills, and how to prepare for the job market. Unfortunately, many students make erroneous assumptions about career fields without conducting a thorough study of the career field. What seems like a good match may not be a match at all. How can you know whether the career field you are interested in is a "fit" or "matches" your interests? Do some background research. By exploring the projected job prospects, typical job duties and responsibilities, opportunities for advancement, educational requirements, salary and benefits, and typical working conditions, you will get a good idea whether a career field or industry is right for you.

Job Prospects

The starving artist, the highly skilled computer programmer, the sophisticated life of a fashion designer—society holds many stereotypes about

Four-Year Plan	
Freshman Year	Make a short list of your educational goals. How do you want to learn and grow during your college experience? Become familiar with general education requirements. Plan courses you will take to complete your general education requirements. Take courses that you find interesting. Get involved with campus activities. Visit the career services center, both in person and online. Take a self-assessment test. If career exploration courses are offered, take one. Research majors offered at your school. Conduct an informational interview with a professor or upperclassman. Research a few majors. Visit professors and ask questions. Take a class in the subject area. Talk to upperclassmen.
Sophomore Year	Continue your general education courses. Conduct another informational interview. Make an appointment with a career services center counselor and begin exploring resources. Prepare your résumé so it will be handy in case a new employment or internship opportunity arises. Do some volunteer work. Declare a major. Begin taking courses in your major.
Junior Year	Make a course plan and meet with your academic advisor. Volunteer in an organization that is in your area of interest. Research internship opportunities. Conduct an informational interview with a professional in your field. Research career opportunities within your major. If you have no job experience, find part-time work now. Participate in internship programs and job fairs on campus. Begin networking with friends and relatives. Let them know what you are majoring in and what your interests are.
Senior Year	Begin your job search. Meet with a career counselor to refine your résumé and to get tips on successful job searching. Consider graduate school. Find out the necessary requirements such as taking the GRE (Graduate Record Exam), MCAT (Medical College Admissions Test), or LSAT (Law School Admissions Test). Meet alumni in your field. Sign up for job interviews. Research companies that interest you. Place your résumé on your college job board and Internet job boards. Network.

Figure 15-1 Use this suggested four-year plan to keep on track toward a career.

certain professions. Should you select a major to prepare for a career field that touts large growth projection in the upcoming years, or should you pursue a career based only on your interests and passions? In order to make an informed decision, it is wise to check into the projected job growth in your fields of interest. If you are attracted to a particular industry but declining employment opportunities are expected for this industry, it is best to be prepared with the knowledge that your job search will necessitate innovation and creativity. It may mean you might be less selective about future jobs in this industry or that you prepare yourself for entrepreneurship rather than corporate work. On the other hand, job markets change. What is considered a promising job market with many opportunities in one year may be a very slow market with limited opportunities five years later. Many career specialists advise their clients to pursue what they enjoy the most and then find a way to make a living at it. Whether or not this is a reasonable option for you depends on your lifestyle goals.

Do the career specialties and industries you are interested in project growth in the upcoming years? How will you gain experience and expertise necessary to be sought after in a growing market? Is the job market or industry you are interested in slowing down or stagnant? How will you market yourself? Information is power, and the more information you have about a particular job market, the more prepared you will be to be successful.

Will there be jobs in your career field of interest in 10 years? in 20 years? Labor market changes are an important consideration when choosing a career or industry to pursue. There are several components to research. For example, you could research occupational trends, or you could research national or state trends and projections for job and industry growth.

Whether you are exploring trends at the local, state, national, or international level, there are several ways of considering labor market growth. You could identify the fastest growing occupations, or you could explore the occupations with the most projected job openings. In some cases, occupations may be growing, but little attrition is expected. Other occupations may expect a large decrease in available workers. You can get more specific and look for the fastest growing occupations by education level, or you can find out which occupations pay the most and which ones are predicted to pay the most in the future. You can explore industry trends and workforce statistics. You can even find out how many graduates are expected to enter the labor market by major.

Should predicted labor market trends affect your career goals? Only you can answer this question. However, being armed with the knowledge can only help you to make an informed career decision.

Job Duties and Responsibilities

Imagine you are a fashion buyer in an urban retail store. You work with department managers from 15 different stores helping them to sell what you have purchased. You travel one week out of the month. These trips are intense and there is not a lot of downtime. You communicate trends to department managers and salespeople, convincing them to "buy into" the newest fashion concepts. You are responsible for the buying plan and budget and spend considerable time "crunching" numbers. Sometimes you take calculated risks with purchases that are fad items. You eagerly wait to see if the items sell or if you will have to take a markdown. You know sales result from great merchandise. Now imagine you went into this career only because you like to shop and thought that travel sounded exciting. You took retail management, retail math, buying, and finance courses in college but never realized how much time you would spend crunching numbers, supervising and directing people, and selling your ideas.

Today, there is no reason to be surprised by the typical duties and job responsibilities of any occupation. Career and industry descriptions abound. You can also gain valuable knowledge about the typical daily tasks and duties and the skills and abilities needed to perform a job from those currently in an occupation or industry. Do not let yourself be surprised. Once again, knowledge is power. The more you know about the duties and responsibilities involved in a particular career or industry, the more informed your decision will be.

Opportunities for Advancement

If you enter your profession as a clinical dietitian, how important is it for you to move into a supervisory position in the next several years? Would you like to advance into a position training other dietitians? Are you interested in private practice, teaching at a local college or university, or using your expertise in a humanitarian relief effort? How important is mobility and change compared to geographical stability to your life satisfaction?

For many young adults, it is difficult to forecast what they may desire in years ahead. Sometimes looking at your current approach to life can give you a clue to what you will desire later in your career. Do you seek out leadership roles or do leadership roles come to you? Do you value change? Do you enjoy teaching or managing others? Have you taken on additional responsibilities as you have progressed in your schooling? If you have answered yes to any of these questions, you may desire opportunities to advance in your career. Many of the topics listed in the next section can give you insight regarding opportunities for advancement that exist in your field of interest.

Educational Requirements

If you plan to be a marriage and family therapist, what type of education do you need to enter the field? If a master's or doctoral degree is required, are you willing to commit to additional years of schooling beyond a bachelor's degree? If you are interested in becoming a registered dietitian, are you eager to do an internship and take the required exam? Is there a difference between educational requirements for entering the field and educational requirements for advancement in the field? Understanding the educational requirements of a given industry or career field is essential to making a career choice that is right for you. Only you know your educational needs, interests, and goals. What you need to figure out is how well your needs, interests, and goals match up with the requirements of a career or industry.

Salary and Benefits

You may be strongly drawn to a career, but will it pay what you desire? Determining

adequate pay is a personal decision based on desired lifestyle. Knowing your needs is an important consideration when researching monetary benefits of a particular career. What level of financial income will meet your needs and help you achieve your goals? Fortunately, you live in an era when a wide variety of salary and wage information is at your fingertips. Salary and wage ranges can be located on the Internet from reputable sources. You search for salary and wage ranges by state. However, there is more to consider than just general salary and wage information. Also consider the geographic location and relative cost of living. The same salary in one city may have much less buying power than in another. Internet resources exist that can help you convert potential wage and salary figures considering the cost of living in one city to another. If you are considering relocating, it is beneficial to look into specific costs such as housing, transportation, and food in the area in which you are interested.

It is important to evaluate salary and benefits in the right context. For example, teacher's salaries must be viewed in the context of the number of months on contract. How much time does a teacher work during noncontracted time? It depends on the school and the school system. This is valuable information to obtain before you pursue a career in education. Other nonsalary *benefits* to consider as you develop career goals may include flexibility in work scheduling, tuition reimbursement, sales discounts, award ticket miles from air travel, holidays and vacations, compensatory time, insurance coverage, or any number of benefits that have value to employees.

Working Conditions

Do you like change? a fast pace? lots of activity? routine and standard operating procedures? There are endless factors to consider when evaluating work conditions. Each industry and occupation has its own personality and culture. It's a good idea to find out as much as you can about a career field or industry before you pursue it further. Do not rule out a career field or industry based on broad generalizations, however. For example, if you love fashion, sales, and working with people but do not like the competitive environment and fast pace of department store sales, look for a segment of the industry that would work well with your needs. A small fashion boutique could offer the factors you enjoy without the fast pace you dislike. A small boutique could offer you the chance to build one-on-one long-term relationships with customers. You might wish to explore owning your own business as a potential career path. If you are passionate about families and children but do not enjoy the everyday interaction with children, research an area of the career field that best utilizes your needs and abilities. Using administrative and management skills to lead programs that benefit families and children may make more sense for you. You are still pursuing your interests, but finding an employment setting that is right for you.

Sources of Career Information

Where do you get information about the job market and specific careers or industries? There are several ways to explore and investigate potential career areas, including job shadowing, volunteering, internships, paid employment, and informational interviews. Good sources of career information include your college career center, career counselors, professors, electronic databases, websites, and publications. All of these resources will be discussed in this section.

Career Centers

One of the most valuable sources of information on a campus is the college or university career center. *Career centers* offer an abundance of resources to students and alumni. Career centers offer counseling, self-assessment tests, internship and job postings and contacts, job

shadowing programs, and help in choosing a major and connecting the chosen major to possible careers. They assist students and graduates in their job search, including assisting with résumé writing, interviewing, identifying job openings, and other job search activities. Each college or university center is different and services provided vary. It is never too early to make your first contact with the campus career center. Typical career center offerings include:

- methods of choosing a major
- connecting your major to a career
- obtaining occupational information
- learning how to network to find information and job opportunities
- locating job opportunities through job fairs, job posting services, and informational interviewing
- resolving on-the-job problems
- finding career resources on the Internet
- discovering your career personality style, interests, values, etc.
- finding internship and volunteer opportunities

Ask an Expert—Informational Interviews

If you are interested in a particular career field, you may wish to talk with someone who works in the field. If you do not know someone to ask, request a recommendation from a professor or the career center. A conversation (or meeting) with a professional or expert in the field does not need to be set up formally. Information can be obtained verbally or through observation during an advising session with a professor or academic counselor, in a casual conversation with someone you happen to meet, or in daily conversations with people with whom you live or work. Do not be afraid to ask questions. If you show genuine interest, most people respond favorably.

Informational interviews are a great way to learn more about a career and make professional contacts in your field. *Informational interviewing* is a networking tactic that allows you to meet professionals, accumulate career information, and explore career options. It also offers an opportunity to obtain advice on job search practices and get referrals to other professionals in the industry. There are two types of informational interviews: industry surveys and networking interviews. Neither type of informational interview should be used as a platform to ask for a job.

The first type of informational interview, the *industry survey*, can tell you many things about an industry. It can tell you whether jobs are available in the field or business that you want to enter and whether your skills and interests fit with a particular industry or specific organization. You can also learn about a specific company, its culture, and how it treats employees.

One of the easiest ways to meet people in the industry is to do the second type of informational interview, the *networking interview*. By setting up an interview, you have the opportunity to have conversations with some of the key professionals in your field of interest. By asking strategic questions, you can gain tremendous knowledge about the industry, career options, and how to enter the field.

Since an informational interview is just that—an interview to obtain information—most professionals are willing to meet with you. Friends and family members may suggest people to contact. Once you have located a person, make a call to introduce yourself and explain why you are calling. It is a good idea to indicate how you were referred and to ask for a short meeting to discuss the occupation. If you have asked for 30 minutes of their time, maintain that time frame during the visit.

When conducting your informational interview, come prepared and dress appropriately. Bring a notepad and pen and a list of questions to ask. For example, you might want to ask:

- How would you describe your typical day?
- What do you like about your job? What do you not like?
- Is your job typical for this occupation?
- How would you describe the company culture?
- How did you get into this field?
- What advice do you have for me as a student?
- Can you refer me to someone else in this field?

Informational interviews are not job interviews. Even so, common etiquette, respect, and gratitude should be shown to the person granting the interview. Do not be discouraged if a professional cannot arrange an interview. Try another person. If you conduct informational interviews, leave a good impression. Write thank-you notes. You never know when this person can support your educational and career goals.

Career Databases

One source of information about careers is right at your fingertips. There are innumerable private and commercial *career databases* on the Internet. However, just because something is available online, that does not mean it is valid or reliable information. Two U.S. government resources available on the Internet are particularly helpful in researching careers: The *Occupational Outlook Handbook* and the *Occupational Information Network*. Both are national databases.

The *Occupational Outlook Handbook* is published by the U.S. Department of Labor, Bureau of Labor Statistics. It is revised every two years and may be accessed online. At the *Occupational Outlook Handbook* website, you can find a variety of career information such as job descriptions, working conditions, wage and salary information, required or desired training and education, and future job prospects. The *Occupational Outlook Handbook* includes a wide variety of career profiles.

The *Occupational Information Network* (O*NET) and *O*NET OnLine* were developed for the U.S. Department of Labor by the National O*NET Consortium. The O*NET includes descriptions and definitions of both public and private career opportunities. It focuses on knowledge, skills, training, and education needed to succeed in each career profiled. In addition, it links labor market data to each career. Although it is an extremely useful tool for job seekers, it is also helpful to employers. The database helps employers structure compensation and reward systems, forecast future human resource requirements, and establish criteria for employee appraisals.

Gaining Experience

One of the best ways to learn about a certain career is to get first-hand knowledge. Opportunities abound for students and include activities from short-term job shadowing to long-term employment. Even if you are sure about a career path, take advantage of these opportunities, many of which are only available to students. Your transition from school to professional career will be easier when you have a variety of experiences.

Job Shadowing

By "shadowing" someone in his or her job for a day, you get a close-up look into what that person's job involves. *Job shadowing* is a short observation consisting of a few hours or a day. The shadowed person can show you just what the benefits and drawbacks of their position are. Although the observation is short, it can give you valuable insight into the daily tasks and activities of a professional. For example, you can see how the person interacts with coworkers and participates in daily activities. You can gain valuable insight into whether a specific job or career is something you might want to aim for yourself. Some students consider job shadowing as a way of capturing "a day in the life of (you name the career professional)."

Since job shadowing is only a short-term activity, you can be creative in selecting people you want to shadow. It is a short-term and worthwhile investment of time and energy. In fact, some people do dozens of job shadows. Each job shadowing experience affords you a new professional contact.

Sometimes college career centers offer job shadowing opportunities. Unless your campus has policies about shadowing, you can set up a job shadowing experience on your own. If you are interested in becoming a clinical dietitian, for example, call your local hospital and ask if you can shadow a clinical dietitian for a day. Your professors and academic advisor are also good sources of contacts for a shadowing experience. As long as safety, security, job schedules, or confidentiality are not issues, most professionals welcome students who shadow them.

Volunteering

Volunteering, or working without financial compensation, for an organization that is related to your career goals is valuable in several ways. First, it provides an important service for the organization. Second, it gives you important experience to include on your résumé. Be sure to list volunteer work as experience on your résumé, not as a hobby or interest. Just because you are not getting paid does not mean the experience is any less valuable. Third, you can learn significant information about the career field by participating in the work. Finally, you can make key contacts with professionals in your field of interest. Consider setting a goal of volunteering for 100 hours or more. This is enough time to make a substantial contribution to an organization and build relationships. It is also feasible to fit into segments of a few hours at a time.

Community service is volunteer work that anyone can do to improve the quality of life in the community. Because FCS focuses on meeting the needs of people, ample opportunity exists in communities for involvement in career-relevant community service. Volunteering in a food pantry, homeless shelter, or secondhand store can help the community. Working as a volunteer for a fashion show, tutoring children, or helping with a community fund-raiser can help you gain experience in your field of interest.

In some cases, volunteer experience and community service learning activities qualify for academic credit, usually as an elective unless it is in your field of study. You may wish to document the experience with credit. Some universities note service learning on the transcript or award a certificate to students who meet specific criteria for volunteer work.

Service Learning

Service learning is the blending of academic study and community service. *Academic study* is learning through textbooks, discussion groups, instructors, and other classroom activities. *Service learning*, on the other hand, provides an opportunity for the student to integrate classroom education with hands-on experience and promotes reflection on its value.

Some examples of service learning are:

- conducting a clothing drive for a local women's shelter
- preparing gift bags with personal hygiene products for families in transitional housing
- leading a session for grade school/middle school girls on self-esteem, appearance, and the media
- presenting an awareness campaign on body image and nutrition
- designing and producing a brochure on sustainable design issues in housing and interiors

Some of the goals of service-learning are:

- to enhance learning through practical experience and reflection
- to gain a lifelong view of community service
- to learn about civic responsibility
- to learn problem-solving skills
- to be of assistance to public and nonprofit organizations that want to serve their communities better

Service learning is tied to specific course learning objectives. Reflective exercises are used to apply concepts learned during service hours to course content and objectives. For example, reflective questions might include:

- What was the community need your service helped meet?

- What were the best things you learned and did during your service?
- What were the challenges you had to face during your service? How did you meet them?
- What did you learn about your value to the community?
- Did the service you performed help or change anything in you? What did it help or change in you? If nothing changed, why do you think it did not change?
- What have you learned from your experience that can be applied to what you have learned in class?

Service learning, community service, and volunteer work can all offer great opportunities to learn more about a career field. When donating your time, make the most of your experience by making a point to meet people. Ask others to introduce you. Ask people questions and observe the inner workings of the organization. Volunteering, community service, and service learning give you an insider's view of the organization's line of work and a better understanding of the multidimensional aspects of communities.

Internships

On most college campuses, students are advised to "get an internship" before they graduate. Sometimes, an internship is a formal requirement to earn a degree. What is an internship? *Internships* and field experiences are similar to employment, but the emphasis is placed on learning over performance. When an internship relationship is established, a company or organization agrees to provide students with an opportunity to gain exposure to an occupational area related to their training. It is a mutually beneficial arrangement for both the organization and the student intern.

How does an internship differ from employment on a daily basis? Internship positions often offer students a more in-depth look at upper-level management decision making and practices. For example, an internship in retail buying might provide an opportunity for a student to sit in on a buying session. For someone working as a retail salesclerk, this opportunity may not be afforded. In other words, internships often give students permission to participate in areas they would not have the opportunity to participate as an employee. This experience can help students identify needed skills, knowledge, and training valued in employees. It helps students appreciate the relevance of their academic preparation. Internship experiences can either be paid or unpaid. Here are some of the benefits of a successful internship:

- self-confidence
- up-to-date, first-hand information about a career field or organization
- insight into how you might fit into a career or company
- understanding how people feel about their work and organization
- interaction and networking with potential employers
- information on ways to approach a job search

What kinds of internships are available? Family service agencies, hospitals, advertising agencies, banks, clothing design and manufacturing companies, performing arts organizations, restaurants, retail stores, interior design firms, schools, and many other types of organizations offer internships to students. An internship is a position that requires you to have taken classes related to the position requirements. Internships are professional-track positions that would not be available to someone who was not pursuing a degree in a related area.

Students majoring in education complete an uncompensated classroom experience under the supervision of a certified, experienced teacher. This experience is called *student teaching*. Student teaching is typically completed in a continuous sequence of weeks for the designated time period. The primary objective of student teaching is to provide opportunity for observing an experienced teacher and developing teaching and classroom management skills. There is usually a phase-in period, when the student teacher initially observes the classes of his or her cooperating teacher(s) and then is gradually given more responsibility. Eventually, student teachers assume the class schedule and supervisory responsibilities of their cooperating teacher(s).

How internships are established and the contractual responsibilities required differ by academic units, degree programs, and the college or university. Some internships are taken for credit, whereas others are not. Your school may require that you enroll in a course at the same time you are completing an internship and may require appointments or meetings with your academic advisor. Be sure to check on your school's internship policy before proceeding.

Where can you find an internship? Most college career centers offer lists of internship possibilities. Your professors and academic advisor are also good sources of information about internships. In the past few years, many internship search engines and databases have become available on the Internet. A professional association in your career field may provide internship opportunities or information. The process of obtaining an internship is good practice for your postgraduation career search. Polish your résumé and prepare a cover letter specific to the desired internship site. Study guidelines for interviewing. Begin several months in advance of the term or summer in which you hope to do your internship to contact the organizations in which you are interested.

Paid Work

There is nothing wrong with being paid for gaining experience in your field of interest. In fact, for many, it is a necessity. Paid work offers valuable experience that provides you with an insider's view of the industry and enhances experiences to include on your résumé.

Students are often faced with the dilemma of choosing work that is unrelated to their career interests and goals but pays well, as compared to work related to their career interests and goals that does not pay as well. Unrelated work is often a financial necessity, but it may offer little related experience for your résumé. For example, if you are interested in interior design, working as a lifeguard does not offer opportunity for developing career-related skills. Unrelated work experience balanced with career-related experience can teach you important transferable skills in leadership. In selecting employment opportunities and internship experiences, it is wise to hone two or more of the following skill areas in your work:

- communication skills
- computer skills
- quantitative skills
- marketing/selling skills
- problem-solving skills
- foreign language skills
- leadership skills

For many students, balancing work and school is a challenge. There are limited hours in a day, and when work consumes too many hours, students find it difficult to study. Many students have additional family responsibilities. Finding a good job that fits with your skills, values, desires, and needs requires patience and persistence, but it can be done. Consider the following questions when securing employment during college:

- Will the work relate to my future career interests or goals?
- Will I gain transferable skills from this job?
- How will I schedule my time to allow for school, work, and personal needs?
- To how many hours can I reasonably adjust?
- Will this job be short-term or long-term?
- Will the energy expended on the job affect my nonworking hours?
- What are my long-term goals and how might working impact these?

Personal Portfolio

As you move through your college years, self-assessment, college planning, career research findings, and your learning experiences can pile up. A *personal portfolio* is a great way to organize the important components of your life that relate to your career goals. Think about why each component is significant to you and how you changed, grew, or what you learned from the experience each component represents.

Items you might include in a personal portfolio include:

- basic information about yourself, including your name, e-mail address, and résumé describing each job held
- essay focusing on career goals or personal attributes and interests (or teaching philosophy if teaching)
- a list of courses taken or a description of your course of study
- sample school or work projects that display your skills
- a list of community activities, including any service learning
- academic recognition, such as letters or certificates of scholarships or honors, team photographs, conferences attended, or leadership opportunities
- documentation of special skills, such as foreign language or computer skills
- work-related experiences, such as letters of recommendation and annual reports of accomplishments

Electronic portfolios are a creative means of organizing, summarizing, and sharing information, along with personal and professional growth, in an easily accessible format. There are benefits to using an electronic portfolio. With traditional portfolios, items included in the portfolio can take up a lot of space and must be stored in boxes, notebooks, binders, or files. With an electronic portfolio, information can be easily stored on a computer hard drive or storage device, transported, and accessed with minimal effort. Electronic portfolios also serve to enhance the creator's computer and technology skills.

Summary

Choosing a major is an important decision every college student must eventually make. Although for many students the task seems overwhelming, choosing a major can be very systematic. As with any significant decision, it should include self-reflection and fact-finding. Facts and perceptions about different majors can be collected by reading course catalogs, talking with current students and alumni, interviewing professors, taking sample courses, and reflecting on what you enjoy studying. Once a major is chosen, it is important to chart out the academic requirements needed to complete your degree.

As you explore potential careers, consider typical job duties and responsibilities, opportunities for advancement, educational requirements, salary and benefits, and typical working conditions. By exploring potential career paths and opportunities, you will be more realistic in deciding whether a career field or industry is right for you. You may repeat this career exploration process several times during your life. The components of effective practical reasoning can also be applied to other important decisions.

An important way to learn more about a career field is to gain experience. This can be done by job shadowing and informational interviews, which require little time and effort but can provide valuable insight. Service learning and volunteer work support preparation for a career. Internships and paid work offer a longer time for observation and for building relationships with people in the career field you have chosen.

Questions for Thought

1. Which is more important to you: doing work for which you have a passion or creating and maintaining a desired lifestyle?

2. What businesses, industries, government agencies, educational institutions, and other employers are predominant in the geographic region in which you prefer to live? What are the opportunities for owning a business in the geographic region you prefer?

3. Review the future trends discussed in Chapter 4. How might these trends change the future job market in your chosen field in 5, 10, 20, and 30 years?

4. Many service-related jobs have moved overseas in recent years. This is commonly referred to as "outsourcing." Are there positions or specific aspects of your chosen career that may become outsourced in the future? Why or why not?

References and Resources

Barkley, N., & Sandburg, E. (1995). *Taking charge of your career.* New York: Workman.

Bolles, R. N. (2012). *What color is your parachute? 2012: A practical manual for job-hunters and career-changers.* New York: Ten Speed Press.

Bolles, R. N. (2010). *What color is your parachute? Job hunter's workbook.* New York: Ten Speed Press.

Bridges, W. (2009). *Managing transitions: Making the most of change* (3rd ed.). Philadelphia, PA: Da Capo Lifelong.

DiTomaso, N., & Post, C. (Eds.). (2004). *Diversity in the workforce.* Oxford, England: Elsevier.

Edwards, P., & Edwards, S. (2003). *Finding your perfect work: The new career guide to making a living, creating a life.* New York: J.P. Tarcher/Putnam.

Han, P. (2005). *Nobodies to somebodies: How 100 great careers got their start.* New York: Portfolio.

Harkness, H. (1997). *The career chase.* Palo Alto, CA: Davies-Black.

Howard, E. (2004). *Career pathways: Preparing students for life.* Thousand Oaks, CA: Corwin Press.

Jansen, J. (2010). *I don't know what I want, but I know it's not this: A step-by-step guide to finding gratifying work.* New York: Penguin Books.

Krumboltz, J. D., & Levin, A. S. (2004). *Luck is no accident: Making the most of happenstance in your life and career.* Atascadero, CA: Impact.

Laster, J. (2008). Nurturing critical literacy through practical problem solving. *Journal of the Japan Association of Home Economics Education, 50*(4). Retrieved from http://www.kon.org/publications/critical-science-paper.pdf

Roofe, N. (n.d.). *The enigmatic profession* [Working Paper]. Kappa Omicron Nu Human Science Archives. Retrieved from http://www.kon.org/hswp/archive/roofe_2.htm

Tieger, P. D., & Barron, B. (2007). *Do what you are: Discover the perfect career for you through the secrets of personality type* (4th ed.). New York: Little, Brown.

Tullier, M. (2004). *Networking for job search and career success.* Indianapolis, IN: Jist.

Zunker, V.G. (2012). *Career counseling: A holistic approach* (8th ed.). Belmont, CA: Brooks/Cole/Cengage Learning.

On the Internet:

https://bigfuture.collegeboard.org/explore—careers, site by the College Board which offers career profiles for many family and consumer sciences careers

http://www.bls.gov/ooh/—the Occupational Outlook Handbook, sponsored by the U.S. Department of Labor, Bureau of Labor Statistics, provides job descriptions, working conditions, wage and salary information, required or desired training and education, and future job prospects for many careers

http://www.careeronestop.org—sponsored by the U.S. Department of Labor, provides information on many careers

Chapter 16

Making Connections

After studying this chapter, you will be able to:

- state objectives and action plans that support career goals.
- conduct a job search using various types of career references and job leads.
- create a résumé and cover letter.
- demonstrate effective job interview skills.
- practice evaluating and replying to job offers.
- describe the process of maneuvering a career change.

Joel and Kylie had great plans. With their new degrees in hotel and restaurant management and nutrition, respectively, they could envision the restaurant they would one day own together. The restaurant would feature healthy entrées made from locally supplied organic ingredients. It would appeal to the young, urban, and trendy. How would they reach their dream?

Joel and Kylie put their plans into specific, achievable goals and designed an action plan with specific steps to meeting their goal. However, between now and then, they needed to gain more restaurant business experience. In other words, they needed to find jobs that would give them experience in restaurant management, ownership, and the daily management of food service. How would they find jobs that offered them creativity, flexibility, mentoring, and management experience, all in the right geographic location? More importantly to them, they needed to find jobs that paid enough for them to save toward their goals, pay off school loans, and make contacts in the industry.

So you know what you want in a career, but how can you find it? How do you let others know you are available? Finally, how can you land that "perfect" job? A job search is known to be hard work and sometimes tough on the ego. Although it is not easy, planning your search strategy can make finding a job a bit simpler. Discovering a job that fits you well requires hard work, patience, and persistence. In this chapter, suggestions that can help you in the job-hunting process will be discussed. These include setting personal and career objectives and goals, finding job leads, writing résumés and cover letters, conducting successful job interviews, evaluating job offers, accepting or rejecting job offers, and changing career directions.

Making Career Decisions

One of the greatest weaknesses of many job seekers is their lack of clear goals and an inability to express what they want in a career. In the previous two chapters, you spent time looking both inward and outward. That is, you looked inward at your interests, skills, and needs and made a connection between yourself and a particular career field or industry. Now it's time to establish your career goals so you can describe your career objective to potential employers in a clear, concise way. Goals will help you establish career objectives, which are more specific than goals.

It is much better to put some thought into your goals and objectives rather than formulating them on the spot when you are conversing with a potential employer. If you formulate them ahead of time, you will come across as focused, motivated, and organized. Your potential employer will understand what drives you and whether a good match exists between you and the company. Thus, the first step in making connections is to spend some time formulating your career goals.

Career Goals

Once you have chosen an occupation, it is time to set career goals, establish career objectives, and form an action plan for achieving them. An action plan to achieve your goals is important for making your dreams become reality.

Career goals are future ambitions or aspirations. For example, you may have a goal to teach, to be an apparel designer, to run a five-star hotel, or run an early childhood arts camp. Career goals state the type of career, industry, environment, or lifestyle you aspire to achieve.

As you begin to make connections with people in the career field or industry you aspire to enter, think about establishing both short-range and long-range career goals. *Long-term goals* are those that may take years to achieve, whereas *short-term goals* include things you can do in six months to a year. For example, a short-term goal may be to become a retail department manager, whereas a long-term goal might be to become a retail department store general manager. Though long-term goals may take years to reach, with a well laid out action plan, you move in the right direction.

Action Plan

Once you have identified an occupation to pursue and established a desired career path, develop an action plan. An *action plan* is a systematic plan for attaining your goals. It requires a thorough analysis of the goals, alternatives,

resources, and obstructions to possible success. From this analysis, steps to achieving the goal are conceived. The more specific a plan is, the more effective it will be toward goal achievement. In life, especially with long-term goals, you must be prepared for curves in the road. Progress may not always be straightforward. You may find yourself moving back to previous steps when you need to gather more information or clarify your choices.

Career Objective

Once you are able to clearly state your career goals, narrow them down to one specific career objective. Make it clear and concise so a potential employer can feel assured you do, in fact, have a clear career direction. Everything you say in your interactions with a potential employer, whether verbally or on paper, should support your career objective. Be prepared to give examples of how your skills and experience support your objective. A portfolio should provide materials to support this.

A *career objective* states what you want to be doing, with what kind of organization you desire to work, or the type of people with whom you want to work. A career objective is directed toward a specific career or position. For example, your objective may be to teach family and consumer sciences in a large urban high school, or your objective may be to have an internship with a commercial interior design firm specializing in retail design. You might be seeking an entry-level copywriter position in a fashion advertising agency where you can use your public speaking, writing, and fashion-forecasting skills.

Although it is tempting to use a general objective that can cover many job prospects, a vague and nondescript objective does not contribute anything. Be specific. Avoid terms and phrases that are overused, such as "opportunity for advancement," "a challenging and interesting position," or a "creative environment."

The process of narrowing your career objective to specific terms will aid you in clearly articulating your desires to prospective employers and to yourself. It will also help you to critically evaluate whether a prospective job matches your career objective.

A career objective should be included on your résumé, in your cover letter, and verbally expressed during interviews. You may find that you need to slightly tweak or customize your objective for each employer. Do not be dishonest, but tailor the objective so the potential employer can easily see how well you match the open position. Emphasize how you can contribute to the organization, rather than what the employer can do for you. For example, "seeking an entry-level position in a nonprofit agency where I can grow professionally" sends a different message than "seeking an entry-level opportunity in a nonprofit agency where I can contribute to an improved quality of life for senior citizens."

Personal Objectives

Besides your stated career objective, you may also have personal objectives relating to your work life. *Personal objectives* tend to be more specific for a particular job. Both career and personal objectives should be measurable and easy to assess. Personal objectives are not usually shared with potential employers, but they may become evident as the career selection process proceeds. For example, you may have an objective to make a very specific dollar salary. If this objective is met, it is easy to know that you have fulfilled your objective. You may have a personal objective to move from assistant to fashion designer in two years or less. Sometimes personal objectives are appropriate to share with your potential employer, and other times it is best to wait. If you do decide to share personal objectives, present them in the least self-serving manner possible. Let the employer know how your personal goals can benefit the organization.

Giving serious thought to your goals, career, and personal objectives will pay off in the long run. You will know what you are looking for in your job search, and it will be easily communicated to your future employer. As in any

relationship, the best communication and "fit" occurs when there is a good match between the interests of both parties.

Sources of Job Leads

Michael is convinced that without his friends, former teammates, and coaches he would never have found the right career path. When he was nearing graduation, Michael let everyone around him know that he was interested in working in the family services field, especially with children in trouble. Although his friends were not in positions of power, they knew people who were. He got his job lead through a former coach's sister-in-law. She was the executive director of the family services agency that provided services and sports programs for at-risk children. Michael's former coach knew him well and gave a great reference. Since she trusted her brother-in-law's ability to choose a team player, she asked for Michael's résumé and eventually hired him. Michael now works as the case manager for the organization. He is living his passion.

Once you have established your career goals and objectives, it is time to begin your job search. Career leads come from a variety of sources, including networking, electronic job boards, company websites, career fairs, and traditional newspaper classified advertisements. Today, the main sources of job leads are networking and electronic sources.

Networking

You have heard it said many times that the key to any job search is networking. *Networking* is the act of meeting and making contact with people, exchanging ideas, and informally interacting for the purpose of increasing business insight. Career specialists frequently report that the vast majority of jobs are found through networking. Sometimes networking sounds like a difficult or, at best, intimidating endeavor, especially for new job seekers. However, networking is really about friendly interactions with people. It can happen anywhere—at family reunions, in the classroom, at a party, in ballparks, at a grocery store, or at any social event. It can take place in quiet conversations, in large group settings, or online. The key to networking is making connections between people. Sounds simple, right?

It is simple, but networking is more than just being friendly. It is also about being focused. When you meet people, let them know your interests, what your passions are, and the specific type of work for which you are looking. Make it succinct and easy to understand. Think of it in terms of a television commercial that must be stated in 60 seconds or less. In fact, you might want to practice so you have the kernel of your message down to a minute or so. Make it logical and concise. You can always expand or subtract based on time or the interest of others.

Referrals really do happen more casually than you might expect, but sometimes results can take a while. The more people you contact, however, the faster connections will be made. If you are positive and upbeat, others will be more likely to feel comfortable recommending you to others. If you are negative and demonstrate low energy, people will be more reluctant to give a referral. After all, people who make referrals put their reputation on the line each time a reference is given.

Networking can be as easy as your college roommate's mother's friend hearing about your desire to enter the commercial interior design field and offering you an "in." However, she can only offer you the job if she knows you are looking for one.

So how do you begin networking? Begin with the old-fashioned method of contacting friends, relatives, and former coworkers and setting up face-to-face meetings with people you already know in the hope of getting job referrals. Ask the people you know for their referrals. While you are in school, network with guest speakers and people you meet on field trips. Students are often seen as nonthreatening. Make use of your student status to make contacts with people with whom you might otherwise not have ready access.

To expand your professional contacts, join a trade or industry group. Most of these groups have college-level organizations. For example, if you desire to enter the fashion industry, join the local fashion professionals group. Join your local or state family and consumer sciences chapter or affiliate. Most professional organizations have state and/or national conferences. Attending a conference is an excellent way to meet many people in addition to staying up to date in your field. There are also structured networking groups in many communities. Do not ask for a job directly, but instead, focus on building relationships. Do not expect to make instant contacts. As with any relationship, it takes time to build trust.

Although you are "selling" yourself, it is important to show interest in others, too. Do not bore others by only focusing on yourself. Ask questions and invite contacts to talk about themselves. If you are hesitant or shy, focusing on others may help you to feel more comfortable. You will be surprised at how much you can learn from listening to the stories of others. Consider printing personal business cards that include your name and contact information. Exchange cards with others when networking. This will allow you to network effectively and follow up with contacts. When you begin networking with professional contacts, you may need to change your voice mail message and your e-mail address to convey a more mature and professional image. Some of your contacts will consider texting too informal for a business relationship; do not text anyone unless they text you first.

The Internet has facilitated networking. You can market yourself through building a personal website, writing a blog, or using social networking sites. For example, LinkedIn is specifically designed for business purposes, such as posting a résumé and joining groups affiliated with professional organizations. People in creative fields can share their work by posting videos on YouTube. However, if you want to create a professional online presence, think carefully about what you post.

Employers are increasingly vetting job candidates by searching online for information about potential hires. Use privacy settings on social networking sites to restrict access to information intended only for family and friends; but be aware that any material posted online may become available to an unintended audience. Periodically search the Internet for your name and view the material through the eyes of a potential employer. You can also establish a Google Alert for your name so that you will be notified when anything new with your name in it appears on the Web. Remove any material under your control that might be problematic, such as profanity, nudity, or criticism of an employer. If other people have posted the material, ask them politely to remove it. If there is negative information about you on the Internet that you cannot remove, you can dilute its impact by generating positive content. For example, start a blog, author an article for your professional organization's website, or write book reviews or letters to the editor. The more recent positive material will probably appear first in search engine results and help to counteract negative information.

Last, do not be selfish or abuse relationships. Even when you are not searching for a job, retain your networking relationships so you can help someone else. Networking is a give-and-take relationship. Networking can be a gratifying lifetime endeavor resulting in professional contacts and support.

The Internet and Electronic Bulletin Boards

Not that long ago, the Sunday newspaper was the prime source of available job openings. Today, finding a job takes more than searching the classified ads in the Sunday paper. It entails several strategies, including using the Internet, an international resource filled with endless possibilities.

One of the most comprehensive Internet sources is *American Job Center*, which is run by the U.S. government. This site provides a single access point for key federal programs and critical local resources to help you research careers, prepare for careers, and locate specific jobs. Because it is a free service for both employers and job seekers, this government site has become the primary electronic source for Internet job leads.

Many commercial electronic bulletin boards exist, however, especially in focused areas. Professional associations are a good place to begin an electronic search. For example, the American Association of Family and Consumer Sciences lists openings in all areas of family and consumer sciences, and the Academy of Nutrition and Dietetics lists open positions in nutrition and dietetics.

It is important to remember that Internet job databases are just one tool to be used in your job search. A very small percentage of jobs are actually obtained through the Internet. Why? Because although there are many jobs listed, there are also millions of people applying for these jobs. Although a job database is a great tool, it is often difficult to set yourself apart from the many other applicants. One way you can set yourself apart is by contacting a few companies and asking them what they are looking for in online applicants.

Searching the Internet for a job is easy and impersonal. That is why it draws so many applicants. On the plus side, it is an efficient way for employers to get the word out about a job opening and it is an easy way for you to apply. It also highlights your ability (or inability) to use computer resources. When you do use the Internet as a job search tool, be careful not to abuse the system. Just because it seems impersonal, do not impersonalize your contact with potential employers. For example, do not send a blanket e-mail message, cover letter, or résumé to dozens of employers. This is the easy way out, and potential employers will interpret it as just that. By not personalizing your submissions to the employer, you become a target for the "delete" key. Also make sure that what you send to employers is computer friendly; that is, short, concise, and visually simple. Complicated graphics or photographs take too long to download or may be distorted when received. Make it as easy as possible for potential employers to read your material.

Company Websites

Is there a particular company in which you are interested? Perhaps there are several key companies in your career field that have a good reputation and with whom you would like to pursue an employment relationship. Check the company website to see if it lists current job openings. If it does, information on pursuing the opening should be included. If not, find out how to contact the human resources department. In this case, a well-written cover letter and well-crafted résumé are essential. Making a telephone inquiry to the human resources department may also be helpful.

Job leads can come from anywhere. As you pursue your career interests, keep your eyes and ears open for organizational changes and restructuring, business and product trends, company buyouts and mergers, and any other changes that might lead to employment opportunities. Keeping up with industry or service trends should be a lifetime pursuit whether you are employed or not.

Career Fairs

Imagine dozens or even hundreds of potential employers in one place at one time. Can it get any better than that? *Career fairs* offer the convenience of interacting with many employers at once, saving you both time and energy in making an initial contact. However, as good as it sounds, career fairs can be overwhelming and ineffective unless you are prepared.

Your first step to successfully navigating a career fair is to find out which organizations will be represented there. Research as many of these companies as possible before attending the career fair. Think of possible questions you might ask recruiters that will demonstrate your interest and your preparedness. Doing this will also help you show how you could fit in with the organization.

Next, prepare by getting your résumé in order. Make plenty of copies. Your résumé should be legible, organized, and error free. Make sure

it is in a form that can be easily scanned if the employer prefers to scan résumés into a computer database. Carry all personal vital statistics and references with you in case you are asked to fill out an application. Have a predetermined system for collecting business cards and company promotional material and for taking notes.

Make sure you are properly attired and professionally groomed. When you walk from booth to booth, smile and make eye contact. Be prepared to offer a firm handshake, introduce yourself, and recite a quick biography about yourself. You may want to consider having a professional name badge made. Office supply stores and some campus bookstores make professional badges. Your introduction should include your:

- name
- major (Be ready with a "one-liner" description of your major.)
- class standing (senior, alumna/alumnus)
- opportunities that you are seeking or your career objective
- relevant experience, skills, and strengths (work, internship, volunteer work)

It is also helpful to make references that demonstrate your knowledge of the company at this time. In order to not ramble, practice your introduction. Make it short, concise, energetic, and sincere. Whatever you do, do not approach a recruiter and say, "Tell me about your company." You have limited time to interact with each recruiter, so use the time wisely. Ending your introduction with a focused question is an engaging way to turn the spotlight off yourself. It will also help engage the recruiter in conversation. For example, you might ask about a new product or service the company is offering or a territory expansion.

Spending time preparing for job fairs can help you exude confidence and personality. Do not short-change yourself. Instead, give yourself the best chance to make positive contacts with potential employers. To really set yourself apart and gain an advantage in job searches, write a thank-you note to those recruiters with whom you spent time conversing. Let them know that you enjoyed learning more about their organization, and if you are interested, let them know what you can offer as an employee.

Résumés and Cover Letters

When you do not have a personal introduction to a potential employer, résumés and cover letters serve as your introduction. Résumés and cover letters act as publicity pieces about you and are designed to "sell" you to potential employers. They tell who you are, what your career objective is, what experience and skills you have, and why you would be a good match for the position. Although résumés will never get you a job, they can get you an interview. Remember, a résumé can be scanned and discarded in 10 seconds. It is essential that you make it the best it can be.

Résumés

You are the product. The consumer is the prospective employer. How are you going to sell yourself on paper? An effective résumé is a sales tool that targets a specific audience. A *résumé* lists and describes your education, work, volunteer, and personal experiences that make you a good candidate for the job. Your message must be clear, concise, and, of course, truthful.

Do you have an up-to-date résumé? As you pursue new endeavors such as internships, graduate school, or a career, you will need to update and hone your résumé to fit the specific tasks for which it is intended. If you think of your résumé as just a list of your education, past jobs, and experiences, you have some work to do.

A good résumé should be carefully constructed and tailored for your audience. It should summarize your relevant experiences while highlighting the aspects of your experiences that might mean the most to a prospective employer. There is no one specific formula for writing a résumé. In some industries, creativity in the form of graphics and colors is valued. In more conservative industries, creativity does not enhance your sales potential and may decrease your chances of being taken seriously. Thus, the first step to writing your résumé is to know your target audience.

Most career specialists agree a résumé should be one page in length. However, if you are a nontraditional student with a great deal of relevant experience, it is better to use a second page than to leave out critical information or to use a font that is too small. Be sure to include your name on the second page and indicate that it is page 2. Because the résumé should be short, make every word count. Résumés should list specific accomplishments. To communicate energy, use active rather than passive verbs. Even if you are trying to conserve space, however, do not assume that potential employers will understand acronyms. For example, not all potential employers will know that FCS or FACS stands for family and consumer sciences. On the other hand, if you are applying for a position as a registered dietitian, you can assume the potential employer knows the meaning of RD.

Many resources are available that can help you write a résumé that fits you. If you are a college student with little work experience, focus on skills and abilities you possess from volunteer and extra-curricular activities rather than your lack of job experience. See **Figure 16-1.** If you do have relevant job experience, highlight this experience in your résumé. See **Figure 16-2.** Counselors in college career centers and college websites are great resources for helping students write résumés that highlight their skills, knowledge, and abilities. Résumé writing advice abounds on the Internet. Also, there are templates available that provide a professional format for résumés. The templates are available as software, and some can be downloaded from websites.

Résumés must be error free. If you cannot produce an effective résumé, others will, and the candidate with the most effective résumé is more likely to get the job. Spelling and grammar should be impeccable. There should be

Skills-Based Résumé

Chris River
2322 E. Oak St., Seattle, WA 98XXX
(206) 555-2485 criver@emailaddress

OBJECTIVE   To obtain a hospitality marketing position in the hospitality industry

EDUCATION   **Bachelor of Arts in Hospitality Management, emphasis in marketing**
Lake University, anticipated graduation, June 20XX
Cumulative GPA 3.52

SKILLS STATEMENT
- Financial analysis, risk analysis, and working knowledge of balance sheets
- Highly proficient in MS Excel, Word, PowerPoint, Internet tools
- Vice President, Hospitality Club. Spearheaded undergraduate hospitality marketing competition
- Innovative problem solver with advanced ability in clarifying problems and evaluating alternatives
- Reliable, purposeful, and solutions-oriented worker

RELATED EXPERIENCE
Computer Information Systems Help Desk: *Lake University, Sept. 20XX–present*
- Respond to phone/e-mail technology questions from faculty, staff, and students
- Equip users with the information and skills needed to effectively use technology
- Assess and forward complex calls to specific information system specialist

Payroll Officer: Creekside Day Spa, Puyallup, WA, Summer 20XX
- Handled, collected, and inspected over 60 employees' timesheets daily
- Calculated and recorded hourly rates for private wages

Administrative Assistant: Creekside Day Spa, Puyallup, WA, Summer 20XX
- Recorded incoming payments to assist accounts receivable daily
- Reconciled bank statements to ensure accurate record

OTHER EXPERIENCE
Part-time Assistant Manager: *Easton Fitness, Summer 20XX*
- Supervised sales associates to encourage and ensure impressive customer service
- Enthusiastically interacted with customers to meet their membership needs
- Calculated and recorded sales outcomes and submitted concise sales reports

University Mailroom Student Leader: *Lake University, 20XX–20XX*
- Organized and implemented the students' quarterly work schedules
- Trained and supervised new employees to ensure adequate training

VOLUNTEER EXPERIENCE
- Recreation Leader, Boys and Girls Club, *Summer 20XX*
- Volunteer, Refugee Camp, Kenya, *Summer 20XX*

Figure 16-1 A skills-based résumé highlights a person's skills.

Experience-Based Résumé

Jordan Hill
1234 North 000th Avenue, Peak, OR 99XXX
(503) 555-1234 jhill@me.email

OBJECTIVE
To obtain a secondary teaching position where my knowledge and skills in family and consumer sciences can facilitate a dynamic learning environment for all students

EDUCATION/CERTIFICATION
Oregon State Residency Teaching Certification, K-8
Bachelor of Arts, Family and Consumer Sciences
Mountain University, Peak, OR, June 20XX
- Overall GPA 3.6
- Dean's List 7 out of 7 semesters

TEACHING EXPERIENCE
Student Teaching, Cascade View High School, Peak School District
(September, 20XX–December, 20XX)
- Planned lessons and long-range units in all areas of family and consumer sciences
- Used a variety of assessment techniques to evaluate student progress and teacher instruction
- Demonstrated effective management of student behavior in various settings, including whole class, small groups, and one-on-one
- Created visual displays and bulletin boards that highlighted student work
- Maintained effective parent communication through phone calls, newsletters, and parent meetings
- Developed and presented long-range units in consumerism
- Evaluated student work through portfolio assessment
- Integrated instructional methods and materials into curriculum
- Effectively tutored students in all areas of curriculum
- Worked efficiently with special needs students to meet teacher-provided objectives
- Independently administered assessments in small group settings

RELATED EXPERIENCE
Pediatric Hospital Volunteer, Pediatric Hospital, Range, Oregon
(January, 20XX–present)
- Create and implement small group activities with children in playroom

LEADERSHIP/HONORS
- Volunteer Tutor, Northwest High School, 20XX
- Floor Advisor, Foothill Hall, MU, 20XX–20XX
- Minority Leader Scholarship, School of Education, MU, 20XX–20XX

Figure 16-2 An experience-based résumé focuses on a person's work-related experiences.

no typographical errors. The appearance of a résumé—layout, fonts, and paper—should not be overlooked as inconsequential. Make sure your language is clear. Do not leave out dates. Do not overrepresent yourself or make false statements, as these can be easily uncovered with simple investigative work. If you are considering including hobbies or activities that may be viewed as controversial or irrelevant to the position, err on the safe side and leave them off your résumé. This does not mean you have to give up these activities, but they are probably not relevant to your potential employer. An exception to this is if the unrelated hobbies show initiative, responsibility, problem solving, or other positive traits. Since it is difficult to edit your own work, have at least two people carefully edit the résumé for you.

Every time you prepare to submit your résumé, review it to see how it can be tailored to meet the needs of the potential employer. It should be a "snapshot" of who you are and what you can contribute. Although it is a critical tool to open the door for further contact, it can only "keep you in the game." It will not get you a job.

Cover Letters

A *cover letter* is a letter of introduction. Cover letters explain who you are and why you are sending your résumé to the reader. A cover letter should give your résumé the proper introduction it deserves. Does a résumé always need a cover letter? In most cases, the answer is yes. If you have an opportunity to verbally introduce yourself to the ultimate decision maker whom you wish to positively impress, a cover letter may not be needed. However, for the vast majority of job seekers, cover letters are critically important.

Cover letters should not be narrative versions of your résumé. Instead, each cover letter should be personally tailored to the potential employer. It should name the position for which you are applying, how you learned about the job, why you are the right person for the job, and how you can be reached. See **Figure 16-3**. If you are applying for an internship, cover letters are also useful. Since you

may not have an abundance of work experience, focus on what you hope to learn and your career goals. See **Figure 16-4.** Generally, three or four paragraphs will suffice. If you make your cover letter too long, it will go unread. If you make it too short, it may come across as hurried or careless. Other considerations include:

- Tailor your letter to the target reader and/or industry. When possible, send the letter to a specific person, whose name and title are included in the salutation. Do not duplicate multiple letters addressed "to whom it may concern."

- Convey your career objective clearly.

- Use bullet points or a boldfaced font to emphasize key words or phrases, but do not overuse graphics and highlighted text.

- Be honest but not overly modest.

- Focus on the positive, not the negative.

- Make your cover letter visually appealing.

- Use sample cover letter templates with caution. (They can be overused and recognized as a template. However, they are an effective way to obtain a professional format for the letter.)

- Focus on what you can offer rather than what you can get from the potential employer.

- Use active rather than passive verbs.

Make sure your letter is factually and grammatically correct. It may not matter if your résumé is hand delivered, mailed, or sent via the Internet, but always check to see which method of delivery is preferred. E-mail etiquette has trained many people to produce short, concise, and quick exchanges. Put your old habits aside when it comes to sending a cover letter through e-mail. No matter which method of delivery you choose, cover letters should be carefully and thoughtfully crafted. If you choose an electronic method of delivery, follow up with a hard copy. Why? Your e-mail may be overlooked; using two methods of delivery increases your chances of being noticed. Be careful when sending attachments via e-mail. The receiver may not be able to open them, and formats and fonts may not

Sample Cover Letter for Employment

Jordan Hill
10987 Snowbelt Lane
Mountain Top, OR 93XXX

June 1, 20XX

Sally Pasture, Director
Human Resources Department
Wildflower School District
1500 Northlake Way
Paradise, OR 93XXX

Dear Ms. Pasture:

I am writing to express my interest in the secondary teaching position available with Wildflower School District. I learned of the opening through the School of Education at Mountain University.

I graduated in May, 20XX, with a Bachelor of Arts degree in secondary education with an emphasis in family and consumer sciences. I believe that the following skills and experience make me an excellent candidate for this position:
- Hold an Oregon State Secondary Teaching Certificate
- Successful teaching experience at Cascade View High School, Peak School District
- Volunteer experience working with children in a hospital setting
- Ability to handle multiple projects and tasks in an accurate and efficient manner
- Strong understanding of teaching plan and unit planning
- Experience in assessing student learning and teaching effectiveness
- Fluency in Spanish and English

I would welcome the opportunity to use my skills, love for learning, and passion for working with students in the Wildflower School District. I look forward to an opportunity to discuss my qualifications with you in person. I will be contacting your office next week to arrange an appointment. Thank you for your consideration.

Sincerely,
Jordan Hill

Enc: résumé

Figure 16-3 This is a sample cover letter of a person interested in an elementary school teaching position.

Sample Cover Letter for an Internship

Pat Sunbelt
1234 Pebble Lane
Dryville, AZ 99XXX
(535) 555-5475
PatSun@my.email

October 3, 20XX

Mr. Sandy Desert
1234 Cactus Lane
Dryville, AZ 99XXX

Dear Mr. Desert:

Dawn Breezleton has shared with me her positive experience of working with Prestige Commercial Interiors and recommended that I contact you. I am seeking an internship or part-time employment in commercial interior design. Enclosed is my résumé detailing my educational and work experience in interior design and home furnishing sales.

As the assistant manager of Sun Creek Fine Home Furnishings for two years, I motivated 11 employees to help customers select and purchase home furnishings that met customer needs. I applied my coursework in CAD, lighting, and textiles and trained employees in these knowledge areas. In turn, we were able to relay technical information in an easy-to-understand manner to our customers. Subsequently, sales rose by 25 percent during my tenure as assistant manager. My experience as an assistant manager taught me excellent communication and organizational skills. In addition, I have a genuine enthusiasm and aptitude for working with others.

I have admired a number of your projects in the community and have found them to be very exciting and creative. I am very interested in having an opportunity to meet with you in person to discuss my qualifications and how they may best benefit your company. I will call in the following week to schedule an appointment. Thank you for your consideration.

Sincerely,
Pat Sunbelt

Enc: résumé

Figure 16-4 This is a sample cover letter of a person applying for an internship.

transfer accurately. For this reason, it is best to convert the résumé and cover letter to PDF (portable document format). The file label should include your name. To test that your materials come through as intended and can be opened, send them to a few friends. If using the mail, print the résumé and cover letter on good-quality #20 paper. Use a large envelope so that the items do not need to be folded.

Sometimes cover letters are read before the résumé. They serve as a letter of introduction. Other times, the résumé is read first, scanned for feasibility, and then the cover letter is read to obtain further information about the candidate. Either way, a winning cover letter and résumé can land you the next step in the job-hunting process, the interview.

Job Interviews

The *job interview*. Is it something you look forward to or something you dread? It may depend on how you view its purpose. For example, do you view the job interview as a form of torture where you are put on the hot seat and grilled, or do you view it as a two-way conversation that allows an interviewer to get to know you and allows you to get to know the organization with the end result of determining whether you are a good match? There are many factors that influence your perception of the job interview, such as your level of need for finding a job, your true interest in potential employment, and whether or not you see it as a good fit. The more you interview, the more you will become comfortable with the process. However, no matter how much experience you have interviewing, preparation is the key to being successful.

Preparing for an Interview

Before you go to an interview, do your homework. Research the organization with which you are interviewing and study the job description. It is very likely you will be asked what you know about the company and how you see yourself fitting in. You may be asked why you want to work for the company. Be prepared for as many types of questions as possible, especially open-ended ones like "tell me about yourself." Make your answers specific to how your skills, experiences, and passions match with the open position. The interviewer is not interested in a 10-minute history of your life.

Knowing about the company and the job description will help you formulate your own questions to ask the interviewer. It will also make you appear prepared and interested. While you are researching the company, look into typical salary ranges so you have a salary range in mind. Also, find out general information about the organization including:

- history
- mission/vision
- culture
- financial status
- organizational structure
- company or agency growth

Instead of going into an interview cold, do several mock interviews with family members or friends. Describe yourself, your goals, your strengths, and your weaknesses and practice giving examples of each. Practice asking questions to your mock interviewer, too. Some job coaches encourage applicants to reframe weaknesses as positives or useful attributes. For example, instead of saying you are compulsive, you say you have high standards. A "negative" can be stated as, "Some people would describe me as overly concerned with details."

You can also prepare for an interview by reviewing and practicing basic business etiquette skills. Many college students are not used to shaking hands, so you may wish to practice giving a firm handshake. Remember to keep your cell phone off throughout the entire interview process, and check it only when you have an opportunity for a break. Some interviews include lunch or dinner, and as a guest you may be asked to order first. Avoid ordering the most expensive items on the menu. Asking your companions for their recommendations can help you make a suitable choice. In general, you should not order alcohol.

Be sure to have your paperwork in order. Carry a résumé, your reference list (with contact information), letters of recommendation, and all other basic information required on job applications. Even if you have provided this information earlier, you may be asked for it again. If immigration work-authorization papers are needed, include these, too. Neatly organize your papers in a briefcase or portfolio. It is a good idea to carry a notepad and a pen. You do not want to ask to borrow a pen during an interview.

Think about what you will wear to the interview. First impressions make a big impact (Howard, 2004; Tullier, 2004). Dress appropriately and practice good hygiene. Dress to appear professional and respectful. Dress professionally but comfortably, and avoid items that cause you to fidget. Do not wear clothing, hairstyles, or accessories that will take the focus off of what you have to say. You want your interviewer to hear your words and not be distracted by what you wear.

Most authorities recommend a traditional, dark-colored suit for an interview. However, for some positions in the fashion industry, it is important to show that you are aware of current fashion and have a creative flair. If you are unsure about the expectations of a particular employer, you may be able to observe employees leaving or entering the business or ask contacts who are familiar with the employer.

Even if employees dress quite casually, more formal attire is expected for an interview. Keep in mind that those who will be interviewing you are likely to be older and more conservative than your college classmates. An interviewer may react negatively to noticeable tattoos, body piercings, and unnatural hair colors. Men with long hair and women with bare legs, short skirts, or visible cleavage may be perceived as unprofessional. Avoid heavy makeup and strong colognes.

Last, it is important to be relaxed. Think of the interview as a two-way conversation. The interviewer is trying to get to know you, but you are trying to get to know the interviewer and the company as well. Thinking of an interview as a conversation may make you feel more comfortable and make the interview seem less like a performance.

During and After an Interview

On the day of your interview, leave home early. You should arrive at your interview between five and ten minutes before the scheduled time. Turn off your cell phone or pager so you will not be interrupted. When you meet your interviewer, introduce yourself with a firm handshake and say something such as, "I am pleased to meet you" or "I have been looking forward to meeting you." Use formal language rather than informal greetings you might use with friends.

When you enter the interview room, wait to be offered a seat and then thank the interviewer. Try to read the mood of the interviewer. If he or she is intense, offer decisive and clear answers. If the interviewer is more casual, mimic the casual tone, while remaining courteous and professional. Use good posture and limit your body movements. Many career specialists recommend mirroring the body position of your interviewer. For example, if he or she is sitting cross-legged, you may want to do the same. That advice can only be taken so far, however. If your interviewer has his or her feet propped on the desk, do not copy him or her, as it is too casual for your role.

Interviewers understand that you are "on the spot" and probably a little nervous. If the interviewer is new or untrained at interviewing, he or she may be nervous, too. Even so, try to avoid appearing apprehensive. Steer clear of nervous habits such as fidgeting, quick or jerky movements, and either staring or avoiding eye contact. Make it your goal to appear confident but not arrogant.

It is a good idea to be ready to ask questions during the interview, but save the bulk of your questions until you are asked. It shows you have prepared and done your homework. Although simple yes or no answers to questions are often not enough, find a balance between providing too much or too little detail. If you are asked to give an example, be sure to provide a direct but brief response. Initiating discussion about pay, benefits, and vacation is usually not recommended for the preliminary interview. Employers may view the inquiry as focused on what you can get from the employer rather than on what you can offer. Once you have received a job offer, salary discussions are most often initiated by employers.

Group interviews are a common way of interviewing potential employees, especially for entry-level positions. The simplest and most common form of a group interview is a company presentation followed by a question-and-answer session. Observing potential employees' interactions with others and their preparedness (shown by questions asked) helps employers do initial screening of potential employees. Another type of group interview places applicants in groups and asks them to perform a task or solve a case. In either situation, group interviews allow employers to observe several things, including:

- interpersonal skills
- communication and persuasion skills
- teamwork and leadership skills
- organizational and planning skills
- stress management strategies

During group interview exercises, it is better to be involved with the active leaders of the group rather than the passive followers.

A flood of information about interviewing is available on the Internet. Sample questions, case studies, simulations, and good questions for you to ask in an interview abound. No one can tell you exactly what to say during an interview, as each interview is different. On the other hand, do all you can to be prepared for the interview.

After interviewing, immediately send a thank-you letter to every person with whom you interviewed. Thank the interviewer for his or her time and reiterate your interest in working for the company. Do not procrastinate. Sometimes a prompt follow-up is a deciding factor in the selection process.

Laws Affecting Job Applications and the Interview Process

In the past several decades, Americans have been offered more protection under the laws regarding employment and hiring. Most regulations focus on antidiscrimination. The *Equal Employment Opportunity Commission (EEOC)* enforces these laws. The commission also supplies supervision and management of all federal equal employment opportunity policies, regulations, and practices.

Federal law prohibits job discrimination in all hiring processes, including applications and interviews. Specifically, *Title VII of the Civil Rights Act of 1964* prohibits employment discrimination based on race, color, religion, sex, or national origin. There are also several federal laws that protect specific groups of workers. For example, the *Equal Pay Act (EPA)* protects men and women who perform substantially equal work in the same establishment from gender-based wage discrimination. Age discrimination is also prohibited under the *Age Discrimination in Employment Act of 1967 (ADEA)*, which protects individuals who are 40 years of age or older.

Americans with disabilities are also a protected group. In 1990, Title I and Title V of the *Americans with Disabilities Act (ADA)* was enacted to prohibit employment discrimination against qualified individuals with disabilities in the private sector and in state and local governments. Federal government employers cannot discriminate against people with disabilities according to Sections 501 and 505 of the *Rehabilitation Act of 1973*. If intentional employment discrimination occurs, the Civil Rights Act of 1991 provides grounds for awarding monetary damages to the person who was discriminated against.

The Americans with Disabilities Act does not prohibit an employer from establishing job-related qualification standards. These standards are under the employer's authority, and employers may seek to hire the most qualified candidate. The ADA requirements are designed to ensure that if a disabled person is deemed the best candidate, he or she is not discriminated against based solely on disability. The following standards and tests necessary for job performance, health, and safety may be used to screen applicants:

- education
- skills
- work experience
- physical test standards
- mental or psychological test standards
- safety requirements
- paper and pencil tests

If candidates with disabilities meet the employment standards, reasonable accommodations must be made to enable employees to perform the job. For example, if an employee has mobility challenges but can perform the job, sensible accommodations such as providing wheelchair access must be provided. However, an employer is not required to lower existing production standards or adjust quality expectations.

The employment application is generally the first piece of paperwork you will fill out when applying for a job. Through an *employment application* a potential employer collects important information for evaluating the experience and skills of an applicant. Besides personal data such as your name, Social Security number, address, and telephone number, you will be asked to list your previous work experience, salaries, and references. You may also be asked why you left a former employer or what value you contributed to that company. Application forms usually include various legal clauses to make sure applicants understand how the information provided will be used.

Interviews involve direct questioning of the potential employee by the employer. Interviews offer the employer a chance to ask more specific, detailed questions. For both applications and interviews, questions that may be used to discriminate

against you are illegal in the United States. The specific areas of concern are:

- age
- color
- disability
- gender
- national origin
- race
- religion or creed
- marital or parenting status

However, employers are required to determine whether a candidate can legally work in the United States, and the U.S. Patriot Act has invoked additional requirements in an effort to increase surveillance and investigative powers in regard to potential terrorist plots. These requirements focus on the job candidate's national origin or past criminal record, particularly when security clearance is involved. The inability to attain security clearance may or may not preclude employment for an individual. It all depends on whether security clearance is needed for a given job. Although an interviewer may have the best intentions and may truly desire to get to know you better, any question that hints at discrimination is considered inappropriate since the potential for a lawsuit exists.

Evaluating Job Offers

Congratulations! After conducting your job search, you have received an offer of employment. Your mind races with possibilities. Perhaps you are mentally running through a list of ways your life will change—maybe you will be able to save to take the trip of your dreams, have a stable living situation, have one employer instead of several, finally leave the job that you have been waiting to leave—or any number of emotional or practical results you have associated with finding a job.

But wait. Is the job all that it is cracked up to be? Should you stop the job search and take the first job offer? Only you can answer this question.

There are many considerations when deciding either to accept or reject a job offer. It may be helpful to break your evaluation process into several categories for your review. These include characteristics of the job or position, the organization, salary and benefits, geographic considerations, and your personal needs. There is no one right answer, but thoughtfully evaluating the selection criteria will help you make an informed, rational decision. If you like the job but are uncertain about whether the job would be a good career move, ask the opinion of others in the field. Remember, jobs can act as stepping stones. Accepting an offer does not mean you will stay in that job forever. To help you evaluate the job offer, consider the following factors.

Evaluating the Position and the Organization

When considering the job itself, think about the following:
- the tasks and responsibilities of the job
- the typical workday
- the people with whom you will work

First, consider exactly what you will be doing in this position. Is the work interesting to you? Knowing what a job entails will help you make the right decision. Explore the tasks and responsibilities of the job you are offered. Think about how you will spend your day. Consider whether the typical daily tasks and responsibilities are ones you enjoy. Contemplate whether you are proud of the products or services of the employer and if the employer has proven to be an ethical organization.

Think about whether the job fits with your lifestyle. Are there spurts of activities balanced by slow times? Will the work hours fit your lifestyle? Will the job impact your personal time commitments, such as recreational sports or family time? Some jobs require long hours of office paperwork, long hours on your feet, or movement to and from locations. Travel and time away from home are also factors to consider.

Another consideration about the job should be the people with whom you will work. Considering your potential relationship with your future boss should not be taken lightly. Communication style, management style, and potential for a mentoring relationship should be evaluated. Having a boss who believes in you and wants to see you succeed is significant. From your early investigative research before the interview and the interview itself, you should have a pretty good idea about the predominant culture of the organization. It is easy to decipher the corporate philosophy, history, products or services, goals, and financial status. What do these say about the organizational culture?

Consider the rigidity versus flexibility of the company. Creative organizations may offer more flexibility, but they may also expect longer work hours. Understanding the organizational structure and chain of command will give you some insight into the culture. To whom will you report? How is your job viewed in the organization? Is there room for advancement?

Consider the organizational culture regarding your personal time. Does the employer require overtime hours? Is overtime work paid? Are work hours flexible when overtime hours are not paid? If you will work with clients or customers, how does the organization approach service to its constituents? Many organizations today foster a family-oriented approach to the work environment. For example, they offer personal time off or flexibility in personal emergencies. Last, consider whether the organization fosters a team environment or an individually competitive one.

Evaluating Salary and Benefits

When it comes to job offers, the first thing many people think is, "How much does it pay?" Compensation involves much more than just salary. For example, in today's economy, a job offer of 26 to 28 hours per week with employer-paid benefits may be more valuable than a full-time (40-hour) job without benefits. In addition to salary, indirect compensation and benefits can significantly contribute toward the total financial package offered by an employer. Some examples of benefits include:

- medical insurance

- dental insurance

- life insurance

- disability insurance

- retirement and savings plans

- paid vacation

- employee leave and/or sabbaticals

- employee assistance programs (EAP)

- company stock and/or ownership options

- "cafeteria" benefits (selecting among benefit options) and/or employee tax-free deductions for health and child care

- additional benefits, such as profit sharing, bonus incentives, or commissions

Medical insurance plans can be complicated and varied. For example, some let you visit any physician you prefer, while others require you to choose a physician from a preferred list. Plans also vary in the amount of out-of-pocket expenses you will incur. Some allow you to enroll dependents and spouses, while others only cover the employee. Because medical costs have soared in recent years, most companies require employees to contribute to health care costs in some way. Some organizations allow you to set aside pretax dollars for medical expenses. As you evaluate the job offer, consider asking for the following information about any form of insurance:

- description of the insurance plan

- benefit eligibility date

- family and dependent benefits

- total employee monthly premium

- premium rate increase history

- copayment and deductibles

- maximum out-of-pocket expenses, lifetime maximum benefits

- prescription drug coverage

- vision care coverage

- availability of insurance for part-time employees

If you are a single, young adult, life insurance may not have entered your mind. Life insurance coverage is an important benefit for many employees, however. Generally, the more you pay into life insurance (premiums), the more your family members will be paid when you die. For people who are the main or sole source of financial support for their families, life insurance coverage with the option of increasing coverage is desired. Disability insurance may also be covered.

For young people just starting their careers, retirement is often difficult to consider, but it is never too early to start saving toward retirement. Retirement plans can be complex, and it is often smart to get the advice of a financial planner. Some employers contribute to retirement funds, some offer a plan to which you can contribute, and others offer a combination of employer and employee participation. Two keys to retirement plans are flexibility and portability. *Flexibility* means that the plan can be changed and adjusted to your life stage. For example, during young adulthood, you may choose to put less money into a retirement program than during another stage in life. *Portability* means that you can move your retirement savings with you if you change employers or you can transfer them to a rollover IRA (individual retirement account). Last, accessibility to your retirement savings account is also a consideration. Some companies fully vest (allow access to funds) immediately, while others require a certain length of employment before you are fully vested.

Employee leave is another consideration. How much paid time off does the company offer? Consider whether paid leave is in the form of sick leave, vacation, or other forms such as jury duty or bereavement. Does the company offer maternity and/or paternity leave? time off without pay? Some employers combine sick days, vacation, and other leaves so that employees have more flexibility in deciding how to use their paid days off. Holidays and planned organization shutdowns or closures should also be considered.

Benefits vary greatly by employer and organization. For example, many universities offer tuition discounts to employees and their dependents. Wholesale and retail companies may offer merchandise discounts. Health care organizations may offer medical services to employees. Flexible work hours, telecommuting options, health club benefits, child care, office equipment, or paid parking may also be valuable benefits, depending on your goals and interests.

When considering compensation, there are factors beyond salary. Only you can decide if the compensation package will meet your needs. Does this mean you have to bombard your potential employer with dozens of questions? The answer is probably not. Most of the answers to these questions can be found in the standard benefits brochure of the organization. Ask the human resources department for a copy. Read the material carefully so you can make an informed decision about the job offer.

Evaluating Geographical Considerations

Consider where the job is located. If it is in another geographic location than where you live presently, consider the climate, the availability of suitable housing, and the size and type of the community. Think about your current lifestyle. If you are looking for a community that supports a social environment for singles, look into the cultural, social, and recreational activities that are offered. You may desire a community that is appropriate for couples or families. If you are a single parent, will you find support services, schools, or child care that will meet your needs? Even if you are staying in your current location, consider how commuting will impact you financially and in time spent.

If the job is in another section of the country, consider the cost of living, the quality of education, recreational facilities and opportunities, the availability of suitable or affordable housing, and the cost of transportation in both time and money. Researching the dominant industries in a location, the majority religious affiliations, and income and educational levels will give you insight into a community and how well you will fit in.

Your environment plays a large role in personal satisfaction. Even if you love the organizational climate, your future coworkers, and boss, you still should consider the community in which you will live. All of your waking hours will not be spent at work. How will your social, emotional, physical, cognitive, and spiritual needs be met outside of work?

Evaluating Your Personal Needs

Although you may be tempted to jump at the offer, take a day or two and think through your decision carefully. The best place to start is to review your self-assessment, especially your life and personal goals and objectives. Is it the best job to meet your current or future personal needs? Is it going to help you on your way in your established action plan? If not, when will you get back to your action plan? For example, imagine you have just graduated from college with a degree in fashion merchandising. You have incurred significant debt in the form of student loans to pay for tuition. You were offered a temporary job working in your college's finance office. The job offers a competitive salary along with subsidized housing in a campus apartment. The job will end at the conclusion of the summer, but you have decided to take it. Why? After reviewing your personal needs, you know you have a need for financial and geographic stability, time to reflect and get your personal matters in order, and time to begin your job search in the fashion field. You know dozens of other recent graduates are looking for jobs. You figure that by fall, you will be ready to start on a concerted effort to find the ideal entry-level job for you in the fashion retail field. Your decision is not in line with your career goals, objectives, and action plan, but you have a designated timeline for going back to your plan.

Searching for a position is difficult and time consuming. It may be tempting to accept an offer after spending many hours on a search. Getting an offer does not necessarily mean you need to take the job, however. Give careful thought to your decision regarding a job offer. Most importantly, make sure it meets your needs, whether short-term or long-term. It is reasonable and generally expected that you will take a few days or a week to make your decision. This does not mean that you will be regarded as indecisive. Instead, you could be perceived as thoughtful, reflective, and capable of making an informed choice.

Accepting or Rejecting Job Offers

Generally, you have three choices to make when presented with a job offer. You can ask for time to consider the offer, you can reject the offer, or you can accept the offer (or counter offer). Each of these options is appropriate under certain conditions.

Asking for more time to make a decision can be useful when you need time to consider the offer or when you are waiting for outside conditions to become apparent. For example, if you are waiting for another offer, it may be to your advantage to delay. In stalling, two things are important. First, you must communicate sincere appreciation and respect for the offer. The offer was extended as an invitation to you to join the organization. Even if you do not believe the offer is fair, it is still an invitation. Professional behavior requires that gratitude be communicated. Second, communicate your reason for delaying as is appropriate. For example, if you applied for a position as a clinical dietitian and were offered a position in the oncology ward but you really want to work in the pediatric ward, you may choose to stall to gather more information such as the availability of the desired position. Again, asking for time to gather information to make an informed choice is generally accepted by employers. However, be careful to not over-extend their patience. The job offer was made because there was a need to fill an open position.

Rejecting an offer is another choice. Only you can decide when to reject an offer. It is very appropriate to ask for or negotiate changes prior to rejecting an offer. If you are interested in the job but one deciding factor is keeping you from accepting it, then put your issue/request on the table. Give the potential employer a chance to respond. If characteristics of the job or compensation will never meet your needs, then sincerely thank the employer for the offer while you reject it. It is a good idea to end your relationship by saying something positive about the organization, the product or service, or the people you encountered. Be careful to not burn bridges, however, as you never know when you will have a future professional relationship with someone in the organization. Even if you reject the offer, leave a positive impression. Typically, a candidate rejects an offer during a meeting or phone conversation and then sends a follow-up letter to the employer. After all, there may be a future opportunity with that organization.

The third alternative is, of course, to accept the job offer. Once again, show your sincere appreciation for the invitation to join their organization. Once you have decided to accept the offer, let the employer know verbally. Follow up with an acceptance in writing. Once you have accepted an offer, do not continue interviewing, as you will run the risk of others relaying this information back to your new employer. Once you have accepted the offer, do not change your mind.

Whether you delay, reject, or accept the job offer, always remember to maintain professional behavior. It may seem that your actions and behaviors are in a vacuum, but in most industries and career fields, people are tightly connected. The networking activity you conducted throughout your job search will continue throughout your career.

When You Are Not Offered the Job

Stephanie had been job hunting for several months. She had yet to have an offer extended, but she felt that this one might be different. Stephanie knew that she nailed both interviews. At the end of the second interview, the hiring manager congratulated her and told her she was the one who was being recommended for the job. Stephanie knew this was the right job for her. She felt well qualified, liked the people she had met in the organization, and knew the company was up and coming. She could easily take the bus to work and relished the opportunity to work in the downtown location. All she needed to do was to wait for the formal offer from the human resources department, maybe negotiate the salary, and get ready to begin. The problem was, the offer never came.

Stephanie had carried her cell phone with her everywhere for days following her interviews. A call never came. She began to wonder. Did she misunderstand the hiring manager? She assured herself that she had heard correctly. She remembered the hiring manager saying she was the most qualified candidate. She supposed that the offer must be tied up in paperwork. More days went by. She felt at the mercy of the human resources department. Finally, she called the hiring manager only to find out that the job had been offered to someone else.

One of the most difficult aspects of job hunting is repeated rejection. When an employer does not make an employment offer, often it is because there was not a good match between your skills and the requirements of the position or there was a better match with someone else. It does not mean you are not capable or valuable. So what should you do?

Before you begin the job search again, ask some questions. If you have the opportunity, ask the employer about the person they did hire. Did the person have more experience? A better alignment of needed skills? Different strengths? Next, tell yourself that it is a matter of finding the right match. You do not need multiple matches, just one.

As soon as you can, begin the job search again. If you are sure this is the right career track for you, begin in full force. If you are unsure, take a step back and review your goals and objectives. Are they right for you? When you do begin the search again, follow multiple leads simultaneously. Your job-searching skills are well honed and you are better prepared after a rejection to obtain the best position for you.

Changing Jobs and Careers

Once you have accepted a job and entered a career field, are you destined to stay there? Traditionally, this was a widely held expectation for new professionals. Today, the answer is that you probably will not stay in one job throughout your career. In fact, you will probably change jobs at least a half-dozen times during your career span. You may even change career fields more than once.

How can you effectively make a career change? The answer is to go back a few steps and repeat the process you have already completed. If you simply desire to change jobs, begin the job-hunting process again. Write your goals and objectives and then make an action plan. This is an important step that will keep you from flitting from one job to another. If you know what you want, job changes can be strategic and well planned. Each job change may take you further along in your action plan. If you have discovered what you do not like in a job, it may help you make a better choice in a new job.

If you do change jobs, consider your employer's predicament. Give ample notice of your leaving. Generally, two weeks is considered adequate notice in business or industry. However the timeline for notification about leaving a job varies by type of employer and contract (such as in a teaching position). To keep relationships positive, offer to train your replacement. Although many career counselors recommend you secure employment prior to leaving your present employer, this may not be the most desirable option in an unpleasant or unsafe environment.

One way to make a career change is to hire oneself! Young professionals are increasingly interested in starting their own business for two reasons: the lack of job security in today's economy and the perceived benefits of self-employment, such as more control over one's schedule and work environment. Family and consumer sciences career fields provide many opportunities for small businesses, such as clothing boutiques, day care centers, restaurants, geriatric care services, interior design firms, and consulting services in nutrition or family financial planning.

If you desire to make a career change, go back to looking inward (self-assessment), followed by looking outward (researching career opportunities), and then finally making connections in your pursuit of a job in a new career field.

Summary

After looking inward and assessing your skills, interests, and needs, you looked outward and made connections to career fields and industries that supported your interests and needs. Your next stage is to find a job that fulfills your interests and needs. Searching for a job is often viewed as hard work, but with focus and organization, it can be an easier and more enjoyable experience.

The first step toward finding a job is to set career goals and objectives and then make an action plan. This will help you in your search. If you find a job that is appropriate to your goals, you will know. If the wrong job becomes available to you, you will also understand why it is not appropriate. In fact, this step will come full circle when you evaluate and eventually accept or reject a job based on your established goals and objectives. These should be the criteria on which to base your decision. If you do not receive a job offer, it will also help you assess why the job was not a good match.

Finding a job is an exercise in selling yourself. Job leads can be found through networking, electronic bulletin boards and databases, job fairs, and company websites. Publicity about yourself in the form of cover letters and résumés must be carefully crafted so that future employers can see your gifts and potential. Cover letters and résumés are your introduction to a potential employer. Manage your online presence as well to create a professional image. A positive first impression can get you the interview that may lead to employment.

The next step in job hunting is a successful interview. It is important to be familiar with employment laws when interviewing. It is also important to be prepared. Preparation for a job interview includes familiarizing yourself with the potential employer, practicing mock interviews, being properly attired, and being prepared with the right information. Plan to arrive early for the job interview. During the interview, offer direct answers and minimize nervous actions. After the interview, send a personal thank-you note to each person who interviewed you.

When you receive a job offer, take time to carefully consider how your goals and objectives match with the employer's objective. Will accepting the job offer help you to move forward in your action plan? Evaluate the position itself, the work you would perform, and the organization as a whole. Consider salary and benefits. Sometimes generous and diverse benefits make up for a lower salary. Other times a generous salary is minimized by inadequate benefits. Also consider the geographic location and overall match between your personal needs and what the employer has to offer.

Job hunting can lead to repeated rejections from potential employers until the right match is made. Remember, not being selected for a job is not a personal rejection; it is a mismatch between you and the potential employer. Take time to research and evaluate why it was not perceived to be a good match. If you believe it could have been a good match, brainstorm ways you can present yourself differently in future interactions with potential employers.

For most people, job changes and even career changes can happen throughout their career path. Changing jobs requires you to go back to the beginning and start the job search steps over again. Changing your career will require you to go back further to looking inward, looking outward, and then beginning the job search again. Sometimes it even requires additional education and retraining.

An effective job search takes hard work, patience, and stretching beyond boundaries of what may be personally comfortable. Careful consideration of opportunities will pay off in a job match that meets both your needs and the needs of the employer.

Questions for Thought

1. Make a list of companies or organizations for which you would like to work. Make your list without regard for what industry they are in or present job openings. What characteristics make these companies or organizations attractive to you?

2. What are common characteristics of résumés in your field of interest?

3. Where would you go to find reference materials on companies in which you have an interest? If you are unsure where to begin, visit your university reference librarian or career counselors.

4. What are your greatest strengths? In what areas could you use the most improvement when interviewing? How can you overcome these challenges?

References and Resources

Bolles, R. (2012). *What color is your parachute? 2012: A practical manual for job-hunters and career-changers.* New York: Ten Speed Press.

Bolles, R. N. (2010). *What color is your parachute? Job hunter's workbook.* New York: Ten Speed Press.

Bridges, W. (2003). *Managing transitions: Making the most of change.* Philadelphia, PA: Perseus.

DiTomaso, N., & Post, C. (Eds.). (2004). *Diversity in the workforce.* Oxford, England: Elsevier.

Edwards, P., & Edwards, S. (2008). *Finding your perfect work* (3rd ed.). [e-book] Distributed by Rosetta Solutions, Inc. www.RosettaSolutions.com

Frazier, B., & Niehm, L.S. (2008). FCS students' attitudes and intentions toward entrepreneurial careers. *Journal of Family and Consumer Sciences, 100*(2), 17-24.

Han, P. (2005). *Nobodies to somebodies: How 100 great careers got their start.* New York: Portfolio.

Howard, E. (2004). *Career pathways: Preparing students for life.* Thousand Oaks, CA: Corwin Press.

Jansen, J. (2003). *I don't know what I want, but I know it's not this: A step-by-step guide to finding gratifying work.* East Rutherford, NJ: Penguin.

Krumboltz, J. D., & Levin, A. S. (2004). *Luck is no accident: Making the most of happenstance in your life and career.* Atascadero, CA: Impact.

Noble, D.F. (2012). *Gallery of best resumes: A collection of quality resumes by professional resume writers.* Indianapolis, IN: JIST Pub.

Pollak, L. (2012). *Getting from college to career.* New York: Harper.

Tieger, P. D., & Barron, B. (2007). *Do what you are: Discover the perfect career for you through the secrets of personality type* (4th ed.). New York: Little, Brown.

Tullier, M. (2004). *Networking for job search and career success.* Indianapolis, IN: JIST.

Zunker, V.G. (2012). *Career counseling: A holistic approach* (8th ed.). Belmont, CA: Brooks/Cole/Cengage Learning.

On the Internet

http://www.aafcs.org/Resources/Careers.asp—the American Association of Family and Consumer Sciences Career Connection where you can post your résumé anonymously and view available jobs

http://www.careeronestop.org—sponsored by the U.S. Department of Labor, provides many tools for job seekers

http://www.chn.org/jobs—the Coalition on Human Needs posts job openings in human services and offers internships for students

http://www.jobhuntersbible.com—a companion site to Dick Bolles' *What color is your parachute?*, this site provides links to many electronic job boards

http://www.linkedin.com—a site specifically designed for professional networking purposes

http://www.socialservice.com—SocialService.Com posts jobs in social services

Chapter 17

Making an Impact

After studying this chapter you will be able to:

- describe work habits, attitudes, and health habits that lead to career success.

- evaluate an organization's culture.

- differentiate between time management and life-work balance.

- compare and contrast different career development models.

- explore possibilities for lifelong learning.

When her alarm clock went off at 6:00 a.m., Jordan was already wide awake. She could not recall the last time she readily woke up at this early hour of the morning, but she knew that today was different. College graduation was weeks behind her, and today was the first day of her new full-time job in the career field she had been hoping to enter for the past two years. She was living in a new apartment, in a different city, and held a new status as a college graduate. What would the day hold? What would her boss and coworkers be like? Did her education adequately prepare her to perform the expected job duties? Did she choose the right major and career? Would she be successful in her career? What would happen to life as she knew it?

Congratulations, you landed a job! So now you can kick back and relax, right? The short answer is no. Now is the time to approach your career with strategies that will enhance your opportunity for success and satisfaction. Leaving school and entering the workforce is an exciting, intimidating time of exploration. You may think of your first professional job as the crowning achievement of your educational experiences, knowledge, and insights. However, changes that will occur in the next few years require willingness to learn and grow. These changes may present themselves as exhilarating opportunities or frustrating challenges. You will encounter situations for which your education did not prepare you.

Change is inevitable but not always easy. It is not always easy because it requires you to bend and to be flexible. Bending and flexing often result in personal growth and development that would not occur without change. Most people resist change to some degree because stretching and growing is not always pleasant. In fact, it may be painful.

It is best to anticipate and approach the changes and challenges that are inevitable as proactively as possible. Try to look beyond the present into the future result or impact on you as a professional. Do not be afraid of mistakes or failure. If you enter the work world with an open mind, open eyes, a willingness to adjust to changes, and common sense, you will fare better than those who resist change. As the old saying goes, "If it does not break you, it will only make you stronger."

Work Habits and Attitudes That Lead to Career Success

You have worked hard to achieve your academic goals and are ready to enter the workforce. You probably put effort into being a good roommate, friend, family member, neighbor, and a responsible citizen. The same skills used in these situations are important in the workplace. However, in many ways, being a good coworker or colleague requires more effort. You may, after all, spend much more time with coworkers than family members, roommates, or neighbors. Coworkers often share small spaces for many hours a day. Sharing the coffeemaker, copier, refrigerator, and company resources can elicit feelings of frustration. It is not always easy to coexist and be productive when deadlines approach and differences in temperaments, opinions, and problem-solving styles emerge.

Your reputation is important to career success. Have you ever heard the expression "reputation is everything"? There is a reason this phrase has endured for some time. Whether it is the reputation of a business, a consumer product, a service, or a person, reputation is directly related to the quality of relationships established. It endures over time and is not based on short-term relationships. When dealing with people, reputations are established over time and with repeated contact. Because workplace environments create repeated contacts over time with both constituents and coworkers, establishing a good personal reputation is critical to your career success.

In specific terms, a reputation for excellence includes dependability, responsibility, showing respect, and the ability to be a team player. Employers also desire workers who can see the big picture, have a can-do attitude, and have a willingness to stretch and grow. These attitudes and behaviors combined with healthy living habits can lead to career success. Although many people dream of career success, common mistakes, such as the following, can keep them from being considered for promotions or increased responsibilities:

- having a negative attitude
- being difficult to work with and/or unable to get along with others
- having a narrow-minded view of your role in the organization
- not paying attention to details
- not treating others with respect, regardless of title or position
- being untrustworthy, spreading rumors, or failing to maintain confidentiality
- blaming others for your mistakes
- not doing your fair share of work
- failing to do what you say you will do
- cheating or stealing
- acting in a vengeful way
- embellishing the truth or lying
- speaking poorly of your former employer or coworkers
- using vulgar language or telling racist, sexist, or off-color jokes
- having an affair with, openly flirting with, or harassing coworkers

Whatever you do, avoid making these common mistakes. Instead, focus on the positive behaviors and attitudes discussed in the following sections. These behaviors and attitudes are not always easy, but your reputation for excellence will develop over time. In the long run, you will reap the benefits.

Dependability

Whom do you depend on in your life? When asked this question, you probably considered the qualities of people in your life and chose those whom you trust and on whom you can depend. These are the people who will come to your aid when needed. In the workplace, dependability or reliability is highly valued. *Dependability* in the workplace includes showing up when agreed on, consistency in temperament and reactions to situations, and willingness to help where needed. People who are dependable are reliable and steadfast. They are trustworthy, loyal, and faithful to the mission of the organization.

It is easy to see why employers and coworkers greatly value employees who are dependable. For example, for interior designers, working with dependable contractors and subcontractors can mean the difference between getting jobs done or not. Contractors who show up when they say they will, provide the level of service expected, and show consistency through their work and behavior are highly valued by interior designers and their clients.

Responsibility

Imagine you are a counselor in a family services organization. It is 6:00 p.m. on a cold, rainy Friday night. A family who was evicted from their home makes a desperate call to you. You are ready to leave the office, and it would be easy for you to tell them to call back on Monday morning. Instead, you take the time to give them information on homeless shelters that are open for the weekend and which ones in particular will take children at the last minute. You go one step further by calling a shelter and arranging for their arrival. You meet them there and offer them meal vouchers for a local restaurant. Because you took the time to follow through, you will now be a few minutes late for dinner with friends. Even so, you follow through with your responsibility to aid homeless families even when it causes you some inconvenience.

Responsibility means being committed 100 percent of the time in all obligations, relationships, and actions. It means not blaming someone else when things do not go exactly as planned. When you are working on a team, responsibility means giving your all even if other team members don't do the same. You will earn respect from others and a reputation for accomplishment and trustworthiness, and you will feel more in control of your own destiny.

Responsibility is related to dependability, but it goes one step further. Responsibility means carrying a project through to the end whether or not the process is easy. If you are given a task, taking responsibility means you will see the task through to completion. You may enlist others to assist you, but you remain the ultimate person who has responsibility to get the job done. The more responsibility you demonstrate to your employer, colleagues, students, clients, or customers, the more responsibility you will be given.

It is easy to be responsible when things are going your way and when all parties involved are in agreement. It is more difficult to complete a task when people and situations seem to go against your efforts. Responsible people often enjoy getting a job done despite hurdles, not because they like to lord authority over others but because the finished task brings satisfaction.

Respect

"The customer is always right." "Always make your boss look good." These are common sayings or words of advice in the workplace. Both of these opinions refer to showing respect. *Respect* means acknowledging people, especially those who are in positions above you, by showing respectful behavior.

It is natural human behavior to want to make yourself look good. Everyone wants to be admired. It is often much more difficult to make your boss look good or to concede a point to a customer. Showing respect does not mean you behave submissively. It also does not require setting aside your own opinions and values. Instead, it means showing regard for another's behavior or expectations, while keeping your place in mind. Showing respect and conceding authority to someone who outranks you is called *deference*. For example, in college, showing deference toward a professor should include respectful behavior in the classroom and respect for his or her course requirements or standards due to the fact that he or she is highly educated or trained in the content area.

Deference means giving the professor the benefit of the doubt that his or her methods of teaching the course content will be effective in the end. Showing deference means you try your best to make the situation a good one. If the professor is abusive or you feel the course content or delivery is ineffective, you have the right and responsibility to respectfully make your opinion known using the appropriate channel and to expect to be heard.

Many new professionals make the mistake of not acknowledging their place in the workplace organization. Even the most casual, unstructured organizations have hierarchies. They may just be more difficult to identify. Be sure you fully understand an organization's hierarchical structure when employment begins. When you know whom you are working for (and those in positions above), be sure to show her or him proper deference. Do not address people who are older or outrank you by their first name unless they specifically ask you to do so. In some organizations, certain nonsupervisory positions are shown deference. Whether a person is your student, another professional, a customer, or your boss, you will be the one who benefits in the long run by understanding the importance of deference.

Team Player

In survey after survey, employers list interpersonal skills as the number one characteristic desired in potential employees. People with good interpersonal skills are able to get along with others in the workplace and are able to participate as effective team players. Being a *team player* means cooperating with others to accomplish a task and being cordial toward your fellow team members. As a child, you learned what it meant to cooperate. Cooperation is not just for the recess playground; it is also a critical skill for the workplace. Cooperative teams are much more creative than teams consisting of individualists. Teams also encourage individual members to use their skills and talents, bringing out the best in every person.

Most people have experienced negative teamwork at some point. Often, this is a result of either an undefined task or, more likely, a lack of teamwork. Team players should be supportive, encouraging, accommodating, and, most importantly, responsible. Always be prepared to share the credit with others and focus on the task rather than differences in personalities or styles of working. Always give credit to the team.

Collaboration is common in the workplace today. Because so much of work is now accomplished through teams, it becomes even more important to be a team player. Expect both departmental and cross-functional teams to be common. By being an effective team player, you build your reputation and increase your value to the organization.

Seeing the Big Picture or Thinking Holistically

A common derogatory statement is, "He cannot see the forest for the trees." Can you see the forest for the trees? Seeing the big picture means seeing past the small details and seeing the larger purpose. Some people get so bogged down in their own tasks that they lose sight of the big picture. They have a myopic view.

Seeing the big picture does not mean you should overlook the details of a job. In fact, many jobs require a high level of attention to details. However, the larger purpose should always be kept in mind. For example, if a fashion merchandiser is caught up in the details of designing and installing a new floor display but misses the larger purpose of selling the product, the work is useless. Likewise, if a dietitian counsels a client to reduce his or her fat intake but forgets the overall goal of better health through total dietary intake and other healthy habits, the larger picture is lost. Seeing the product or service through from beginning to end is a good way to keep the big picture in mind. In other words, focus on the bottom line and understand the steps needed to get there.

Developing a Positive Attitude

Why do some people love their work and others hate it? Although the type of work performed is important to personal satisfaction, theory and research suggest that a positive attitude also plays a large role in transcendent work. Having a positive attitude—a can-do attitude—means having the optimism and energy to positively relate to others and to complete a job. It is the desire to "make something happen." It is satisfaction with your work and your work environment.

Your coworkers will appreciate your positive attitude. Instead of continually complaining to fellow workers, a person with a positive attitude can see the good in situations. These people are generally more pleasant to be around, and their positive attitude often rubs off on coworkers.

Attitude is one side of the equation, while actual work is the other side. Sometimes it is difficult to change a person's attitude. Changing a person's work environment is much easier. High-quality and personally meaningful work is, therefore, the first step toward improving your work attitude. What high-quality or personally meaningful work entails is very individual and personal and requires much self-reflection. For most people, high-quality work is challenging, actualizing work that gives meaning and purpose to life. As you can imagine, it is much easier to have a positive attitude when meaningful work is before you. After establishing meaningful work, your reaction to your work is up to you.

Sometimes it takes a while to find meaningful work. How can you demonstrate a positive attitude that will aid you on your way to finding meaningful work? A positive attitude is still very important and highly valued by employers. Although you may not find long-lasting satisfaction in your current work, look for ways you can grow personally. Look for ways you can help other people grow personally and professionally as well. Your satisfaction may not come from your work, but you can be optimistic about your growth, development, and preparation for future work.

Understanding Organizational Culture

Imagine this. You show up for your first company picnic wearing shorts, a tank top, and flip-flops. You are ready for a good time. When you arrive, everyone else is dressed in well-coordinated sportswear such as khaki pants, button-down shirts, and sundresses. Is it all in your mind or is everyone a little guarded in their conversations with you? Did you miss a memo or do you not understand the organizational culture?

What is *organizational culture*? It is the assumptions, values, behaviors, and actions of people, the group norms and tangible signs of an organization. The *tangible* signs are easy to recognize. These include the "look" of the space, the typical clothing worn, and which accomplishments are highlighted. The *intangible* signs of organizational culture are basically the personality traits of the organization. Just as it is often difficult to capture the personality of a person, it is difficult to capture the personality of an organization in words. However, understanding the organizational culture of a company or other organization is critical to career success. Just as there are good matches between people, there are good matches between personalities of organizations and employees. When a good match is made, job stress is lower and employees are more productive.

So how can you figure out the culture of an organization? A good place to start is with the systems (company policies and procedures) and structures. Organizational systems include both inputs and outputs. Inputs are the processes used to create a product or service. They include how the organization values and uses people, facilities, space, and other resources such as technology. Outputs focus on the products or services that come out of the organization. The company image of an organization is promoted through advertising and marketing, while the product or service itself is a good indicator of organizational outputs.

The next step to understanding organizational culture is to listen to daily conversations and negotiations between members of the organization. These conversations are the result of negotiations or ongoing agreements on the policies, standards of practice, and procedures within the organization. Take time to listen and figure out the organizational culture of your workplace. Understanding and assessing the organizational culture can mean the difference between success and failure in the workplace. In addition to formal policies and procedures, often presented in an employee handbook, some questions to ask yourself and fellow employees to learn about your workplace culture are given in **Figure 17-1.**

Finally, review the published mission and goals of the organization. Although these should give you an idea about the organization, in reality there is sometimes a disparity between the published and actual mission and goals of an organization.

Business Etiquette

Tom had been working in his first post-college professional position for three months when he had his first evaluation conference with his supervisor. Tom expected to be praised for his work ethic, productivity, and creativity. He had been on time or early every day, frequently worked late, completed several projects, and made many suggestions about how to improve procedures in the office. He was genuinely shocked when the boss said that Tom was receiving a "below expectations" rating in his quarterly review. The reason? Coworkers and customers had complained that Tom was "rude," "inconsiderate," "too informal," and "immature." He gave several specific examples of Tom's inappropriate behavior. The boss handed him a book on etiquette, asked him to read it, and to meet with him in a week to discuss what he was going to do differently in the future. Tom thought, "Etiquette! Why do I need to learn a bunch of old-fashioned rules for which fork to use at a formal dinner?"

Etiquette simply means the socially accepted norms for behavior in interpersonal interactions. Etiquette for the workplace differs somewhat from etiquette in the social realm, and it differs from culture to culture. However, certain underlying principles apply: make people feel comfortable, respect privacy, respect shared space, and show appreciation.

Manners are passed from generation to generation, but when new technologies are introduced, it takes a while before a consensus is reached on the etiquette involving their use. For example, if you ask some acquaintances about the appropriate use of cell phones, you are likely to hear a litany of complaints. These include having to listen to others' cell phone conversations, being interrupted by ringtones during presentations, and coworkers who text and check e-mails during meetings. Such behaviors indicate a lack of respect for others. Turn off your phone or set it to vibrate when in a meeting. If you must take an important call, excuse yourself and speak out of earshot. Focus on the people who are physically present and remain engaged in the discussion rather than texting or checking e-mails.

Telephone etiquette for business, whether using landlines or cell phones, also includes the following:

- Identify yourself immediately with your full name when answering the phone or placing a call.

Workplace Culture Questions
What 10 adjectives describe your (or a selected) work organization?
What is valued and considered important?
Who gets promoted, and which behaviors get rewarded?
Who fits in and who does not?
Which projects/work tasks are valued the most?
Who gets the most resources allocated to their projects?
How and when does change occur in the organization?
Are policies and procedures strictly enforced or are they "guidelines"?

Figure 17-1 Discovering the answers to these questions can help you determine the type of culture that exists in your workplace.

- State the purpose of your call at once if the phone is answered by support staff.

- When leaving voice mail messages, say your name and number very slowly. Leave the number at the beginning and end of the message so that the recipient does not have to replay the entire message several times to catch the number.

- Return calls promptly and avoid putting a caller on hold for a long period of time.

- Avoid taking a call if you are in a scheduled appointment with someone. Remember the guideline that the person who is physically present takes priority.

The Internet has created a need for another area of etiquette sometimes called "netiquette." The business use of e-mail differs significantly from personal, social use. Keep in mind that your work e-mails are not private communications; they belong to your employer. Be sure to read and follow company policies about use of the Internet. Do not send anything in an e-mail that you would not want made public. Show respect for the recipients by using correct spelling, grammar, and punctuation. Failure to do so will convey that you are either careless or uneducated. In general, avoid texting abbreviations and emoticons. Carefully consider whether a request for a return receipt is absolutely necessary, because some people consider such a request intrusive. Think twice before forwarding an e-mail without the original sender's permission. If sending an e-mail to a number of people, you can protect the privacy of their e-mail addresses by sending the e-mail to yourself and putting the recipients in the BCC (blind carbon copy) section. Save jokes for social, not business, e-mail. Always remember that sensitive issues are best handled face-to-face, where nonverbal cues can make communication more effective.

Business meals are another situation where certain etiquette is expected. Whether your position involves only one meal function a year or several lunches per week with customers, you can create a negative or positive impression with manners. "Rules" for dining are designed to show consideration for others. For example, wait until everyone at the table has been served before beginning to eat (unless you are at a very long banquet table). If you remember that food is always in front of you or to your left and beverages to your right, you won't end up with your fork in someone else's salad. The napkin belongs on your lap, and if you leave the table, it goes on your chair until you return. The guidelines for cell phone use during meetings also apply to meal functions.

College students generally have more experience with fast-food outlets than fine dining, so you may feel ill at ease in more formal settings. Consult one of the many available business etiquette books for more guidance, and then plan a dinner at a nice restaurant with friends. With practice, following the rules of etiquette will become second nature and you can be confident in any situation.

Professional Image

You may believe the old saying that you "can't judge a book by its cover," but research shows that appearance is an important factor in career success. Deciding what to wear to an interview is probably easier than choosing a work wardrobe once you have been offered a position. Formal business clothing as described in Chapter 16 is the generally accepted dress for an interview for a professional position. However, appropriate attire for work differs and is based on the type of industry, the nature of the work, your level within the organizational hierarchy, geographic location, the events of the day, and possibly the day of the week.

In creative fields, fashion-forward, unusual, casual clothing may be acceptable. Other employers, such as government agencies, financial and educational institutions, and health organizations expect more traditional, conservative clothes. Employers may have written dress codes or unwritten but generally understood expectations. It is perfectly appropriate to contact your new supervisor or human resources office to ask about dress expectations before reporting to work. In the first days, it is wiser to dress more formally than too casually. You can easily remove a jacket or tie if your coworkers are dressed more casually.

Even within the same organization, you will find levels of formality of dress. Employees who do not interact with the public may dress more casually than those who represent the company to clients. Individuals at the top of an organization tend to dress more formally; their appearance reinforces their authority. Image consultants suggest that you dress for the job you want, rather than the job you have. Dressing like those one or two levels above you in the hierarchy helps others picture you in that position.

In your personal life, self-expression and comfort might guide your clothing choices, but at work your appearance reflects on your employer. Your image should be one that makes other people comfortable and inspires confidence in your professional capabilities. Keep generational differences in mind. Your definition of "too short" likely differs from that of older coworkers who expect skirts to be no shorter than two inches above the knee. Young men should realize that many people consider wearing hats indoors, except for religious reasons, to be rude. Likewise, keeping sunglasses on inside is interpreted as an attempt to avoid eye contact, and wearing earphones in the presence of others signals "don't talk to me." For more detailed suggestions on dressing for success, refer to one of the many books on the topic.

Health Habits for Career Success

Imagine you have a big presentation in an hour. Your client is ready to see your preliminary design for her new home. You had planned to spend yesterday and today preparing for the presentation, but the computers went down in your office. Yesterday, you spent an hour looking for your lost keys. Your boss stopped by

your office to chat several times and ended up giving you an additional project to do. This morning, you noticed your cat was lethargic and appeared ill. You were late coming to work anyway due to heavy traffic. Your mom sends an e-mail wondering why she has not heard from you. As the hour approaches, you feel the stress in your stomach. You did not have time for lunch and are feeling light-headed. Your boss stops by to tell you she will be sitting in on the meeting. Your client shows up and your heart races.

Life is full of time pressures and turmoil. Trying to meet deadlines, unexpected events, family issues—all of these combine to create a situation that makes your body react as if it were facing a physical threat. Being constantly in this state has many negative long-term effects. As you enter the workforce, make use of the variety of resources available that will help you deal with, avoid, or control your reaction to stress. These include stress management, time management, eating well and staying fit, and achieving life-work balance. The effort is worth it because the payoff is huge.

Stress Management

Stressed out. Overwhelmed. Anxious. Frazzled. Everyone has felt this way at some time or other. Stress is a fact of life, and it continues to plague workers. In fact, stress has been increasingly reported by workers in the past few decades. With all of the conveniences and technological advances, why is stress increasing? Some believe it comes from the difficulty in separating work from personal life. For many, it is difficult to leave work behind when cell phones and e-mail make work accessible 24 hours a day. Others believe it comes from increased choices. In earlier generations, fewer choices existed. Today, you are constantly faced with a multitude of options and information to promote those choices.

Stress comes from many sources. In the workplace, it can come from interactions with coworkers or your boss, the nature of the work itself, customer or client interactions, work expectations, or simply too much work. Environmental conditions such as lack of privacy, little natural lighting, or stagnant air can also cause stress. Although these are all common workplace conditions, personal stressors such as family issues, personal financial worries, and other demands can also add to stress in the workplace. Employers are concerned about the effect of stress on worker productivity and the long-term effects of stress on employee health and wellness.

How can you lower your stress level? It is really a matter of knowing yourself and maintaining control over your surroundings. The first step is to recognize its true source. Often, the source of stress is misidentified. For example, heavy traffic on the way to work is frustrating, and you may be late to work as a result. It is probably not the traffic itself that is causing the stress but your concern over not having enough time to finish your presentation and, ultimately, how you will be perceived by your boss and client. Although you may not have control over traffic, you do have some control over how you react.

Second, change your environment so demands are not so high. Stress develops when the demands in your life exceed your ability to cope with them. Often, perceived demands are self-established and may be unattainable. Third, learn how to better cope with the demands of your environment. Planning and forecasting can help relieve many stressful situations. It is impossible to eliminate all stress and, in some instances, stress or pressure can result in innovative solutions. Remember, different people react to stress differently. Find your own ways to manage stress and keep at it every day. When the big things come up, such as unexpected illness, job changes, or a work crisis, you will be better prepared to deal with them.

Eating Well and Staying Fit

Numerous research studies and employee surveys show that a healthy body can lead to increased energy and, subsequently, improved work performance (Tennant & Sperry, 2003). For many professionals, however, the workplace can be physically and emotionally taxing. You need energy to do your best work. How can you get it? There are several factors that play a role in your level of work energy. Some of these factors are individual, whereas others are environmental and work-related, such as excessive noise or poor lighting. Healthy eating habits and physical fitness are two important factors that lead to increased energy.

Healthy eating and active living not only increase energy levels, but they also play an important role in preventing and treating many diseases and conditions. For example, together they reduce the risk of heart disease and some forms of cancer as they reduce anxiety and stress. Healthy eating and exercise also elevate mood and self-esteem.

Many companies support employee wellness programs that incorporate a healthy balance between good nutrition and physical activity. Some employers offer on-site fitness centers, in-house weight loss programs, and incentive programs for employees who achieve and maintain healthy lifestyles. If your employer does not offer a wellness program, design your own. An abundance of solid nutrition and fitness information is readily available. Healthy eating requires well balanced, varied, and proportioned servings. Physical fitness can be incorporated throughout your day through walking and stretching. Remember, the connection between body and mind is far stronger then we sometimes are willing to accept.

Promoting Life-Work Balance

Moving from high school to college required new time-management skills. Studying between classes, juggling work or family responsibilities, and pursuing extracurricular interests required time-management skills from early morning to late afternoon that you may not have needed when you attended high school. In college, you probably spent less time in the classroom but more hours juggling study, work, extracurricular activities, and family and friends. Going into the workforce as a professional requires a new adjustment in time management. However, managing time does not necessarily equate to healthy life-work balance. For example, you may be very efficient in managing your time and completing tasks, but family relationships, volunteerism, personal health, spiritual development, and work toward future goals may suffer. Today, career experts emphasize life-work balance over time-management skills.

Life-work balance involves finding the fragile balance among the needs of family and friends; the organizations and causes you choose to serve; activities that promote your spiritual and/or physical health; intellectual and emotional growth; and the demands of a career. For most people, the concern is about more than just finding balance; it also includes making a difference in people's lives, in organizations, and in the community. Is life-work balance even a possibility or an elusive dream?

As you move through adult life stages, life-work balance may become more challenging rather than less challenging. Marriage, parenting, single-parenting, and taking care of other family members can make life-work balance more challenging to achieve. As people enter midlife, they often devote considerably more time to community service and other interests. In addition, midlife and older adults often find themselves in leadership roles in their homes, work, and communities.

Life-work balance requires a person to look at his or her life as a whole rather than compartmentalizing it into work, family, and other pursuits. Of course, the more overlap there is, the easier it is to balance different components. In today's environment, people are faced with more diversity, more choices, and greater access to a variety of experiences and responsibilities that demand time and effort. Some futurists believe that seeing life whole, finding the balance, is the ultimate challenge for the workforce of today and tomorrow.

The beginning of your career is the perfect time to consider how you can balance all of the parts of your life. With a background in family and consumer sciences, you are uniquely trained to understand the dynamics of issues surrounding life-work balance. For example, you understand families are unique ecosystems that are influenced by the input of their environment. You understand there will be competing interests, responsibilities, and needs among individuals. There will also be competing opportunities. Likewise, there will be people who will tell you how to balance your life-work. Ultimately, however, only you can figure out how to pack it all into one lifetime journey. It is a challenge that must be revisited again and again as your life and work change.

The Career Life Cycle

When many people begin their careers, their view of the future includes finding a professional position related to their education and training, subsequent pay raises and promotions, and finally retirement. Some people envision themselves moving from company to company, but still they often see their career as linear. Although many people still follow this traditional career path, it is far less common than it was for past generations. The *traditional linear career development model*, which progresses from education to employment to retirement, makes up a much smaller percentage of the total workforce than in previous years. Many futurists believe linear career paths will become even less common in upcoming years. Free-form and mixed-form career paths are becoming more common (Dolliver, 1999; Sterrett, 1999).

Free-form careers include entrepreneurial ventures, consulting work, contract and temporary work, and part-time work. They can also include volunteer or unpaid work. *Mixed-form careers* include some linear career tracks combined with periods of free-form career paths. For example, you may enter the workforce with a linear trajectory only to find yourself taking some time to pursue entrepreneurial ventures after a decade of experience. Later, you may reenter the traditional workforce, change careers, and consult during your later career years.

Changing career life cycles carry both positive and negative attributes, depending on the worker. Linear career paths are perceived to be much more stable and predictable. However, when the relationship between a long-term employer and employee is severed due to downsizing, layoffs, or termination, the impact on the employee is great. Free-form and mixed-career life cycles are much more flexible and often work well with a person's private life. However, stability of work and income is not present in most free-form career life cycles. There is no one right path for every individual. Certainly age, gender, social role, and cultural background play a significant role in career life cycle choices and the impact of these choices.

Lifelong Learning

Learning does not end when one or more academic degrees are earned. Learning continues throughout life. Learning throughout life does not just occur through life experiences. Today, people of all ages are enrolled in undergraduate degree programs, graduate degree programs, vocational training, apprenticeships, and formal mentoring programs. Classes in recreational pursuits and hobbies, such as cooking, gardening, and computer programming, are offered in community colleges and cooperative extension programs. Professional associations also support continuing education and professional development along with licensing requirements, certification, community involvement, and public policy advocacy. These forms of lifelong learning are discussed in the following pages.

Professional Association Membership

One of the best ways to know what is happening in your field is to join and actively participate in a *professional organization*. Most

professions have associations that provide leadership and service opportunities along with educational and employment resources for members. Membership in professional organizations not only provides resources but also provides networking opportunities. Most professional organizations hold conferences and meetings that serve to update professionals in their field of expertise. At these conferences and meetings, both formal and informal interactions create valuable networking contacts. Professionals who are active in their association(s) can access a network of colleagues and a ready support group when needed.

Several umbrella organizations for family and consumer sciences exist. The American Association of Family and Consumer Sciences (AAFCS) and the International Federation for Home Economics (IFHE) are two of the organizations that welcome members from diverse areas of specialization. Each family and consumer sciences specialization has several of its own professional organizations, such as the American Society for Interior Designers (ASID) and the American Apparel Manufacturers Association (AAMA). There are many advantages to joining a professional organization, especially as a beginning professional. Through newsletters, journals, online communities, webinars, and conferences, you can keep up with current events and future trends. Leadership positions are often available. These positions demonstrate commitment to the profession. Furthermore, joining a professional organization may help you to access job banks and career networking sessions open only to members.

Graduate School

For some college students, graduate school is in their immediate plans. For many others, graduate school is not considered until many years after they have established themselves in their field. For example, many people in the family services field choose to complete a master's degree or doctorate in their field in order to complete the credentials necessary to perform a given role such as a counselor, college professor, or social worker. To become a registered dietitian, a post-baccalaureate internship or master's degree is necessary unless you completed an accredited coordinated program in dietetics as an undergraduate. In other family and consumer sciences specializations, such as apparel design, a person may choose to complete a graduate degree later in his or her career in order to open up new career opportunities in supervisory roles or education.

The best way to approach the possibility of continuing your education with a graduate degree is to "never say never." Education levels are rising around the world, as discussed in Chapter 4, and many college graduates may find it desirable to further their education. With that in mind, it is a good idea to keep your options open. Academically, strive to do your best so your academic record reflects positively on you if and when you apply to graduate school. Academic references are also important in the process of applying to graduate school, so foster and maintain positive relationships with your professors and advisors.

Continuing Education

Continuing your education may not include completing a graduate degree. Instead, you may find the need or desire to gain further knowledge or skills without completing a degree. For example, you might find that taking an accounting course would greatly benefit your business background. If you are working in the design field, a course that teaches the newest computer-aided design software may make you more marketable or more efficient in your job. Teachers often take continuing education courses to learn new ways of teaching a subject to their students. In fact, many professional certifications require continuing education credits.

Required continuing education is usually very specific, and the number of credits and time allowance guidelines are spelled out. Professionals who are certified in family and consumer sciences (CFCS) must complete continuing education credits during a specified period in order to maintain their credentials. Registered dietitians must also complete continuing education credits to maintain their credentials. Depending on individual state requirements, counselors and teachers generally have continuing education requirements as well. Continuing education is considered essential for maintaining a current knowledge base for all of these specializations.

Community Involvement

In Chapter 3, the marks of a professional and professional ethics were discussed. Within the six pillars of professional ethics, caring and citizenship were highlighted. Caring involves being kind and compassionate to fellow human beings by expressing gratitude, forgiving others, and helping people in need. Citizenship involves doing what you can to make your community a better place. Becoming personally involved with issues in the community can be very gratifying, especially when your professional knowledge and skills can be put to use. Communities become better places for everyone, your professional and personal skills are enhanced, and networking with others can improve your interpersonal skills.

Community involvement can give you the opportunity to build your confidence as a professional in a setting that may be more flexible than an employment setting. Many career counselors advise college students and job seekers to utilize community service opportunities as a way to increase experience in their field. For people who take time off from their careers due to family or other personal responsibilities, community involvement, especially when professional skills are utilized, provides an effective forum for keeping professionally current.

Public Policy Advocacy

Public policy includes community and government policies, laws, standards, and regulations. In Chapter 5, the importance of public policy involvement for family and consumer sciences professionals was highlighted. It was noted that family and consumer sciences professionals have influenced public policy for over 100 years, beginning with the discipline's founder, Ellen Swallow Richards. Thousands of family and consumer sciences leaders have followed in her steps by advocating for public policies that improve individual well-being and family life as well as protecting consumers. Examples include personal hygiene and food sanitation education and legislation, career and technical training in public schools, textile safety and trade legislation, food labeling, housing standards, and early childhood care and education.

The mark of a family and consumer sciences professional is a concern for improving the life of individuals, families, and communities. For family and consumer sciences professionals, it is imperative that they advocate for public policies that improve quality of life. The benefits to the advocate and his or her community are immense.

Summary

As you leave school and prepare to enter the workforce, you will find the same skills for doing well in school are important in the workplace. However, in many ways, being a good coworker or colleague requires more effort than being a good student. Coworkers often share small spaces for many hours a day, and it is not always easy to coexist and be productive when deadlines approach and differences in temperaments, opinions, and problem-solving styles emerge.

Your reputation is important to career success. When dealing with people, reputations are established over time and with repeated contact. Because workplace environments create repeated contacts with both constituents and coworkers, establishing a good personal reputation is critical to your career success. A reputation for excellence includes dependability, responsibility, showing respect, and the ability to be a team player. Employers also desire workers who can see the big picture, have a can-do attitude, and have a willingness to stretch and grow.

Understanding the organizational culture of a company or other organization is critical to career success. This includes the assumptions, values, behaviors and actions of people, group norms, and tangible signs of an organization. Adapting to the organizational culture includes recognizing expected etiquette and standards for personal appearance. Just as there are good matches between people, there are good matches between personalities of organizations and employees. When a good match is made, job stress is lower and employees are more productive. Company policies and procedures, advertising and marketing, and the product or service offered are good indicators of organizational culture. Understanding and assessing the organizational culture can mean the difference between success and failure in the workplace.

Life is full of time pressures and turmoil. Being constantly in a state of stress and turmoil can have many negative long-term effects. As you enter the workforce, make use of the variety of resources available that will help you deal with, avoid, or control your reaction to stress. These include stress management, time management, eating well and staying fit, and achieving life-work balance. The benefit will be well worth the effort.

Entering the workforce as a professional requires a new adjustment in life-work balance. Life-work balance involves finding the fragile balance among the needs of family and friends, organizations and causes you choose to serve, activities that promote your spiritual and/or physical health, intellectual and emotional growth, and the demands of a career.

Learning does not end when one or more academic degrees are earned; it continues throughout life. Graduate degree programs, career training, apprenticeships, formal mentoring programs, recreational pursuits, and hobbies all play a part in continuing education. Professional associations also support continuing education and professional development along with licensing requirements, certification, community involvement, and public policy advocacy.

Questions for Thought

1. You have heard it said that "Attitude is everything." Perhaps you have heard the well-worn advice "What goes around, comes around," "Don't burn bridges," or "Patience is

a virtue." You can be assured career advice abounds. These adages offer wisdom that can be hard to remember on a daily basis. Ask someone you know who has been employed for at least 20 years which adages he or she finds to be the most important. Ask the person why he or she considers the adages to be important.

2. Seeing the big picture is an important personal attitude to cultivate. It takes practice to become aware of this attitude. For one week, look for examples of "seeing the big picture" and "focusing only on the details" in your daily conversations with people around you. Jot these examples down. Note whether the approach used was the best for solving the problem at hand.

3. Most advice related to attitudes that lead to successful careers can be condensed into cultivating a positive attitude. Having a positive attitude and a willingness to personally stretch and grow will often lead to career success. If a person is not naturally optimistic, how can this attitude be cultivated? Is perception more important than reality? Can a person be so overly optimistic that it becomes a detriment in the workplace?

References and Resources

Albion, M. (2000). *Making a life, making a living: Reclaiming your purpose and passion in business and in life*. New York: Warner Books.

Barkley, N., & Sandburg, E. (1995). *Taking charge of your career*. New York: Workman.

Bennis, W. (1997). *Leading people is like herding cats*. Provo, UT: Executive Excellence.

Bolles, R. (2012). *What color is your parachute? 2012: A practical manual for job-hunters and career-changers*. New York: Ten Speed Press.

Bossidy, L., & Charan, R. (2004). *Confronting reality: Doing what matters to get things right*. New York: Crown Business.

Butterfield, J. (2011). *Professionalism*. Boston, MA: Course Technology Cengage Learning.

Clayton, M. (2011). *Brilliant stress management: How to manage stress in any situation*. Harlow, England: Pearson Education.

Connellan, T. (2003). *Bringing out the best in others*. Austin: Bard Press.

Cook, R.A., & Cook, G.O. (2011). *Guide to business etiquette*. Upper Saddle River, NJ: Prentice Hall.

Covey, S. (1997). *The seven habits of highly effective families*. New York: Golden Books.

Covey, S. (2004). *The seven habits of highly effective people*. New York: Free Press.

Covey, S. (2004). *The 8th habit: From effectiveness to greatness*. New York: Free Press.

DeMarco, T. (2001). *Slack: Getting past burnout, busywork, and the myth of total efficiency*. New York: Broadway Books.

DiTomaso, N., & Post, C. (Eds.). (2004). *Diversity in the workforce*. Oxford, England: Elsevier.

Dolliver, M. (1999). Maybe it's not too late to become a fireman. *Adweek, 40*(36), 40.

Edwards, P., & Edwards, S. (2003). *Finding your perfect work: The new career guide to making a living, creating a life*. New York: J.P. Tarcher/Putnam.

Han, P. (2005). *Nobodies to somebodies: How 100 great careers got their start*. New York: Portfolio.

Howard, E. (2004). *Career pathways: Preparing students for life*. Thousand Oaks, CA: Corwin Press.

Jones, L. B. (2005). *The four elements of success*. Nashville, TN: Nelson Business.

Kegan, R., & Lahey, L. (2001). *How the way we talk can change the way we work: Seven languages for transformation*. San Francisco: Jossey-Bass.

Post, P., Post, A., Post, L., & Senning, D.P. (2011). *Emily Post's etiquette: Manners for a new world* (18th ed.). New York: Harper Collins.

Schneider, B., & Waite, J. (Eds.). (2005). *Being together, working apart: Dual-career families and the work-life balance*. New York: Cambridge University Press.

Scholl, A.T. (2010). *No sneakers at the office*. Crockett, TX: LandMarc Press.

Seligman, Martin E. P. (1990). *Learned optimism: How to change your mind and your life*. New York: Pocket Books.

Sterrett, E. (1999). A comparison of women's and men's career transitions. *Journal of Career Development*, *25*(4), 249-259.

Tennant, G., & Sperry, L. (2003). Work-family balance: Counseling strategies to optimize health. *The Family Journal*, *11*(4), 404-408.

Whitemore, J. (2011). *Poised for success*. New York: St. Martin's Press.

Zunker, V.G. (2012). *Career counseling: A holistic approach* (8th ed.). Belmont, CA: Brooks/Cole/Cengage Learning.

On the Internet

http://www.netmanners.com—provides information on e-mail etiquette including an opportunity to ask questions

http://www.emilypost.com—includes the Etipedia® an online etiquette encyclopedia with sections on interview etiquette and business manners

Appendix

National Standards for Family and Consumer Sciences Education

Standard 1: **Career, Community and Family Connections:** Integrate multiple life roles and responsibilities in family, work, and community settings.

Standard 2: **Consumer and Family Resources:** Evaluate management practices related to the human, economic, and environmental resources.

Standard 3: **Consumer Services:** Integrate knowledge, skills, and practices needed for a career in consumer services.

Standard 4: **Education and Early Childhood:** Integrate knowledge, skills, and practices required for careers in early childhood, education, and services.

Standard 5: **Facilities Management and Maintenance:** Integrate knowledge, skills, and practices required for careers in facilities management and maintenance.

Standard 6: **Family:** Evaluate the significance of family and its effects on the well-being of individuals and society.

Standard 7: **Family and Community Services:** Synthesize knowledge, skills, and practices required for careers in family and community services.

Standard 8: **Food Production and Services:** Integrate knowledge, skills, and practices required for careers in food production and services.

Standard 9: **Food Science, Dietetics, and Nutrition:** Integrate knowledge, skills, and practices required for careers in food science, food technology, dietetics, and nutrition.

Standard 10: **Hospitality, Tourism, and Recreation:** Synthesize knowledge, skills, and practices required for careers in hospitality, tourism, and recreation.

Standard 11: **Housing and Interior Design:** Integrate knowledge, skills, and practices required for careers in housing and interior design.

Standard 12: **Human Development:** Analyze factors that influence human growth and development.

Standard 13: **Interpersonal Relationships:** Demonstrate respectful and caring relationships in the family, workplace, and community.

Standard 14: **Nutrition and Wellness:** Demonstrate nutrition and wellness practices that enhance individual and family well-being.

Standard 15: **Parenting:** Evaluate the effects of parenting roles and responsibilities on strengthening the well-being of individuals and families.

Standard 16: **Textiles, Fashion, and Apparel:** Integrate knowledge, skills, and practices required for careers in textiles and apparel.

Developed by the National Association of State Administrators of Family and Consumer Sciences (NASAFACS) http://nasafacs.org/national-standards--competencies.html/

Glossary

A

academic study. Learning through textbooks, discussion groups, instructors, and other classroom activities. (15)

Academy of Nutrition and Dietetics (AND). The largest organization for food and nutrition professionals. It includes the Accreditation Council for Education in Nutrition and Dietetics (ACEND), which grants accreditation status to approved higher education programs. The AND also provides educational programs and conferences, research updates, and information on current trends. In addition, the AND credentials individuals through the Commission on Dietetic Registration. (6)

account manager. A professional in a business setting who is responsible for the overall satisfaction of a major client or customer, selling products or services, and understanding the desires, needs, and problems of individuals within the client company. (13)

accredited financial counselor. A financial counselor who has received certification from the Association for Financial Counseling and Planning Education. (13)

action plan. A systematic plan for attaining your goals. (16)

activity assistant. One who assists an activity director. (12)

activity director. A professional who works to meet the leisure and educational needs of the elderly or disabled. Activity directors may work in adult day care programs, retirement communities, senior citizen centers, hospices, and assisted living or long-term care facilities. Their clients may also include individuals of any age who have disabilities. (12)

administrative dietitian. A dietitian who manages food service operations, often in noncommercial food service organizations such as educational institutions, health care facilities, correctional institutions, businesses and industries, government agencies, and the military. Responsibilities include menu planning, purchasing, and supervising staff in food preparation and delivery. (6)

adult education. Educational opportunities for adults outside the traditional degree-seeking programs of colleges and universities. Generally administered through state and community agencies, adult education may include adult literacy programs, workforce development programs, technical training, high school degree equivalency programs, English as a second language (ESL) programs, or basic academic skill development in math, science, or computers. (10)

Age Discrimination in Employment Act of 1967 (ADEA). A law that protects individuals who are 40 years of age or older from discrimination because of age. (16)

American Job Center. A comprehensive online source that provides a single access point for key federal programs and critical local resources to help you research careers, prepare for careers, and locate specific jobs. (16)

Americans with Disabilities Act (ADA). A federal law that prohibits employment discrimination against qualified individuals with disabilities in the private sector and in state and local governments. (16)

apparel design. The segment of the apparel industry that conceives and creates garments. (8)

apparel designer. A professional who is involved in tasks such as cutting and sewing sample garments as well as selecting fabrics, trimmings, and notions for designs. Other activities include selling a design line (collection of related designs) to company merchandisers, working with manufacturing and production managers, and collecting sales data. (8)

apparel industry. The industry responsible for all fashion apparel processes from conception through final production. In this segment of the industry, apparel designers create clothing that will meet the needs of consumers, and manufacturers produce apparel that meets the functional, fashion, and financial desires and constraints of consumers. (8)

apparel production management. The segment of the fashion industry that involves the administration of all aspects of the apparel manufacturing process from start to finish. (8)

apparel trade. The business segment that focuses on the conception, production, marketing, and sales of textile and apparel products. (Also called the fashion industry.) (8)

appraiser. A professional who determines the relative value of a property. (9)

asset property manager. A professional who oversees the financial status of properties and reports relevant information such as occupancy rates, the status of leases, and other financial matters to property owners. (9)

assets. All the things you have going for you, including your personal characteristics, experiences, resources, education, and skills. (14)

benefits. Nonsalary services or rights provided by an employer. Benefits may include flexible schedules, tuition or sales discounts, award ticket miles from air travel, holidays and vacations, compensatory time, insurance coverage, or any number of benefits that have value to employees. (15)

career center. A resource located on college and university campuses that offers an abundance of career information to students and alumni, such as counseling, self-assessment tests, résumé writing help, internship and job postings and contacts, job shadowing programs, and help in choosing a major and connecting the chosen major to possible careers. (15)

career databases. Private and commercial resources available to students and job seekers on the Internet. (15)

career fair. A formal gathering of dozens or even hundreds of potential employers in one place at one time. (16)

career goal. A future career ambition or aspiration. (16)

career objective. A specific and measurable statement about what you want to be doing, what kind of organization you desire to work with, or the type of people with whom you want to work. (16)

caregiver specialist. A professional who provides information and resource and referral services to support caregivers. Caregiver specialists typically work for government agencies, such as an Area Agency on Aging. (12)

case manager. (Sometimes called a case coordinator or caseworker.) A professional who works directly with clients from all representative populations. Case managers are responsible for developing appropriate case plans as well as helping direct care managers develop specific plans. (11)

catering. Providing food and beverages for special occasions, one-time or infrequent events, or regularly scheduled events. (7)

Certified Family Life Educator (CFLE). A designation that recognizes the educational, preventive, and enriching nature of the work of family life educators. (11)

certified financial planner. A financial planning expert who has been credentialed by the Certified Financial Planner Board of Standards. (13)

Certified Personal and Family Finance Educator. A credential awarded by the American Association of Family and Consumer Sciences to individuals who pass the required exam. (13)

child care center director. A professional who is responsible for the overall operation of a day care center. (12)

child life assistant. One who works under the direction of a child life specialist. (12)

child life specialist. A professional who helps children and their families deal with the stress of hospitalization and traumatic events such as injury, chronic illness, health care procedures, or the death of a loved one. (12)

civic engagement. A process by which different voices, opinions, and perspectives are shared and oriented toward mutual understanding with the goal of making a difference in the life of the community. (5)

clinical dietitian. A health care professional who holds the credentials of registered dietitian. (6)

collaboration. The process of partnering with others to accomplish a goal. (5)

colorist. A textile designer who creates a variety of different color combinations for a design. (8)

commercial food service. Food service establishments that prepare and serve food to the general public for profit . (7)

commercial interior design. Design that encompasses all kinds of nonresidential interior spaces, such as offices, restaurants, religious facilities, recreational and community centers, health care facilities, schools, libraries, museums, and retail spaces. (9)

commercial interior designer. A professional who focuses on creating safe, efficient, functional, and aesthetically pleasing interior spaces for commercial uses. (9)

communication skills. Skills (spoken, written, or nonverbal) needed to interact with others. (14)

community association manager. A professional who oversees the common property in multifamily residences such as apartment or condominium complexes. (9)

community dietitian. A nutritionist who works to identify nutrition and food consumption issues and helps individuals and families resolve problems and improve their quality of life. (6)

community service. Volunteer work to improve the quality of life in a community. (15)

consumer affairs specialist. A professional who advocates for consumer rights and mediates between interested parties. (13)

consumer credit counselor. A professional who works with consumers by educating them on ways to avoid and reduce personal debt. (13)

consumerism. The idea that increased consumption of goods is good for individuals and the economy. (1)

consumer researcher. A professional who collects data about consumer decision making, spending, savings, and values and disseminates it in a usable form. (13)

convention service manager. A hospitality professional who plans, coordinates, and implements events in hotels, including conferences, meetings, trade shows, or other special events. (7)

cooperative extension agent. A professional who provides educational programs in family and consumer sciences, 4-H youth development, agriculture, and community and rural development. (10)

cooperative extension service. Also known as the Extension Service of the United States Department of Agriculture (USDA), this service provides nonformal educational programs designed to help people use research-based knowledge to improve their lives. (10)

corporate trainer. A business professional who designs, conducts, and supervises development programs for employees or members of organizations. (10)

counselor. A professional who offers psychological evaluation and care for clients. (11)

course planner. A plan that structures the courses and terms remaining to complete your degree. (15)

cover letter. A letter of introduction to a potential employer. (16)

critical care specialist. A clinical dietitian who works with patients who are critically or terminally ill, sometimes called a *nutrition support dietitian*. (6)

customer service representative. A professional who serves as the direct contact between a company and the customer before, during, and after a customer purchase. (13)

D

dependability. A quality of employees who are consistent in temperament and reactions to situations, willing to help where needed, reliable and steadfast, trustworthy, loyal, and faithful to the mission of the organization. (17)

development director. A family and community services professional who implements strategies for securing funding to meet program goals and objectives. (11)

diabetes specialist. In reference to a clinical dietitian: one who develops nutrition care plans and helps patients and their families manage diabetes through nutrition and exercise. (6)

dietetics. The science of helping people to apply and use nutrition knowledge to improve their health and wellness. (6)

dietetic technician, registered. *See* registered dietetic technician.

dualistic economy. An economy in which critical masses can be found at the two ends of the economic spectrum with a diminishing middle class between the two. (4)

E

early intervention specialist. A professional who works to improve the life prospects for children who may be at risk because of poverty, low birth weight, disabilities, or other factors that may hinder their development. Professionals in this field may also be called case managers, service coordinators, or home visitors. (12)

ecological theory of development. Developmental psychologist Urie Bronfenbrenner's theory to describe a person's social, emotional, physical, and cognitive development within the context of his or her environment. (2)

ecosystem. The interdependence of humans on many factors both within and with the environment as referred to in the ecological theory of development. (2)

electronic portfolio. A creative means of organizing, summarizing, and sharing information, along with personal and professional growth, in an electronic format. (15)

employment application. A form used by employers to collect important information from potential employees, such as their name, Social Security number, address, telephone number, previous work experience, salaries, and references. (16)

Equal Employment Opportunity Commission (EEOC). A U.S. government commission that oversees and enforces all federal equal employment opportunity policies, regulations, and practices. (16)

Equal Pay Act (EPA). A federal law that protects men and women who perform substantially equal work in the same establishment from gender-based wage discrimination. (16)

escrow officer. A professional who coordinates the conduct and the transfer of property ownership. (In more complex transactions, attorneys and accountants are involved.) (9)

event planner. A professional who works with clients to plan events such as weddings, festivals, or conventions. Event planners meet with clients to understand the purpose of the event and determine the budget, time, location, and activities. They contract for services from vendors such as florists, photographers, and musicians and arrange for food service and lodging. (7)

executive chef. A food service professional in charge of the menu planning and food preparation in a restaurant. (7)

executive director. A family and community services professional responsible for the overall management and leadership of an organization. (11)

exhibit designer. A professional who creates displays for trade shows, libraries, and other organizations. (9)

F

family. The basic unit in which two or more people are sharing emotional, social, physical, and economic resources. (2)

Family, Career, and Community Leaders of America (FCCLA). A nonprofit student leadership group that promotes application of family and consumer sciences content in schools, at home, and in the community. (10)

family and consumer sciences. A discipline and a profession that focuses on an integrative approach to the reciprocal relationships among individuals, families, and communities, as well as the environments in which they function. (1)

Family and Medical Leave Act (FMLA). A law that allows eligible workers up to 12 weeks per year of unpaid leave for family caregiving without loss of job security or health benefits. (4)

family day care home provider. A professional who provides day care for a limited number of children in his or her own home. (12)

family ecosystem model. A theoretical model for a family's interaction with its environments. (2)

family policy. Programs and legislation that specifically benefit individuals and families. (5) (11)

fashion. Apparel design that undergoes frequent changes because of social, psychological, and economic factors; the latest and most admired styles of apparel and appearance. (8)

fashion forecaster. A professional who reviews significant social developments, political events, economic trends, and weather changes to determine what consumers will demand in clothing in the future. The forecaster conveys trends through forecasting publications, subscription websites, and training seminars. (8)

fashion industry. The business segment that focuses on the conception, production, marketing, and sales of textile and apparel products. (Also called the apparel trade.) (8)

fashion journalist. A professional who disseminates information about fashion and beauty trends for consumers. (8)

fashion merchandiser. A professional who performs the duties of marketing and selling fashion. (8)

fashion merchandising. The umbrella term used for the business side of fashion that involves the buying and selling of fashion, product development, retail management, and fashion marketing. (8)

fashion publicist. A professional who tries to influence celebrities to wear a client's new designs. Fashion publicists may work for design houses or public relations firms. (8)

financial manager. A professional responsible for providing financial guidance to clients by overseeing the preparation of financial reports, executing cash management strategies, and guiding investment activities. (13)

food production. The natural or human-constructed sources of food and the production, product development, distribution, marketing, and sales of food products. (6)

food science technician. A professional who assists food scientists in tasks such as maintaining safe and sterile laboratories, preparing and analyzing samples, and testing food, additives, or containers. (6)

food scientist. A professional trained to apply knowledge of biochemistry, human biology, microbiology, toxicology, biotechnology, and other sciences to determine new or better ways to prepare, distribute, package, use, and store foods. (6)

food service industry. All the establishments that serve meals and snacks prepared outside the home. Generally, the food service industry can be divided into commercial and noncommercial ventures. (7)

food service manager. A food service professional who directs and coordinates the operations of businesses that prepare and serve food. (7)

free-form careers. Careers that include entrepreneurial ventures, consulting work, contract and temporary work, and part-time work. They may also include volunteer or unpaid work. (17)

G

general manager. The professional with the overall responsibility for the operation of a hospitality venue. This person performs the administrative duties and provides general business oversight in assignments that include maintaining employee work records and payroll; completing paperwork to comply with licensing, tax, wage and hour, unemployment compensation, and Social Security laws; and maintaining, ordering, and paying for new equipment. (7)

geriatric care manager. A professional who helps older adults remain in their homes by providing resource and referral services, education, and support to families. He or she may connect clients with a variety of service providers, such as companion services, chore services, and home health care. (12)

geriatric nutrition. A specialty that focuses on the needs of older adults. Clinical dietitians in this specialty work in long-term care, assisted living facilities, home health care,

community meal programs, and other settings that serve older adults. (6)

global family. The relationships and interactions of a family unit with the outside culture, often worldwide. (2)

green design. Design that attempts to diminish the impact of new buildings on the environment. Green design tends to minimize use of fossil fuels and environmentally adverse building materials, to conserve energy, and to lower the output of pollution. (9)

group interview. A common way of interviewing potential employees, especially for entry-level positions. The simplest and most common form of a group interview is a company presentation followed by a question-and-answer session. (16)

H

historic costume preservationist. A professional who cares for antique textiles and clothing so they can be maintained for years of enjoyment in exhibitions, museums, libraries, and other historic or educational institutions. (8)

home. The place where a person resides during nonwork hours, that stores material goods, and that is a reflection of a person's values, interests, and personality. (9)

home furnishings. The segment of the interior design industry that focuses on functional and aesthetic items such as furniture, rugs, lighting, linens, and decorative accents. (9)

hospitality industry. The industry that serves to meet food, shelter, and other needs of people away from home. A multifaceted industry that includes several major segments: food service, lodging, travel and tourism, recreation, and event and meeting management. (6) (7)

housing industry. An industry that focuses on the behavioral, social, economic, functional, and aesthetic aspects of housing, interiors, and other built environments. (9)

housing specialist. A professional who plans, organizes, and directs activities relating to affordable and market housing. (9)

human ecosystem model. A theoretical model in which the environments in which families and individuals live are differentiated into the natural environment, the human constructed environment, and the human behavioral environment. (2)

human resources. Refers to the individuals working within an organization and also to the portion of the organization that deals with hiring, training, maintaining, firing, and other personnel issues. Human resources workers analyze an organization's competitive strengths by linking insight into workforce trends and characteristics with the most effective methods for enhancing the productivity, motivation, and well-being of the workers. (7)

human resources specialist. A professional who deals with hiring, firing, training, benefits, and other personnel issues within an organization. (13)

I

industry survey. A type of informational interview that can tell you whether jobs are available in the field or business that you want to enter and whether your skills and interests fit with a particular industry or specific organization. (15)

informational interview. A networking tactic that allows a person to meet professionals, accumulate career information, explore career options, get advice on job search practices, and get referrals to other professionals in the industry. However, it should not be used to ask for a specific job. (15)

inspector. In the real estate field, a professional who looks for physical problems with a property. (9)

insurance agent. A professional who sells insurance coverage. (9)

interior decorator. Someone who focuses on the aesthetic aspects of interior furnishings with the intent of making the space pleasing. Interior decorators help people choose colors, textures, flooring, window coverings, furniture, and other home furnishings. (9)

interior design. The process of shaping the experience of interior space through the manipulation of the space, the application of the elements and principles of design, and the use of materials. (9)

interior designer. A professional who is responsible for the design, functionality, safety, performance, and aesthetic image of a client's residential or business space. A professional who is qualified through education, training, experience, and professional examination to create both functional and quality interior environments. (9)

internship. Job experience, similar to employment, with emphasis placed on learning over performance. It is a professional-track position, may be paid or unpaid, that would not be available to someone who was not pursuing a degree in a related area. (15)

J

job interview. A conversation between an employer and a potential employee in order to ascertain whether there is a good match between them. (16)

job shadowing. A short observation period that can give valuable insight into the daily tasks and activities of a professional. (15)

K

key accomplishments. Positive experiences from your past in which you take pride. (14)

kitchen and bath designer. An interior designer who specializes in kitchens and bathrooms, which are the most costly and often the most complex rooms to design. (9)

L

land-grant universities. Universities made possible through the Morrill Act of 1862. They were established to extend educational opportunities that promoted agricultural, industrial, and domestic economy (which was later known as home economics). (1)

leadership. The process of leading others toward an established goal. (3)

leadership skills. Skills that help an individual to influence, motivate, and enable others toward a goal. (14)

life coach. A professional who partners with clients to help them create fulfilling results in their personal and professional lives. (12)

life-work balance. Balance among the needs of family and friends; organizations and causes you choose to serve; activities that promote your spiritual and/or physical health; intellectual and emotional growth; and the demands of a career. (17)

lighting designer. A professional who uses different intensities and colors of light to create a functional and pleasing environment. (9)

loan officer. A professional who works with a team of "back office" support personnel who do credit checks and process the paperwork required to qualify a buyer and obtain a loan. (9)

lodging. Temporary housing. It takes many forms, such as hotels, motels, lodges, camps, inns, bed-and-breakfasts, ranches, resorts, and cruise ships. (7)

long-term goals. Goals that may take years to achieve. (16)

M

marriage and family therapist. A counselor who helps individuals, couples, family groups, or organizations resolve conflicts. (11)

mental health counselor. A counselor who helps people assess, address, and treat mental and emotional disorders. (11)

mentors. People you learn from and admire. They have guided you, modeled appropriate behaviors or attitudes, and have taken an active role in your development. (14)

mixed-form careers. Careers that include some linear career tracks combined with periods of free-form career paths. (17)

Morrill Act of 1862. An act that designated a parcel of land in each state to be used for establishing a university, called a land-grant university. (1)

mortgage broker. A professional who does sales and marketing for loan sources by gathering data from buyers and connecting buyers with lenders. The brokers do not provide funds themselves. (9)

mortgage lender. A professional who provides the funding for the purchase of property. (9)

multiculturalism. An approach for managing cultural diversity in a multiethnic society, stressing mutual respect and appreciation for cultural differences. (4)

multiracialism. A person's racial heritage that is based on multiple racial ancestry. (4)

museum exhibit designer. A professional who creates museum displays that showcase artifacts or works of art in a way that is pleasing, emphasizes the object, keeps it safe, and preserves it. (9)

N

National Standards for FCS. Standards developed by family and consumer sciences educators and other professionals that offer specific guidelines and communicate direction for family and consumer sciences curriculum across the United States. (10)

networking. The act of meeting and making contact with people, exchanging ideas, and informally interacting for the purpose of increasing business insight. (16)

networking interview. A type of informational interview that provides the opportunity to have conversations with some of the key professionals in your field of interest. (15)

noncommercial food service. Businesses that provide food service within established organizations such as schools, hospitals, and other establishments. (7)

nutrition. The study of how nutrients interact with biological organisms and how an organism assimilates food and uses it for growth and maintenance. (6)

nutrition educator. A professional who provides nutrition information to students and food service workers in both public and private education, from child care centers through universities. (6)

Occupational Information Network (O*NET). A resource developed for the U.S. Department of Labor by the National O*NET Consortium that includes descriptions and definitions of both public and private career opportunities and focuses on knowledge, skills, training, and education needed to succeed in each career profiled. (15)

Occupational Outlook Handbook. A resource published by the U.S. Department of Labor, Bureau of Labor Statistics, that offers a variety of career information, including job descriptions, working conditions, wage and salary information, required or desired training and education, and future job prospects. (15)

organizational culture. The assumptions, values, behaviors, and actions of people; group norms; and tangible signs of an organization. (17)

pediatric dietitian. A clinical dietitian who specializes in the nutritional health and care of children. (6)

Perkins Act. Vocational education legislation that supports secondary and post-secondary programs in agriculture, business, and technology. (1)

personal essentials. Values, needs, and wants that are critical to a person. (14)

personal financial planner. A professional who provides guidance to individuals to help them with their budgeting, spending, income, insurance, credit, and other financial decisions. (13)

personal objective. A specific and measurable statement directed toward a specific career or position but held confidentially rather than shared with an employer. (16)

personal portfolio. A tangible collection of the important components of your life that relate to your career goals. (15)

personal statement. A written statement that works as a promotional piece about an individual and serves as an introduction to prospective employers, typically used in personal portfolios. (14)

personal values. Motivations that create beliefs, actions, and behaviors that are important in your personal life. (14)

preschool director. A professional who is responsible for the overall operation of a preschool. (12)

preschool teacher. A teacher who works with children aged three to five. Professionals in this field may work in a traditional preschool or in a day care center. (12)

prescriptive advice. Advice that encourages you toward a certain decision or life path. (14)

product developer. An apparel designer who modifies successful and popular designs to meet a specific customer niche. For example, a product developer may create a simpler, less expensive version of a popular design that can be sold by mass retailers. (8)

professional ethics. The moral decisions that are made in professional activities. (3)

professionalism. Exemplifying competence, complex decision making, decisiveness, and community awareness in your profession. (3)

professional organization. An association of professionals who work in the same or related fields. It provides leadership, service, and networking opportunities along with educational and employment resources for members. (17)

program director. A family and community services professional who oversees the mission, goals, and programs of an organization. (11)

prohibitive advice. Advice that warns against a certain decision or life path. (14)

property manager. A professional who oversees the overall performance of income-producing commercial or residential properties. (9)

psychological family. The modern nuclear family that is shaped by romantic love between adult partners, parental love for children, and the belief that bonds among nuclear family members grow more intense and binding. (2)

psychological wants. The fundamental desires you have that lead to personal well-being and self-satisfaction. (14)

public health nutritionist. A nutritionist who works for a government agency, such as a county health department. (6)

public policy. Guidelines, regulations, and laws enacted by the government. (5)

R

real estate agent. A professional who lists property for sale and facilitates the offer and acceptance process. (9)

recreation industry. A segment of the hospitality industry that focuses on recreational, leisure, sports, adventure, and cultural activities. (7)

registered dietetic technician (DTR). A trained food and nutrition professional who works under the supervision of a registered dietitian when providing nutrition care. Dietetic technicians also work independently as part of the food production and food service industries. (6)

registered dietitian (RD). A nutritionist who

holds a bachelor's degree from an approved program (designated by the ACEND), has completed a supervised internship, and has achieved a passing score on the national examination administered by the Commission on Dietetic Registration. (6)

Rehabilitation Act of 1973. A federal law that prohibits the government from discriminating against people with disabilities. (16)

rehabilitation counselor. A counselor who helps people deal with the effects of disabilities, including personal, social, physical, and vocational ramifications. (11)

renal specialist. In reference to a clinical dietitian, one who counsels patients experiencing kidney problems, such as those who have had transplants or require dialysis. (6)

research dietitian. A clinical dietitian specializing in research. For example, research dietitians may work in health care or academic institutions, exploring and defining the role of nutrition in acute and chronic diseases. They may also work in the food industry or for pharmaceutical/nutraceutical companies to examine the role of functional foods, supplements, and/or drugs on intake of foods/nutrients and eating behavior. (6)

residential interior design. Design that includes single-family houses, multifamily houses such as duplexes, apartments, and condominiums, and any other form of residence. (9)

residential interior designer. A professional who focuses on the design needs of individuals and families in their interior home living environment. (9)

respect. Acknowledging people, especially those who are in positions above you, by showing respectful behavior. (17)

responsibility. A quality of employees who are committed 100 percent of the time in all obligations, relationships, and actions. (17)

résumé. A document that targets a specific audience and lists and describes education, work, volunteer, and personal experiences that make a person a good candidate for a job. (15)

retail buyer. A professional who works with fashion merchandisers to select apparel that will meet the needs of a target customer base, establish an image identity for a department or store, and increase revenue. (8)

retail fashion merchandiser. A professional who is the point person for ensuring that the right apparel products are in the right retail store at the right time. (8)

retail manager. A professional who has total responsibility over all aspects of a retail store's daily functioning, including managing stock, reviewing inventory and sales records, developing merchandising plans, and coordinating sales promotions as well as managing the physical facilities, security and loss prevention programs, and general operating procedures. (8)

sales and marketing manager. A professional who uses all available communication media in the effort to reach the target market. (7)

school food service consultant. An administrative dietitian who works for a government agency and helps schools comply with government regulations through activities such as staff training. (6)

school food service director. An administrative dietitian who works with teachers in nutrition education programs or serves on the district's wellness committee. (6)

self-assessment. A lifetime looking-inward process that helps you reflect on and identify your personal values, needs, wants or desires, resources, and abilities. (14)

service learning. A blend of academic study and community service that provides an opportunity for the student to integrate classroom education with hands-on experience and promotes reflection upon its value. (15)

short-term goals. Goals that include things you can do in six months to a year. (16)

skill. The ability to do something well, which was learned over time through experiences, practice, or instruction. (14)

Smith-Hughes Act of 1917. Federal legislation that set vocational education apart from the regular high school curriculum and established federal funds to support vocational education. (1)

Smith-Lever Act of 1914. The act that established the Cooperative Extension Service. (1)

social system. A task performance group that meets the needs of its members as well as other societal groups. (2)

social worker. A family and community services professional who interviews, coordinates, and plans programs and activities to meet the social and emotional needs of clients. (11)

space planner. A professional who creatively solves complex problems that involve the organization and layout of interior spaces. (9)

sports nutritionist. A clinical dietitian who specializes in the specific needs of athletes in sports and physical activity. (6)

student teaching. An uncompensated classroom experience for education majors under the supervision of a certified and experienced teacher. (15)

stylist. A fashion professional who chooses clothing and accessories for clients in order to create a desired image. (8)

sustainable textiles. Environmentally friendly textiles that are safe, use recycled and/or safely biodegradable materials, and implement safe manufacturing processes. (8)

system. An informal network of elements that are interrelated in a more or less stable fashion within a given time period. (2)

T

team player. A person who has good interpersonal skills and is able to get along with others in order to cooperatively accomplish a task. (17)

technology skills. Learned skills that relate to technological literacy. (14)

textile design. The art of creating or changing the appearance of a fabric. (8)

textile designer. A professional who is concerned with the structural and surface design components of fabrics. Because these two areas are so technically different, textile designers usually specialize in one or the other. (8)

textile industry. An agricultural and chemical industry that produces fibers, yarns, and finished fabrics. (8)

textile market analyst. A professional who researches the market for trends and forecasts future supply and demand of particular fibers and fabrics. (8)

textile sales representative. A sales professional who shows a manufacturer's fabric line to designers at the beginning of each season and whenever new fabrics are added. The representative may be employed by a textile production company or work independently. (8)

textile scientist. A professional who studies textiles from raw materials through manufacturing and finishing of fabrics as related to durability, comfort, care, and aesthetics. (8)

Title VII of the Civil Rights Act of 1964. A federal law that prohibits employment discrimination based on race, color, religion, sex, or national origin. (16)

traditional linear career development model. A traditional career path that typically progresses from education to employment and then to retirement. (17)

transferable skill. A skill, such as the ability to orally express an idea, that can be transferred from one situation to another. (15)

travel and tourism industry. A segment of the hospitality industry that focuses on modes of transportation and travel guidance. (7)

U

universal design. Design that adapts to the needs of users in changing environments rather than being suitable only for the specific needs of one user, or in the case of accessible design, the specific needs of a particular disability. (4)

V

values. Beliefs that certain behaviors, attitudes, and actions are preferable to others. Values are what a person holds to be important. (14)

visual merchandiser. A professional who works to place merchandise in front of a target market and capture the consumer's attention through skillful manipulation of color, texture, light, sound, and styles. (8)

vocational counselor. A counselor who assists people with finding employment. (11)

W

wants. The psychological requirements that give you satisfaction in life. (14)

wedding planner. An event planner who works directly for the bride and groom. Wedding planners consult with the couple to plan the event and are present to troubleshoot activities on the actual wedding day. (7)

wholesale representative. A professional who carries one or more manufacturers' clothing lines and sells them to retail buyers. Generally, the representative specializes in one fashion category, such as children's sportswear. (8)

work values. Motivations that create beliefs, actions, and behaviors that are important in your work life. (14)

Index